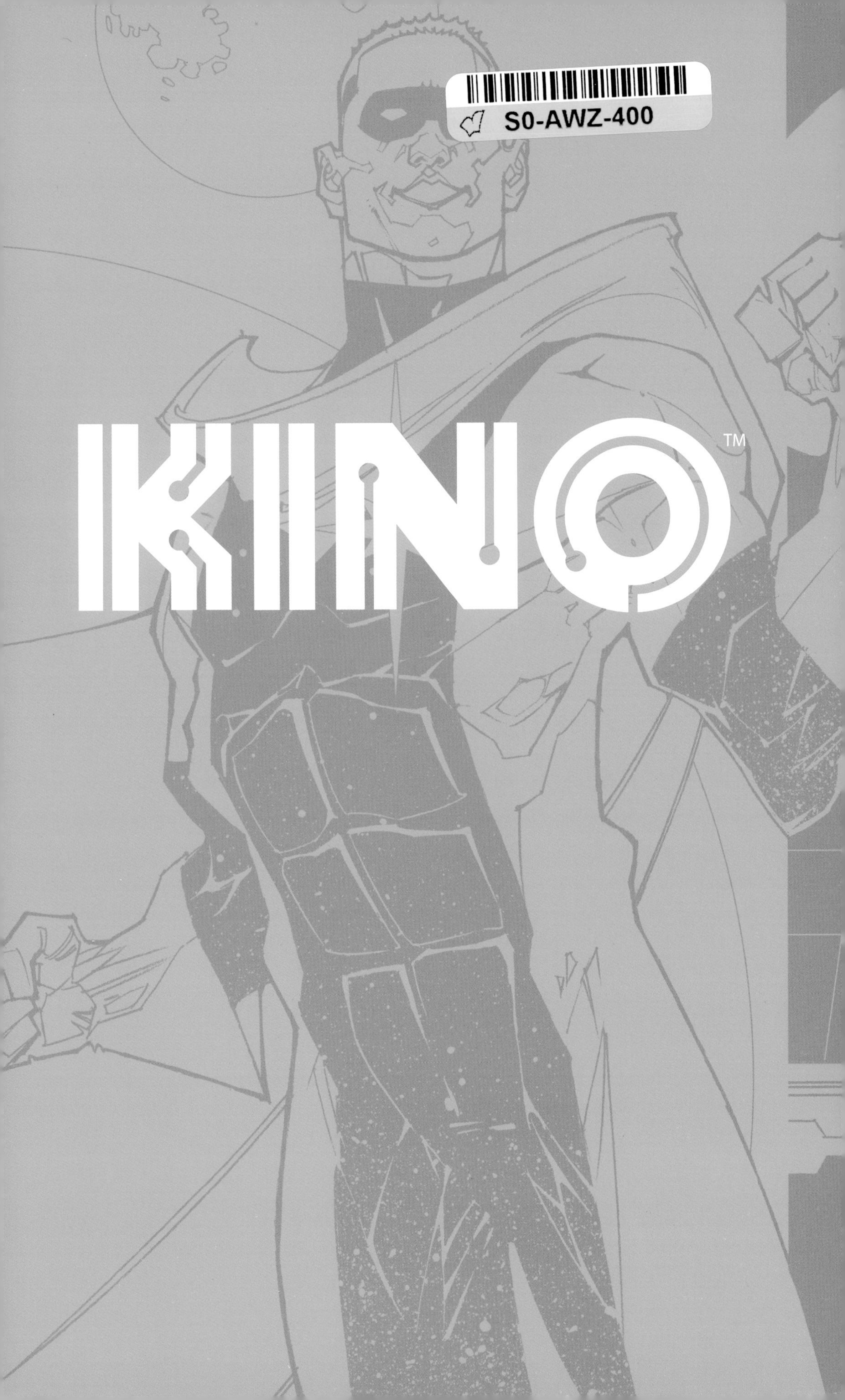

KINO™

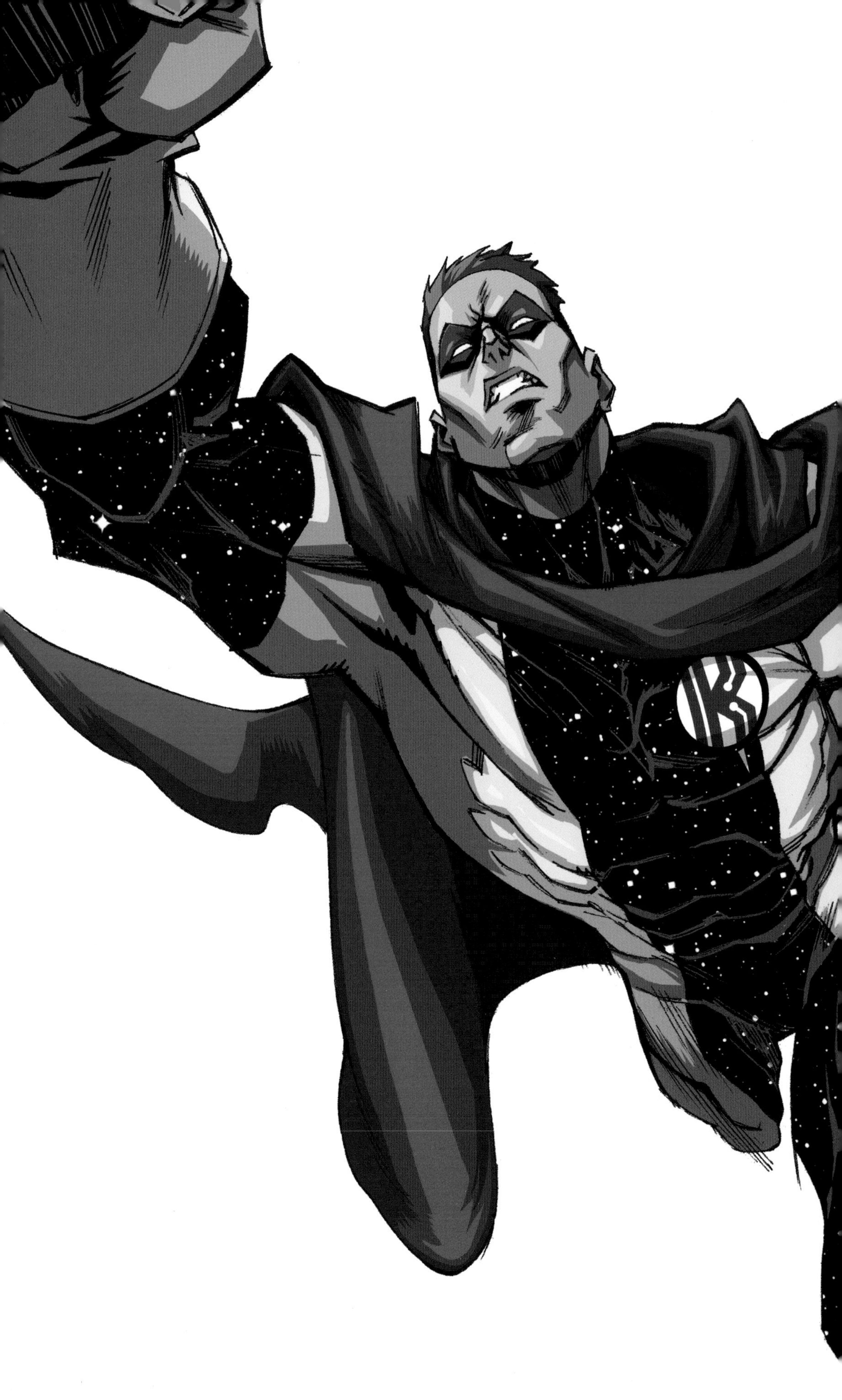

KINO™

ESCAPE FROM THE ABYSS

written by **JOE CASEY**
illustrated by **JEFTE PALO**
lettered by **TODD KLEIN**
colored by **CHRIS SOTOMAYOR**

THE EVENT

written by **PRIEST** and
JOSEPH PHILLIP ILLIDGE
illustrated by **MARCO TURINI** and **WILL ROSADO**
lettered by **ANDWORLD DESIGN**
colored by **JESSICA KHOLINNE**

JOSEPH ILLIDGE · senior editor
DESIREE RODRIGUEZ · editorial assistant
cover by **JEFTE PALO** and **CHRIS SOTOMAYOR**

LION FORGE™

ISBN: 978-1-941302-65-1

Library of Congress Control Number: 2017961064

CHAPTER ONE

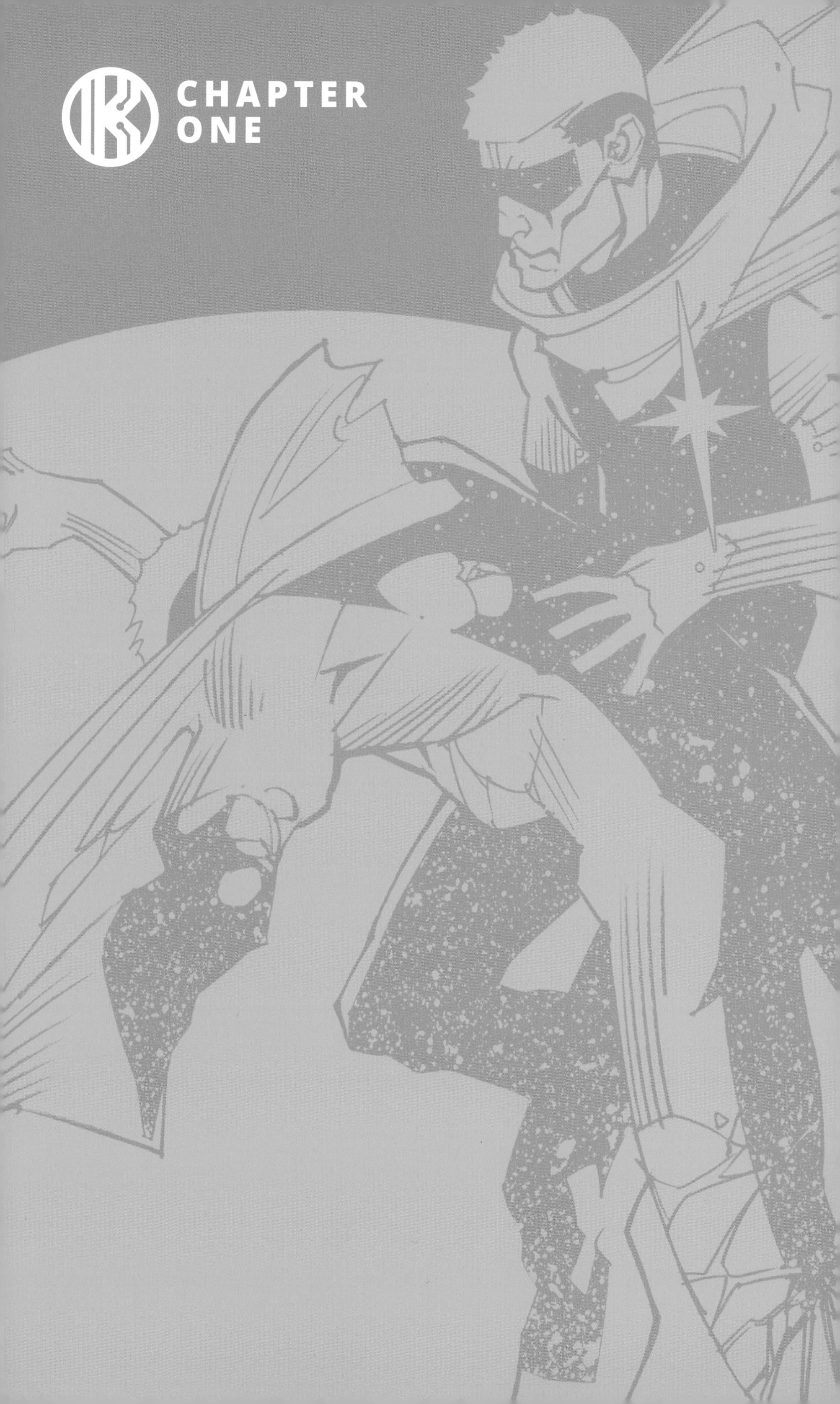

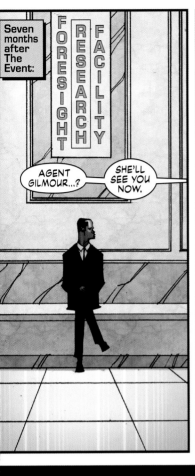

Seven months after The Event:
FORESIGHT RESEARCH FACILITY
AGENT GILMOUR...?
SHE'LL SEE YOU NOW.
YOU'RE LUCKY SHE WAS ABLE TO FIT YOU IN. MISS PAYAN IS QUITE BUSY.
SORRY, IS THAT A LONDON ACCENT...?
MMM... I'M SURE SHE IS.
BRISTOL, ACTUALLY.
SO...
...THIS IS AN UNEXPECTED PLEASURE.
WELCOME TO FORESIGHT.

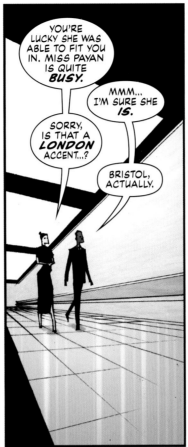

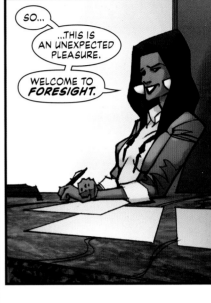

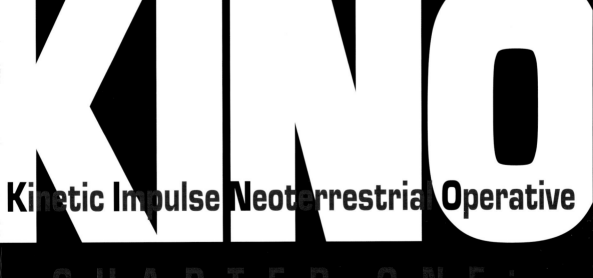

KINO

Kinetic Impulse Neoterrestrial Operative

CHAPTER ONE:

The Sleep Of The Just

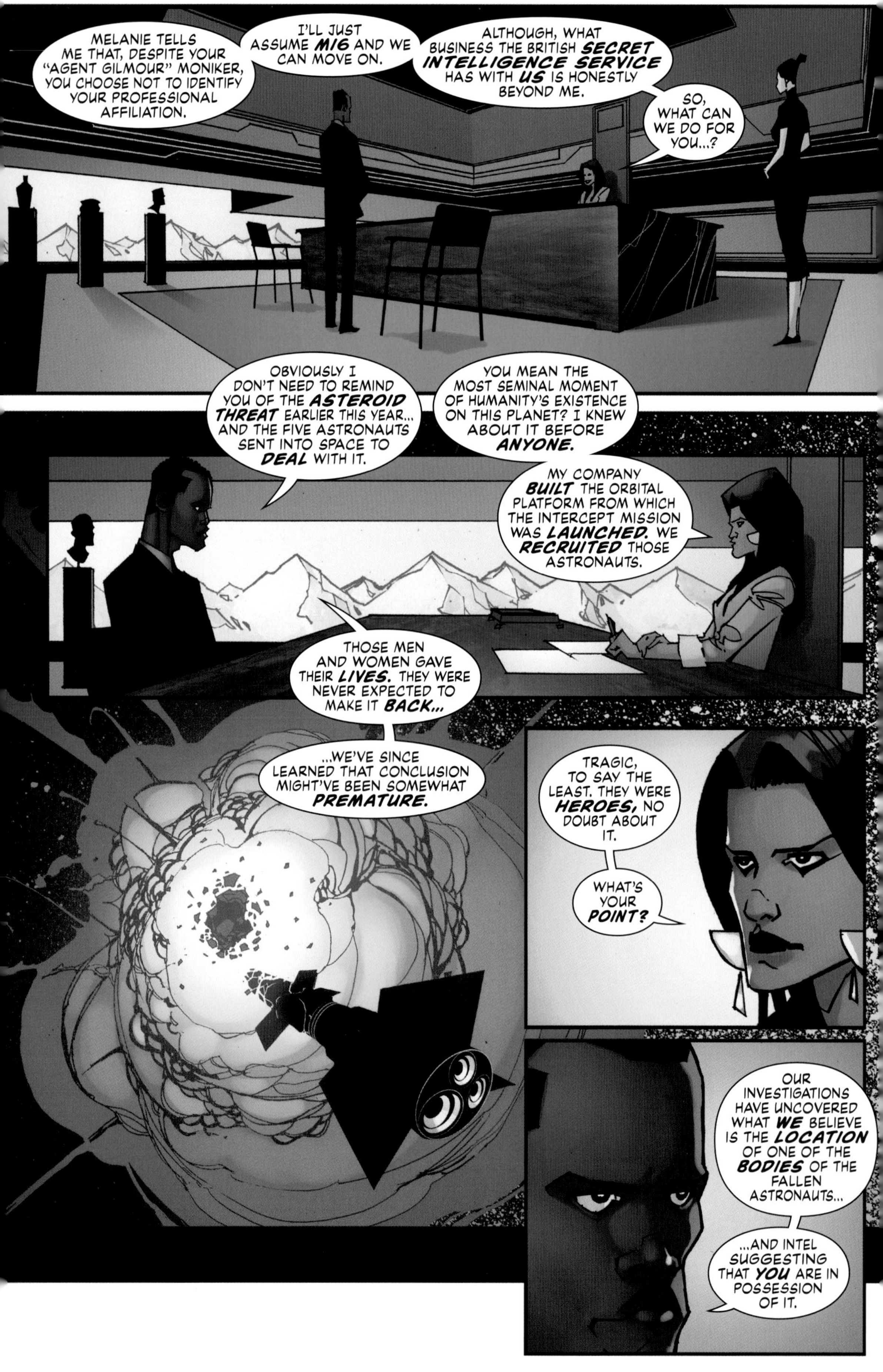

MELANIE TELLS ME THAT, DESPITE YOUR "AGENT GILMOUR" MONIKER, YOU CHOOSE NOT TO IDENTIFY YOUR PROFESSIONAL AFFILIATION.
I'LL JUST ASSUME MI6 AND WE CAN MOVE ON.
ALTHOUGH, WHAT BUSINESS THE BRITISH SECRET INTELLIGENCE SERVICE HAS WITH US IS HONESTLY BEYOND ME.
SO, WHAT CAN WE DO FOR YOU...?
OBVIOUSLY I DON'T NEED TO REMIND YOU OF THE ASTEROID THREAT EARLIER THIS YEAR... AND THE FIVE ASTRONAUTS SENT INTO SPACE TO DEAL WITH IT.
YOU MEAN THE MOST SEMINAL MOMENT OF HUMANITY'S EXISTENCE ON THIS PLANET? I KNEW ABOUT IT BEFORE ANYONE.
MY COMPANY BUILT THE ORBITAL PLATFORM FROM WHICH THE INTERCEPT MISSION WAS LAUNCHED. WE RECRUITED THOSE ASTRONAUTS.
THOSE MEN AND WOMEN GAVE THEIR LIVES. THEY WERE NEVER EXPECTED TO MAKE IT BACK...
...WE'VE SINCE LEARNED THAT CONCLUSION MIGHT'VE BEEN SOMEWHAT PREMATURE.
TRAGIC, TO SAY THE LEAST. THEY WERE HEROES, NO DOUBT ABOUT IT.
WHAT'S YOUR POINT?
OUR INVESTIGATIONS HAVE UNCOVERED WHAT WE BELIEVE IS THE LOCATION OF ONE OF THE BODIES OF THE FALLEN ASTRONAUTS...
...AND INTEL SUGGESTING THAT YOU ARE IN POSSESSION OF IT.

EXCUSE ME...?

AGENT GILMOUR, YOU CAN'T BE SERIOUS.

YOUR REPUTATION FOR CUTTING-EDGE RESEARCH IS WELL-KNOWN. IT MAKES PERFECT SENSE THAT YOU'D WANT TO STUDY WHATEVER MIGHT'VE RETURNED FROM THAT ILL-FATED MISSION.

AS YOU KNOW, ONE OF THOSE ASTRONAUTS WAS ENGLISH...

"...MAJOR ALISTAIR MEATH.

"HIS ROLE IN THE DELIVERY OF A MULTIFACETED NUCLEAR PAYLOAD HELPED TURN A PLANET-KILLER ASTEROID INTO SOMETHING THAT EARTH COULD SURVIVE...

British Aerospace Age

"...EVEN IF HE DIDN'T.

"AT LEAST, THAT'S WHAT THE WORLD WAS LED TO BELIEVE."

SIMPLY PUT, WE WANT HIS BODY BACK.

I'M NOT HERE TO ENACT ANY OFFICIAL MANDATE. NOT YET, ANYWAY.

I'M SIMPLY HERE TO RETRIEVE THE EXCLUSIVE PROPERTY OF THE BRITISH EMPIRE.

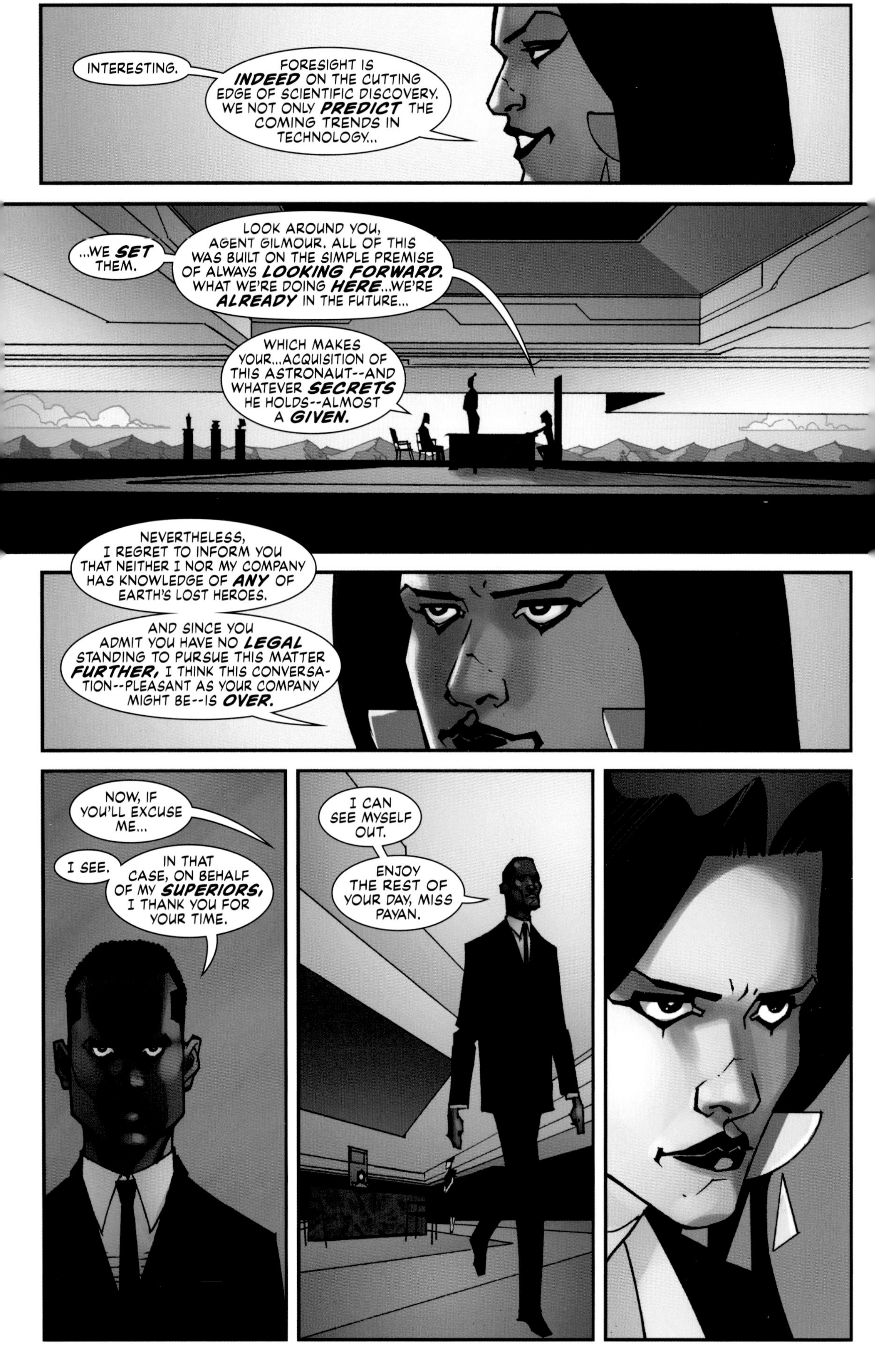
INTERESTING.
FORESIGHT IS INDEED ON THE CUTTING EDGE OF SCIENTIFIC DISCOVERY. WE NOT ONLY PREDICT THE COMING TRENDS IN TECHNOLOGY...
...WE SET THEM.
LOOK AROUND YOU, AGENT GILMOUR. ALL OF THIS WAS BUILT ON THE SIMPLE PREMISE OF ALWAYS LOOKING FORWARD. WHAT WE'RE DOING HERE...WE'RE ALREADY IN THE FUTURE...
WHICH MAKES YOUR...ACQUISITION OF THIS ASTRONAUT--AND WHATEVER SECRETS HE HOLDS--ALMOST A GIVEN.
NEVERTHELESS, I REGRET TO INFORM YOU THAT NEITHER I NOR MY COMPANY HAS KNOWLEDGE OF ANY OF EARTH'S LOST HEROES.
AND SINCE YOU ADMIT YOU HAVE NO LEGAL STANDING TO PURSUE THIS MATTER FURTHER, I THINK THIS CONVERSATION--PLEASANT AS YOUR COMPANY MIGHT BE--IS OVER.
NOW, IF YOU'LL EXCUSE ME...
I SEE.
IN THAT CASE, ON BEHALF OF MY SUPERIORS, I THANK YOU FOR YOUR TIME.
I CAN SEE MYSELF OUT.
ENJOY THE REST OF YOUR DAY, MISS PAYAN.

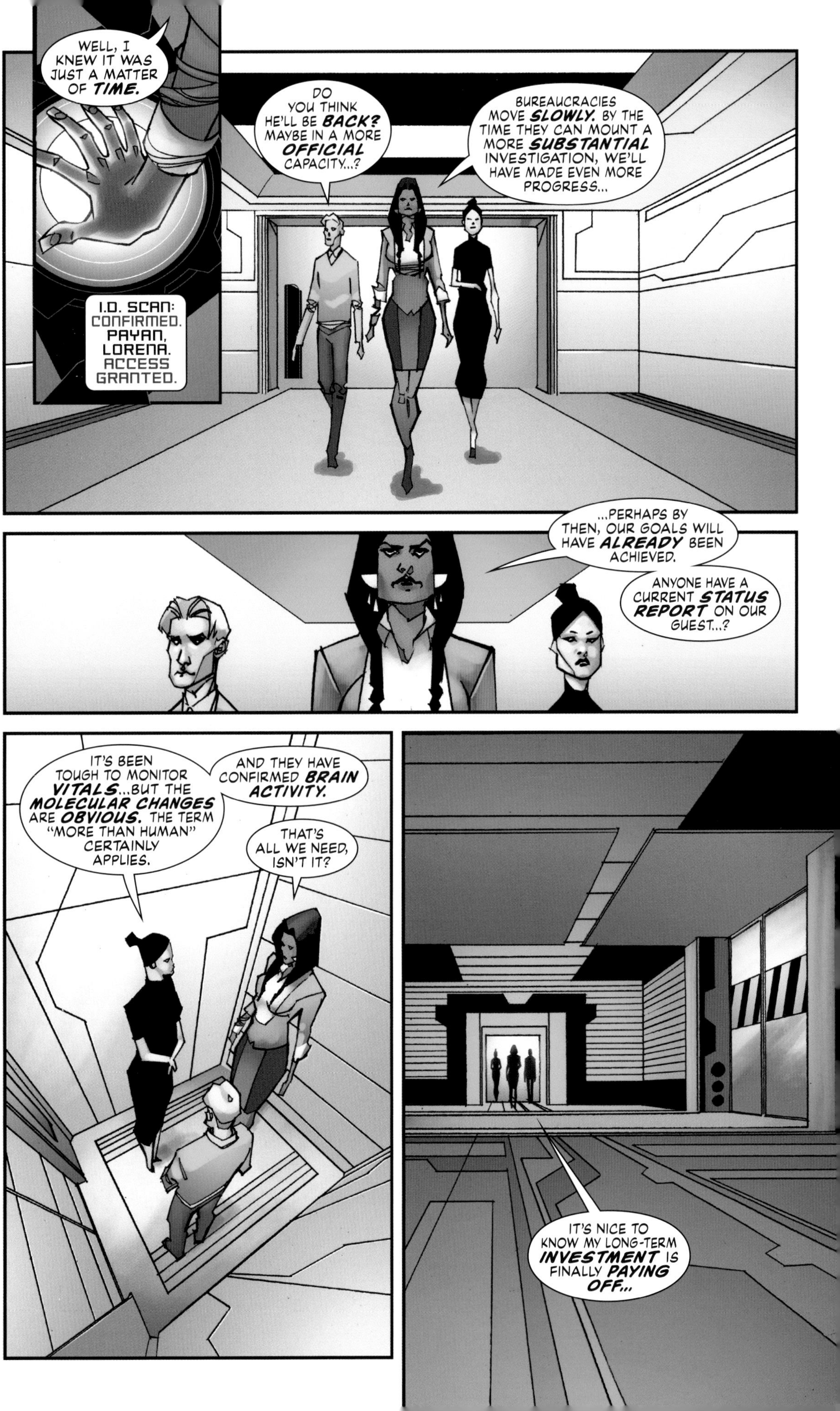
WELL, I KNEW IT WAS JUST A MATTER OF TIME.
I.D. SCAN: CONFIRMED. PAYAN, LORENA. ACCESS GRANTED.
DO YOU THINK HE'LL BE BACK? MAYBE IN A MORE OFFICIAL CAPACITY...?
BUREAUCRACIES MOVE SLOWLY. BY THE TIME THEY CAN MOUNT A MORE SUBSTANTIAL INVESTIGATION, WE'LL HAVE MADE EVEN MORE PROGRESS...
...PERHAPS BY THEN, OUR GOALS WILL HAVE ALREADY BEEN ACHIEVED.
ANYONE HAVE A CURRENT STATUS REPORT ON OUR GUEST...?
IT'S BEEN TOUGH TO MONITOR VITALS...BUT THE MOLECULAR CHANGES ARE OBVIOUS. THE TERM "MORE THAN HUMAN" CERTAINLY APPLIES.
AND THEY HAVE CONFIRMED BRAIN ACTIVITY.
THAT'S ALL WE NEED, ISN'T IT?
IT'S NICE TO KNOW MY LONG-TERM INVESTMENT IS FINALLY PAYING OFF...

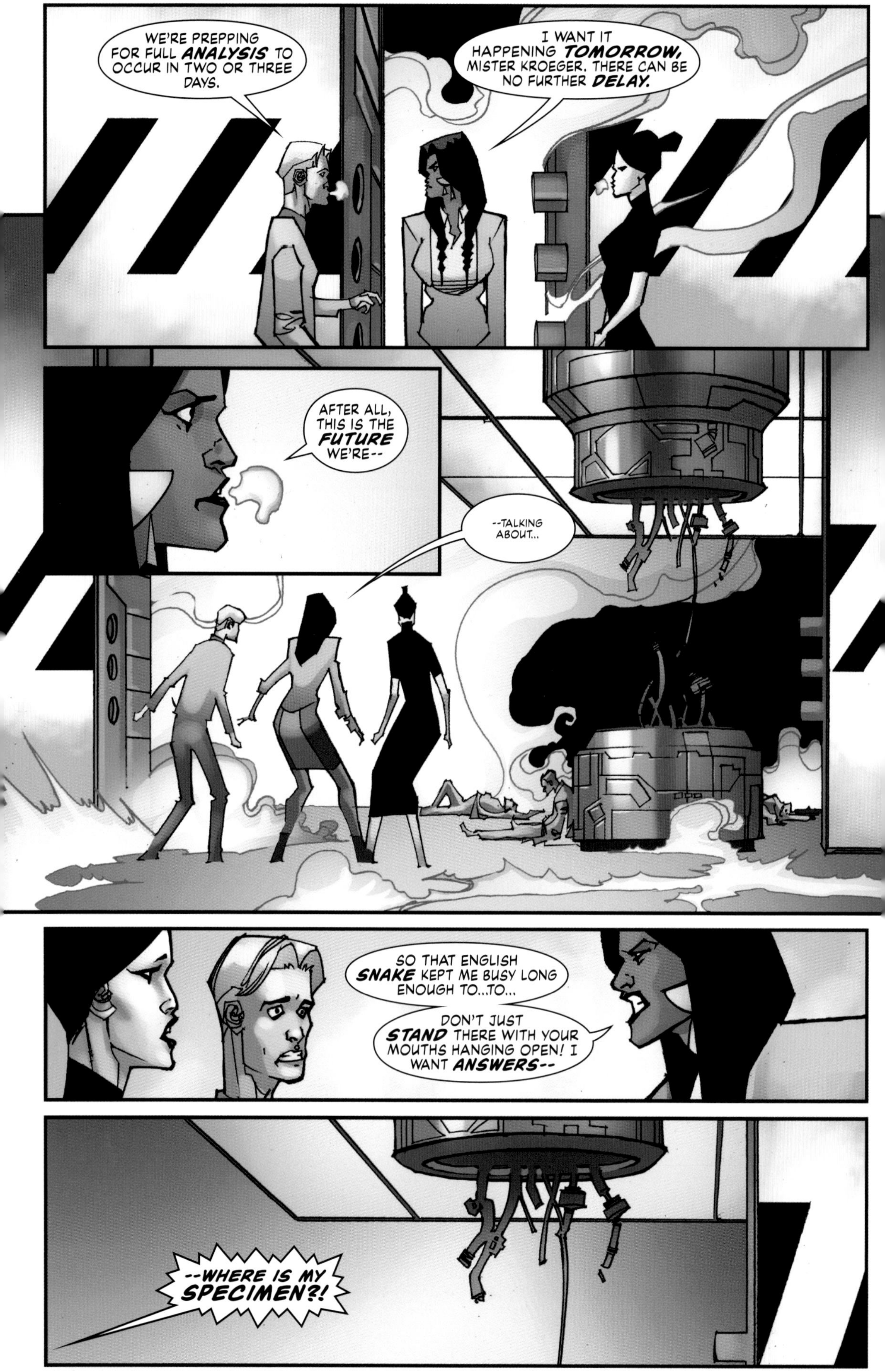
WE'RE PREPPING FOR FULL ANALYSIS TO OCCUR IN TWO OR THREE DAYS.
I WANT IT HAPPENING TOMORROW, MISTER KROEGER. THERE CAN BE NO FURTHER DELAY.
AFTER ALL, THIS IS THE FUTURE WE'RE--
--TALKING ABOUT...
SO THAT ENGLISH SNAKE KEPT ME BUSY LONG ENOUGH TO...TO...
DON'T JUST STAND THERE WITH YOUR MOUTHS HANGING OPEN! I WANT ANSWERS--
--WHERE IS MY SPECIMEN?!

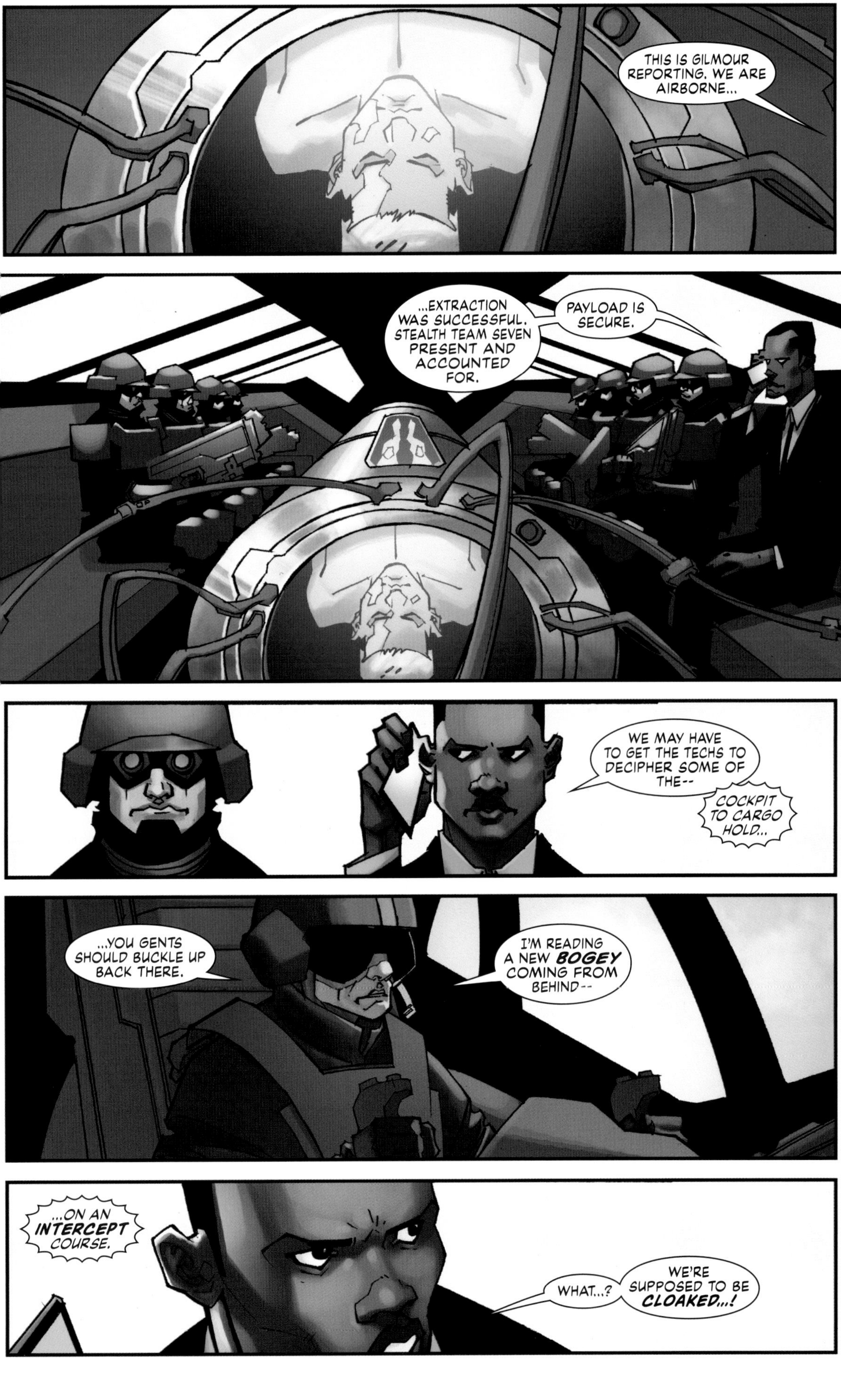
THIS IS GILMOUR REPORTING. WE ARE AIRBORNE...
...EXTRACTION WAS SUCCESSFUL. STEALTH TEAM SEVEN PRESENT AND ACCOUNTED FOR.
PAYLOAD IS SECURE.
WE MAY HAVE TO GET THE TECHS TO DECIPHER SOME OF THE--
COCKPIT TO CARGO HOLD...
...YOU GENTS SHOULD BUCKLE UP BACK THERE.
I'M READING A NEW BOGEY COMING FROM BEHIND--
...ON AN INTERCEPT COURSE.
WHAT...?
WE'RE SUPPOSED TO BE CLOAKED...!

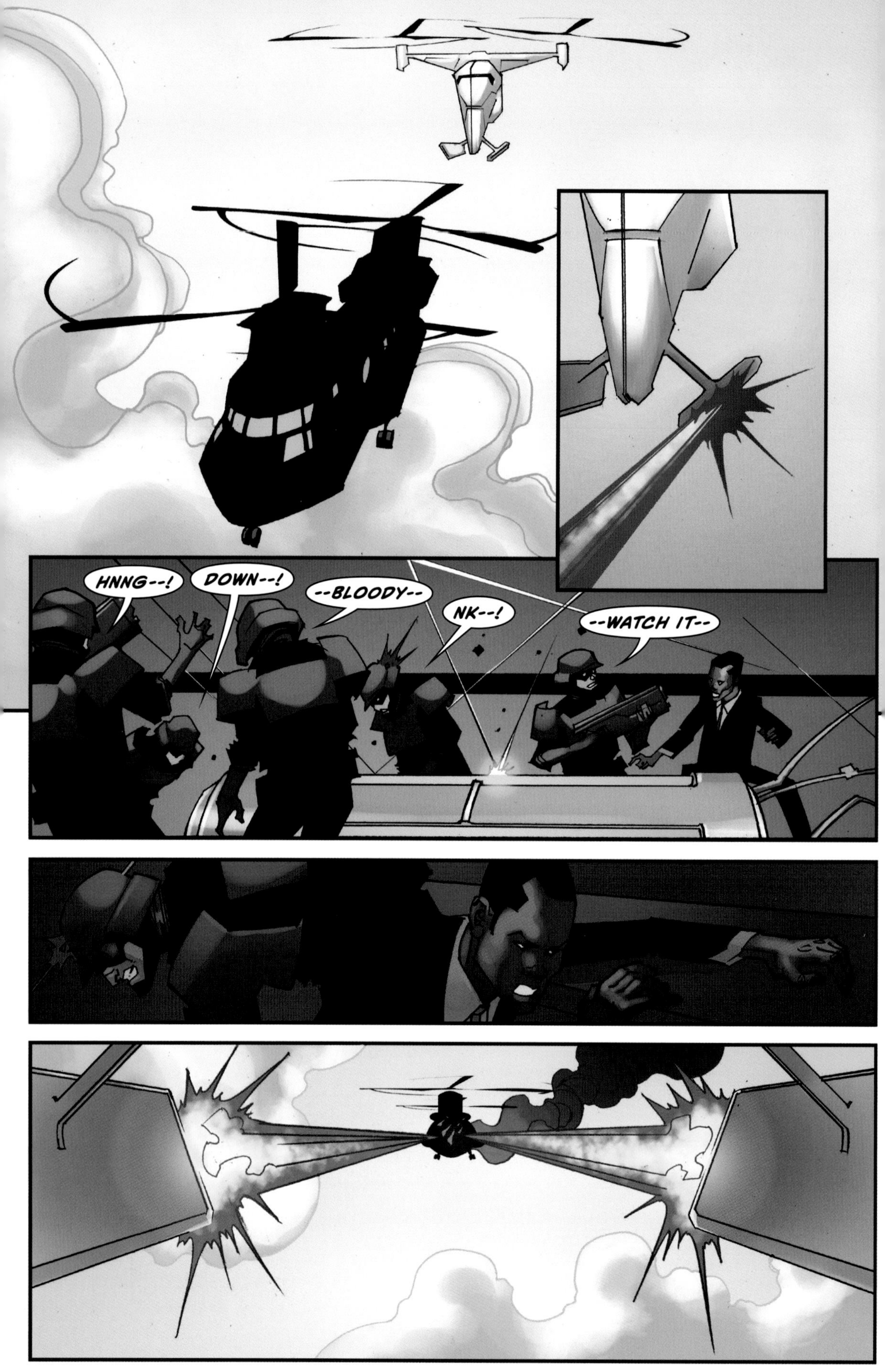
HNNG--!
DOWN--!
--BLOODY--
NK--!
--WATCH IT--

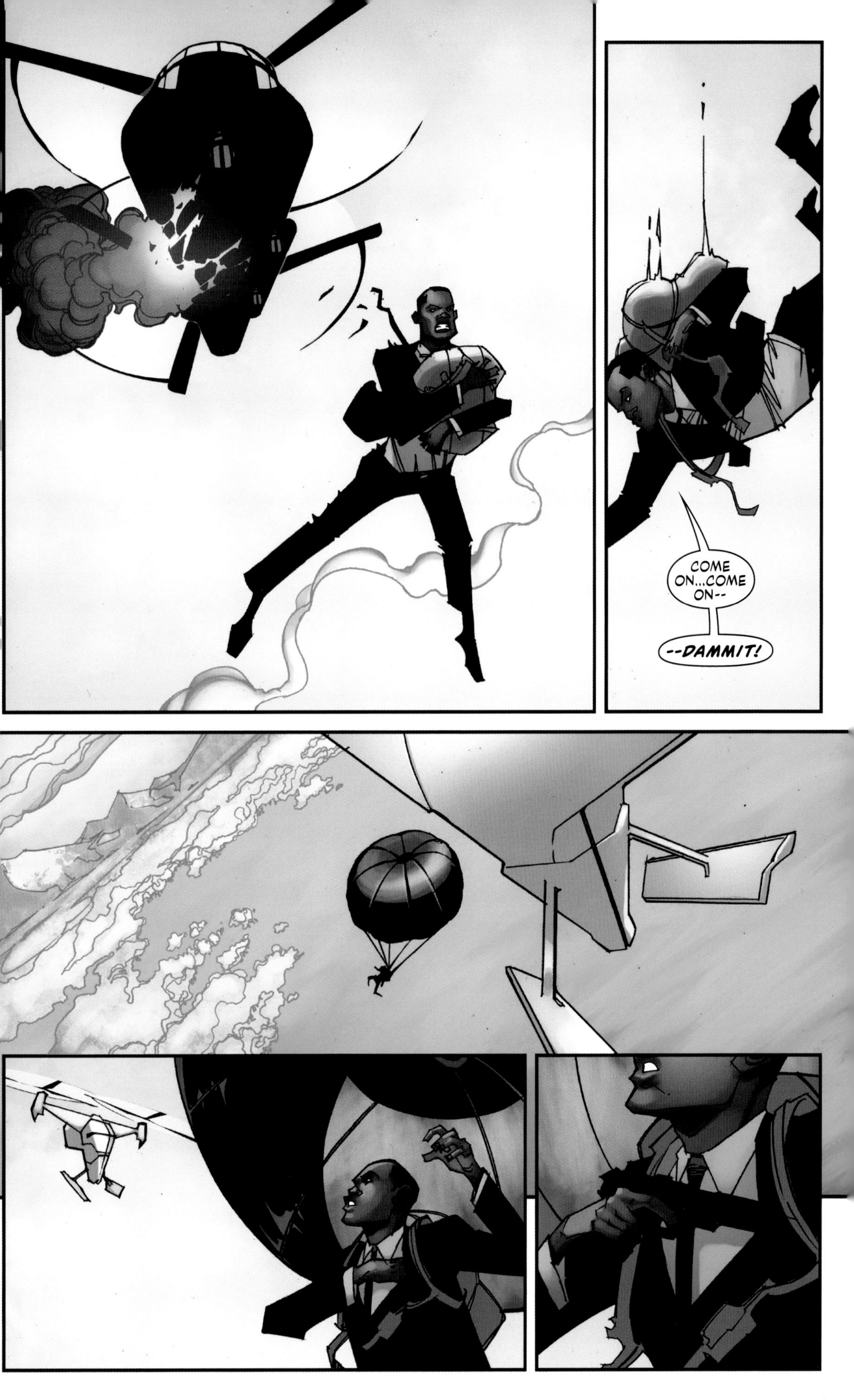
COME ON...COME ON--
--DAMMIT!

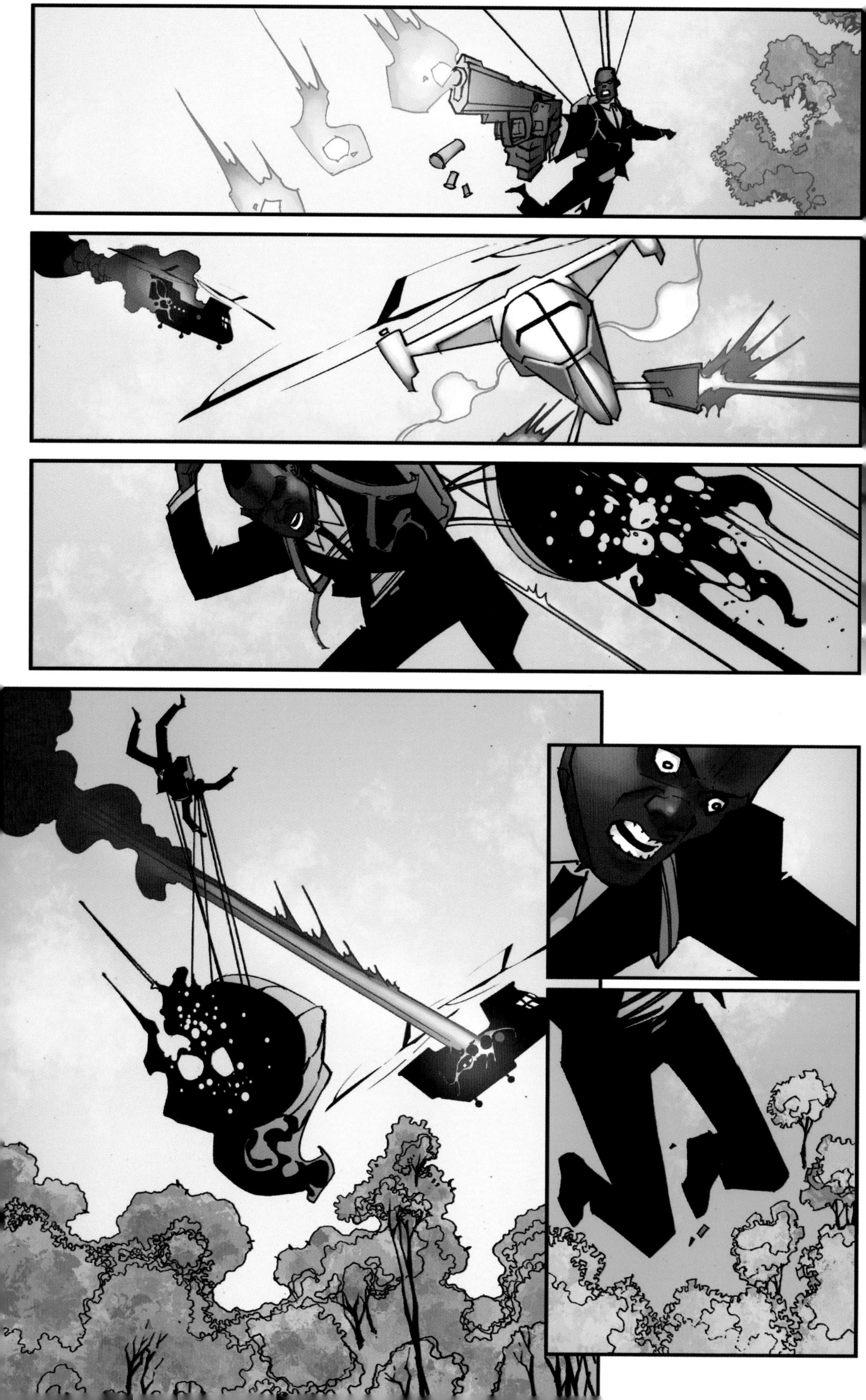

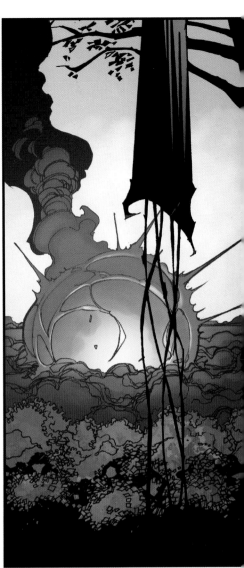

...NNNN...

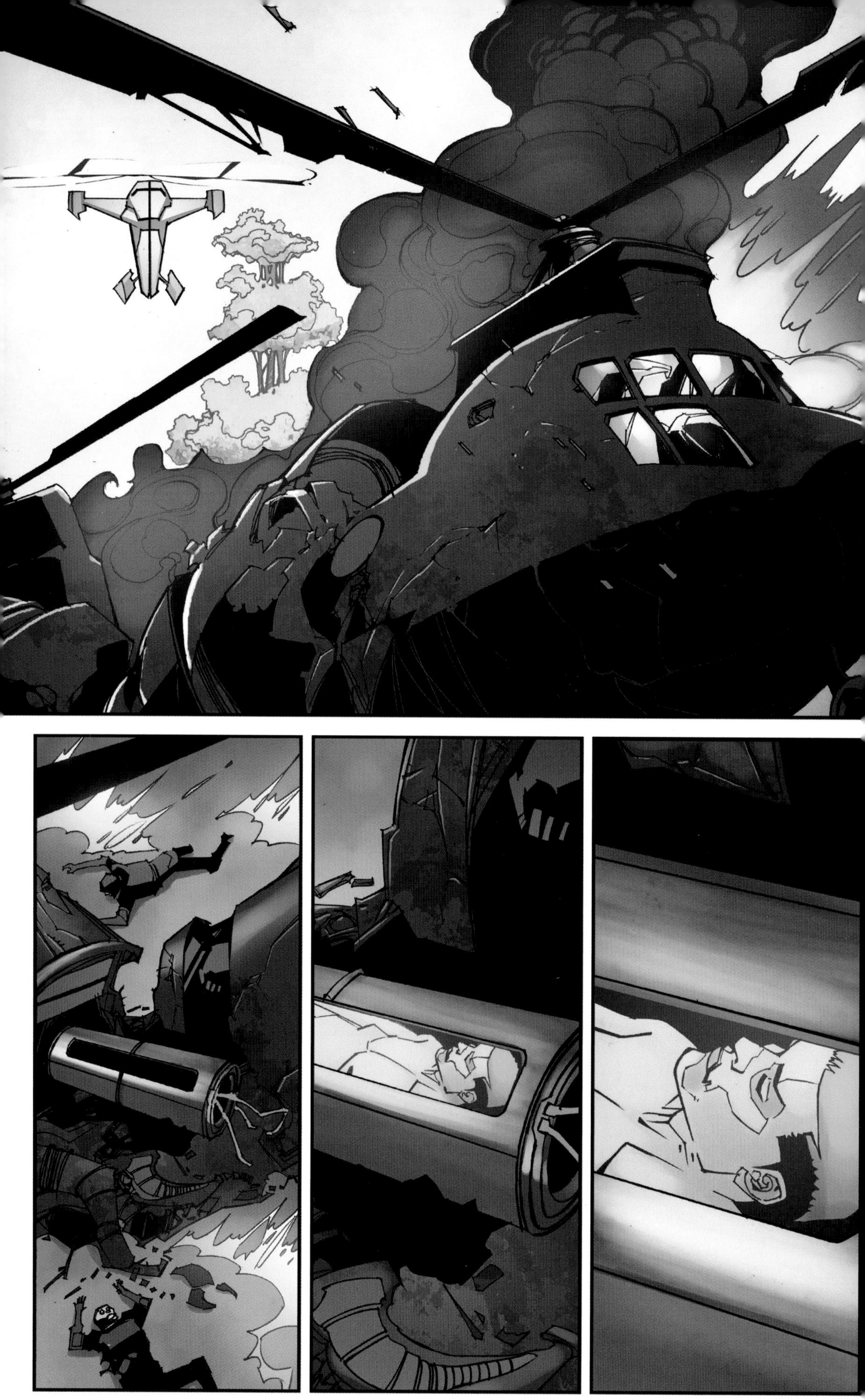

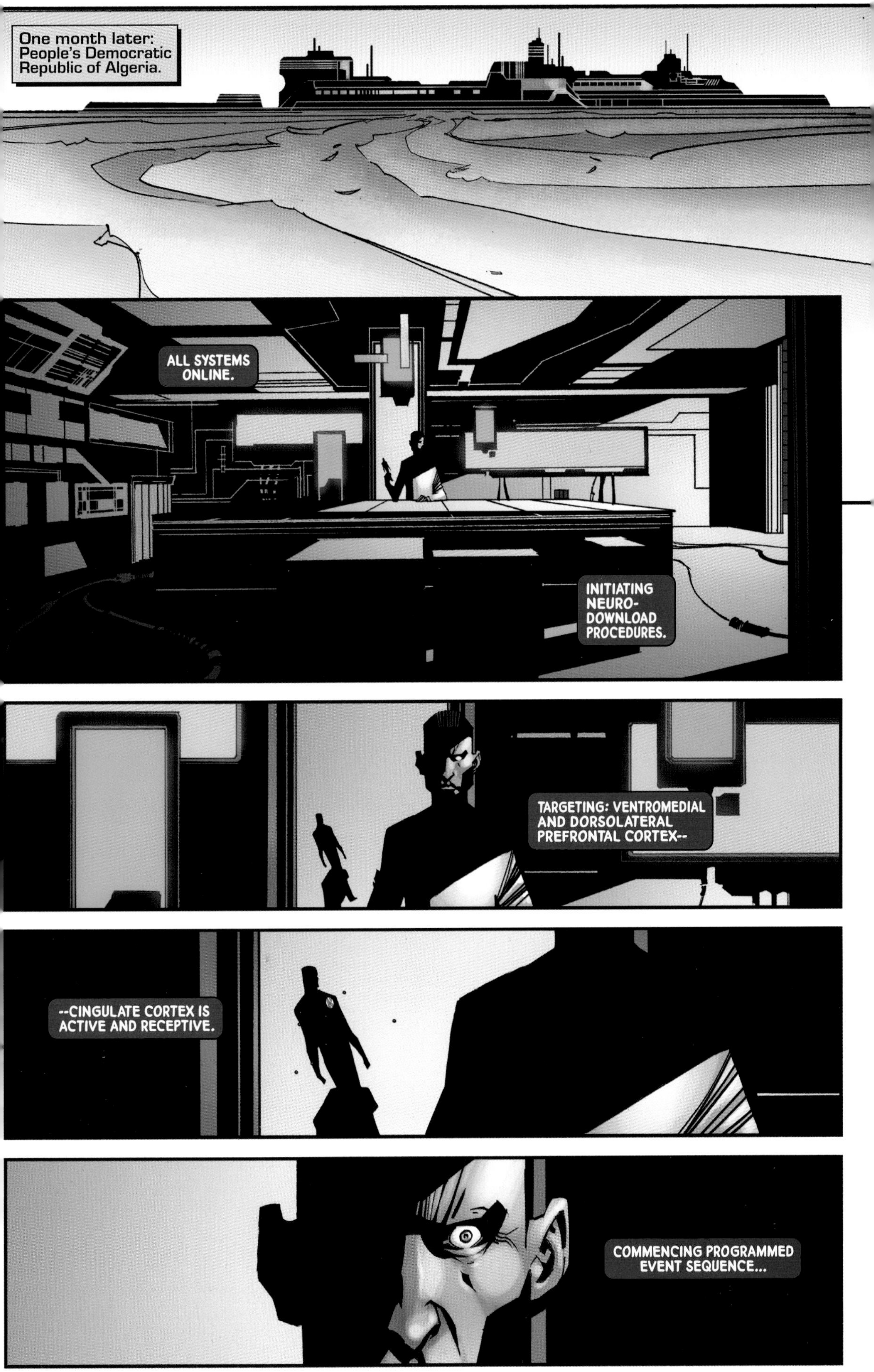
One month later: People's Democratic Republic of Algeria.
ALL SYSTEMS ONLINE.
INITIATING NEURO-DOWNLOAD PROCEDURES.
TARGETING: VENTROMEDIAL AND DORSOLATERAL PREFRONTAL CORTEX--
--CINGULATE CORTEX IS ACTIVE AND RECEPTIVE.
COMMENCING PROGRAMMED EVENT SEQUENCE...

THERE ARE THOSE WHO POSSESS GREAT *VIRTUE.* THERE ARE THOSE WHO POSSESS GREAT *WISDOM!* BUT WHEN THE GATES OF HUMANITY ARE *THREATENED*--IT TAKES A TRUE *HERO* TO STAND TALL AND FACE THAT THREAT!

*L*UCKILY, WE *HAVE* ONE! AND SUCH A THREAT *HAS* ARISEN! BUT *WHAT IS IT?* AND WHAT KIND OF *DAMAGE* IS IT CAPABLE OF? CAN THIS HERO SAVE THE DAY IN TIME? OF *COURSE* HE CAN! HE IS A *K*INETIC! *I*MPULSE! *N*EOTERRESTRIAL! *O*PERATIVE!

IF I DON'T *STOP* THIS CREATURE *NOW*--THE ENTIRE *CITY* WILL GO UP IN *FLAMES!*

KINO VS. CREEPING DEATH!

*I*T BEGINS IN THE HEART OF THE CITY, DEEP WITHIN A HIGH-TECH *LABORATORY*--

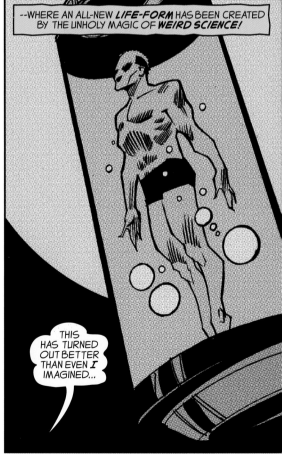

--WHERE AN ALL-NEW *LIFE-FORM* HAS BEEN CREATED BY THE UNHOLY MAGIC OF *WEIRD SCIENCE!*

THIS HAS TURNED OUT BETTER THAN EVEN *I* IMAGINED...

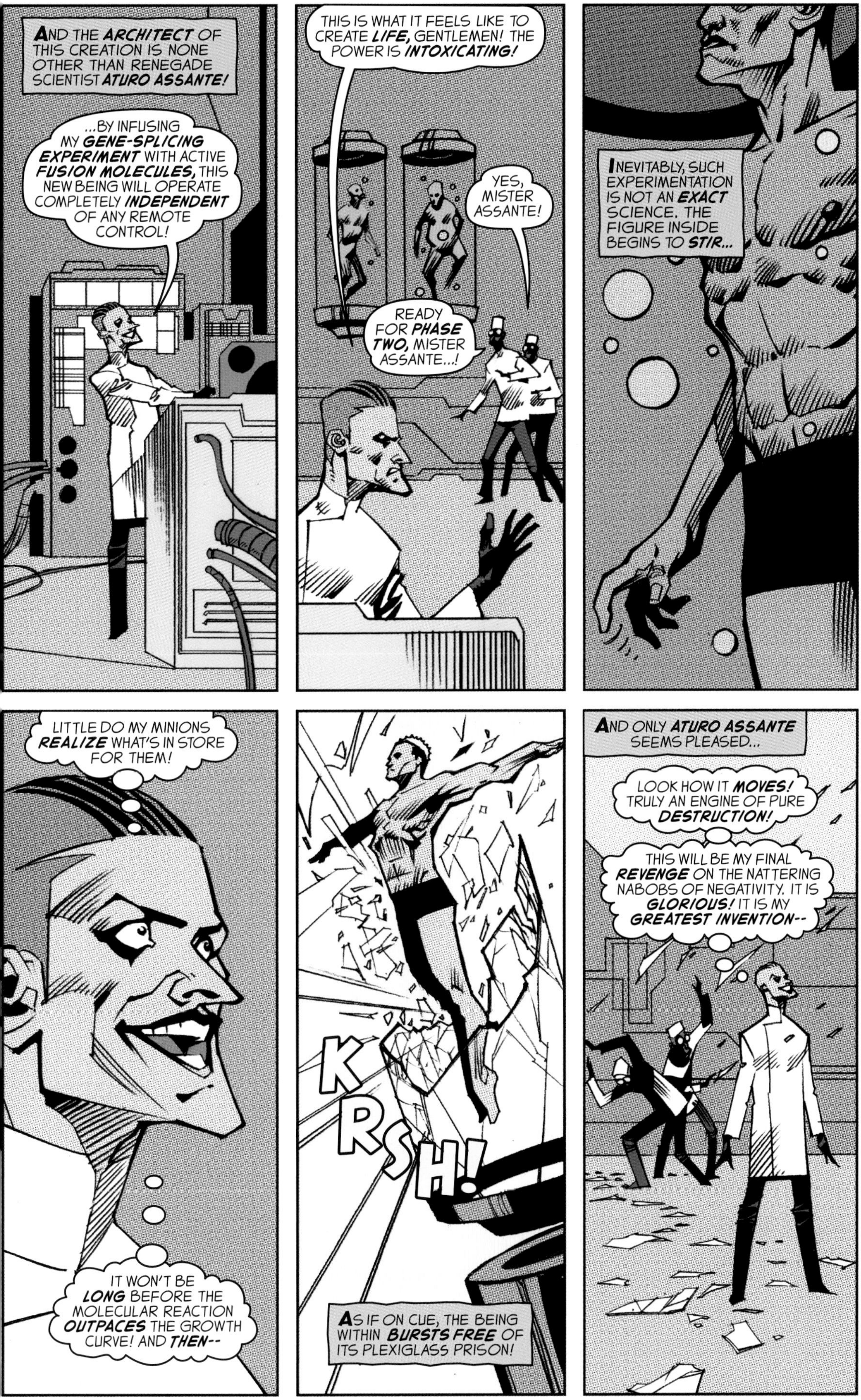
AND THE ARCHITECT OF THIS CREATION IS NONE OTHER THAN RENEGADE SCIENTIST ATURO ASSANTE!
...BY INFUSING MY GENE-SPLICING EXPERIMENT WITH ACTIVE FUSION MOLECULES, THIS NEW BEING WILL OPERATE COMPLETELY INDEPENDENT OF ANY REMOTE CONTROL!
THIS IS WHAT IT FEELS LIKE TO CREATE LIFE, GENTLEMEN! THE POWER IS INTOXICATING!
YES, MISTER ASSANTE!
READY FOR PHASE TWO, MISTER ASSANTE...!
INEVITABLY, SUCH EXPERIMENTATION IS NOT AN EXACT SCIENCE. THE FIGURE INSIDE BEGINS TO STIR...
LITTLE DO MY MINIONS REALIZE WHAT'S IN STORE FOR THEM!
IT WON'T BE LONG BEFORE THE MOLECULAR REACTION OUTPACES THE GROWTH CURVE! AND THEN--
KRSH!
AS IF ON CUE, THE BEING WITHIN BURSTS FREE OF ITS PLEXIGLASS PRISON!
AND ONLY ATURO ASSANTE SEEMS PLEASED...
LOOK HOW IT MOVES! TRULY AN ENGINE OF PURE DESTRUCTION!
THIS WILL BE MY FINAL REVENGE ON THE NATTERING NABOBS OF NEGATIVITY. IT IS GLORIOUS! IT IS MY GREATEST INVENTION--

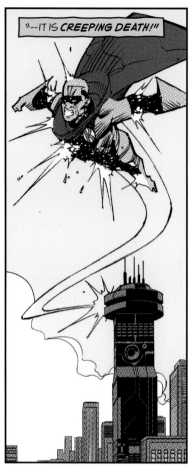

"--IT IS *CREEPING DEATH!*"

MEANWHILE, AT THE NEWLY RENOVATED *SPACELAND THEME PARK* LOCATED JUST OUTSIDE THE CITY, A GRAND *CEREMONY* IS TAKING PLACE...WITH A VERY *SPECIAL GUEST...*

...WE ARE PROUD TO HAVE THE FAMOUS INTERNATIONAL ASTRONAUT *MAJOR ALISTAIR MEATH* OF THE ROYAL AIR FORCE HERE TO CUT THE RIBBON!

SAY SOMETHING, MAJOR...!

I'M JUST HAPPY TO *BE* HERE ON THIS AUSPICIOUS OCCASION...

...HOPEFULLY, THESE RIDES WILL *INSPIRE* AS MUCH AS THEY *ENTERTAIN.*

SPACE TRAVEL IS THE FUTURE OF HUMANITY. WHATEVER IT TAKES TO *PROMOTE* THAT IDEA, I'LL BE RIGHT THERE!

EVEN AS THE CEREMONY BEGINS, A *REPORTER* RECEIVES A *DIFFERENT* KIND OF NEWS BULLETIN...

HEY! I'M GETTING SOMETHING FROM DOWNTOWN...!

SOUNDS LIKE SOME KIND OF MONSTER IS RUNNING WILD IN THE STREETS...

...GETTING REPORTS OF SEVERE CIVILIAN *CASUALTIES!*

EH...?

WELL, I CERTAINLY CAN'T HANG AROUND *HERE* IF INNOCENT CITIZENS ARE IN *DANGER...!*

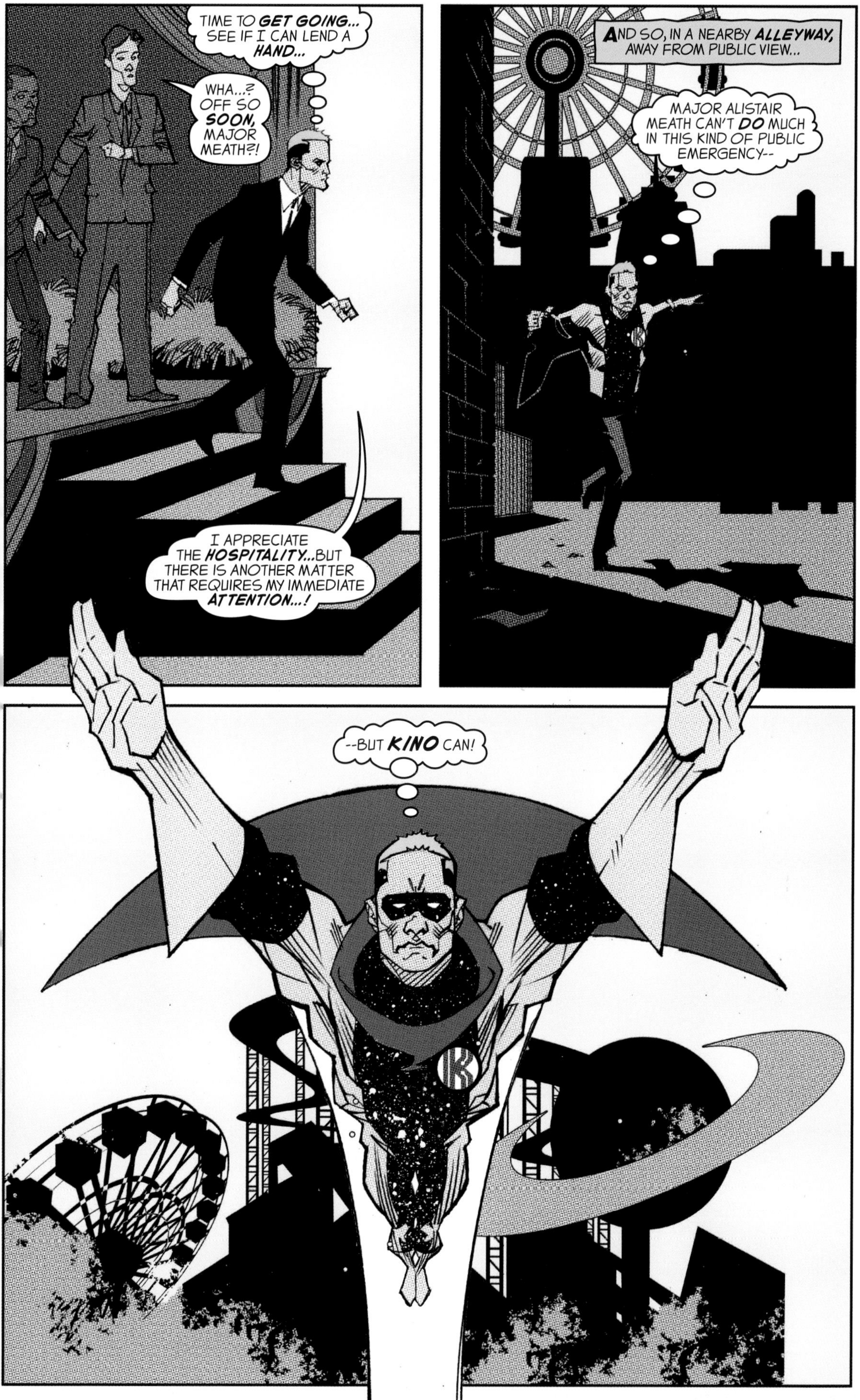
TIME TO GET GOING... SEE IF I CAN LEND A HAND...
WHA...? OFF SO SOON, MAJOR MEATH?!
I APPRECIATE THE HOSPITALITY...BUT THERE IS ANOTHER MATTER THAT REQUIRES MY IMMEDIATE ATTENTION...!
AND SO, IN A NEARBY ALLEYWAY, AWAY FROM PUBLIC VIEW...
MAJOR ALISTAIR MEATH CAN'T DO MUCH IN THIS KIND OF PUBLIC EMERGENCY--
--BUT KINO CAN!

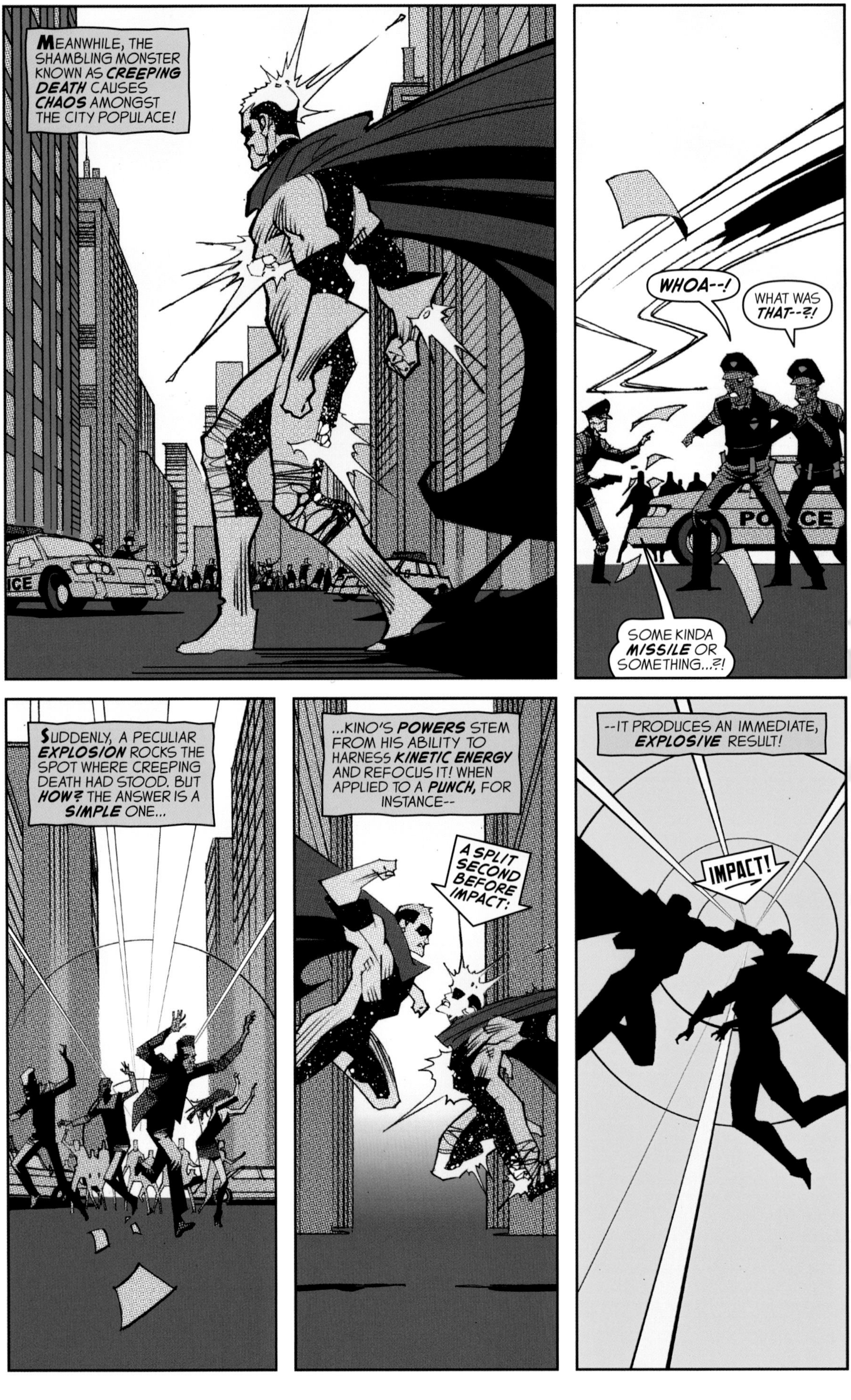
MEANWHILE, THE SHAMBLING MONSTER KNOWN AS **CREEPING DEATH** CAUSES **CHAOS** AMONGST THE CITY POPULACE!
WHOA--!
WHAT WAS **THAT--?!**
SOME KINDA **MISSILE** OR SOMETHING...?!
SUDDENLY, A PECULIAR **EXPLOSION** ROCKS THE SPOT WHERE CREEPING DEATH HAD STOOD. BUT **HOW?** THE ANSWER IS A **SIMPLE** ONE...
...KINO'S **POWERS** STEM FROM HIS ABILITY TO HARNESS **KINETIC ENERGY** AND REFOCUS IT! WHEN APPLIED TO A **PUNCH,** FOR INSTANCE--
A SPLIT SECOND BEFORE IMPACT:
--IT PRODUCES AN IMMEDIATE, **EXPLOSIVE** RESULT!
IMPACT!

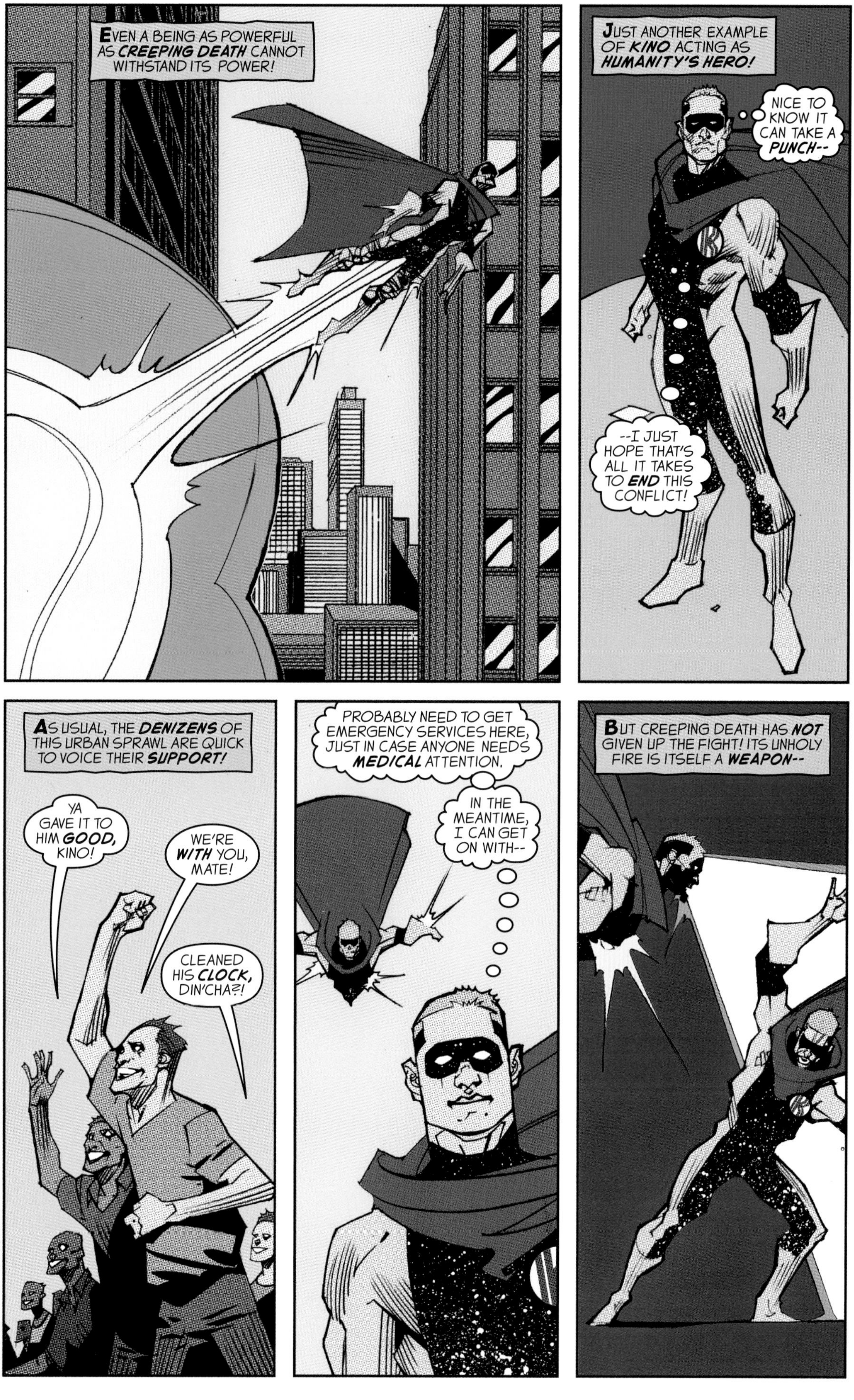
EVEN A BEING AS POWERFUL AS CREEPING DEATH CANNOT WITHSTAND ITS POWER!
JUST ANOTHER EXAMPLE OF KINO ACTING AS HUMANITY'S HERO!
NICE TO KNOW IT CAN TAKE A PUNCH--
--I JUST HOPE THAT'S ALL IT TAKES TO END THIS CONFLICT!
AS USUAL, THE DENIZENS OF THIS URBAN SPRAWL ARE QUICK TO VOICE THEIR SUPPORT!
YA GAVE IT TO HIM GOOD, KINO!
WE'RE WITH YOU, MATE!
CLEANED HIS CLOCK, DIN'CHA?!
PROBABLY NEED TO GET EMERGENCY SERVICES HERE, JUST IN CASE ANYONE NEEDS MEDICAL ATTENTION.
IN THE MEANTIME, I CAN GET ON WITH--
BUT CREEPING DEATH HAS NOT GIVEN UP THE FIGHT! ITS UNHOLY FIRE IS ITSELF A WEAPON--

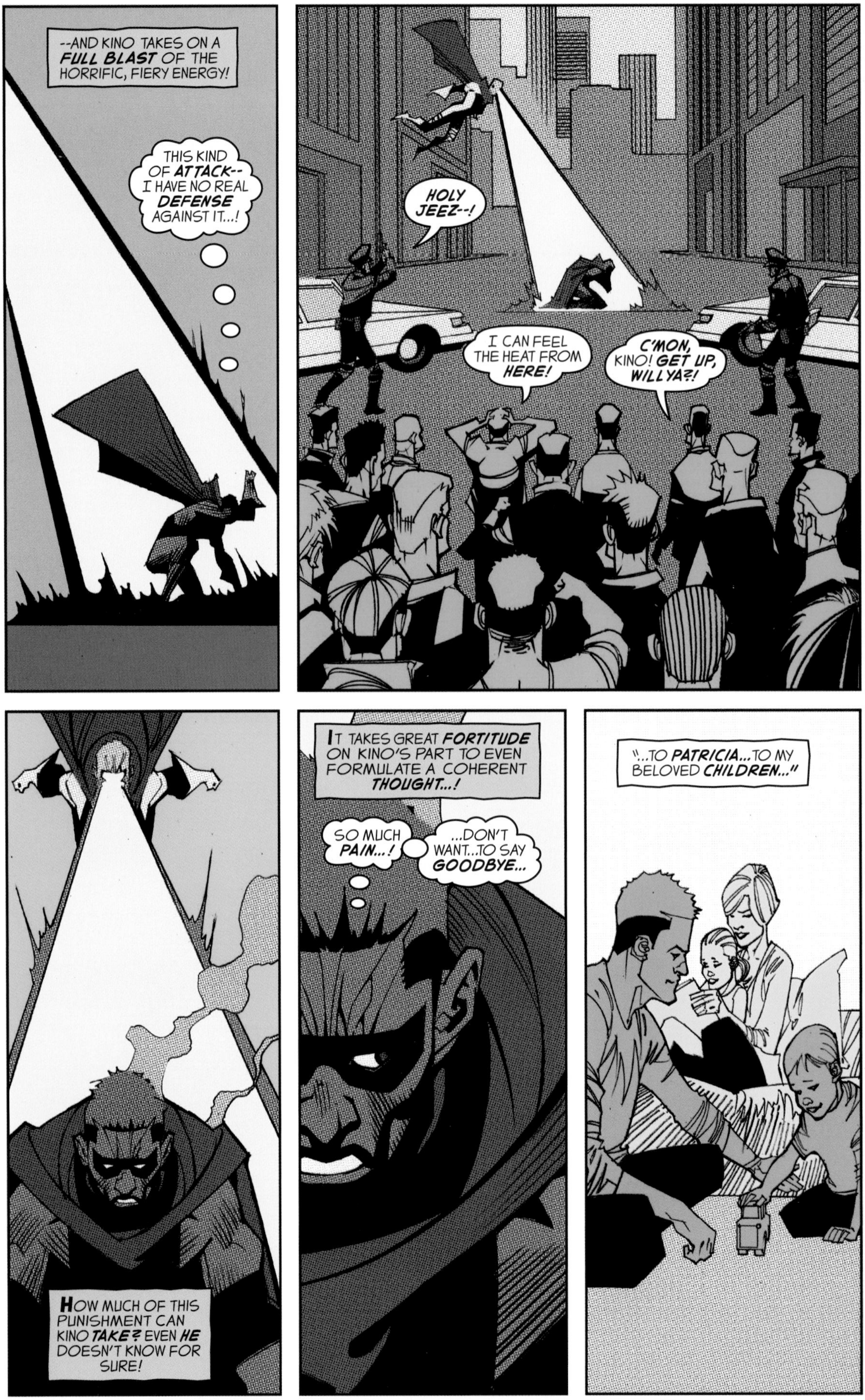
--AND KINO TAKES ON A FULL BLAST OF THE HORRIFIC, FIERY ENERGY!
THIS KIND OF ATTACK-- I HAVE NO REAL DEFENSE AGAINST IT...!
HOLY JEEZ--!
I CAN FEEL THE HEAT FROM HERE!
C'MON, KINO! GET UP, WILLYA?!
HOW MUCH OF THIS PUNISHMENT CAN KINO TAKE? EVEN HE DOESN'T KNOW FOR SURE!
IT TAKES GREAT FORTITUDE ON KINO'S PART TO EVEN FORMULATE A COHERENT THOUGHT...!
SO MUCH PAIN...!
...DON'T WANT...TO SAY GOODBYE...
"...TO PATRICIA...TO MY BELOVED CHILDREN..."

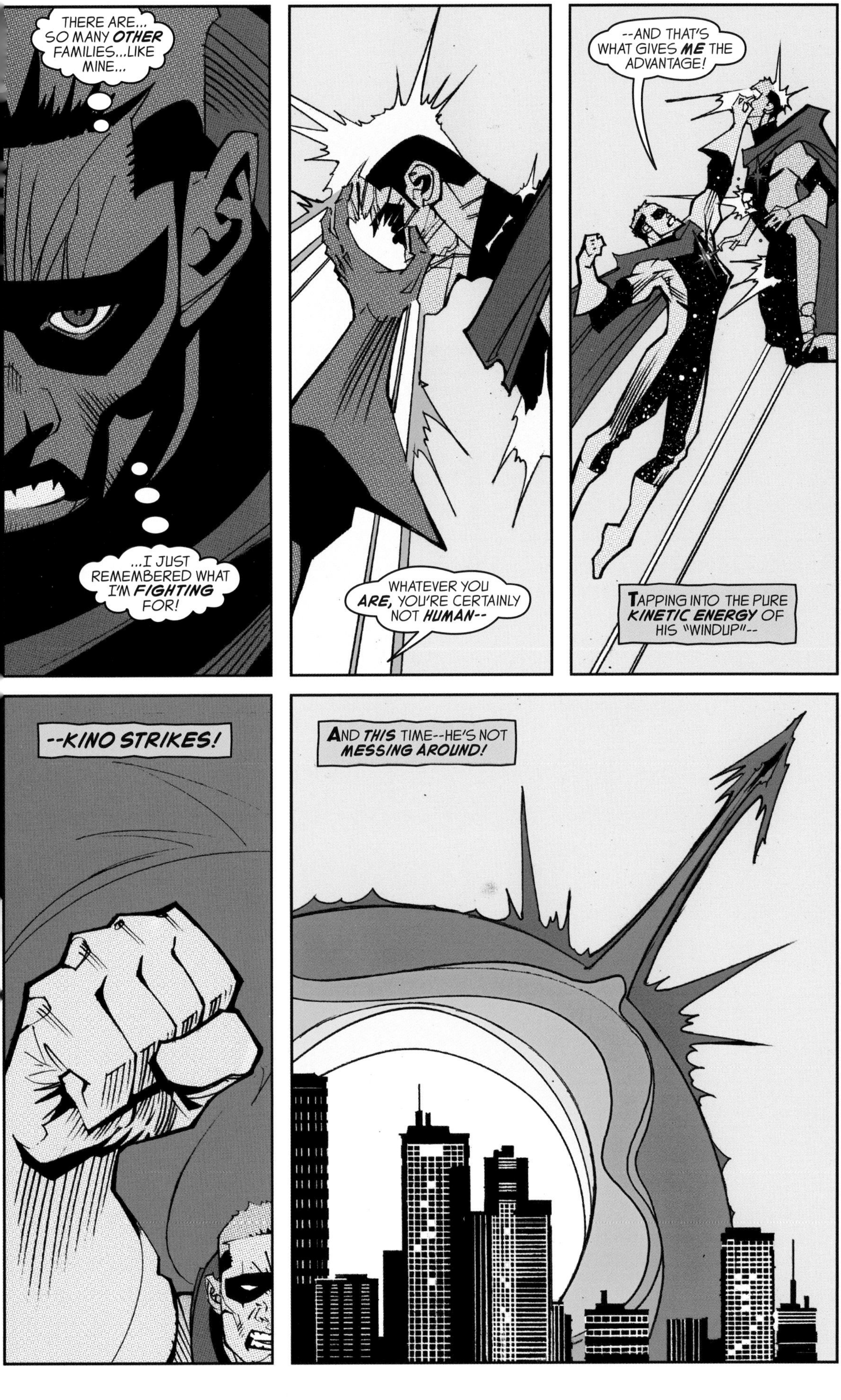
THERE ARE... SO MANY **OTHER** FAMILIES...LIKE MINE...
...I JUST REMEMBERED WHAT I'M **FIGHTING** FOR!
WHATEVER YOU **ARE,** YOU'RE CERTAINLY NOT **HUMAN--**
--AND THAT'S WHAT GIVES **ME** THE ADVANTAGE!
TAPPING INTO THE PURE **KINETIC ENERGY** OF HIS "WINDUP"--
--KINO STRIKES!
AND **THIS** TIME--HE'S NOT **MESSING AROUND!**

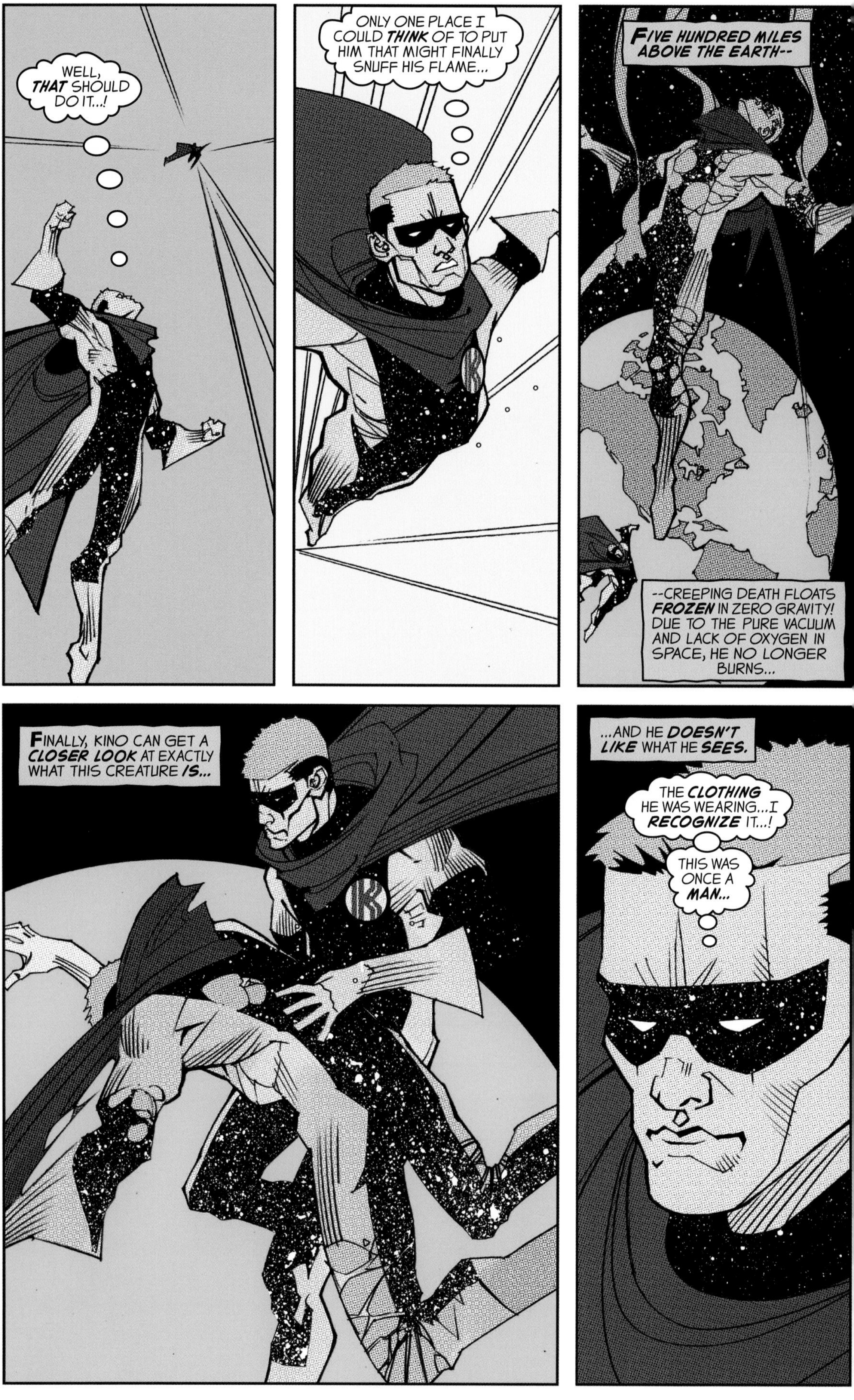
WELL, THAT SHOULD DO IT...!
ONLY ONE PLACE I COULD THINK OF TO PUT HIM THAT MIGHT FINALLY SNUFF HIS FLAME...
FIVE HUNDRED MILES ABOVE THE EARTH--
--CREEPING DEATH FLOATS FROZEN IN ZERO GRAVITY! DUE TO THE PURE VACUUM AND LACK OF OXYGEN IN SPACE, HE NO LONGER BURNS...
FINALLY, KINO CAN GET A CLOSER LOOK AT EXACTLY WHAT THIS CREATURE IS...
...AND HE DOESN'T LIKE WHAT HE SEES.
THE CLOTHING HE WAS WEARING...I RECOGNIZE IT...!
THIS WAS ONCE A MAN...

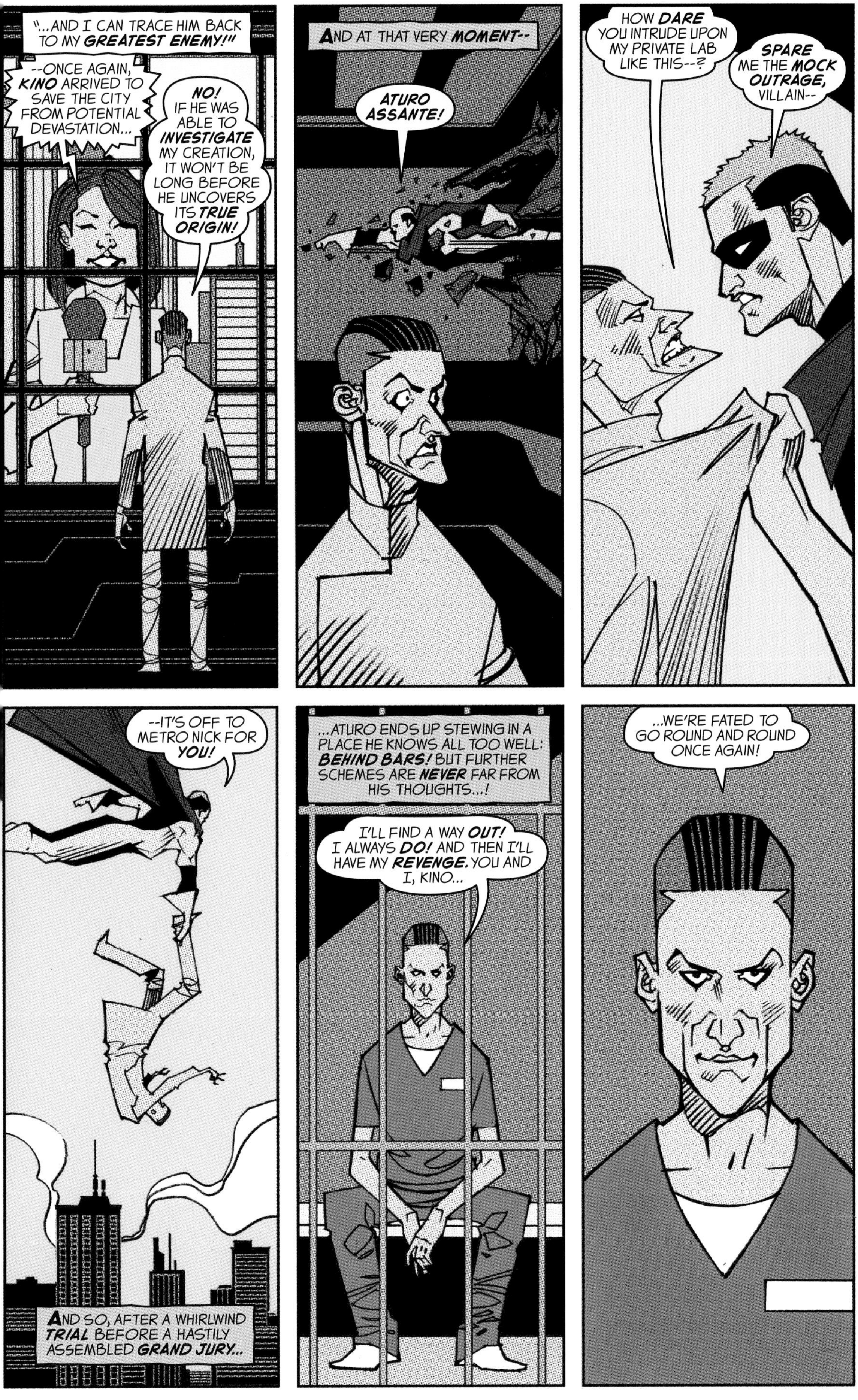
"...AND I CAN TRACE HIM BACK TO MY GREATEST ENEMY!"
--ONCE AGAIN, KINO ARRIVED TO SAVE THE CITY FROM POTENTIAL DEVASTATION...
NO! IF HE WAS ABLE TO INVESTIGATE MY CREATION, IT WON'T BE LONG BEFORE HE UNCOVERS ITS TRUE ORIGIN!
AND AT THAT VERY MOMENT--
ATURO ASSANTE!
HOW DARE YOU INTRUDE UPON MY PRIVATE LAB LIKE THIS--?
SPARE ME THE MOCK OUTRAGE, VILLAIN--
--IT'S OFF TO METRO NICK FOR YOU!
AND SO, AFTER A WHIRLWIND TRIAL BEFORE A HASTILY ASSEMBLED GRAND JURY...
...ATURO ENDS UP STEWING IN A PLACE HE KNOWS ALL TOO WELL: BEHIND BARS! BUT FURTHER SCHEMES ARE NEVER FAR FROM HIS THOUGHTS...!
I'LL FIND A WAY OUT! I ALWAYS DO! AND THEN I'LL HAVE MY REVENGE. YOU AND I, KINO...
...WE'RE FATED TO GO ROUND AND ROUND ONCE AGAIN!

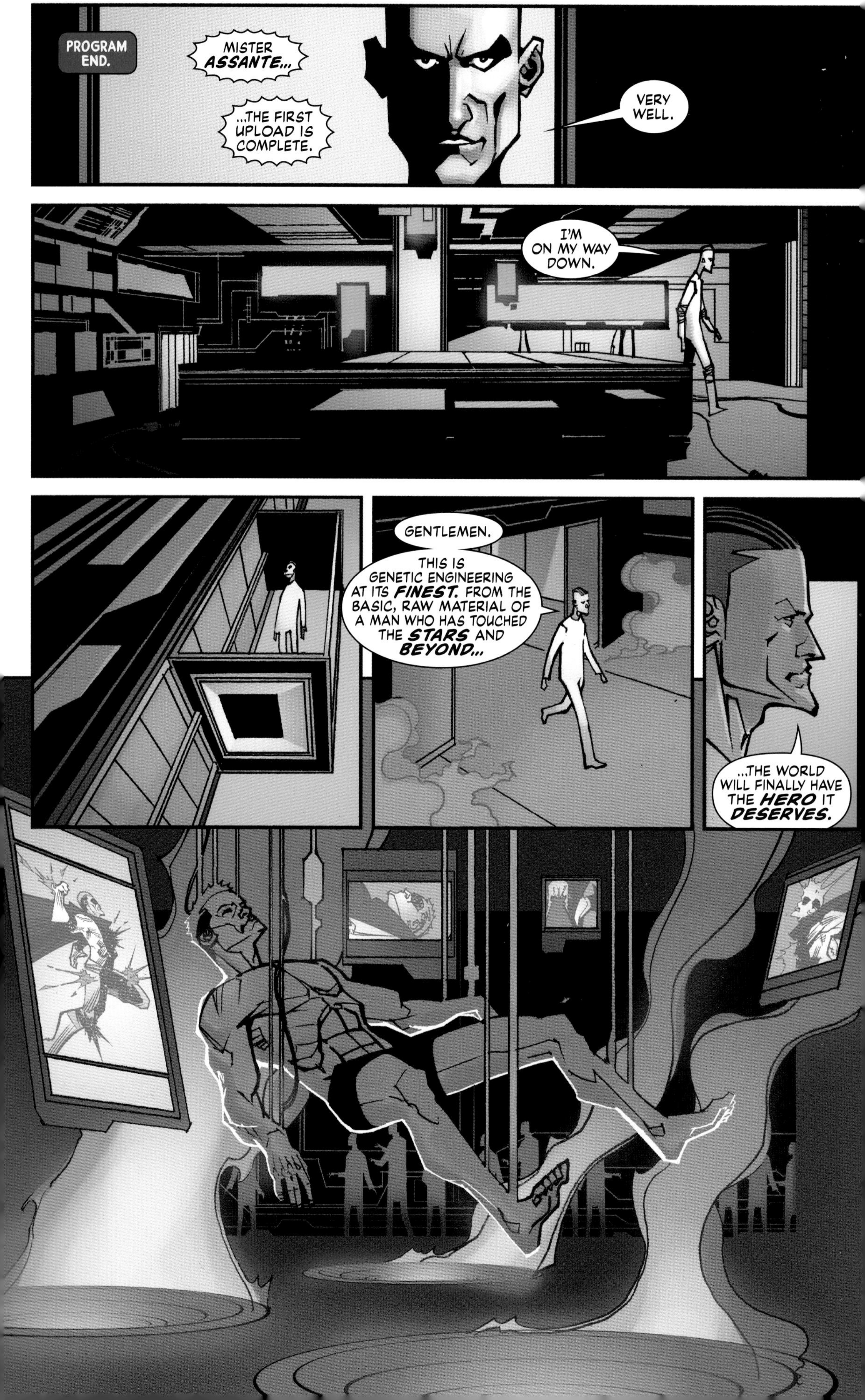
PROGRAM END.
MISTER ASSANTE...
...THE FIRST UPLOAD IS COMPLETE.
VERY WELL.
I'M ON MY WAY DOWN.
GENTLEMEN.
THIS IS GENETIC ENGINEERING AT ITS FINEST. FROM THE BASIC, RAW MATERIAL OF A MAN WHO HAS TOUCHED THE STARS AND BEYOND...
...THE WORLD WILL FINALLY HAVE THE HERO IT DESERVES.

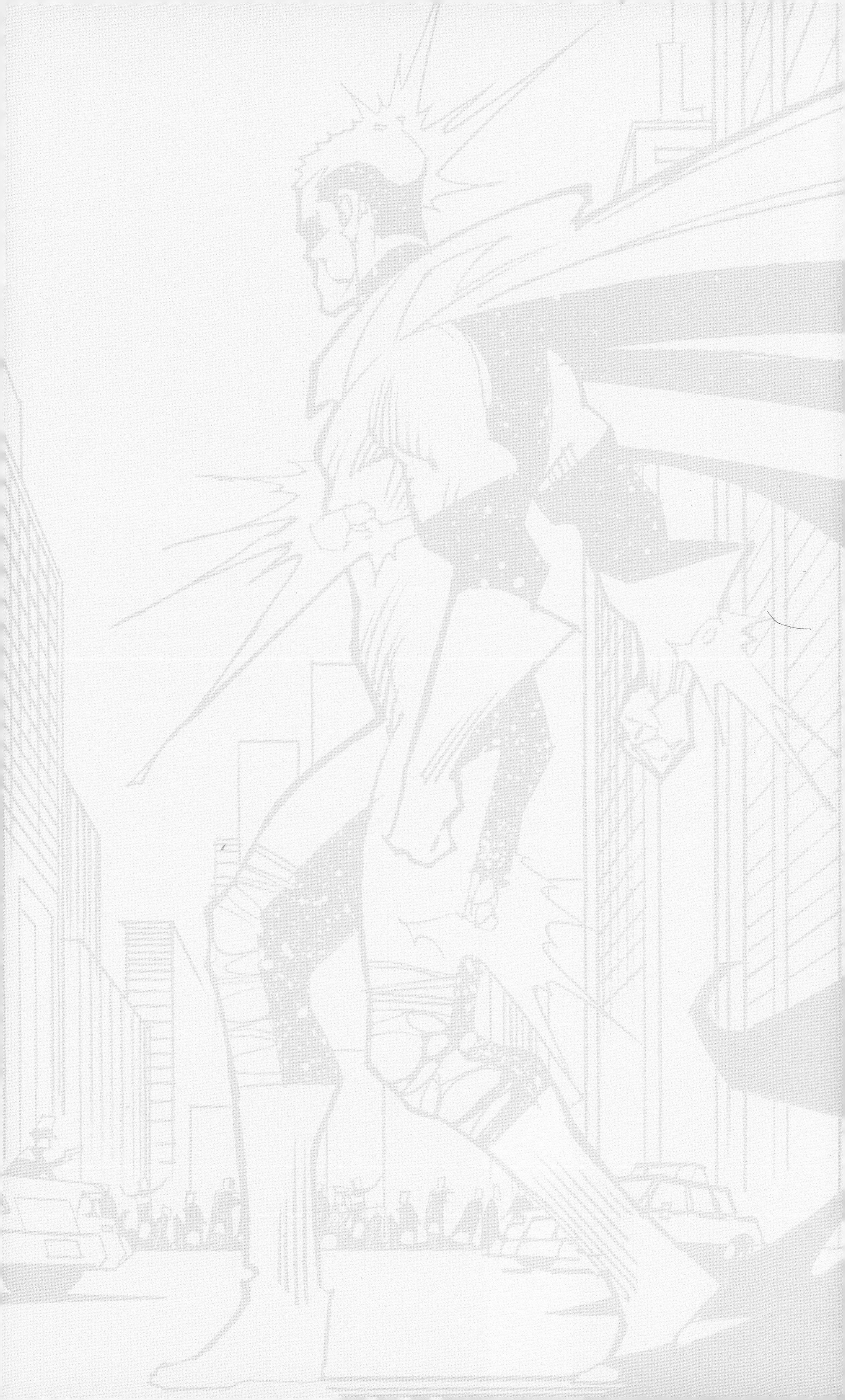

CHAPTER TWO

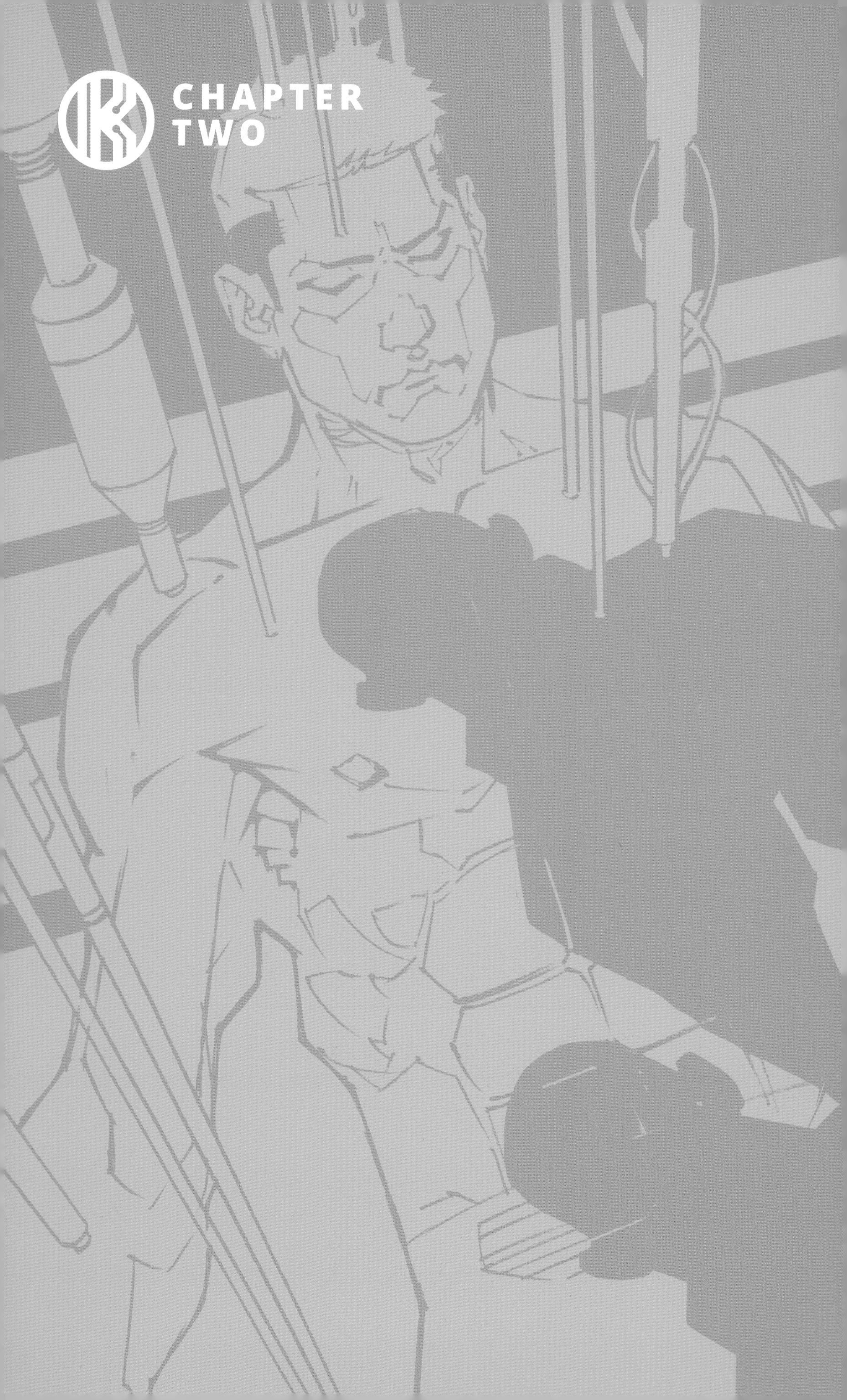

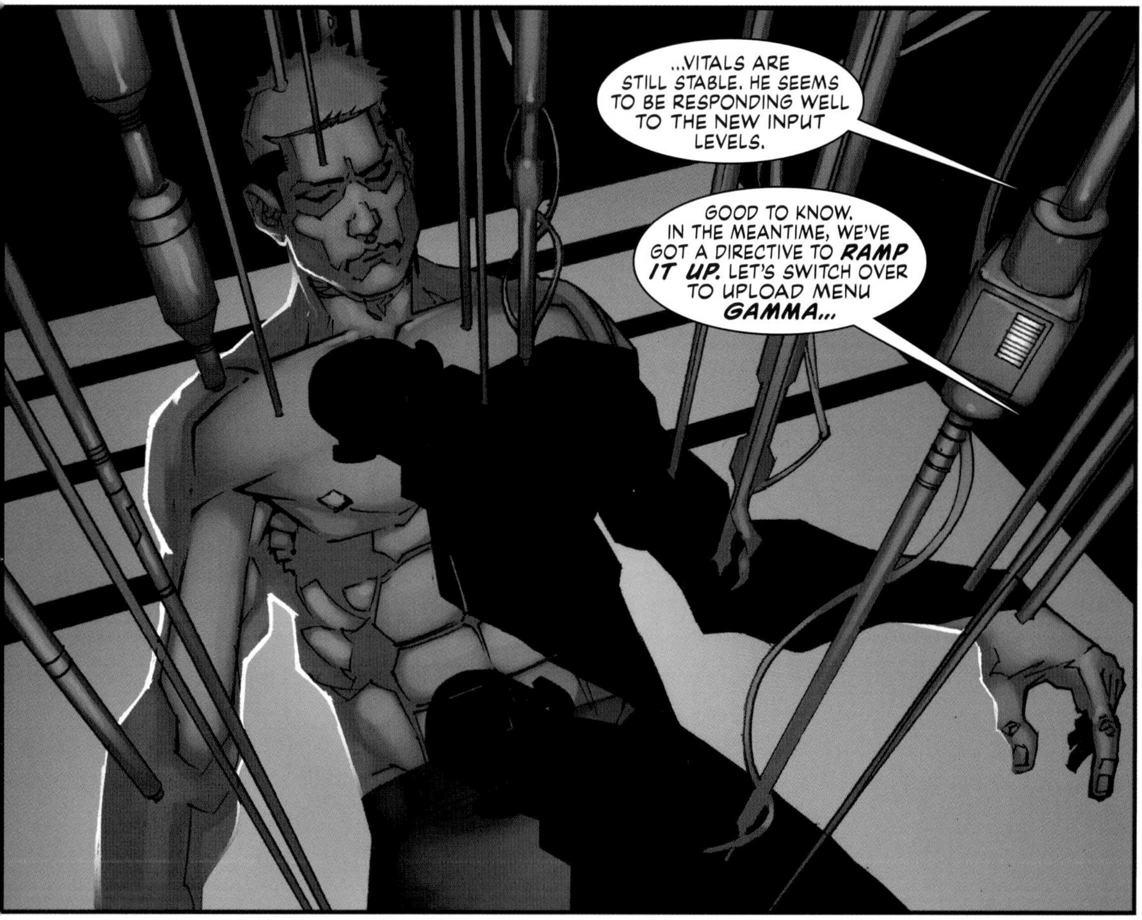
...VITALS ARE STILL STABLE. HE SEEMS TO BE RESPONDING WELL TO THE NEW INPUT LEVELS.
GOOD TO KNOW. IN THE MEANTIME, WE'VE GOT A DIRECTIVE TO RAMP IT UP. LET'S SWITCH OVER TO UPLOAD MENU GAMMA...
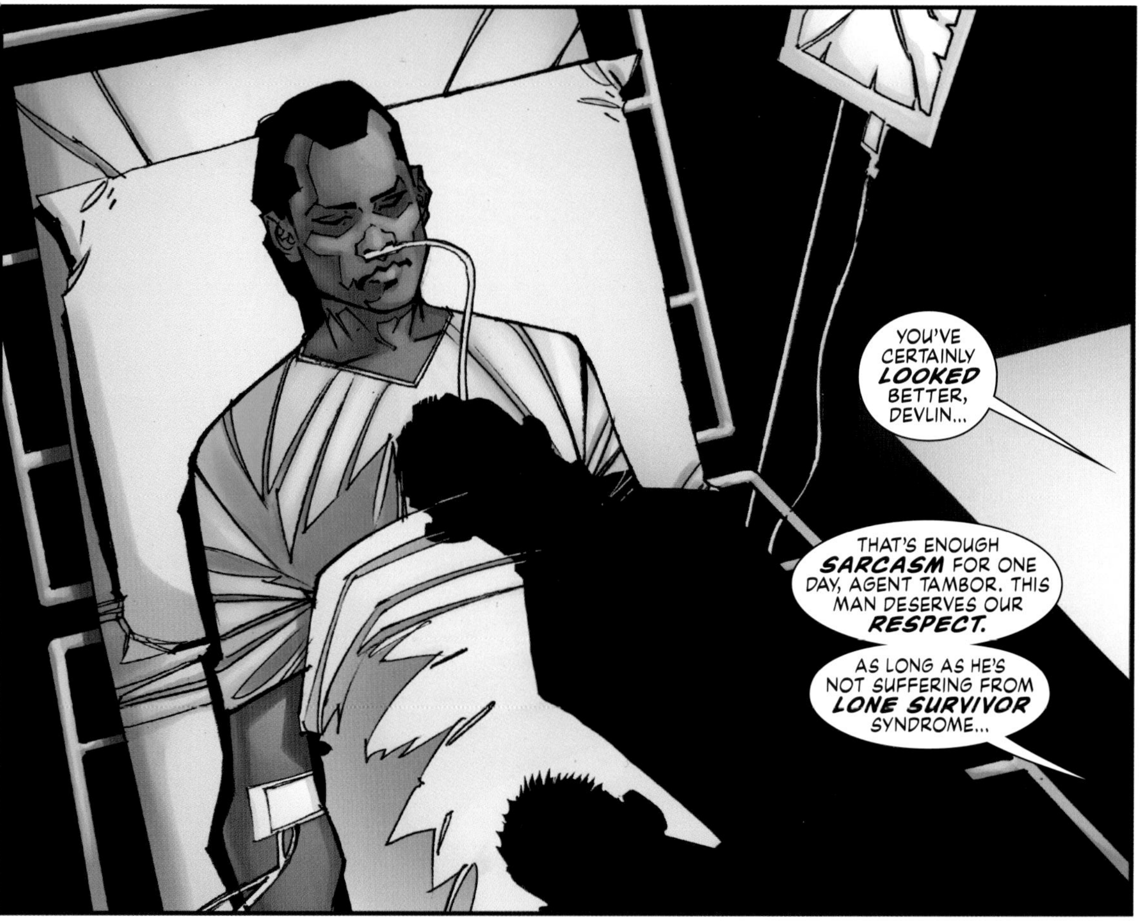
YOU'VE CERTAINLY LOOKED BETTER, DEVLIN...
THAT'S ENOUGH SARCASM FOR ONE DAY, AGENT TAMBOR. THIS MAN DESERVES OUR RESPECT.
AS LONG AS HE'S NOT SUFFERING FROM LONE SURVIVOR SYNDROME...

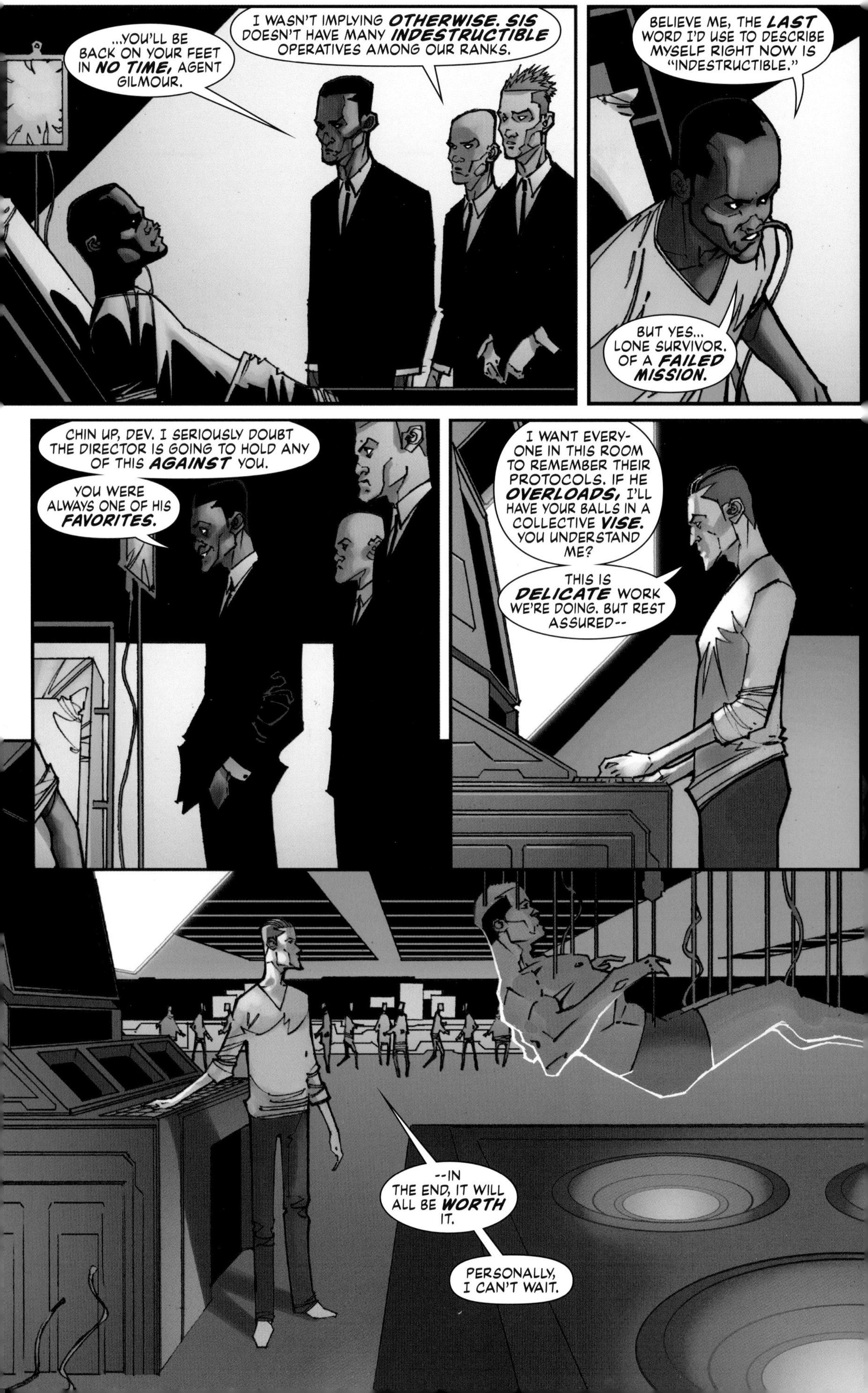

...YOU'LL BE BACK ON YOUR FEET IN NO TIME, AGENT GILMOUR.
I WASN'T IMPLYING OTHERWISE. SIS DOESN'T HAVE MANY INDESTRUCTIBLE OPERATIVES AMONG OUR RANKS.
BELIEVE ME, THE LAST WORD I'D USE TO DESCRIBE MYSELF RIGHT NOW IS "INDESTRUCTIBLE."
BUT YES... LONE SURVIVOR. OF A FAILED MISSION.
CHIN UP, DEV. I SERIOUSLY DOUBT THE DIRECTOR IS GOING TO HOLD ANY OF THIS AGAINST YOU.
YOU WERE ALWAYS ONE OF HIS FAVORITES.
I WANT EVERY-ONE IN THIS ROOM TO REMEMBER THEIR PROTOCOLS. IF HE OVERLOADS, I'LL HAVE YOUR BALLS IN A COLLECTIVE VISE. YOU UNDERSTAND ME?
THIS IS DELICATE WORK WE'RE DOING. BUT REST ASSURED--
--IN THE END, IT WILL ALL BE WORTH IT.
PERSONALLY, I CAN'T WAIT.

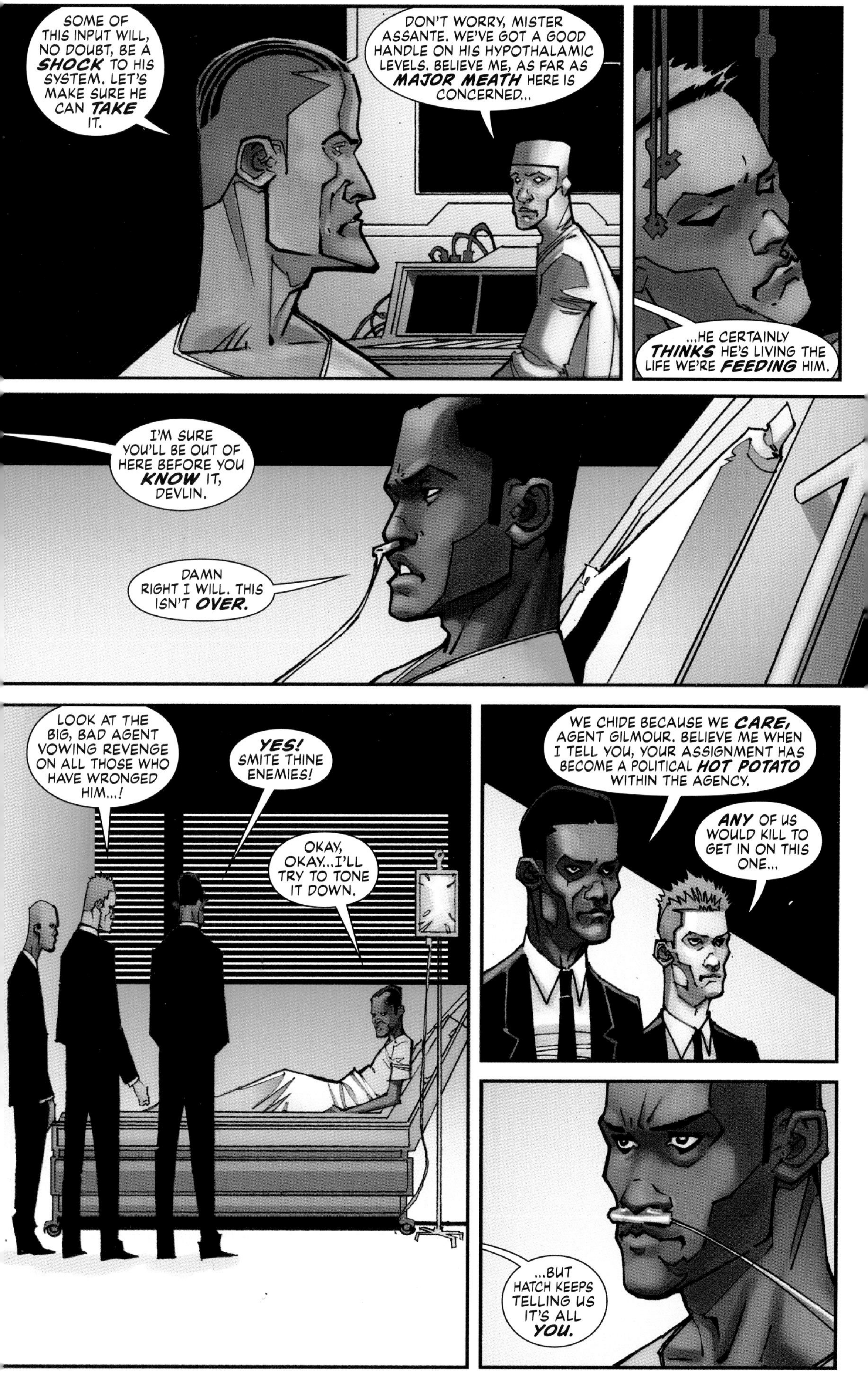
SOME OF THIS INPUT WILL, NO DOUBT, BE A SHOCK TO HIS SYSTEM. LET'S MAKE SURE HE CAN TAKE IT.
DON'T WORRY, MISTER ASSANTE. WE'VE GOT A GOOD HANDLE ON HIS HYPOTHALAMIC LEVELS. BELIEVE ME, AS FAR AS MAJOR MEATH HERE IS CONCERNED...
...HE CERTAINLY THINKS HE'S LIVING THE LIFE WE'RE FEEDING HIM.
I'M SURE YOU'LL BE OUT OF HERE BEFORE YOU KNOW IT, DEVLIN.
DAMN RIGHT I WILL. THIS ISN'T OVER.
LOOK AT THE BIG, BAD AGENT VOWING REVENGE ON ALL THOSE WHO HAVE WRONGED HIM...!
YES! SMITE THINE ENEMIES!
OKAY, OKAY...I'LL TRY TO TONE IT DOWN.
WE CHIDE BECAUSE WE CARE, AGENT GILMOUR. BELIEVE ME WHEN I TELL YOU, YOUR ASSIGNMENT HAS BECOME A POLITICAL HOT POTATO WITHIN THE AGENCY.
ANY OF US WOULD KILL TO GET IN ON THIS ONE...
...BUT HATCH KEEPS TELLING US IT'S ALL YOU.

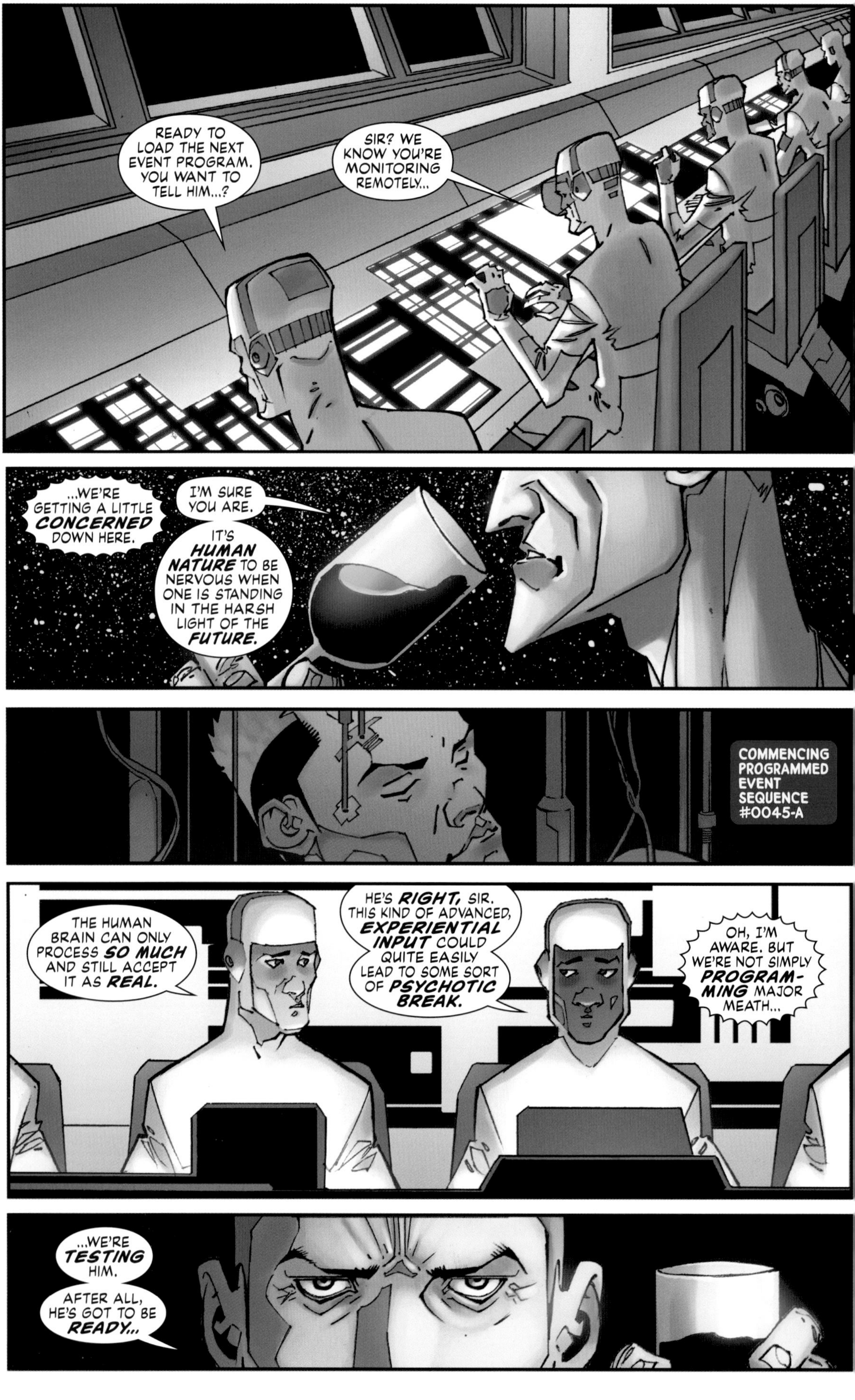
READY TO LOAD THE NEXT EVENT PROGRAM. YOU WANT TO TELL HIM...?
SIR? WE KNOW YOU'RE MONITORING REMOTELY...
...WE'RE GETTING A LITTLE CONCERNED DOWN HERE.
I'M SURE YOU ARE.
IT'S HUMAN NATURE TO BE NERVOUS WHEN ONE IS STANDING IN THE HARSH LIGHT OF THE FUTURE.
COMMENCING PROGRAMMED EVENT SEQUENCE #0045-A
THE HUMAN BRAIN CAN ONLY PROCESS SO MUCH AND STILL ACCEPT IT AS REAL.
HE'S RIGHT, SIR. THIS KIND OF ADVANCED, EXPERIENTIAL INPUT COULD QUITE EASILY LEAD TO SOME SORT OF PSYCHOTIC BREAK.
OH, I'M AWARE. BUT WE'RE NOT SIMPLY PROGRAM-MING MAJOR MEATH...
...WE'RE TESTING HIM.
AFTER ALL, HE'S GOT TO BE READY...

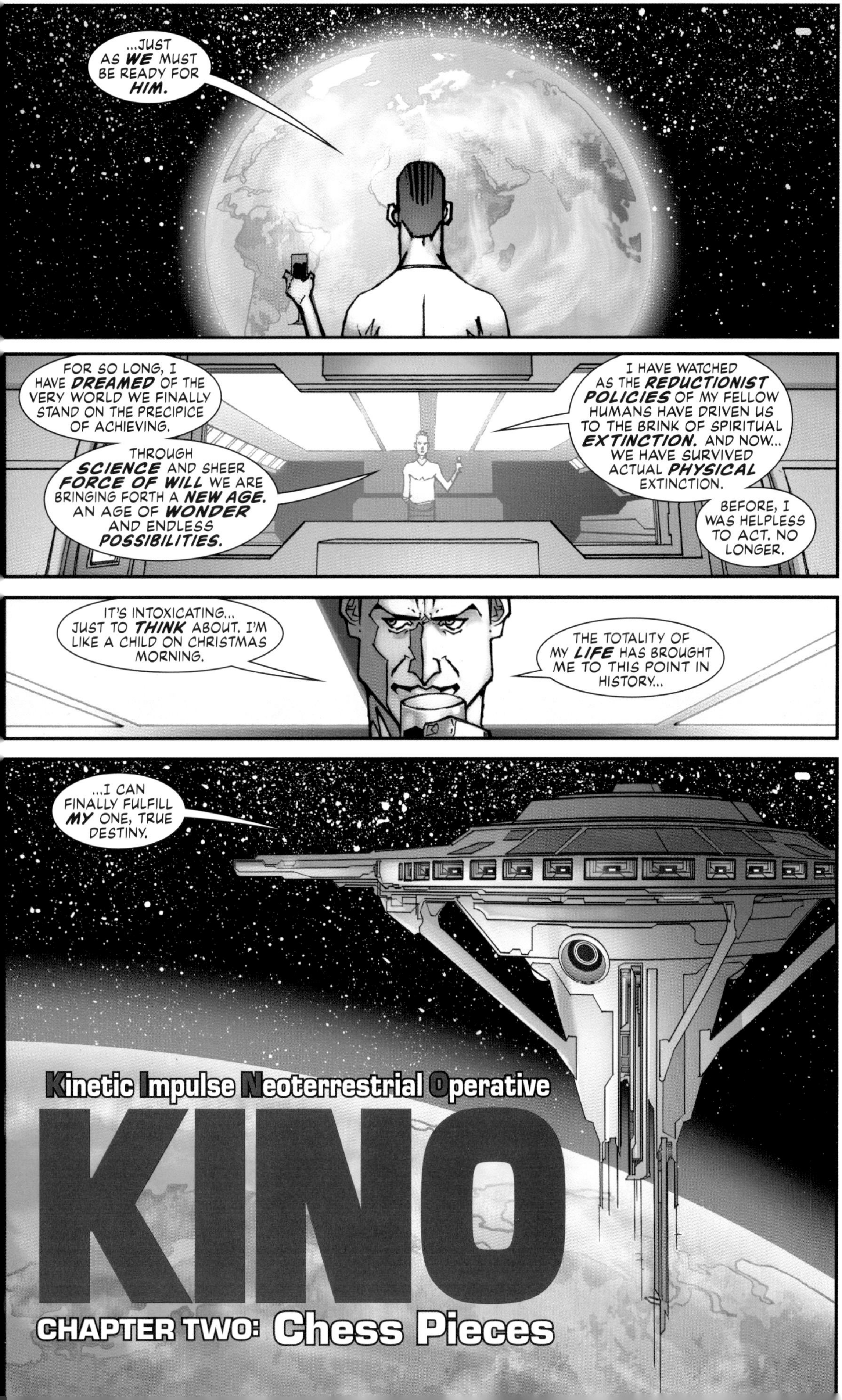
...JUST AS WE MUST BE READY FOR HIM.
FOR SO LONG, I HAVE DREAMED OF THE VERY WORLD WE FINALLY STAND ON THE PRECIPICE OF ACHIEVING.
THROUGH SCIENCE AND SHEER FORCE OF WILL WE ARE BRINGING FORTH A NEW AGE. AN AGE OF WONDER AND ENDLESS POSSIBILITIES.
I HAVE WATCHED AS THE REDUCTIONIST POLICIES OF MY FELLOW HUMANS HAVE DRIVEN US TO THE BRINK OF SPIRITUAL EXTINCTION. AND NOW... WE HAVE SURVIVED ACTUAL PHYSICAL EXTINCTION.
BEFORE, I WAS HELPLESS TO ACT. NO LONGER.
IT'S INTOXICATING... JUST TO THINK ABOUT. I'M LIKE A CHILD ON CHRISTMAS MORNING.
THE TOTALITY OF MY LIFE HAS BROUGHT ME TO THIS POINT IN HISTORY...
...I CAN FINALLY FULFILL MY ONE, TRUE DESTINY.
Kinetic Impulse Neoterrestrial Operative
KINO
CHAPTER TWO: Chess Pieces

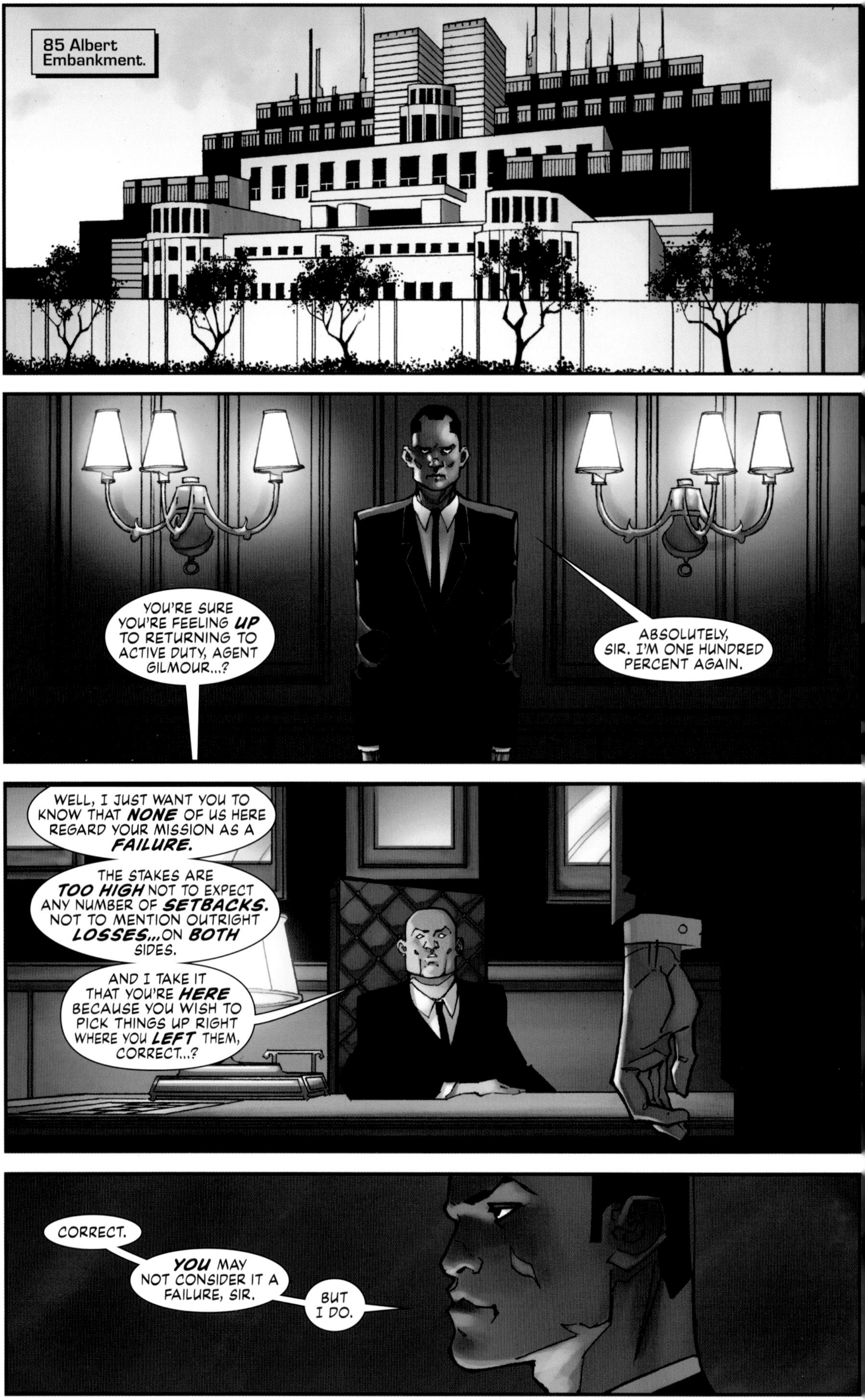
85 Albert Embankment.
YOU'RE SURE YOU'RE FEELING *UP* TO RETURNING TO ACTIVE DUTY, AGENT GILMOUR...?
ABSOLUTELY, SIR. I'M ONE HUNDRED PERCENT AGAIN.
WELL, I JUST WANT YOU TO KNOW THAT *NONE* OF US HERE REGARD YOUR MISSION AS A *FAILURE.*
THE STAKES ARE *TOO HIGH* NOT TO EXPECT ANY NUMBER OF *SETBACKS.* NOT TO MENTION OUTRIGHT *LOSSES*...ON *BOTH* SIDES.
AND I TAKE IT THAT YOU'RE *HERE* BECAUSE YOU WISH TO PICK THINGS UP RIGHT WHERE YOU *LEFT* THEM, CORRECT...?
CORRECT.
YOU MAY NOT CONSIDER IT A FAILURE, SIR.
BUT I DO.

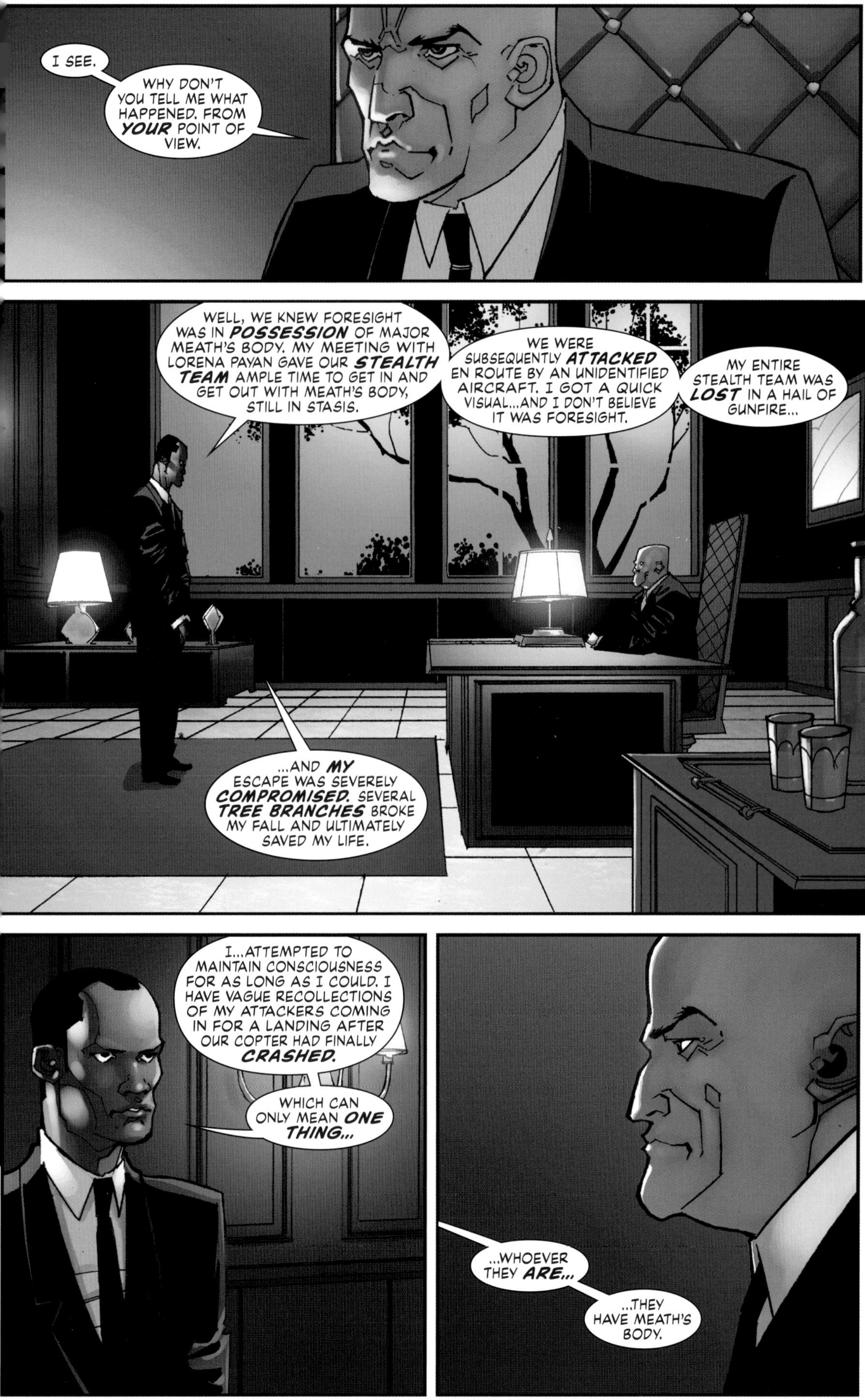
I SEE.
WHY DON'T YOU TELL ME WHAT HAPPENED. FROM YOUR POINT OF VIEW.
WELL, WE KNEW FORESIGHT WAS IN POSSESSION OF MAJOR MEATH'S BODY. MY MEETING WITH LORENA PAYAN GAVE OUR STEALTH TEAM AMPLE TIME TO GET IN AND GET OUT WITH MEATH'S BODY, STILL IN STASIS.
WE WERE SUBSEQUENTLY ATTACKED EN ROUTE BY AN UNIDENTIFIED AIRCRAFT. I GOT A QUICK VISUAL...AND I DON'T BELIEVE IT WAS FORESIGHT.
MY ENTIRE STEALTH TEAM WAS LOST IN A HAIL OF GUNFIRE...
...AND MY ESCAPE WAS SEVERELY COMPROMISED. SEVERAL TREE BRANCHES BROKE MY FALL AND ULTIMATELY SAVED MY LIFE.
I...ATTEMPTED TO MAINTAIN CONSCIOUSNESS FOR AS LONG AS I COULD. I HAVE VAGUE RECOLLECTIONS OF MY ATTACKERS COMING IN FOR A LANDING AFTER OUR COPTER HAD FINALLY CRASHED.
WHICH CAN ONLY MEAN ONE THING...
...WHOEVER THEY ARE...
...THEY HAVE MEATH'S BODY.

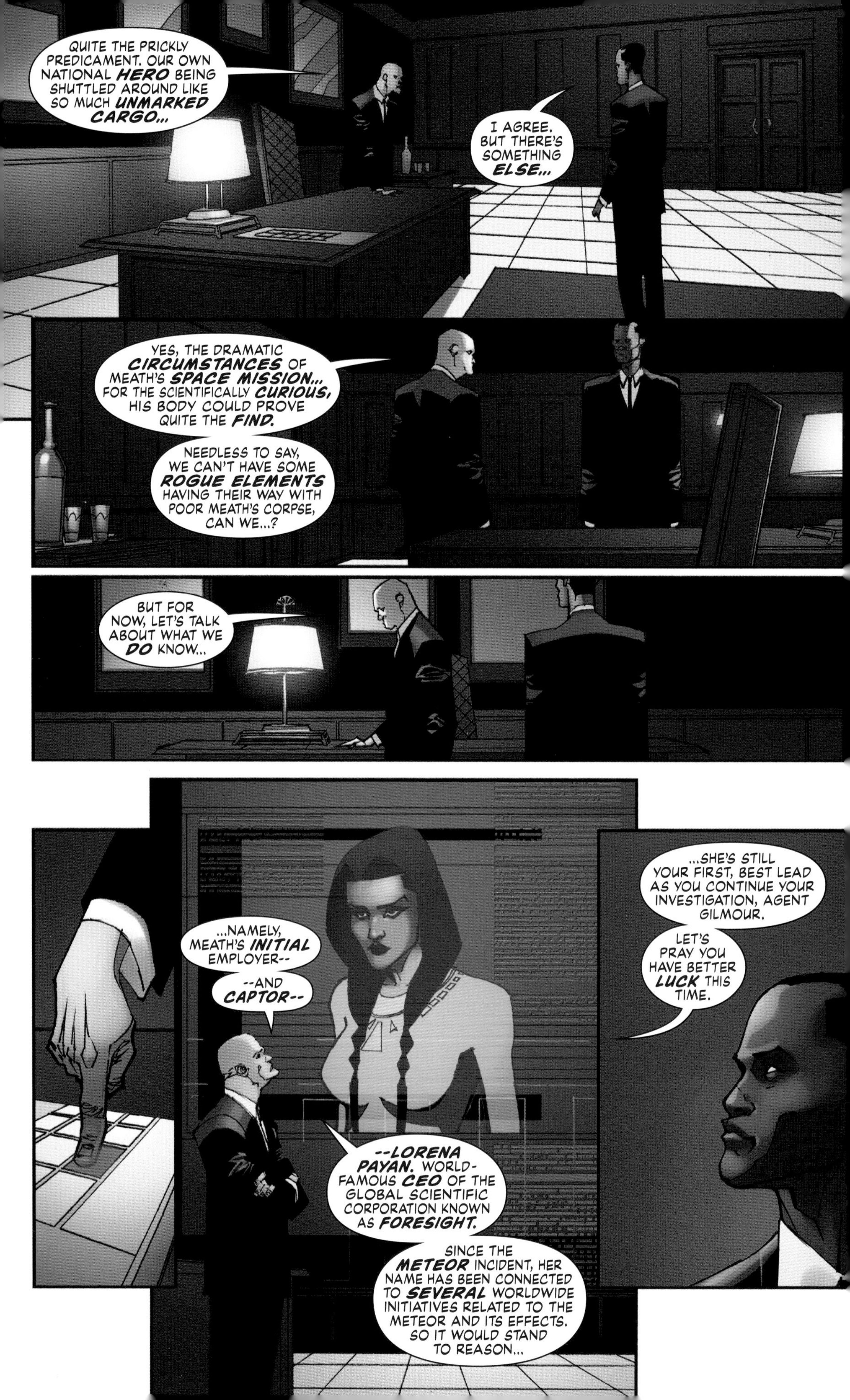
QUITE THE PRICKLY PREDICAMENT. OUR OWN NATIONAL HERO BEING SHUTTLED AROUND LIKE SO MUCH UNMARKED CARGO...
I AGREE. BUT THERE'S SOMETHING ELSE...
YES, THE DRAMATIC CIRCUMSTANCES OF MEATH'S SPACE MISSION... FOR THE SCIENTIFICALLY CURIOUS, HIS BODY COULD PROVE QUITE THE FIND.
NEEDLESS TO SAY, WE CAN'T HAVE SOME ROGUE ELEMENTS HAVING THEIR WAY WITH POOR MEATH'S CORPSE, CAN WE...?
BUT FOR NOW, LET'S TALK ABOUT WHAT WE DO KNOW...
...NAMELY, MEATH'S INITIAL EMPLOYER--
--AND CAPTOR--
--LORENA PAYAN. WORLD-FAMOUS CEO OF THE GLOBAL SCIENTIFIC CORPORATION KNOWN AS FORESIGHT.
SINCE THE METEOR INCIDENT, HER NAME HAS BEEN CONNECTED TO SEVERAL WORLDWIDE INITIATIVES RELATED TO THE METEOR AND ITS EFFECTS. SO IT WOULD STAND TO REASON...
...SHE'S STILL YOUR FIRST, BEST LEAD AS YOU CONTINUE YOUR INVESTIGATION, AGENT GILMOUR.
LET'S PRAY YOU HAVE BETTER LUCK THIS TIME.

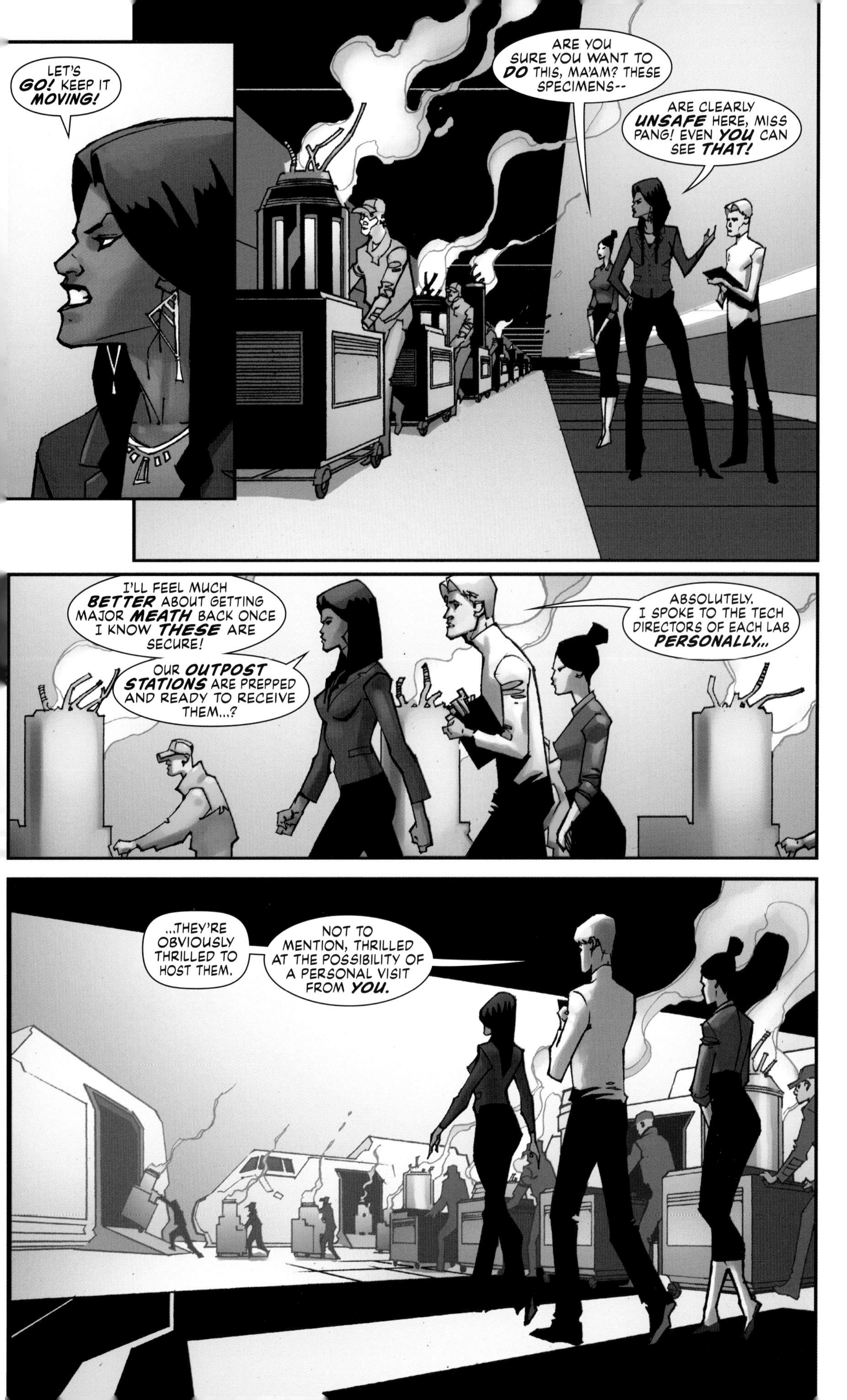

LET'S GO! KEEP IT MOVING!
ARE YOU SURE YOU WANT TO DO THIS, MA'AM? THESE SPECIMENS--
ARE CLEARLY UNSAFE HERE, MISS PANG! EVEN YOU CAN SEE THAT!
I'LL FEEL MUCH BETTER ABOUT GETTING MAJOR MEATH BACK ONCE I KNOW THESE ARE SECURE!
OUR OUTPOST STATIONS ARE PREPPED AND READY TO RECEIVE THEM...?
ABSOLUTELY. I SPOKE TO THE TECH DIRECTORS OF EACH LAB PERSONALLY...
...THEY'RE OBVIOUSLY THRILLED TO HOST THEM.
NOT TO MENTION, THRILLED AT THE POSSIBILITY OF A PERSONAL VISIT FROM YOU.

WELL, THAT'S A FOREGONE **CONCLUSION,** ISN'T IT? WE'VE PUT OFF FULL ANALYSIS LONG ENOUGH.

IT JUST... MAKES ME **NERVOUS,** MA'AM.

I'M WITH MELANIE ON THIS, BOSS. **SEPARATING** THE SPECIMENS? PUTTING THEM ON OPPOSITE CORNERS OF THE **GLOBE,** PRACTICALLY--

FOR THE **FINAL** TIME, THIS IS A **NECESSARY** STEP TO ENSURE THEY REMAIN **SECURE,** NOT TO MENTION FORESIGHT'S **PROPRIETARY CONTROL** OVER EACH OF THEM.

IN THE MEANTIME, **YOU TWO** SHOULD CONCERN YOURSELVES WITH A MORE **PRESSING** MATTER...

...GETTING MEATH **BACK** FROM THE BRITISH BASTARDS WHO **TOOK** HIM FROM ME.

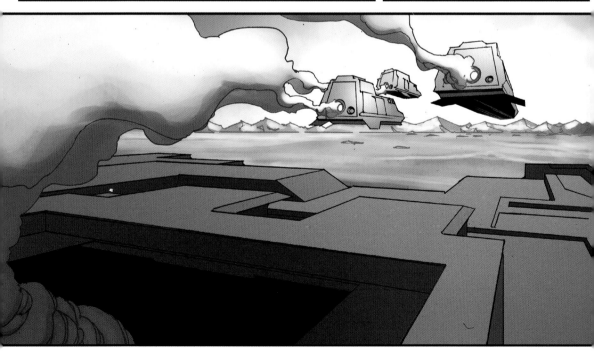

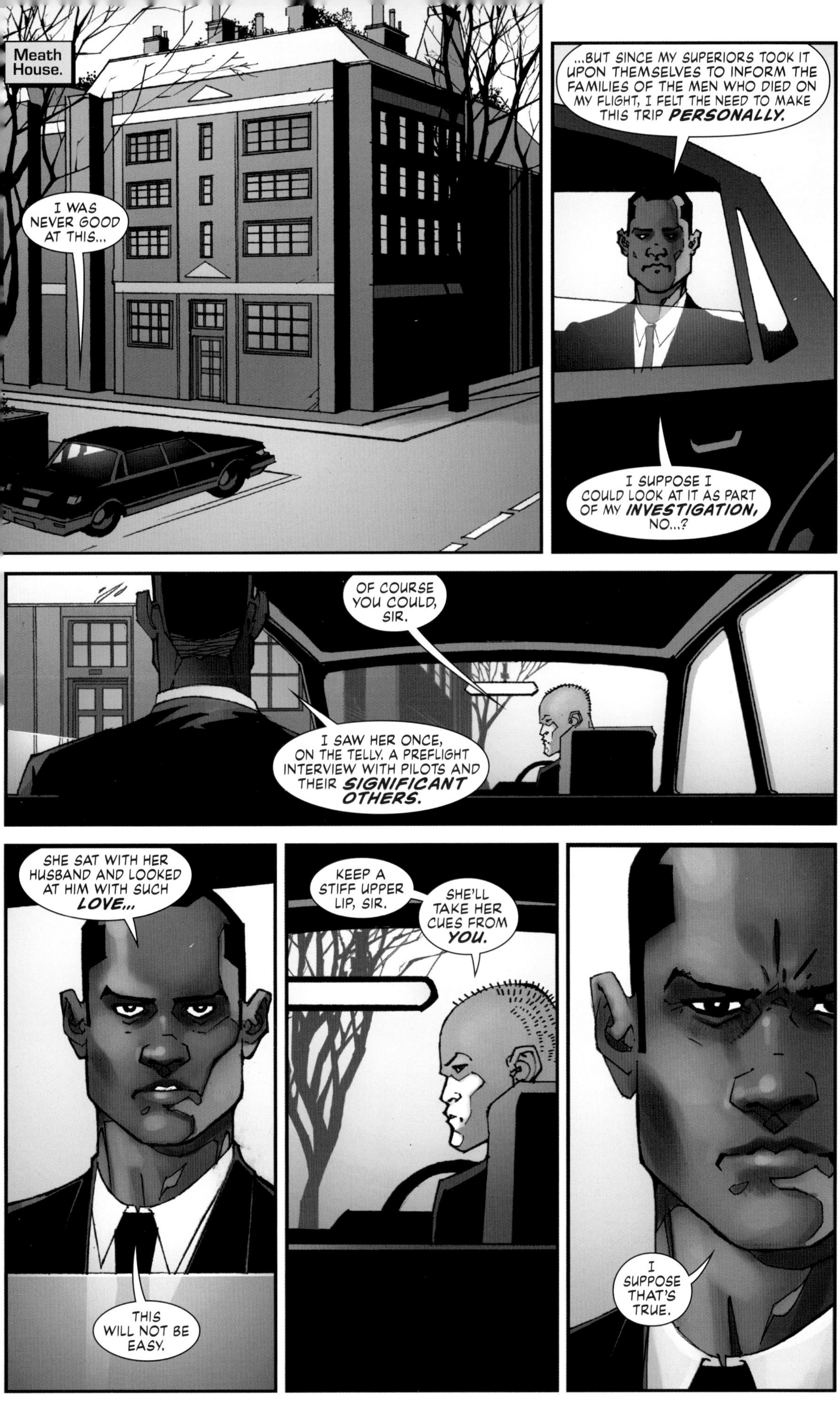
Meath House.
I WAS NEVER GOOD AT THIS...
...BUT SINCE MY SUPERIORS TOOK IT UPON THEMSELVES TO INFORM THE FAMILIES OF THE MEN WHO DIED ON MY FLIGHT, I FELT THE NEED TO MAKE THIS TRIP PERSONALLY.
I SUPPOSE I COULD LOOK AT IT AS PART OF MY INVESTIGATION, NO...?
OF COURSE YOU COULD, SIR.
I SAW HER ONCE, ON THE TELLY. A PREFLIGHT INTERVIEW WITH PILOTS AND THEIR SIGNIFICANT OTHERS.
SHE SAT WITH HER HUSBAND AND LOOKED AT HIM WITH SUCH LOVE...
THIS WILL NOT BE EASY.
KEEP A STIFF UPPER LIP, SIR.
SHE'LL TAKE HER CUES FROM YOU.
I SUPPOSE THAT'S TRUE.

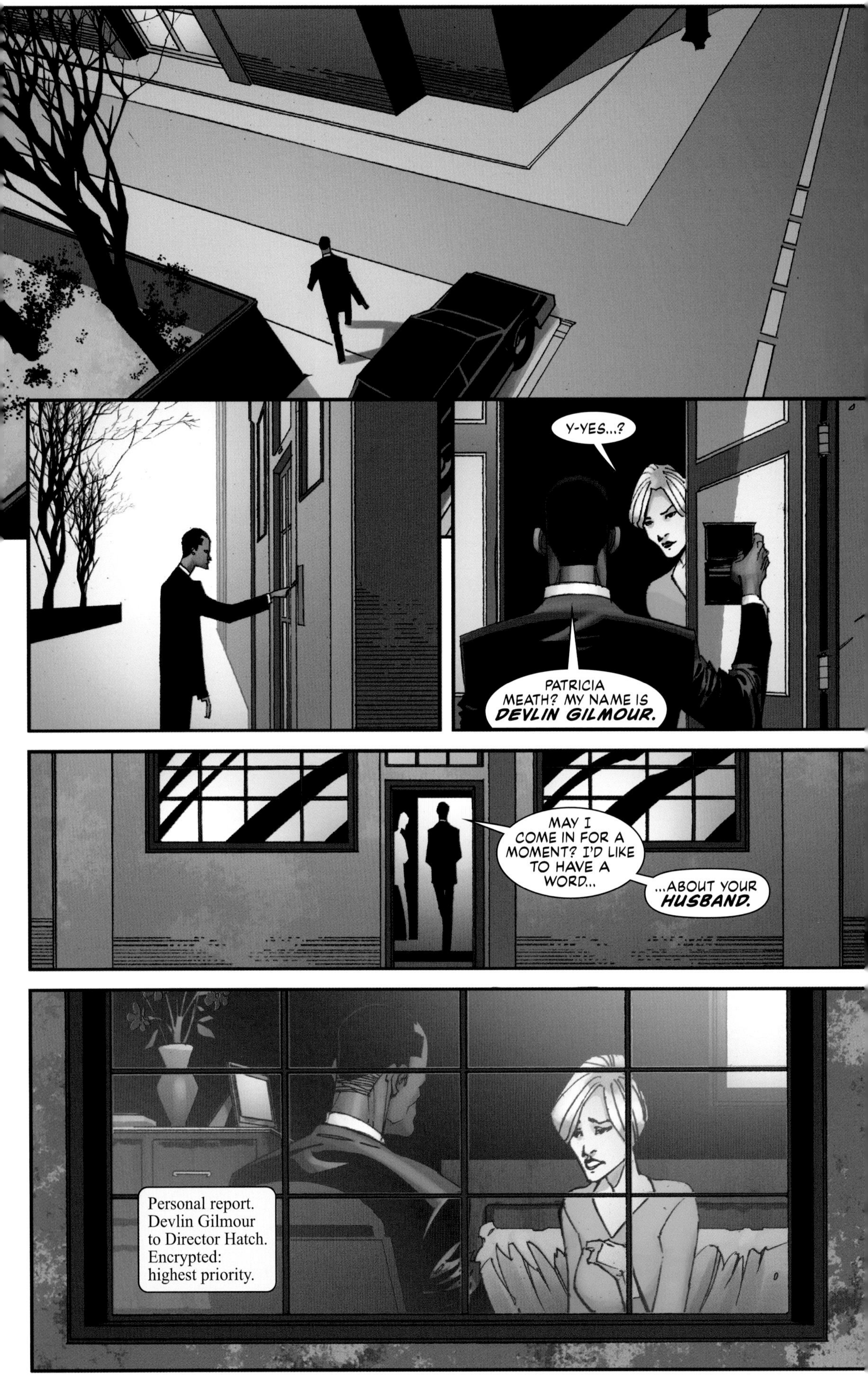
Y-YES...?
PATRICIA MEATH? MY NAME IS DEVLIN GILMOUR.
MAY I COME IN FOR A MOMENT? I'D LIKE TO HAVE A WORD...
...ABOUT YOUR HUSBAND.
Personal report. Devlin Gilmour to Director Hatch. Encrypted: highest priority.

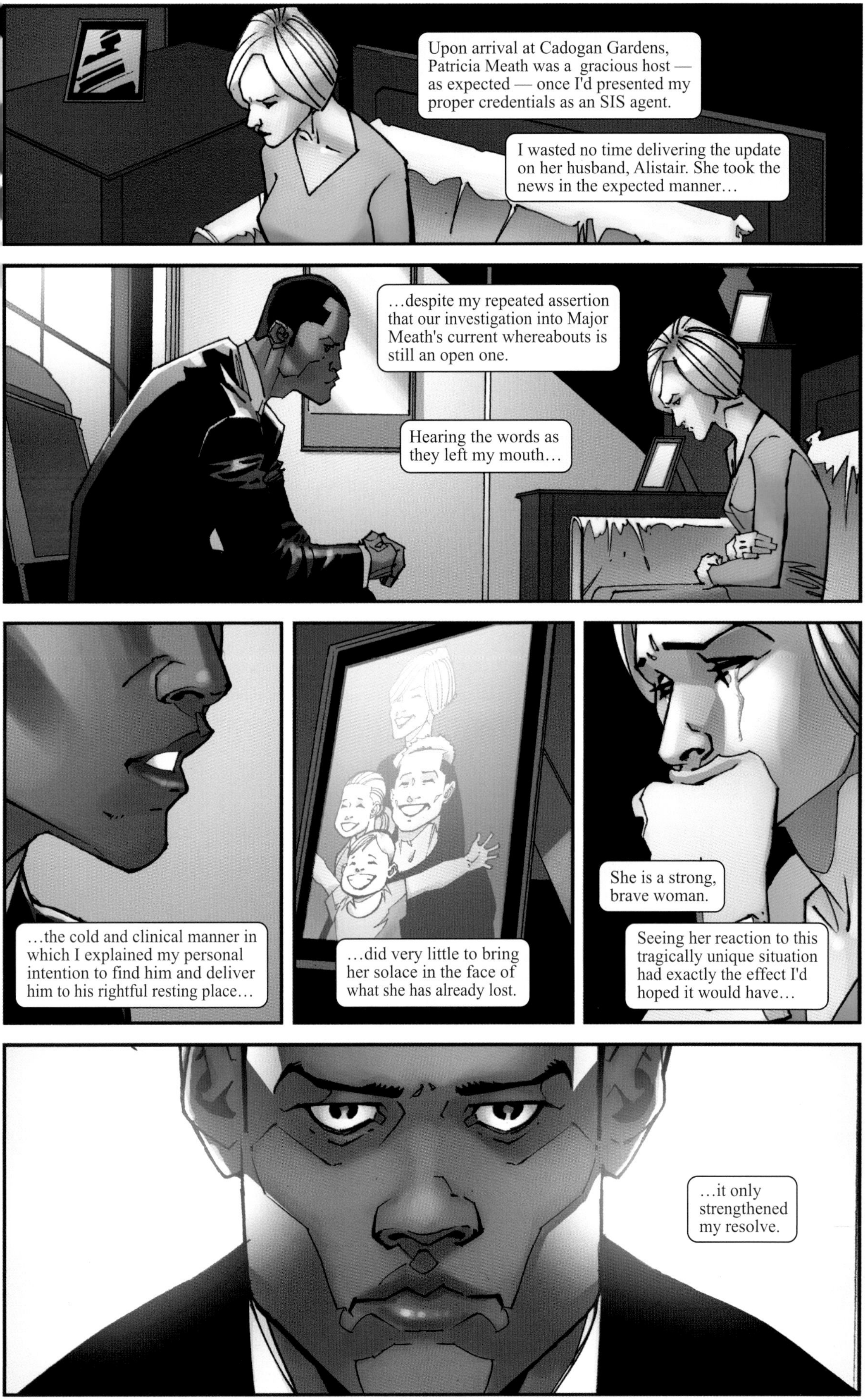
Upon arrival at Cadogan Gardens, Patricia Meath was a gracious host — as expected — once I'd presented my proper credentials as an SIS agent.
I wasted no time delivering the update on her husband, Alistair. She took the news in the expected manner…
…despite my repeated assertion that our investigation into Major Meath's current whereabouts is still an open one.
Hearing the words as they left my mouth…
…the cold and clinical manner in which I explained my personal intention to find him and deliver him to his rightful resting place…
…did very little to bring her solace in the face of what she has already lost.
She is a strong, brave woman.
Seeing her reaction to this tragically unique situation had exactly the effect I'd hoped it would have…
…it only strengthened my resolve.

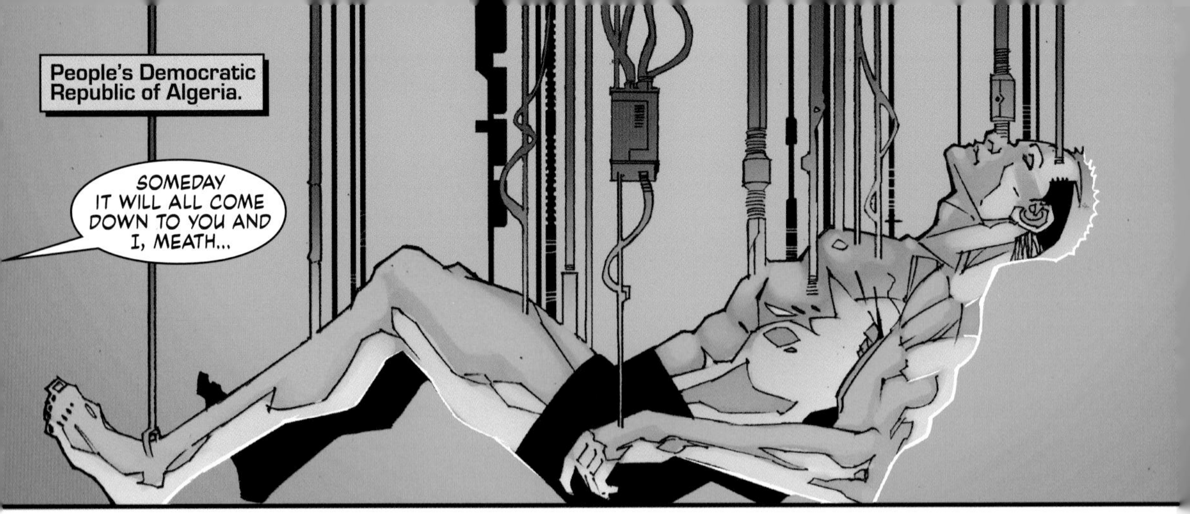
People's Democratic Republic of Algeria.
SOMEDAY IT WILL ALL COME DOWN TO YOU AND I, MEATH...

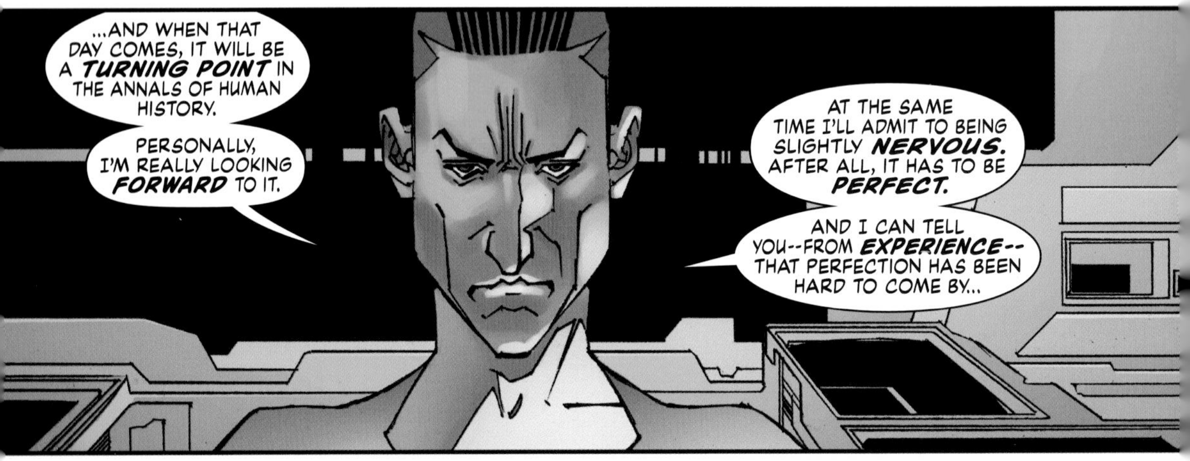
...AND WHEN THAT DAY COMES, IT WILL BE A TURNING POINT IN THE ANNALS OF HUMAN HISTORY.
PERSONALLY, I'M REALLY LOOKING FORWARD TO IT.
AT THE SAME TIME I'LL ADMIT TO BEING SLIGHTLY NERVOUS. AFTER ALL, IT HAS TO BE PERFECT.
AND I CAN TELL YOU--FROM EXPERIENCE--THAT PERFECTION HAS BEEN HARD TO COME BY...

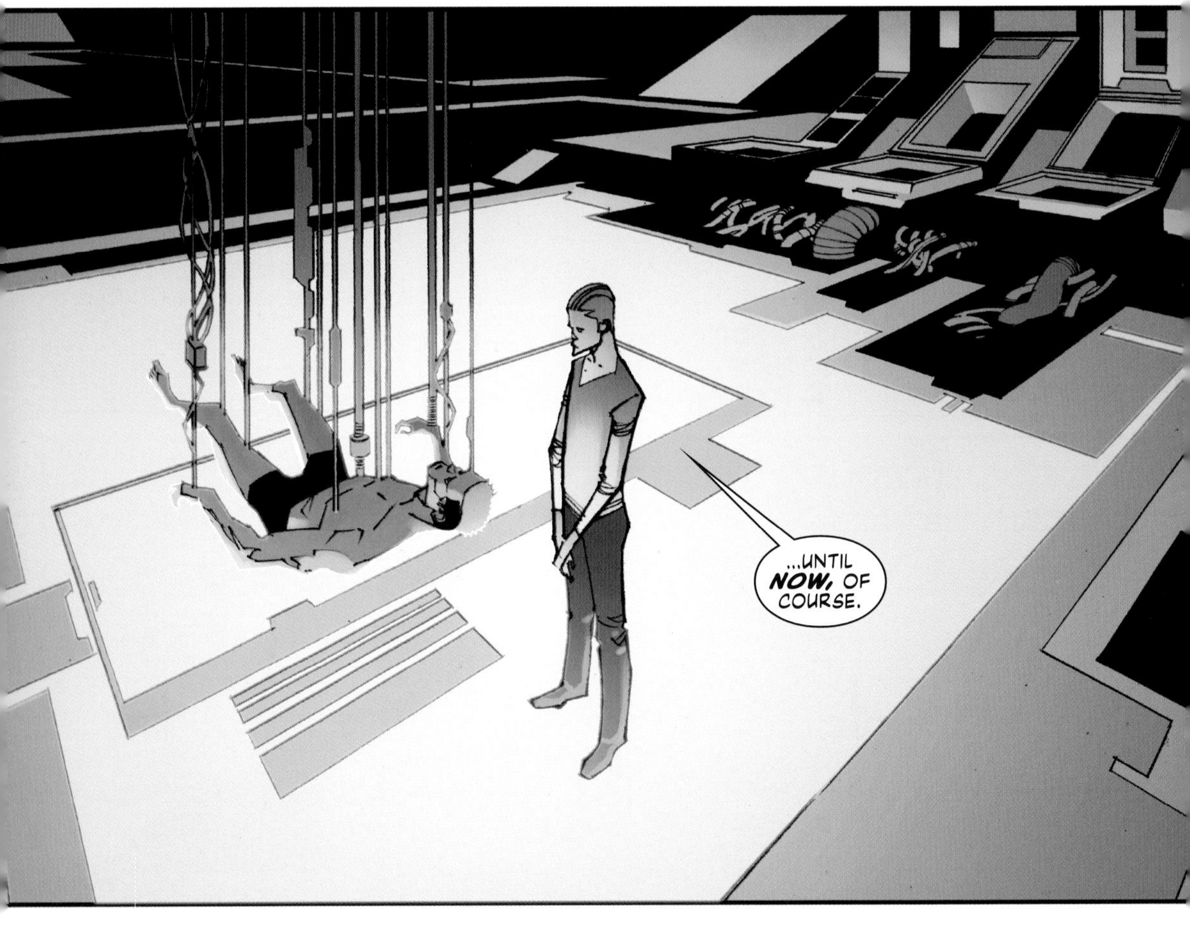
...UNTIL NOW, OF COURSE.

WE'RE GETTING CLOSER WITH EACH AND EVERY DAY. I DON'T KNOW IF *YOU* CAN FEEL IT...BUT I CAN ASSURE YOU, IT'S *HAPPENING.*

WITH EACH *MANIPULATION,* WE'RE BRINGING YOU THAT MUCH *CLOSER* TO YOUR ULTIMATE EXISTENCE...

...ONE THAT WILL BE PERFECTLY SUITED TO MATCH MY *OWN.*

GENTLEMEN, TAKE YOUR STATIONS.

YES, MISTER ASSANTE.

AS YOU'LL SEE ON YOUR DESKTOPS, I HAVE FORMULATED A *NEW* SET OF SCENARIOS FOR THE VIRTUAL PLEASURE OF OUR GUEST.

REFER TO THE PULL-DOWN MENU AND PROCEED.

WARMING UP THE FEEDS. VITALS CHECK.

ALL VITALS CURRENTLY STABLE.

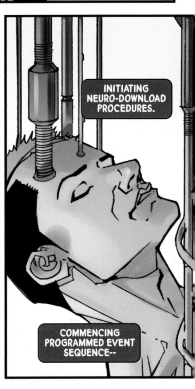

INITIATING NEURO-DOWNLOAD PROCEDURES.

COMMENCING PROGRAMMED EVENT SEQUENCE--

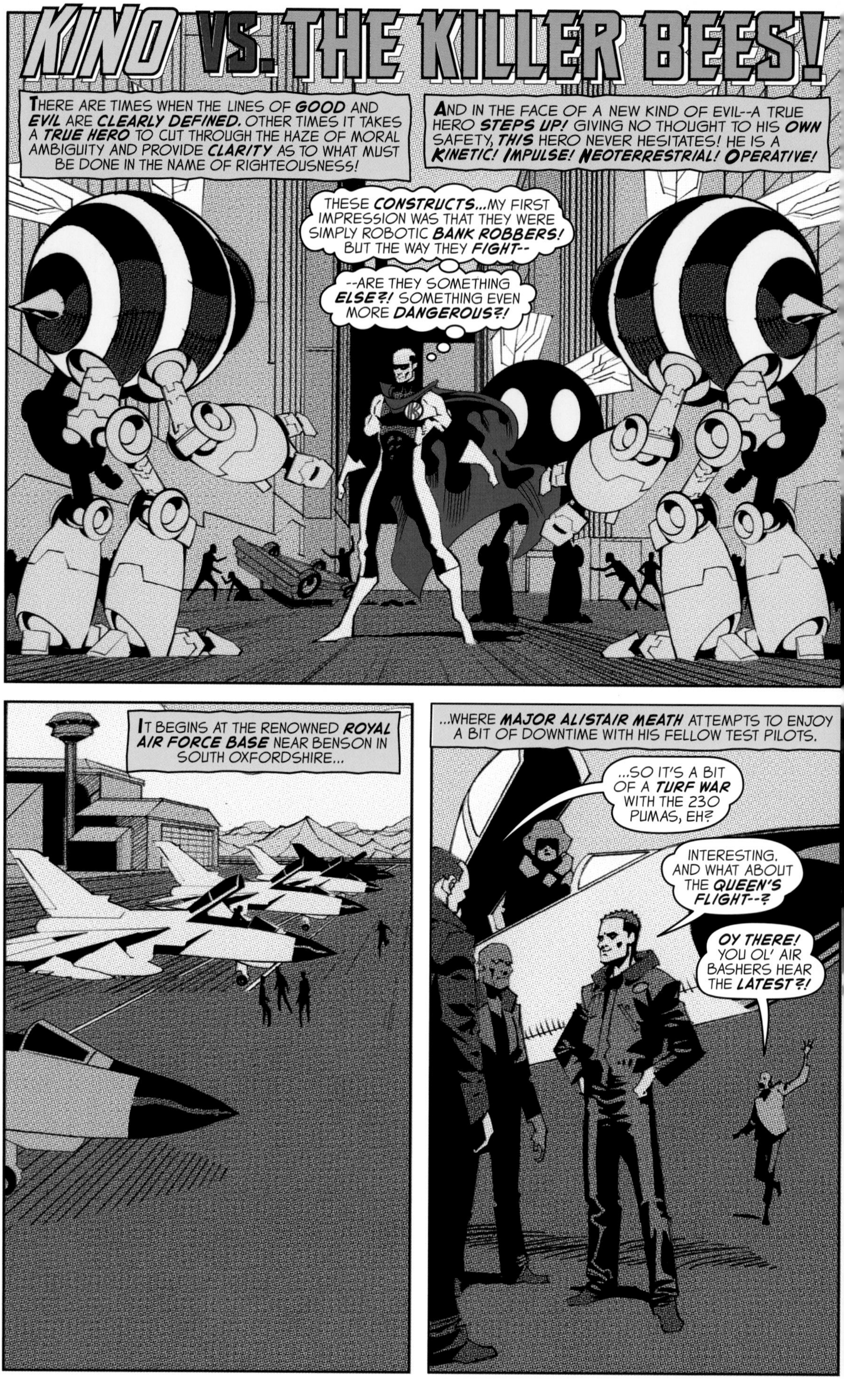
KINO VS. THE KILLER BEES!
THERE ARE TIMES WHEN THE LINES OF GOOD AND EVIL ARE CLEARLY DEFINED. OTHER TIMES IT TAKES A TRUE HERO TO CUT THROUGH THE HAZE OF MORAL AMBIGUITY AND PROVIDE CLARITY AS TO WHAT MUST BE DONE IN THE NAME OF RIGHTEOUSNESS!
AND IN THE FACE OF A NEW KIND OF EVIL--A TRUE HERO STEPS UP! GIVING NO THOUGHT TO HIS OWN SAFETY, THIS HERO NEVER HESITATES! HE IS A KINETIC! IMPULSE! NEOTERRESTRIAL! OPERATIVE!
THESE CONSTRUCTS...MY FIRST IMPRESSION WAS THAT THEY WERE SIMPLY ROBOTIC BANK ROBBERS! BUT THE WAY THEY FIGHT--
--ARE THEY SOMETHING ELSE?! SOMETHING EVEN MORE DANGEROUS?!
IT BEGINS AT THE RENOWNED ROYAL AIR FORCE BASE NEAR BENSON IN SOUTH OXFORDSHIRE...
...WHERE MAJOR ALISTAIR MEATH ATTEMPTS TO ENJOY A BIT OF DOWNTIME WITH HIS FELLOW TEST PILOTS.
...SO IT'S A BIT OF A TURF WAR WITH THE 230 PUMAS, EH?
INTERESTING. AND WHAT ABOUT THE QUEEN'S FLIGHT--?
OY THERE! YOU OL' AIR BASHERS HEAR THE LATEST?!

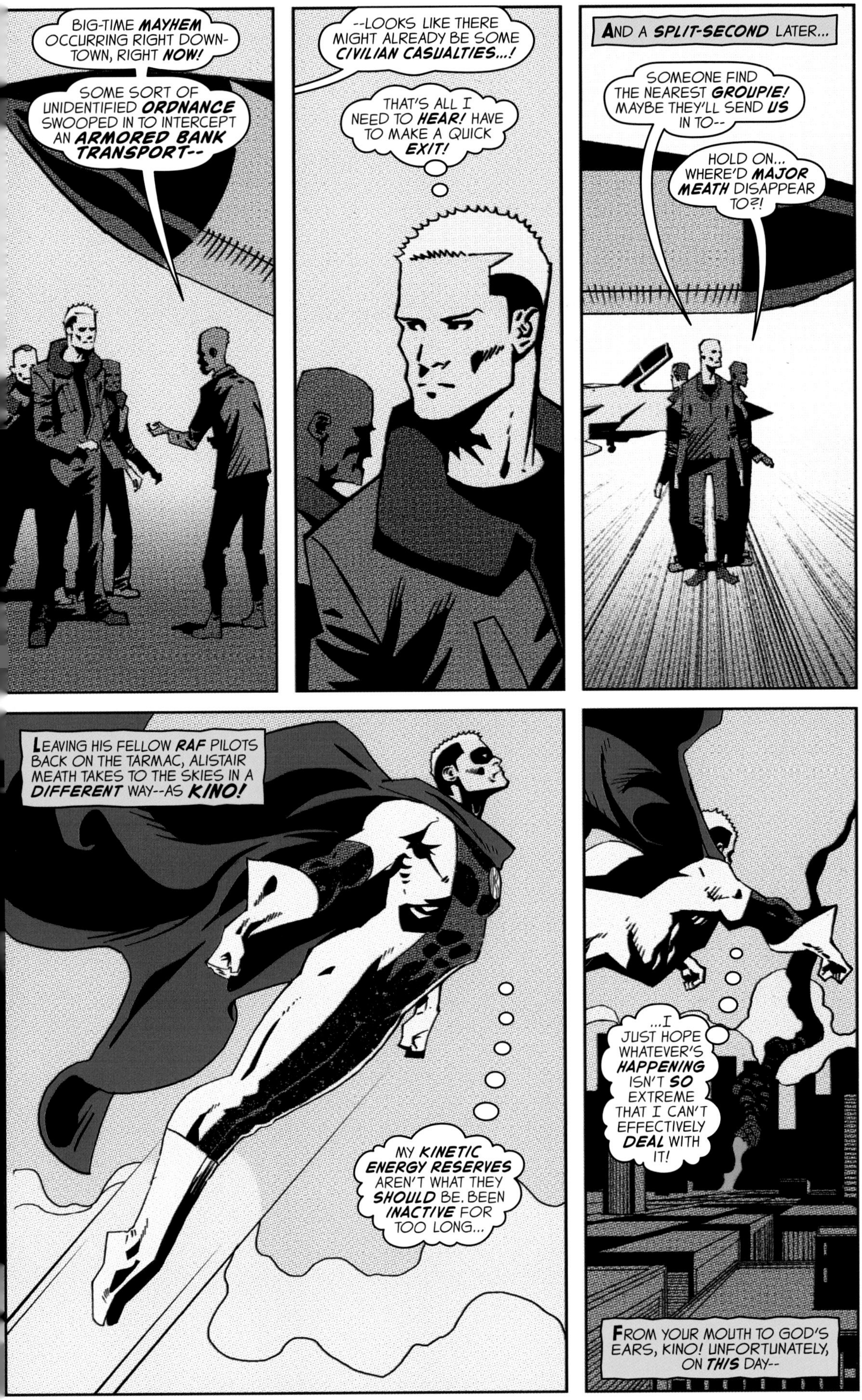
BIG-TIME MAYHEM OCCURRING RIGHT DOWN-TOWN, RIGHT NOW!
SOME SORT OF UNIDENTIFIED ORDNANCE SWOOPED IN TO INTERCEPT AN ARMORED BANK TRANSPORT--
--LOOKS LIKE THERE MIGHT ALREADY BE SOME CIVILIAN CASUALTIES...!
THAT'S ALL I NEED TO HEAR! HAVE TO MAKE A QUICK EXIT!
AND A SPLIT-SECOND LATER...
SOMEONE FIND THE NEAREST GROUPIE! MAYBE THEY'LL SEND US IN TO--
HOLD ON... WHERE'D MAJOR MEATH DISAPPEAR TO?!
LEAVING HIS FELLOW RAF PILOTS BACK ON THE TARMAC, ALISTAIR MEATH TAKES TO THE SKIES IN A DIFFERENT WAY--AS KINO!
MY KINETIC ENERGY RESERVES AREN'T WHAT THEY SHOULD BE. BEEN INACTIVE FOR TOO LONG...
...I JUST HOPE WHATEVER'S HAPPENING ISN'T SO EXTREME THAT I CAN'T EFFECTIVELY DEAL WITH IT!
FROM YOUR MOUTH TO GOD'S EARS, KINO! UNFORTUNATELY, ON THIS DAY--

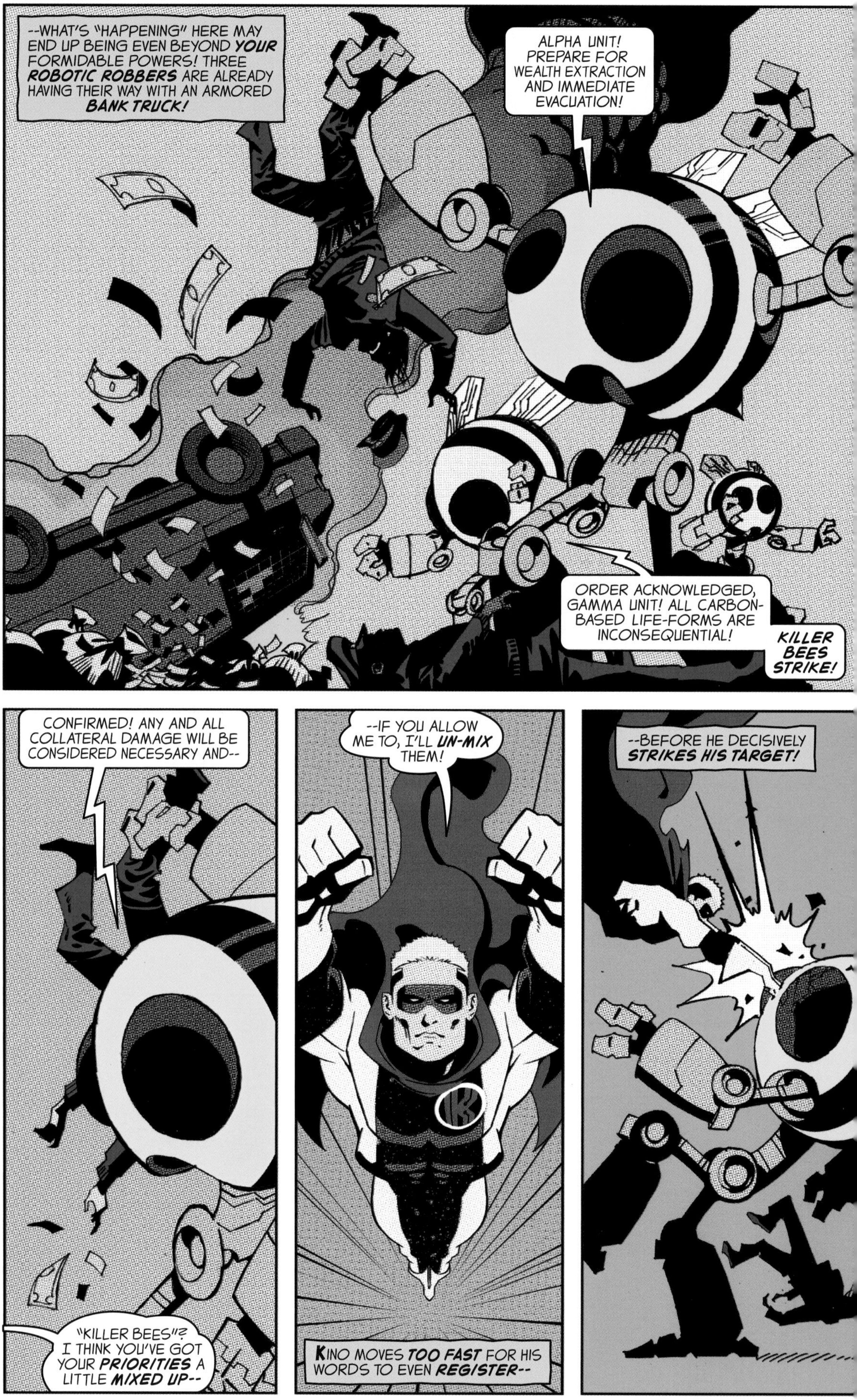
--WHAT'S "HAPPENING" HERE MAY END UP BEING EVEN BEYOND **YOUR** FORMIDABLE POWERS! THREE **ROBOTIC ROBBERS** ARE ALREADY HAVING THEIR WAY WITH AN ARMORED **BANK TRUCK!**
ALPHA UNIT! PREPARE FOR WEALTH EXTRACTION AND IMMEDIATE EVACUATION!
ORDER ACKNOWLEDGED, GAMMA UNIT! ALL CARBON-BASED LIFE-FORMS ARE INCONSEQUENTIAL!
KILLER BEES STRIKE!
CONFIRMED! ANY AND ALL COLLATERAL DAMAGE WILL BE CONSIDERED NECESSARY AND--
"KILLER BEES"? I THINK YOU'VE GOT YOUR **PRIORITIES** A LITTLE **MIXED UP**--
--IF YOU ALLOW ME TO, I'LL **UN-MIX** THEM!
KINO MOVES **TOO FAST** FOR HIS WORDS TO EVEN **REGISTER**--
--BEFORE HE DECISIVELY **STRIKES HIS TARGET!**

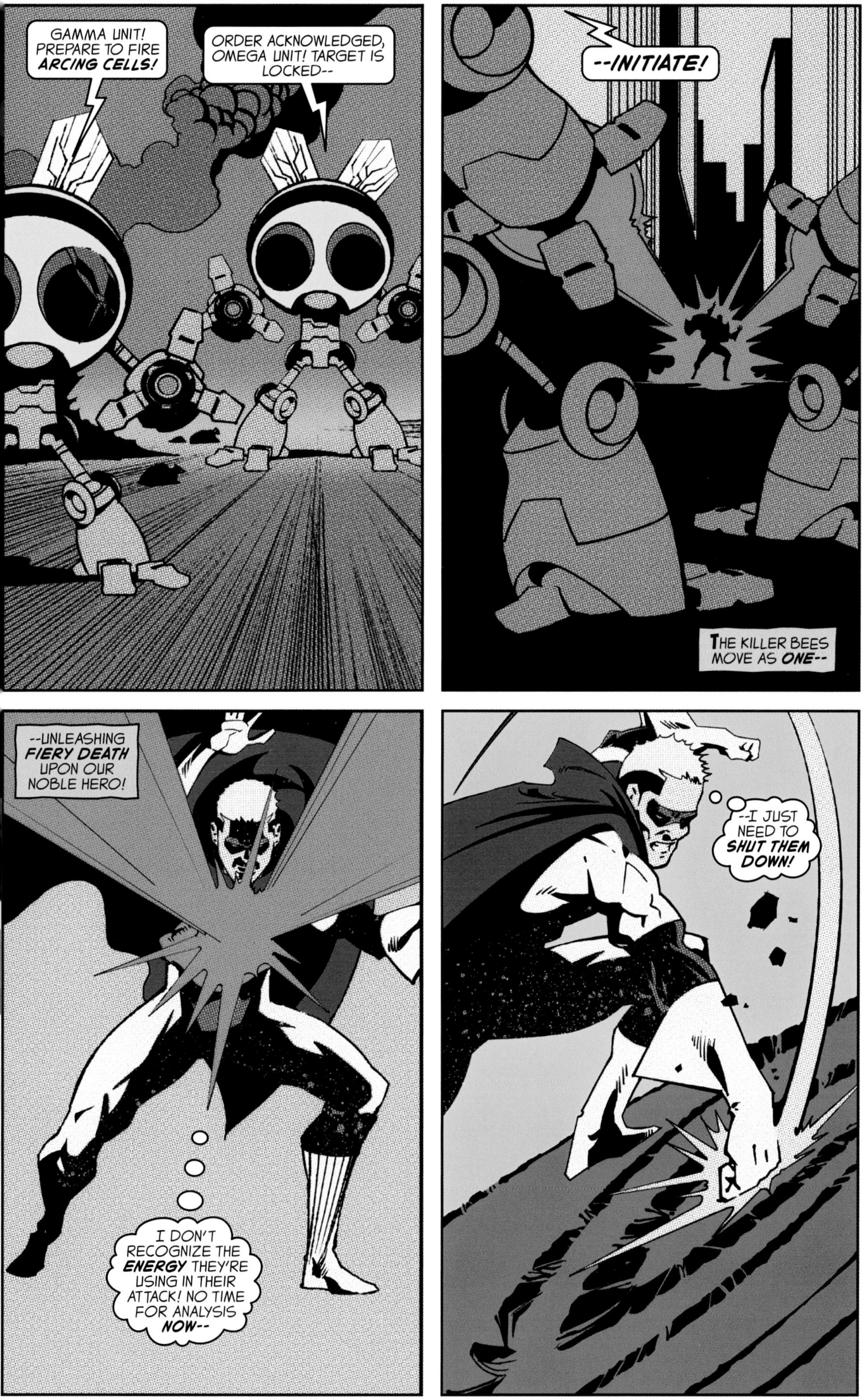
GAMMA UNIT! PREPARE TO FIRE ARCING CELLS!
ORDER ACKNOWLEDGED, OMEGA UNIT! TARGET IS LOCKED--
--INITIATE!
THE KILLER BEES MOVE AS ONE--
--UNLEASHING FIERY DEATH UPON OUR NOBLE HERO!
I DON'T RECOGNIZE THE ENERGY THEY'RE USING IN THEIR ATTACK! NO TIME FOR ANALYSIS NOW--
--I JUST NEED TO SHUT THEM DOWN!

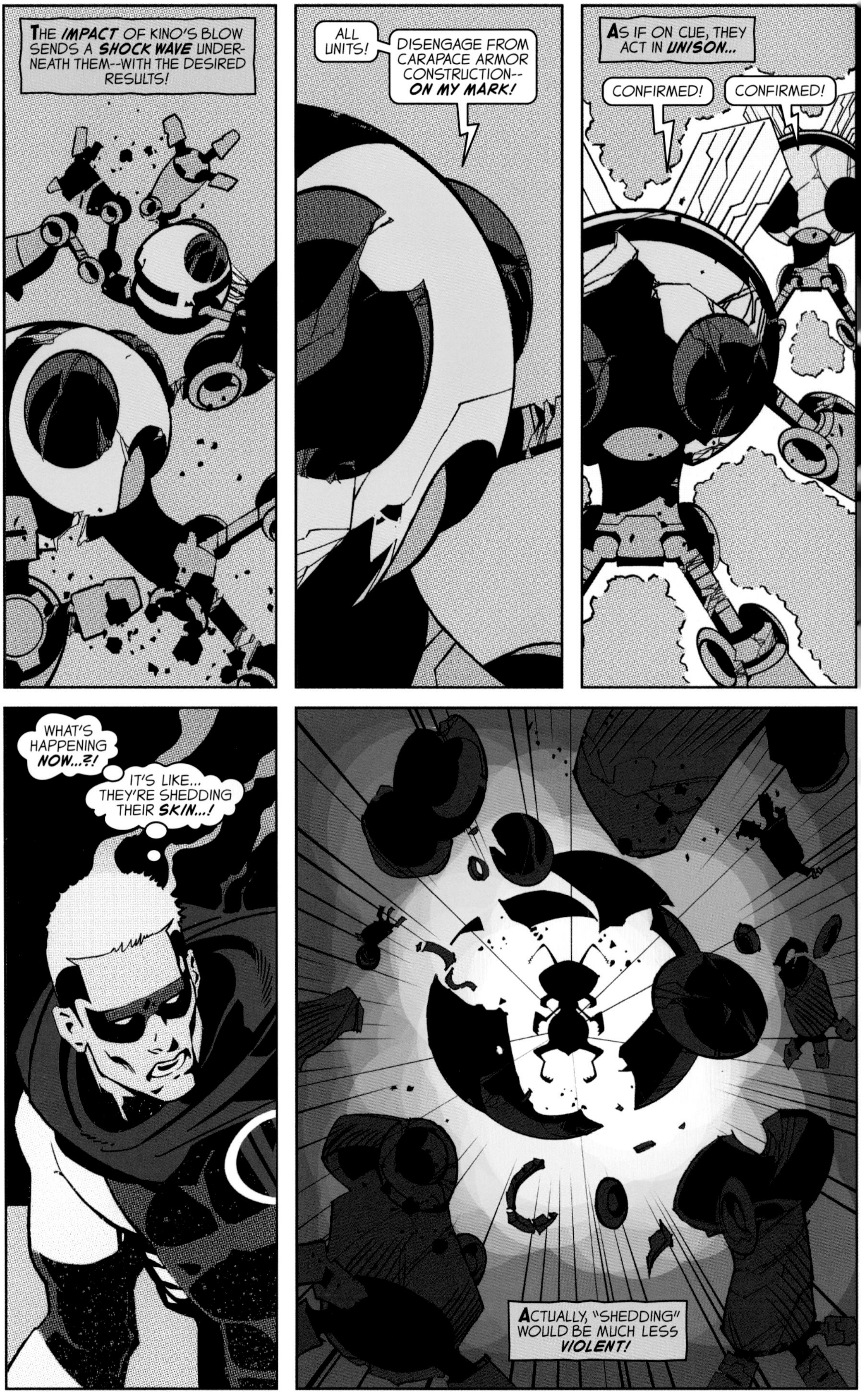
THE IMPACT OF KINO'S BLOW SENDS A SHOCK WAVE UNDERNEATH THEM--WITH THE DESIRED RESULTS!
ALL UNITS!
DISENGAGE FROM CARAPACE ARMOR CONSTRUCTION-- ON MY MARK!
AS IF ON CUE, THEY ACT IN UNISON...
CONFIRMED!
CONFIRMED!
WHAT'S HAPPENING NOW...?!
IT'S LIKE... THEY'RE SHEDDING THEIR SKIN...!
ACTUALLY, "SHEDDING" WOULD BE MUCH LESS VIOLENT!

OH NO...I JUST *ASSUMED* THE KILLER BEES WERE *ATURO ASSANTE'S* HANDIWORK...!

NORMALLY, THAT WOULD BE AN EXTREMELY *ACCURATE* ASSUMPTION--

--BUT IN *THIS* PARTICULAR CASE, A SECRET EVEN *STRANGER* IS REVEALED!

⟨THE SUBTERFUGE OF ARMORED *EARTH CRIMINALS* WOULD ONLY TAKE US SO FAR *ANYWAY...!*⟩

*TRANSLATED FROM AN UNKNOWN ALIEN LANGUAGE.

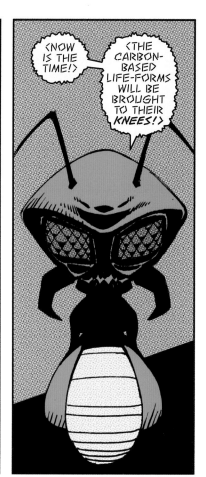

⟨NOW IS THE TIME!⟩

⟨THE CARBON-BASED LIFE-FORMS WILL BE BROUGHT TO THEIR *KNEES!*⟩

I DON'T RECOGNIZE THE LANGUAGE. NEVERTHELESS, I'D BETTER TRY TO *COMMUNICATE...*

ATTENTION, NON-TERRESTRIAL ENTITIES...

...AS A REPRESENTATIVE OF THE HUMAN RACE, I MUST *WARN* YOU THAT IF YOU INTEND FURTHER *HARM* TO THE POPULATION, I WILL NOT *ALLOW* SUCH ACTIONS TO--

THEIR *RESPONSE* IS AN EAR-SPLITTING *ALIEN SHRIEK* AIMED SQUARELY AT THE HEAVENS...

SKKRREEE!

NOW WHAT--?!

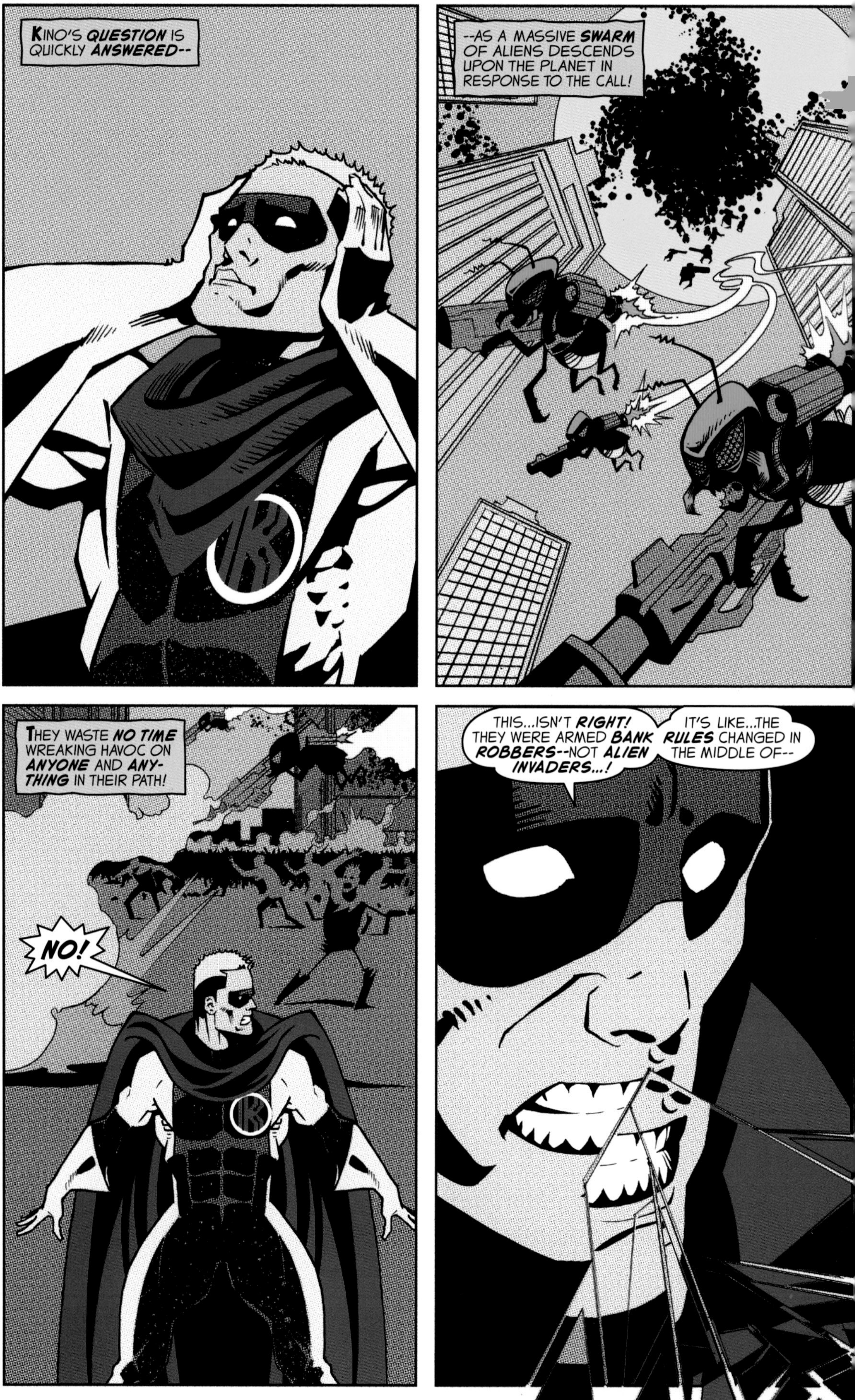
KINO'S QUESTION IS QUICKLY ANSWERED--
--AS A MASSIVE SWARM OF ALIENS DESCENDS UPON THE PLANET IN RESPONSE TO THE CALL!
THEY WASTE NO TIME WREAKING HAVOC ON ANYONE AND ANYTHING IN THEIR PATH!
NO!
THIS...ISN'T RIGHT! THEY WERE ARMED BANK ROBBERS--NOT ALIEN INVADERS...!
IT'S LIKE...THE RULES CHANGED IN THE MIDDLE OF--

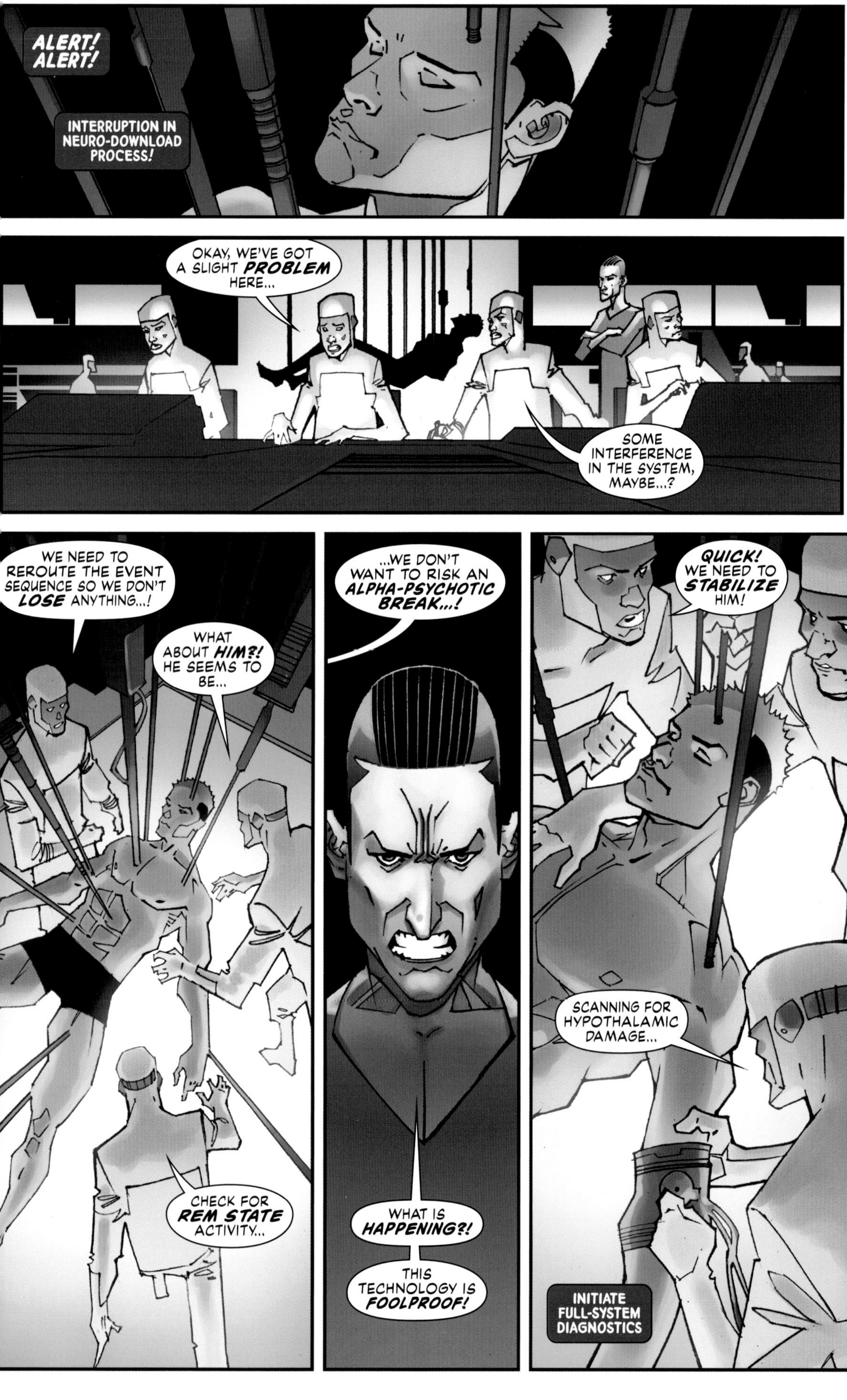
ALERT! ALERT!
INTERRUPTION IN NEURO-DOWNLOAD PROCESS!
OKAY, WE'VE GOT A SLIGHT PROBLEM HERE...
SOME INTERFERENCE IN THE SYSTEM, MAYBE...?
WE NEED TO REROUTE THE EVENT SEQUENCE SO WE DON'T LOSE ANYTHING...!
WHAT ABOUT HIM?! HE SEEMS TO BE...
CHECK FOR REM STATE ACTIVITY...
...WE DON'T WANT TO RISK AN ALPHA-PSYCHOTIC BREAK...!
WHAT IS HAPPENING?!
THIS TECHNOLOGY IS FOOLPROOF!
QUICK! WE NEED TO STABILIZE HIM!
SCANNING FOR HYPOTHALAMIC DAMAGE...
INITIATE FULL-SYSTEM DIAGNOSTICS

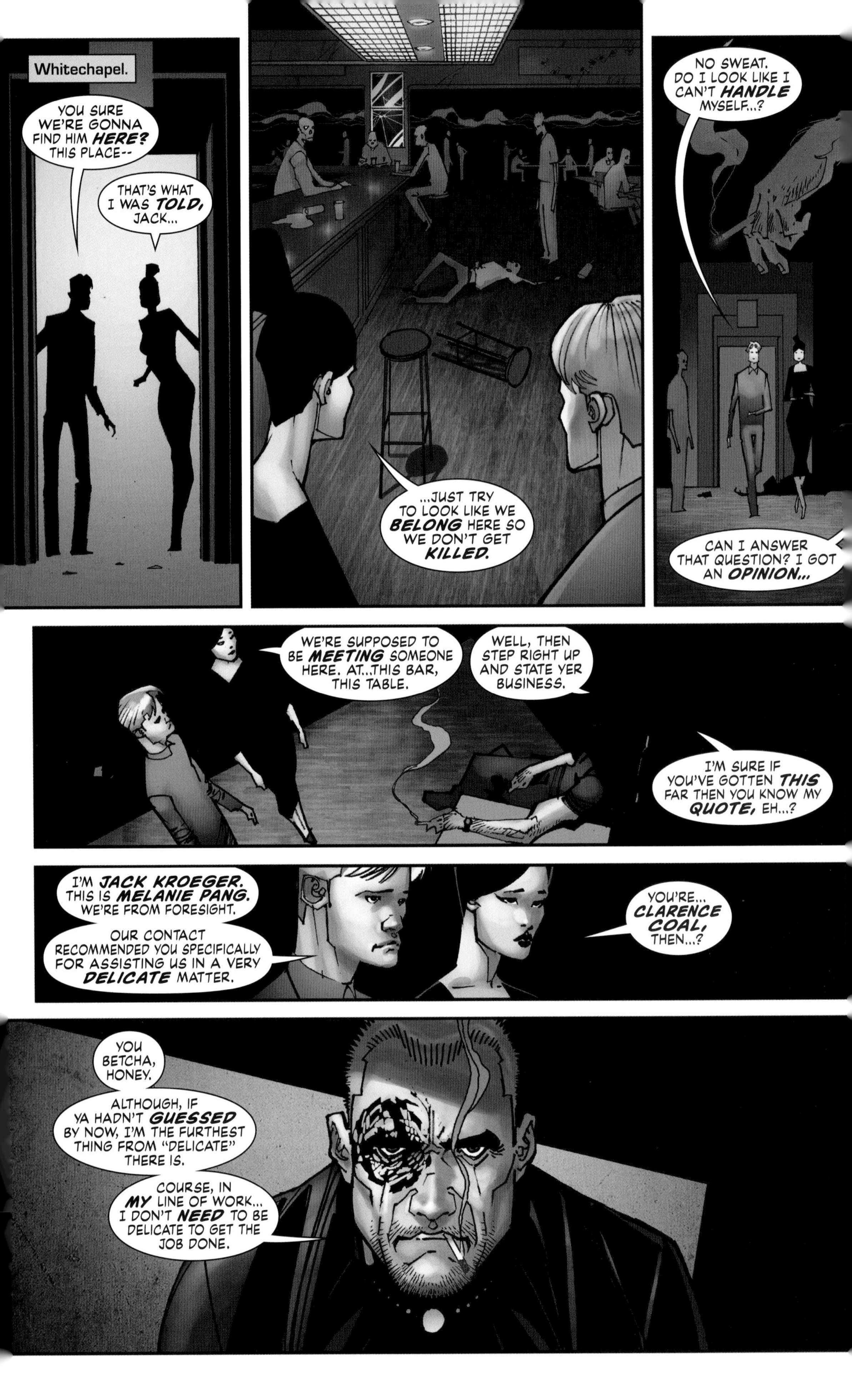
Whitechapel.
YOU SURE WE'RE GONNA FIND HIM HERE? THIS PLACE--
THAT'S WHAT I WAS TOLD, JACK...
...JUST TRY TO LOOK LIKE WE BELONG HERE SO WE DON'T GET KILLED.
NO SWEAT. DO I LOOK LIKE I CAN'T HANDLE MYSELF...?
CAN I ANSWER THAT QUESTION? I GOT AN OPINION...
WE'RE SUPPOSED TO BE MEETING SOMEONE HERE. AT...THIS BAR, THIS TABLE.
WELL, THEN STEP RIGHT UP AND STATE YER BUSINESS.
I'M SURE IF YOU'VE GOTTEN THIS FAR THEN YOU KNOW MY QUOTE, EH...?
I'M JACK KROEGER. THIS IS MELANIE PANG. WE'RE FROM FORESIGHT.
OUR CONTACT RECOMMENDED YOU SPECIFICALLY FOR ASSISTING US IN A VERY DELICATE MATTER.
YOU'RE... CLARENCE COAL, THEN...?
YOU BETCHA, HONEY.
ALTHOUGH, IF YA HADN'T GUESSED BY NOW, I'M THE FURTHEST THING FROM "DELICATE" THERE IS.
COURSE, IN MY LINE OF WORK... I DON'T NEED TO BE DELICATE TO GET THE JOB DONE.

CHAPTER THREE

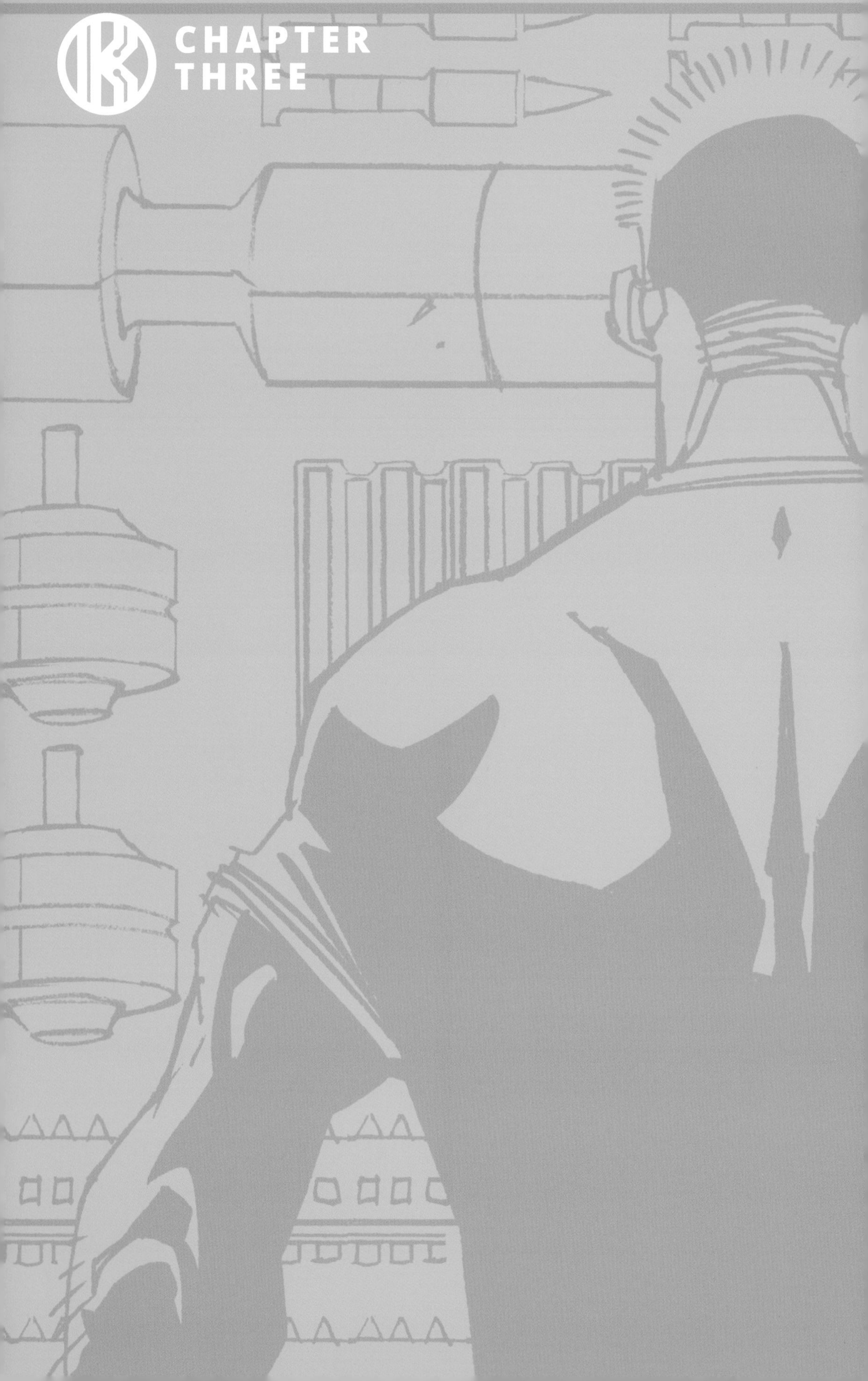

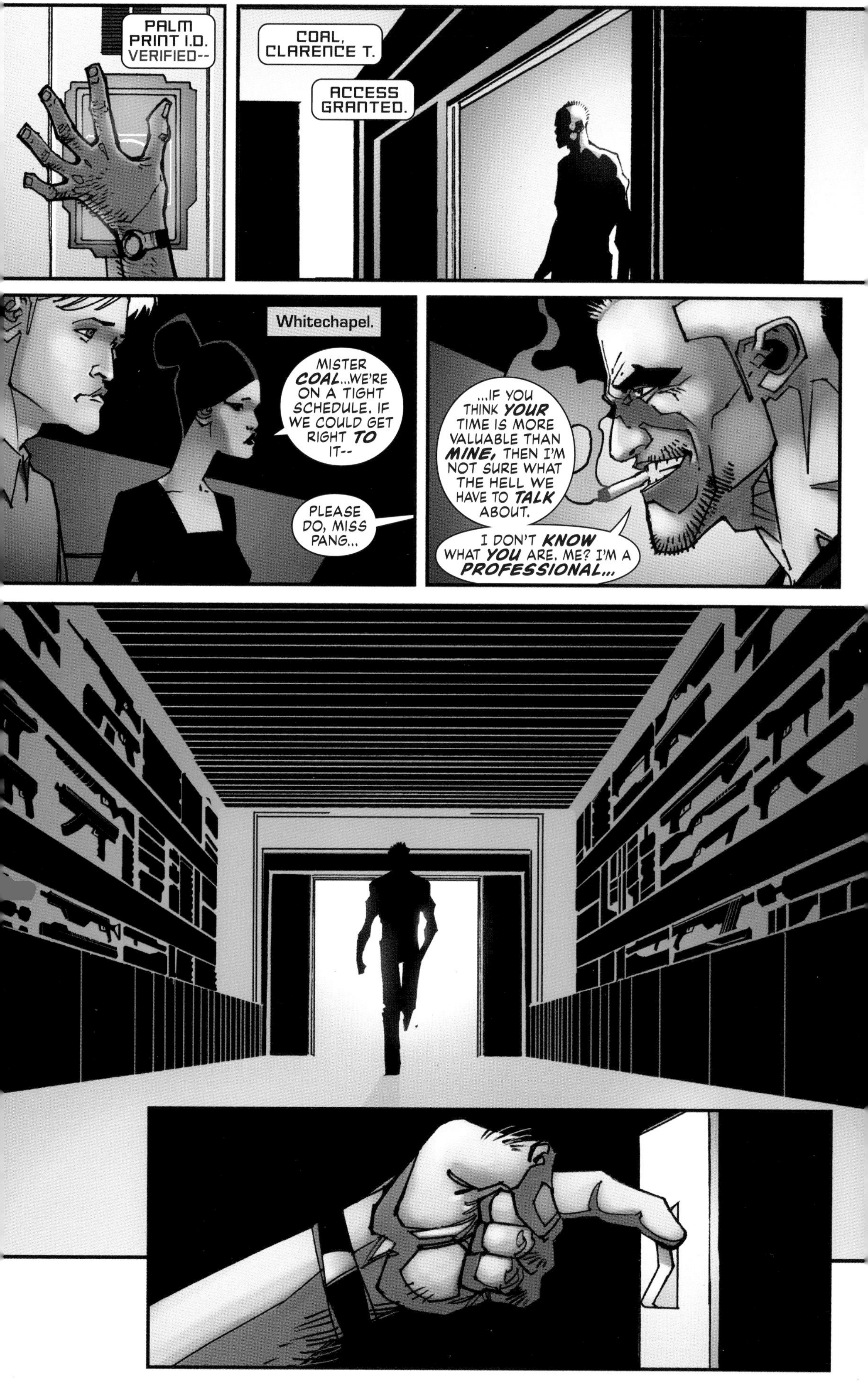
PALM PRINT I.D. VERIFIED--
COAL, CLARENCE T.
ACCESS GRANTED.
Whitechapel.
MISTER COAL...WE'RE ON A TIGHT SCHEDULE. IF WE COULD GET RIGHT TO IT--
PLEASE DO, MISS PANG...
...IF YOU THINK YOUR TIME IS MORE VALUABLE THAN MINE, THEN I'M NOT SURE WHAT THE HELL WE HAVE TO TALK ABOUT.
I DON'T KNOW WHAT YOU ARE. ME? I'M A PROFESSIONAL...

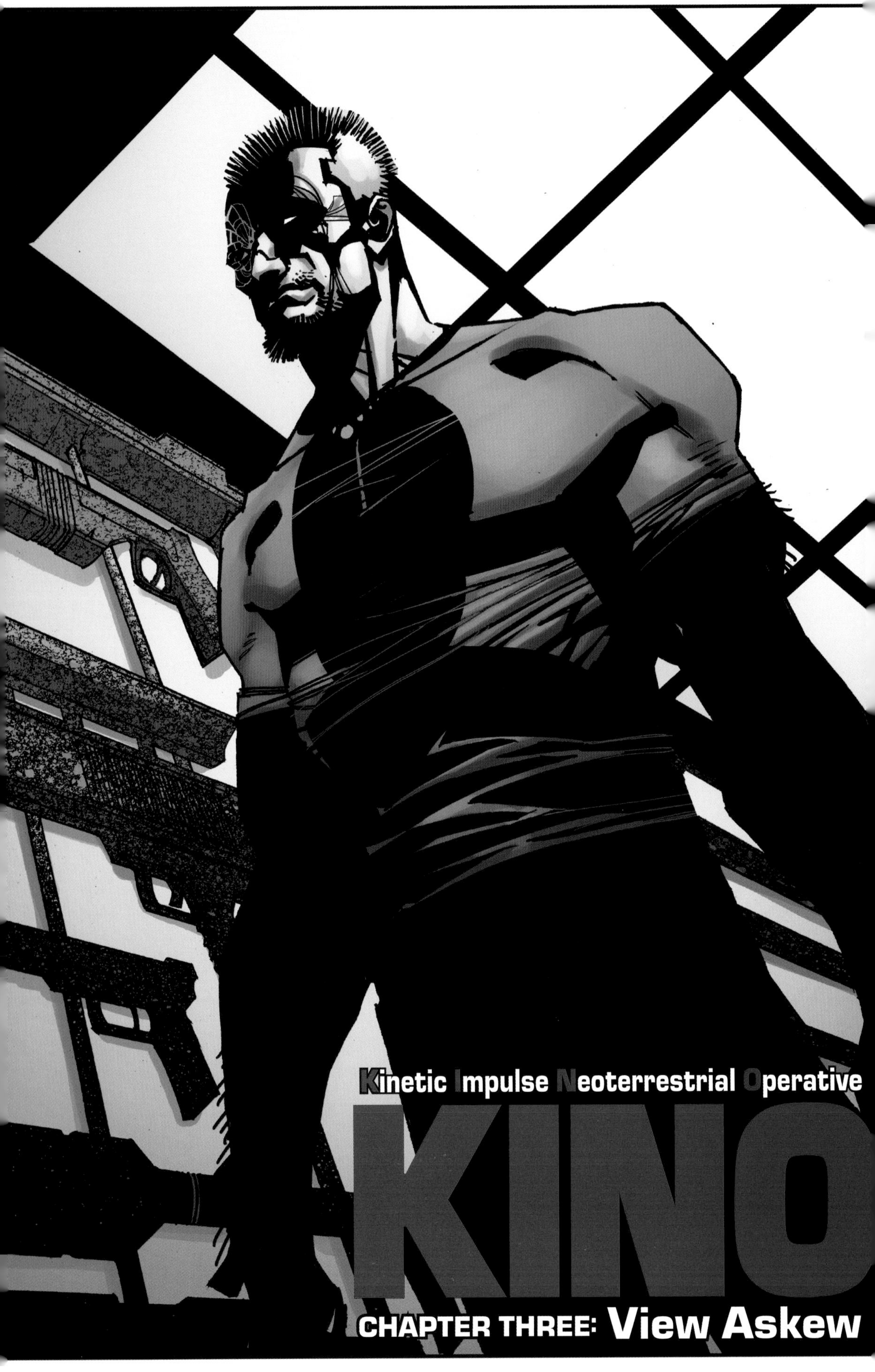
Kinetic Impulse Neoterrestrial Operative
KINO
CHAPTER THREE: View Askew

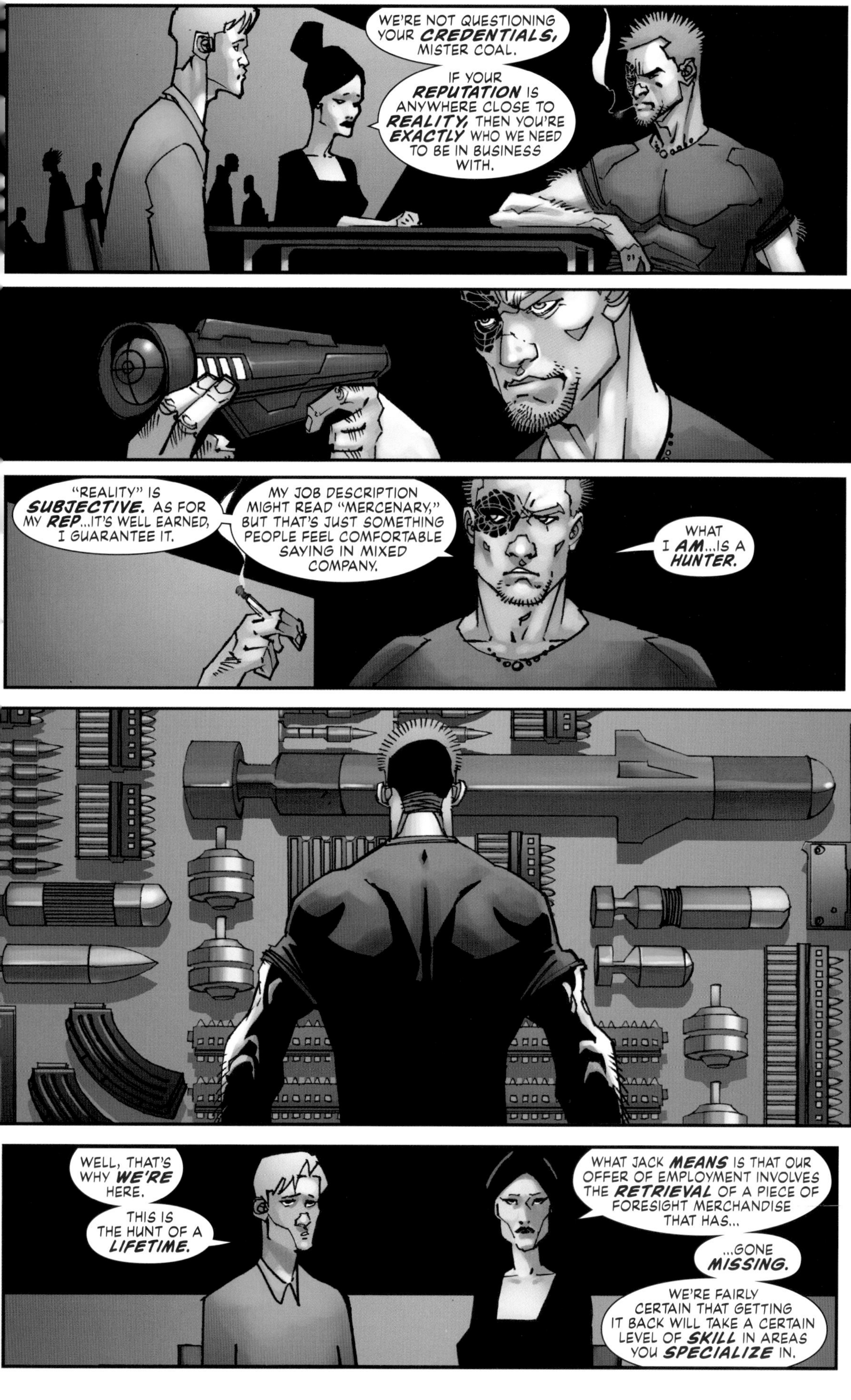
WE'RE NOT QUESTIONING YOUR CREDENTIALS, MISTER COAL.
IF YOUR REPUTATION IS ANYWHERE CLOSE TO REALITY, THEN YOU'RE EXACTLY WHO WE NEED TO BE IN BUSINESS WITH.
"REALITY" IS SUBJECTIVE. AS FOR MY REP...IT'S WELL EARNED, I GUARANTEE IT.
MY JOB DESCRIPTION MIGHT READ "MERCENARY," BUT THAT'S JUST SOMETHING PEOPLE FEEL COMFORTABLE SAYING IN MIXED COMPANY.
WHAT I AM...IS A HUNTER.
WELL, THAT'S WHY WE'RE HERE.
THIS IS THE HUNT OF A LIFETIME.
WHAT JACK MEANS IS THAT OUR OFFER OF EMPLOYMENT INVOLVES THE RETRIEVAL OF A PIECE OF FORESIGHT MERCHANDISE THAT HAS...
...GONE MISSING.
WE'RE FAIRLY CERTAIN THAT GETTING IT BACK WILL TAKE A CERTAIN LEVEL OF SKILL IN AREAS YOU SPECIALIZE IN.

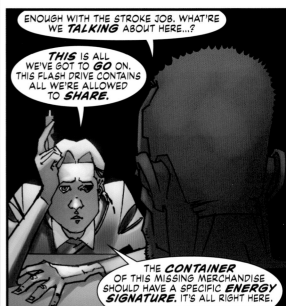

ENOUGH WITH THE STROKE JOB. WHAT'RE WE *TALKING* ABOUT HERE...?

THIS IS ALL WE'VE GOT TO *GO* ON. THIS FLASH DRIVE CONTAINS ALL WE'RE ALLOWED TO *SHARE*.

THE *CONTAINER* OF THIS MISSING MERCHANDISE SHOULD HAVE A SPECIFIC *ENERGY SIGNATURE.* IT'S ALL RIGHT HERE.

WELL, THIS IS GOING TO MAKE IT *EASY,* ISN'T IT?

AND HERE I WAS HOPING FOR A BIT OF A *CHALLENGE.*

CONFIGURING FREQUENCY SWEEP PROGRAMS.

INITIATING ORBITAL SAT FEEDS.

MAPPING IN PROGRESS...

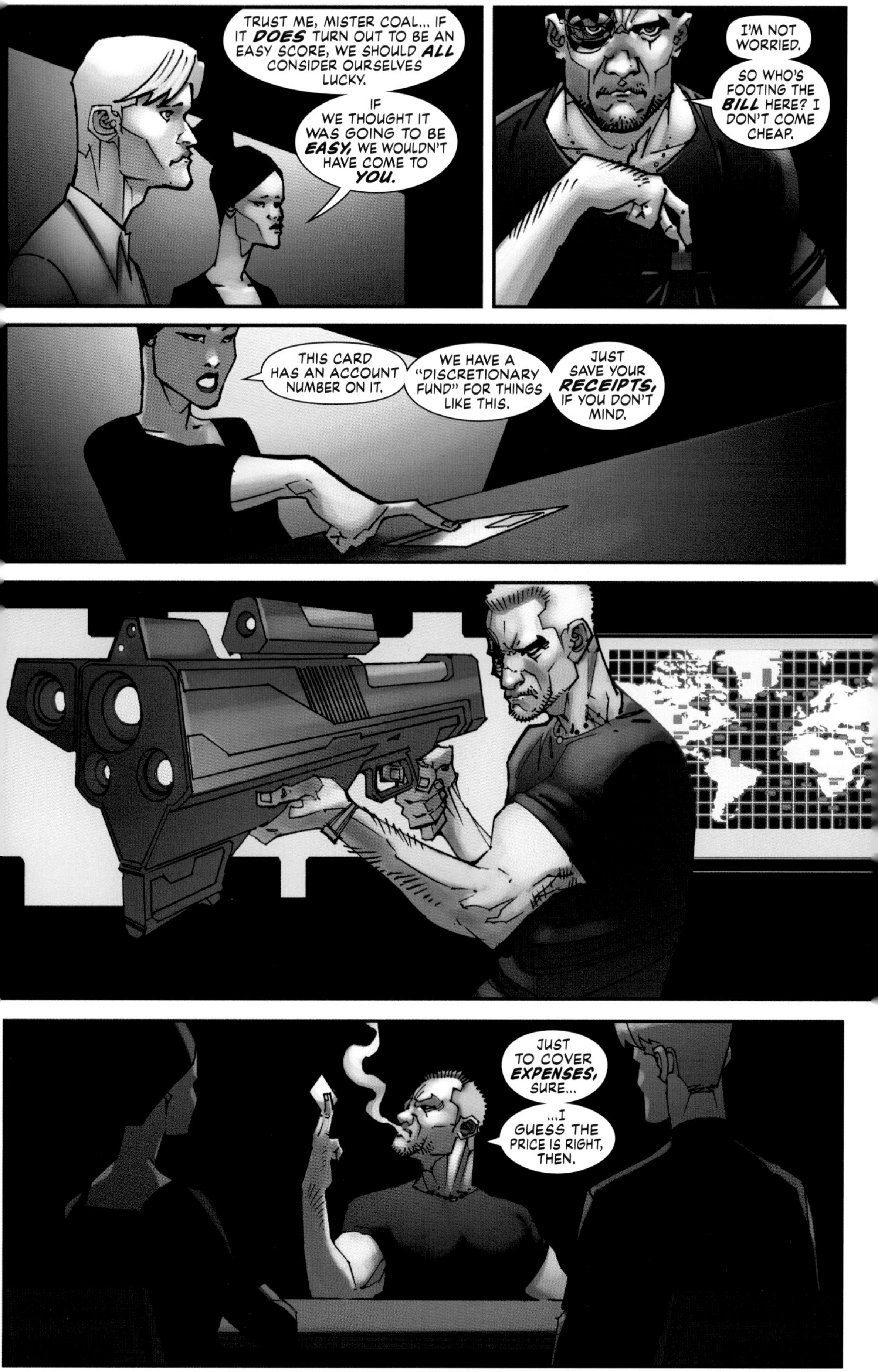
TRUST ME, MISTER COAL... IF IT DOES TURN OUT TO BE AN EASY SCORE, WE SHOULD ALL CONSIDER OURSELVES LUCKY.
IF WE THOUGHT IT WAS GOING TO BE EASY, WE WOULDN'T HAVE COME TO YOU.
I'M NOT WORRIED.
SO WHO'S FOOTING THE BILL HERE? I DON'T COME CHEAP.
THIS CARD HAS AN ACCOUNT NUMBER ON IT.
WE HAVE A "DISCRETIONARY FUND" FOR THINGS LIKE THIS.
JUST SAVE YOUR RECEIPTS, IF YOU DON'T MIND.
JUST TO COVER EXPENSES, SURE...
...I GUESS THE PRICE IS RIGHT, THEN.

THEN WE'RE *DONE* HERE, AREN'T WE?

MAKE NO MISTAKE, MISTER COAL... YOUR *EXPENDABILITY* IS ONE OF YOUR MOST *ATTRACTIVE* QUALITIES.

IN OTHER WORDS, THIS MEETING NEVER TOOK PLACE. UNDERSTOOD?

STORY OF MY LIFE. LOVE 'EM AND LEAVE 'EM.

WE'LL BE IN TOUCH WITHIN THE WEEK FOR AN INITIAL *PROGRESS REPORT.*

JUST MAKE SURE THERE *IS* SOME PROGRESS TO REPORT, WILLYA?

UH-HUH.

RUN ON BACK TO YOUR *CUBICLE,* WHITE MAN...

...THIS IS THE BEST INVESTMENT YOU EVER MADE.

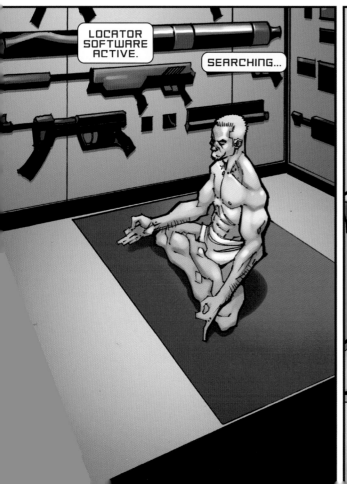

LOCATOR SOFTWARE ACTIVE.

SEARCHING...

SEARCHING...

SEARCHING...

ALERT.

SIGNAL MATCH IDENTIFIED.

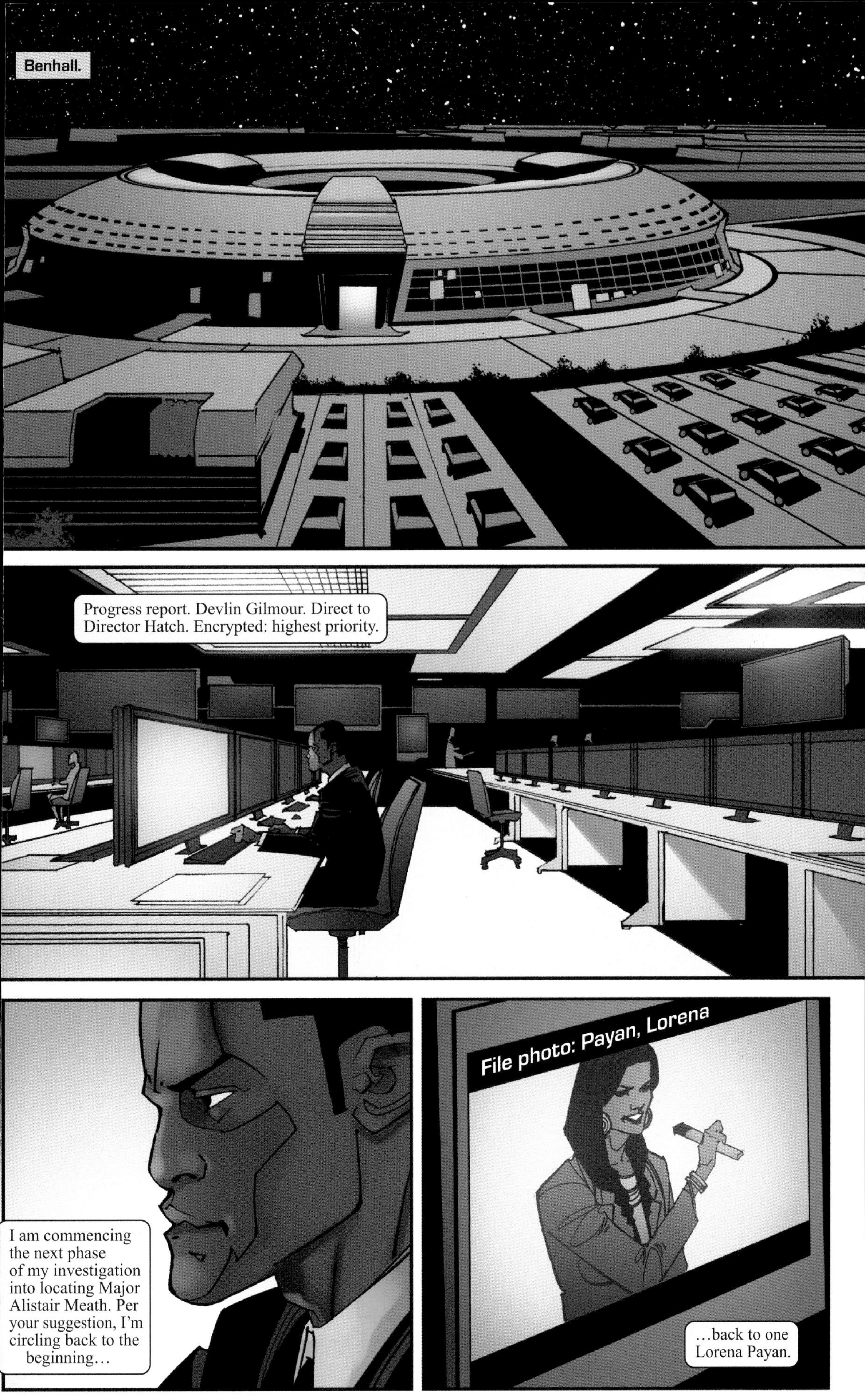
Benhall.
Progress report. Devlin Gilmour. Direct to Director Hatch. Encrypted: highest priority.
I am commencing the next phase of my investigation into locating Major Alistair Meath. Per your suggestion, I'm circling back to the beginning…
File photo: Payan, Lorena
…back to one Lorena Payan.

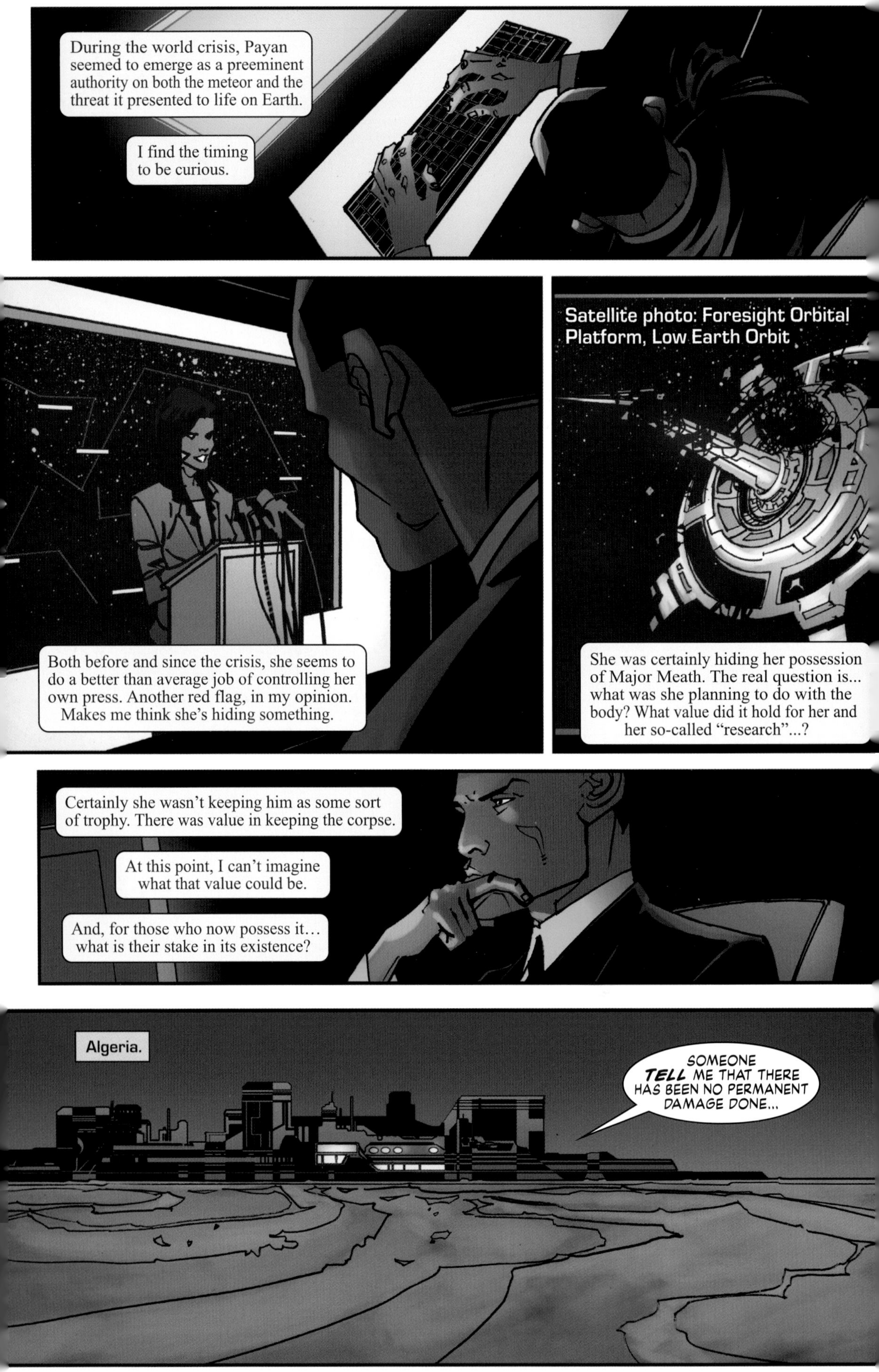
During the world crisis, Payan seemed to emerge as a preeminent authority on both the meteor and the threat it presented to life on Earth.
I find the timing to be curious.
Both before and since the crisis, she seems to do a better than average job of controlling her own press. Another red flag, in my opinion. Makes me think she's hiding something.
Satellite photo: Foresight Orbital Platform, Low Earth Orbit
She was certainly hiding her possession of Major Meath. The real question is... what was she planning to do with the body? What value did it hold for her and her so-called "research"...?
Certainly she wasn't keeping him as some sort of trophy. There was value in keeping the corpse.
At this point, I can't imagine what that value could be.
And, for those who now possess it… what is their stake in its existence?
Algeria.
SOMEONE *TELL* ME THAT THERE HAS BEEN NO PERMANENT DAMAGE DONE...

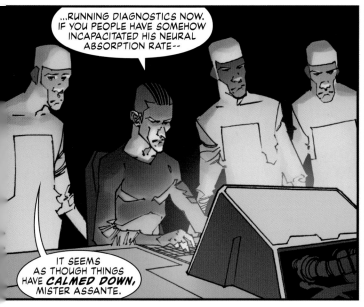

...RUNNING DIAGNOSTICS NOW. IF YOU PEOPLE HAVE SOMEHOW INCAPACITATED HIS NEURAL ABSORPTION RATE--

IT SEEMS AS THOUGH THINGS HAVE *CALMED DOWN,* MISTER ASSANTE.

I DESIGNED THESE PROGRAMS FOR HIS BRAIN WAVE PATTERN. THEY *SHOULD* BE SELF-MODULATING...!

DIAGNOSTICS COMPLETE-- LEVELS ARE NOMINAL.

RECOMMENCING NEURO-DOWNLOAD PROCESS.

I'M ADJUSTING THE EVENT SEQUENCE. WE NEED TO EASE HIM BACK INTO IT.

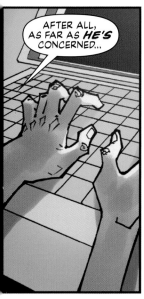

AFTER ALL, AS FAR AS *HE'S* CONCERNED...

...THIS IS THE *ONLY* LIFE HE'S EVER KNOWN.

FOR NOW, WE'LL PROVIDE HIM WITH A MORE *LOW-IMPACT* EXPERIENCE AND SEE HOW HE RESPONDS.

RESUMING PROGRAMMED EVENT SEQUENCE.

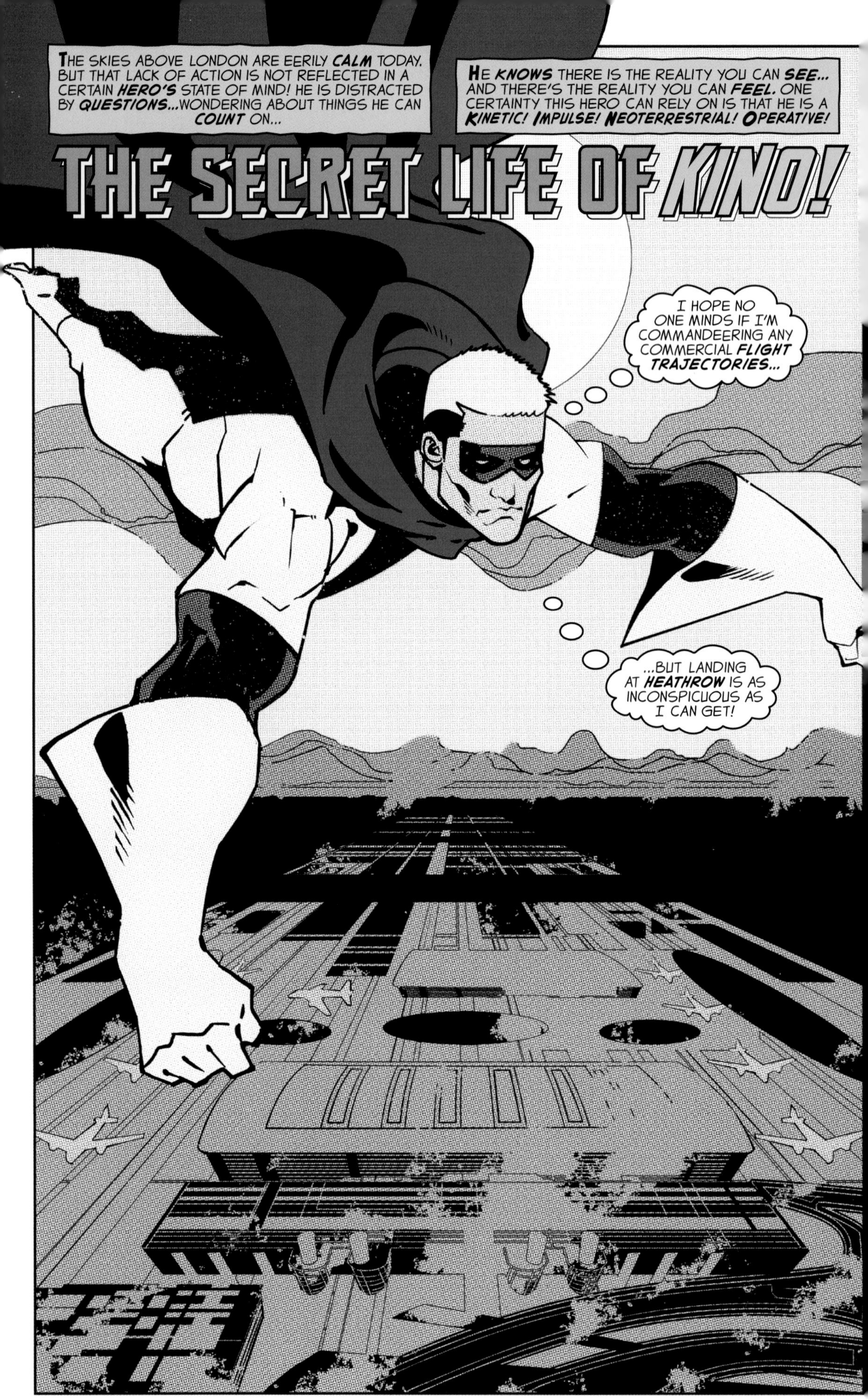
THE SKIES ABOVE LONDON ARE EERILY CALM TODAY. BUT THAT LACK OF ACTION IS NOT REFLECTED IN A CERTAIN HERO'S STATE OF MIND! HE IS DISTRACTED BY QUESTIONS...WONDERING ABOUT THINGS HE CAN COUNT ON...
HE KNOWS THERE IS THE REALITY YOU CAN SEE... AND THERE'S THE REALITY YOU CAN FEEL. ONE CERTAINTY THIS HERO CAN RELY ON IS THAT HE IS A KINETIC! IMPULSE! NEOTERRESTRIAL! OPERATIVE!
THE SECRET LIFE OF KINO!
I HOPE NO ONE MINDS IF I'M COMMANDEERING ANY COMMERCIAL FLIGHT TRAJECTORIES...
...BUT LANDING AT HEATHROW IS AS INCONSPICUOUS AS I CAN GET!

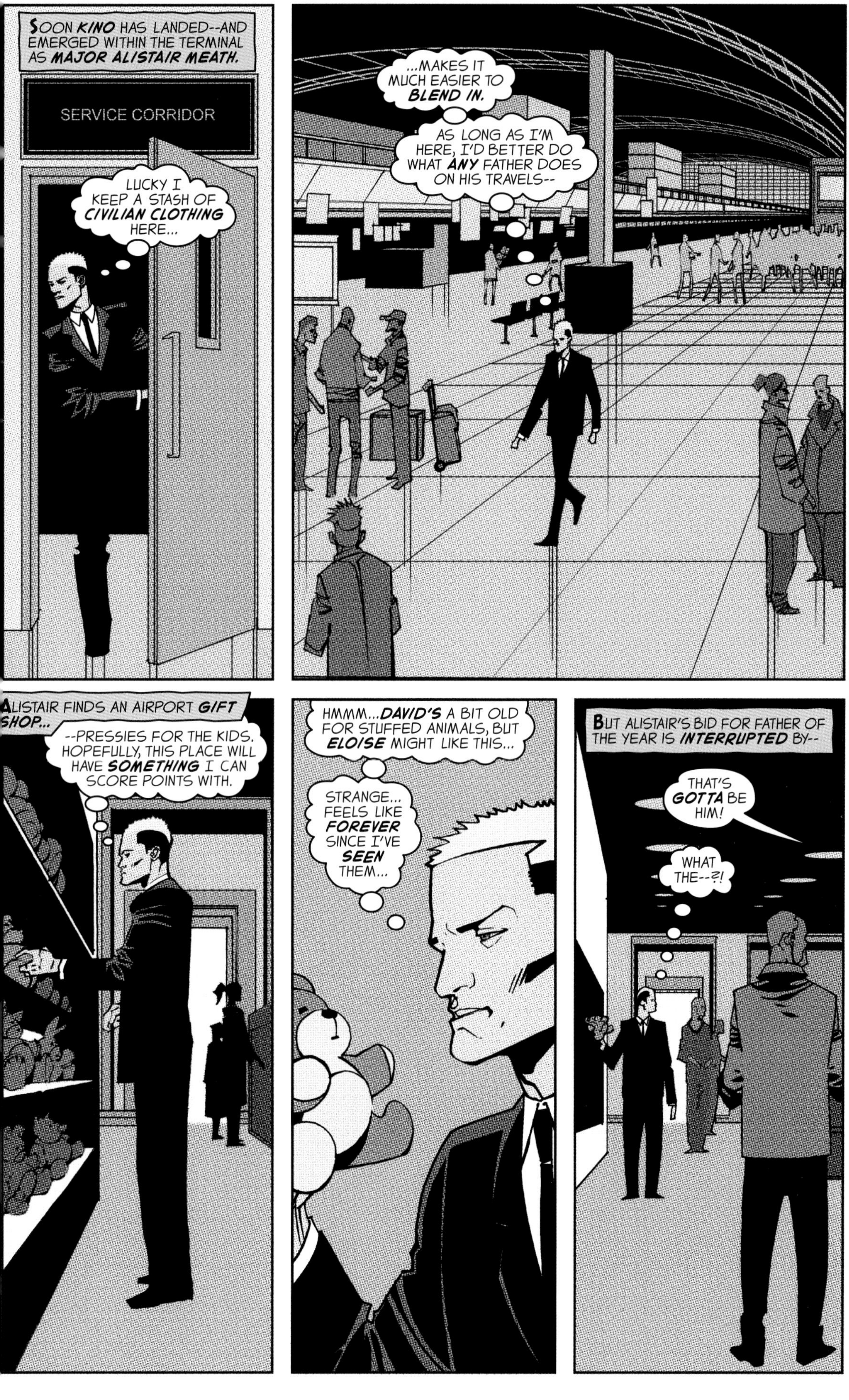
SOON KINO HAS LANDED--AND EMERGED WITHIN THE TERMINAL AS MAJOR ALISTAIR MEATH.
SERVICE CORRIDOR
LUCKY I KEEP A STASH OF CIVILIAN CLOTHING HERE...
...MAKES IT MUCH EASIER TO BLEND IN.
AS LONG AS I'M HERE, I'D BETTER DO WHAT ANY FATHER DOES ON HIS TRAVELS--
ALISTAIR FINDS AN AIRPORT GIFT SHOP...
--PRESSIES FOR THE KIDS. HOPEFULLY, THIS PLACE WILL HAVE SOMETHING I CAN SCORE POINTS WITH.
HMMM...DAVID'S A BIT OLD FOR STUFFED ANIMALS, BUT ELOISE MIGHT LIKE THIS...
STRANGE... FEELS LIKE FOREVER SINCE I'VE SEEN THEM...
BUT ALISTAIR'S BID FOR FATHER OF THE YEAR IS INTERRUPTED BY--
THAT'S GOTTA BE HIM!
WHAT THE--?!

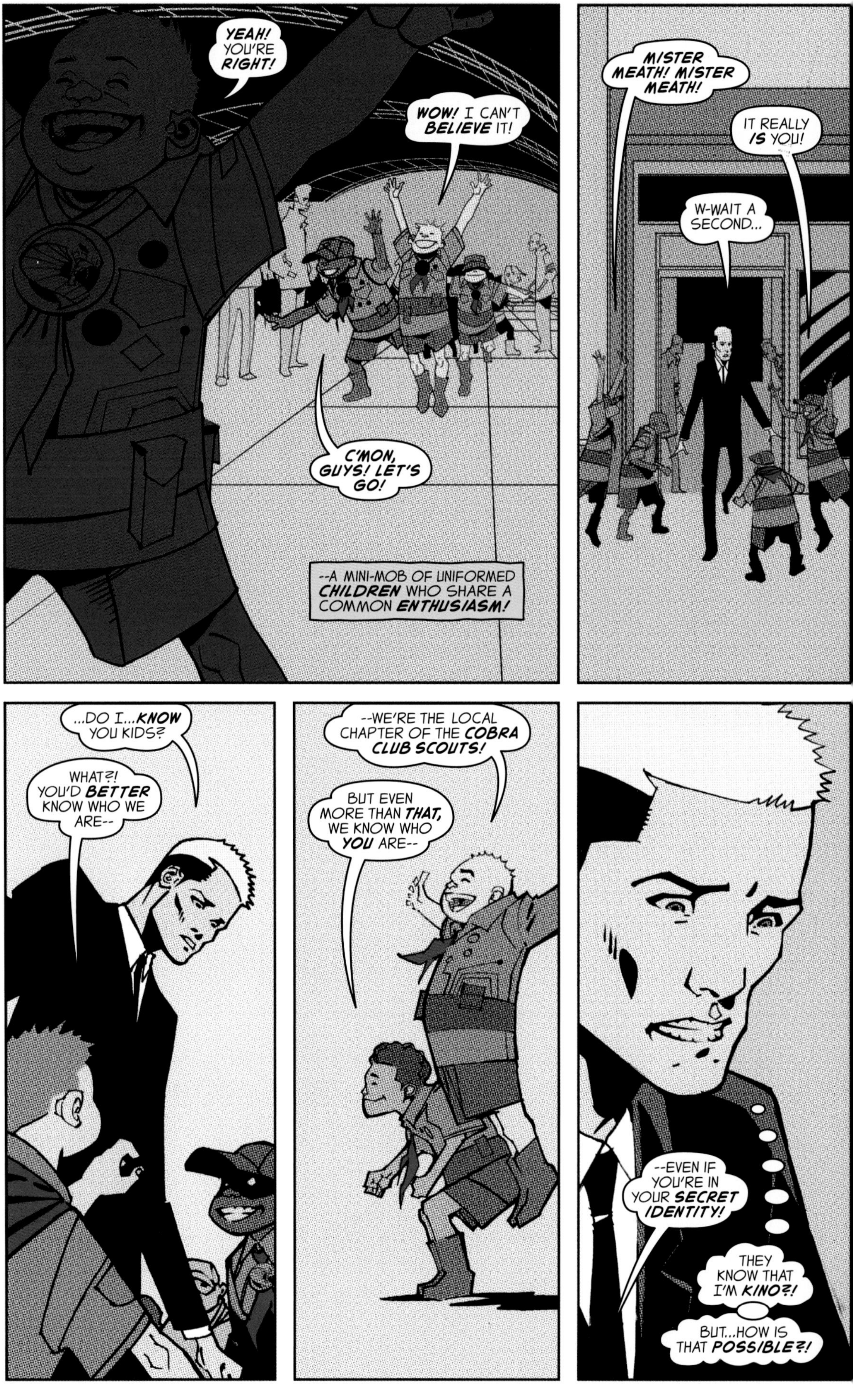
YEAH! YOU'RE RIGHT!
WOW! I CAN'T BELIEVE IT!
C'MON, GUYS! LET'S GO!
--A MINI-MOB OF UNIFORMED CHILDREN WHO SHARE A COMMON ENTHUSIASM!
MISTER MEATH! MISTER MEATH!
IT REALLY IS YOU!
W-WAIT A SECOND...
...DO I...KNOW YOU KIDS?
WHAT?! YOU'D BETTER KNOW WHO WE ARE--
--WE'RE THE LOCAL CHAPTER OF THE COBRA CLUB SCOUTS!
BUT EVEN MORE THAN THAT, WE KNOW WHO YOU ARE--
--EVEN IF YOU'RE IN YOUR SECRET IDENTITY!
THEY KNOW THAT I'M KINO?!
BUT...HOW IS THAT POSSIBLE?!

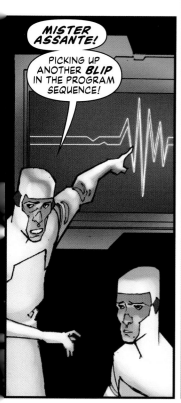

MISTER ASSANTE! PICKING UP ANOTHER *BLIP* IN THE PROGRAM SEQUENCE!

INTERESTING. LOOKS TO BE MORE OF AN *EMOTIONAL* RESPONSE THAN A *LOGIC* ONE.

LET IT RIDE FOR NOW. PERHAPS WE CAN *LEARN* SOME-THING.

THIS MUST BE HOW *GOD* FELT WHEN HE LOOKED DOWN UPON THE PROTO-UNIVERSE...

...PONDERING EXACTLY *WHERE* HE WOULD IGNITE THE *DIVINE SPARK.*

WHO IS HE *TALKING* TO, EXACTLY...?

NEVER MIND THAT. JUST HELP ME RECALCULATE THE *IDENTITY VARIABLES...!*

WHAT WILL HISTORY *RECORD* OF THIS MOMENT...

...THE MOMENT WHERE *EVOLUTION* TRANSFORMED INTO AN ACT OF SHEER *WILL...?*

I AM NOTHING LESS THAN THE NEW *PROMETHEUS.*

I BRING FORTH A NEW *KIND* OF FIRE.

HONESTLY, I CAN'T *WAIT* TO SEE THE EFFECTS OF *THIS* DRAMATIC TURN.

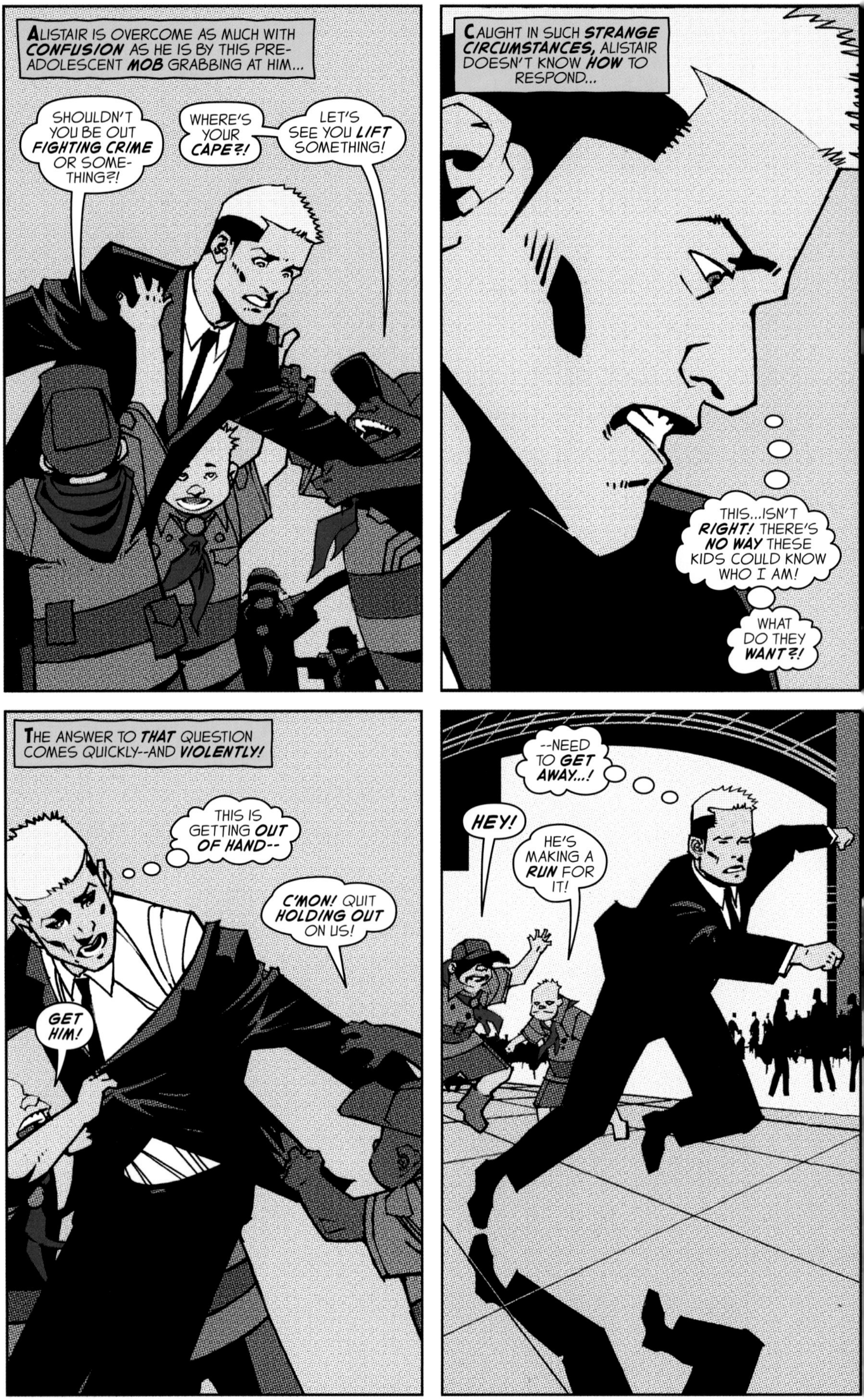
ALISTAIR IS OVERCOME AS MUCH WITH CONFUSION AS HE IS BY THIS PRE-ADOLESCENT MOB GRABBING AT HIM...
SHOULDN'T YOU BE OUT FIGHTING CRIME OR SOME-THING?!
WHERE'S YOUR CAPE?!
LET'S SEE YOU LIFT SOMETHING!
CAUGHT IN SUCH STRANGE CIRCUMSTANCES, ALISTAIR DOESN'T KNOW HOW TO RESPOND...
THIS...ISN'T RIGHT! THERE'S NO WAY THESE KIDS COULD KNOW WHO I AM!
WHAT DO THEY WANT?!
THE ANSWER TO THAT QUESTION COMES QUICKLY--AND VIOLENTLY!
THIS IS GETTING OUT OF HAND--
C'MON! QUIT HOLDING OUT ON US!
GET HIM!
--NEED TO GET AWAY...!
HEY!
HE'S MAKING A RUN FOR IT!

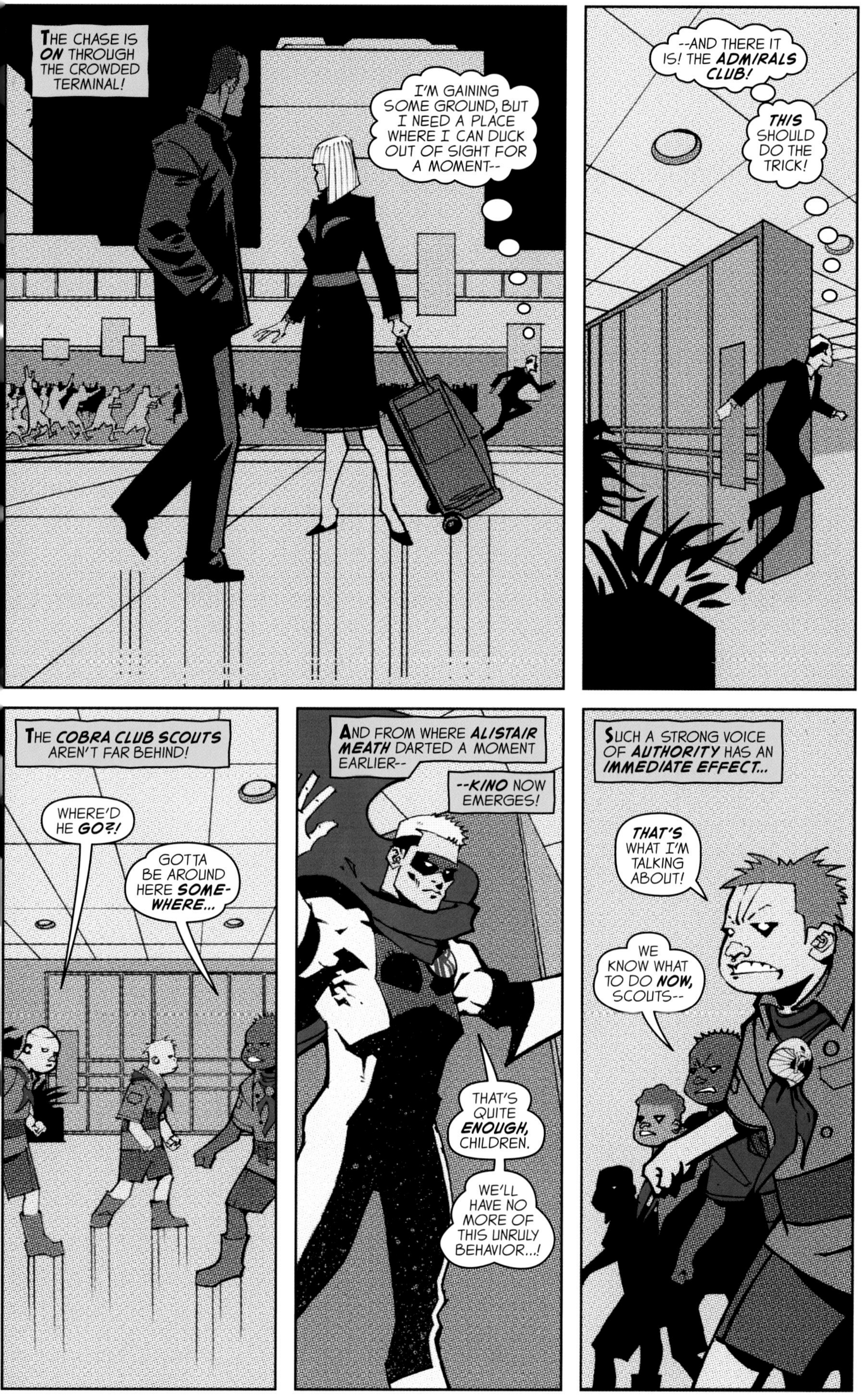
THE CHASE IS ON THROUGH THE CROWDED TERMINAL!
I'M GAINING SOME GROUND, BUT I NEED A PLACE WHERE I CAN DUCK OUT OF SIGHT FOR A MOMENT--
--AND THERE IT IS! THE ADMIRALS CLUB!
THIS SHOULD DO THE TRICK!
THE COBRA CLUB SCOUTS AREN'T FAR BEHIND!
WHERE'D HE GO?!
GOTTA BE AROUND HERE SOME-WHERE...
AND FROM WHERE ALISTAIR MEATH DARTED A MOMENT EARLIER--
--KINO NOW EMERGES!
THAT'S QUITE ENOUGH, CHILDREN.
WE'LL HAVE NO MORE OF THIS UNRULY BEHAVIOR...!
SUCH A STRONG VOICE OF AUTHORITY HAS AN IMMEDIATE EFFECT...
THAT'S WHAT I'M TALKING ABOUT!
WE KNOW WHAT TO DO NOW, SCOUTS--

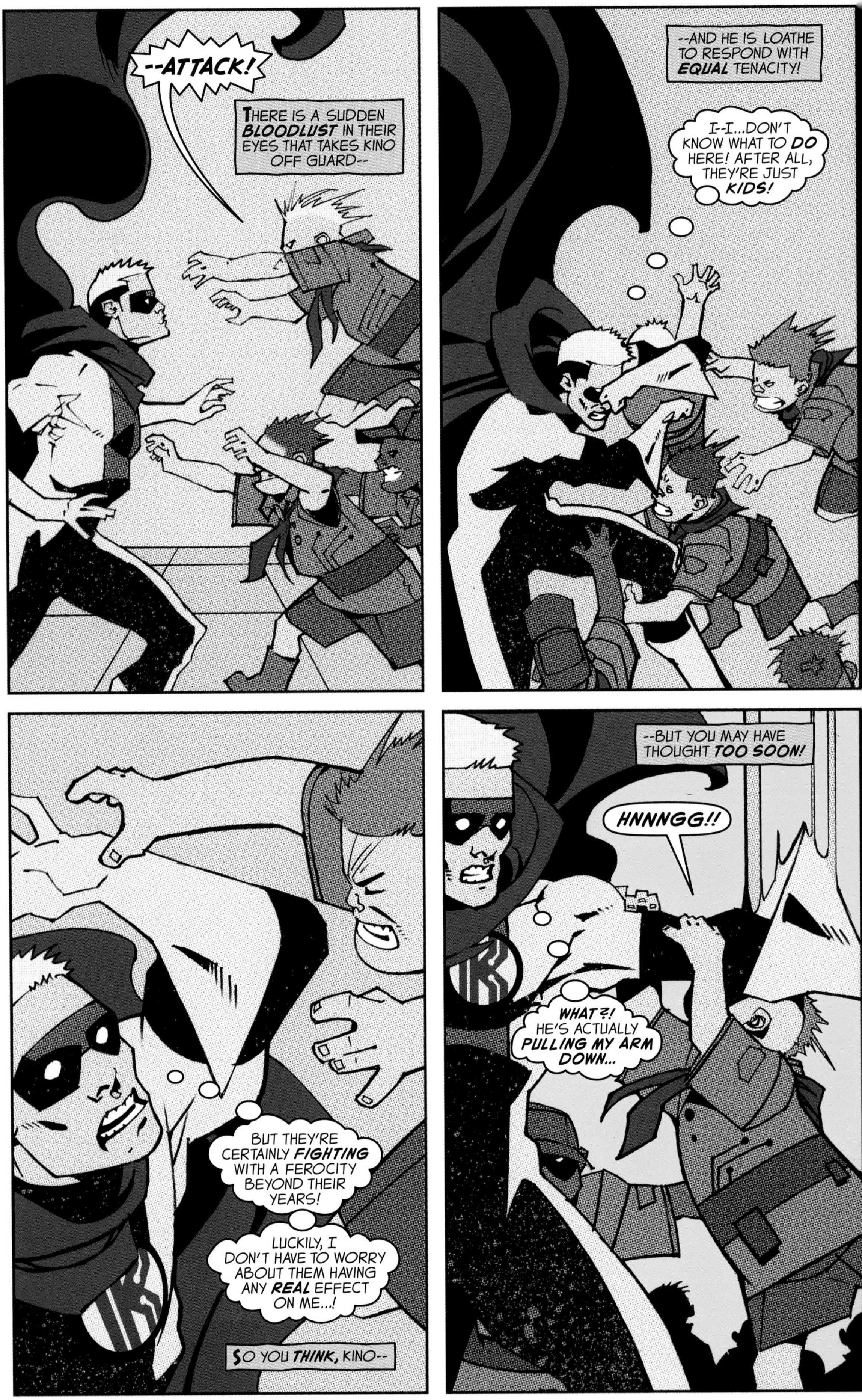
--ATTACK!
THERE IS A SUDDEN BLOODLUST IN THEIR EYES THAT TAKES KINO OFF GUARD--
--AND HE IS LOATHE TO RESPOND WITH EQUAL TENACITY!
I--I...DON'T KNOW WHAT TO DO HERE! AFTER ALL, THEY'RE JUST KIDS!
BUT THEY'RE CERTAINLY FIGHTING WITH A FEROCITY BEYOND THEIR YEARS!
LUCKILY, I DON'T HAVE TO WORRY ABOUT THEM HAVING ANY REAL EFFECT ON ME...!
SO YOU THINK, KINO--
--BUT YOU MAY HAVE THOUGHT TOO SOON!
HNNNGG!!
WHAT?! HE'S ACTUALLY PULLING MY ARM DOWN...

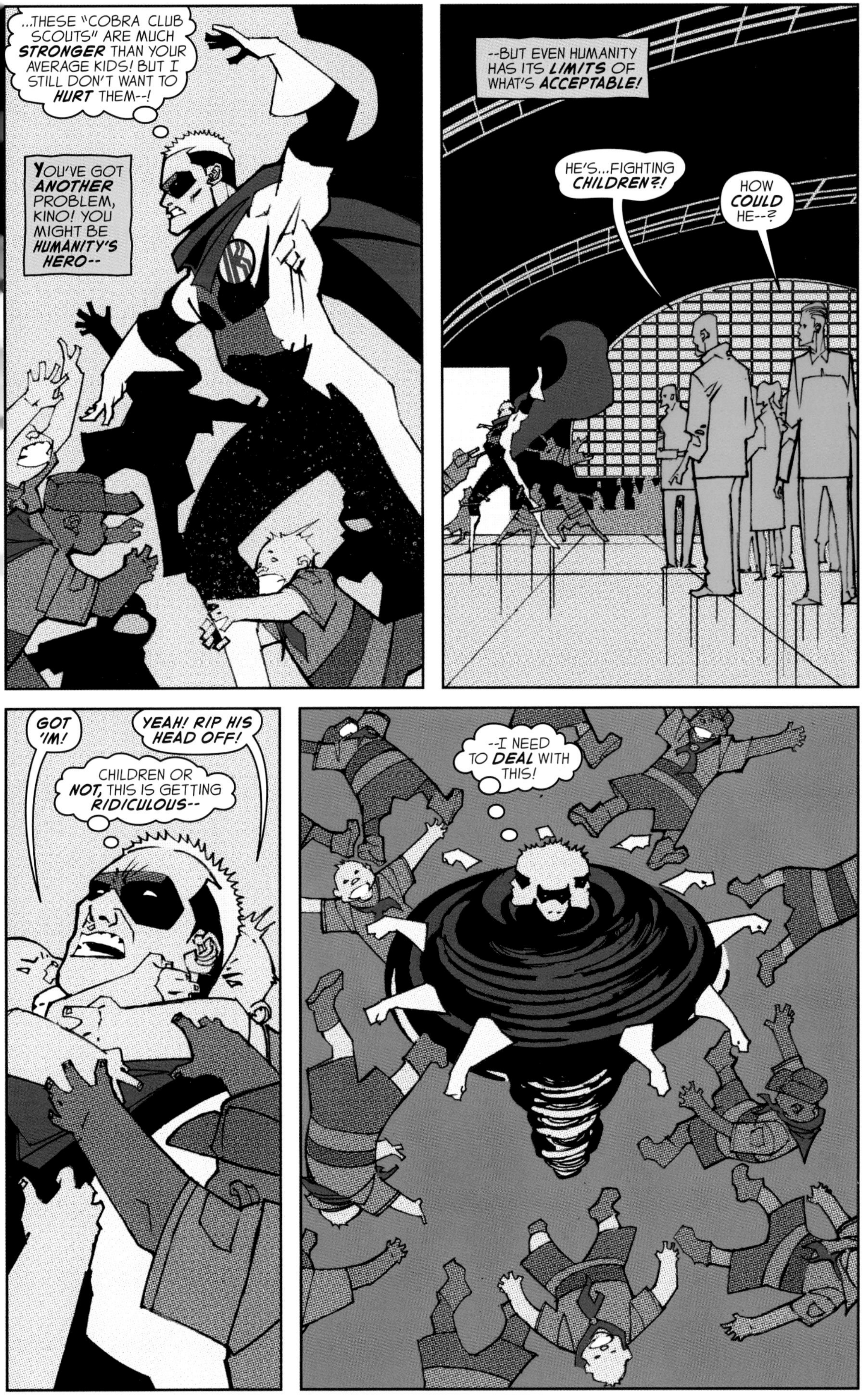
...THESE "COBRA CLUB SCOUTS" ARE MUCH STRONGER THAN YOUR AVERAGE KIDS! BUT I STILL DON'T WANT TO HURT THEM--!
YOU'VE GOT ANOTHER PROBLEM, KINO! YOU MIGHT BE HUMANITY'S HERO--
--BUT EVEN HUMANITY HAS ITS LIMITS OF WHAT'S ACCEPTABLE!
HE'S...FIGHTING CHILDREN?!
HOW COULD HE--?
GOT 'IM!
YEAH! RIP HIS HEAD OFF!
CHILDREN OR NOT, THIS IS GETTING RIDICULOUS--
--I NEED TO DEAL WITH THIS!

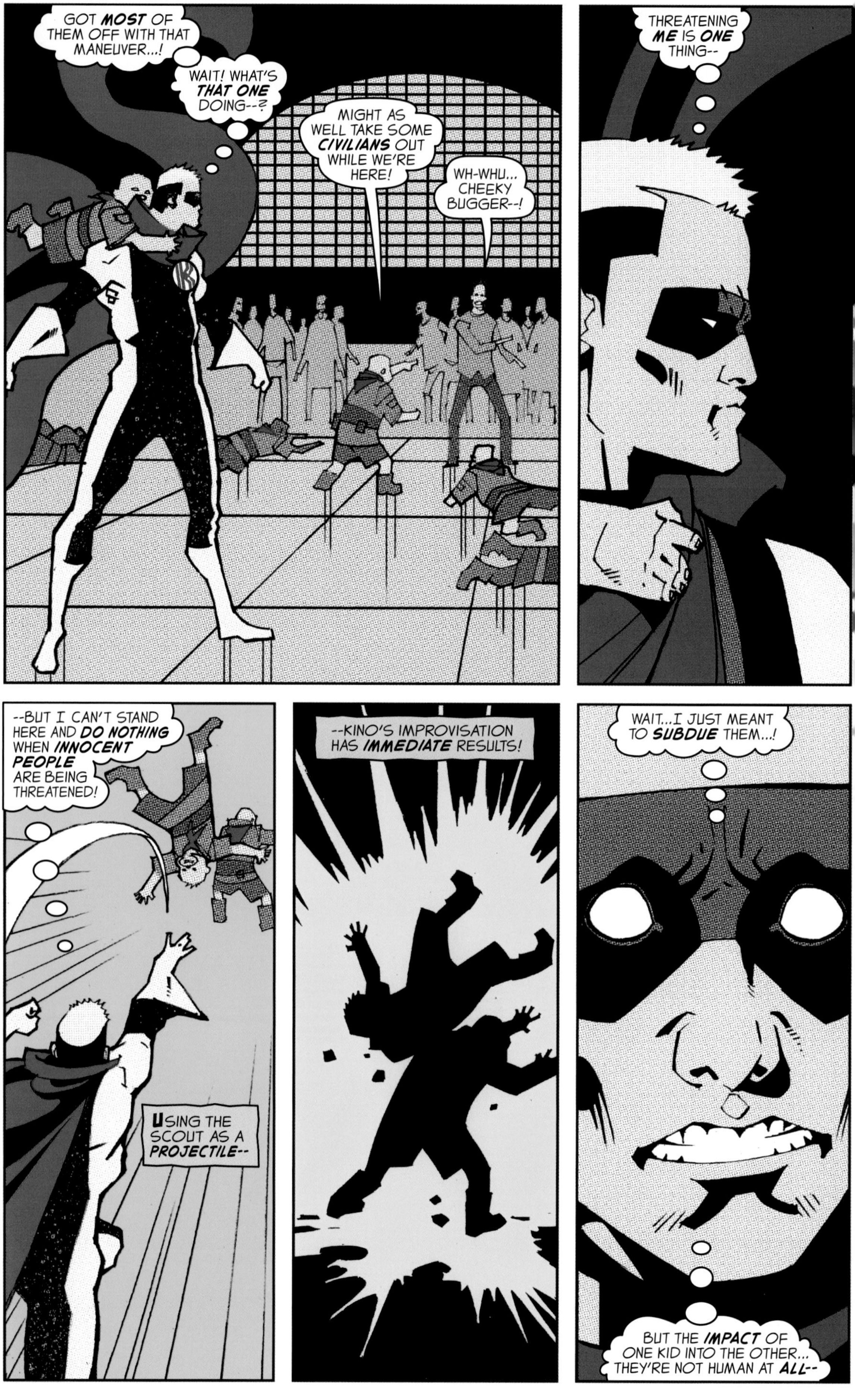
GOT MOST OF THEM OFF WITH THAT MANEUVER...!
WAIT! WHAT'S THAT ONE DOING--?
MIGHT AS WELL TAKE SOME CIVILIANS OUT WHILE WE'RE HERE!
WH-WHU... CHEEKY BUGGER--!
THREATENING ME IS ONE THING--
--BUT I CAN'T STAND HERE AND DO NOTHING WHEN INNOCENT PEOPLE ARE BEING THREATENED!
USING THE SCOUT AS A PROJECTILE--
--KINO'S IMPROVISATION HAS IMMEDIATE RESULTS!
WAIT...I JUST MEANT TO SUBDUE THEM...!
BUT THE IMPACT OF ONE KID INTO THE OTHER... THEY'RE NOT HUMAN AT ALL--

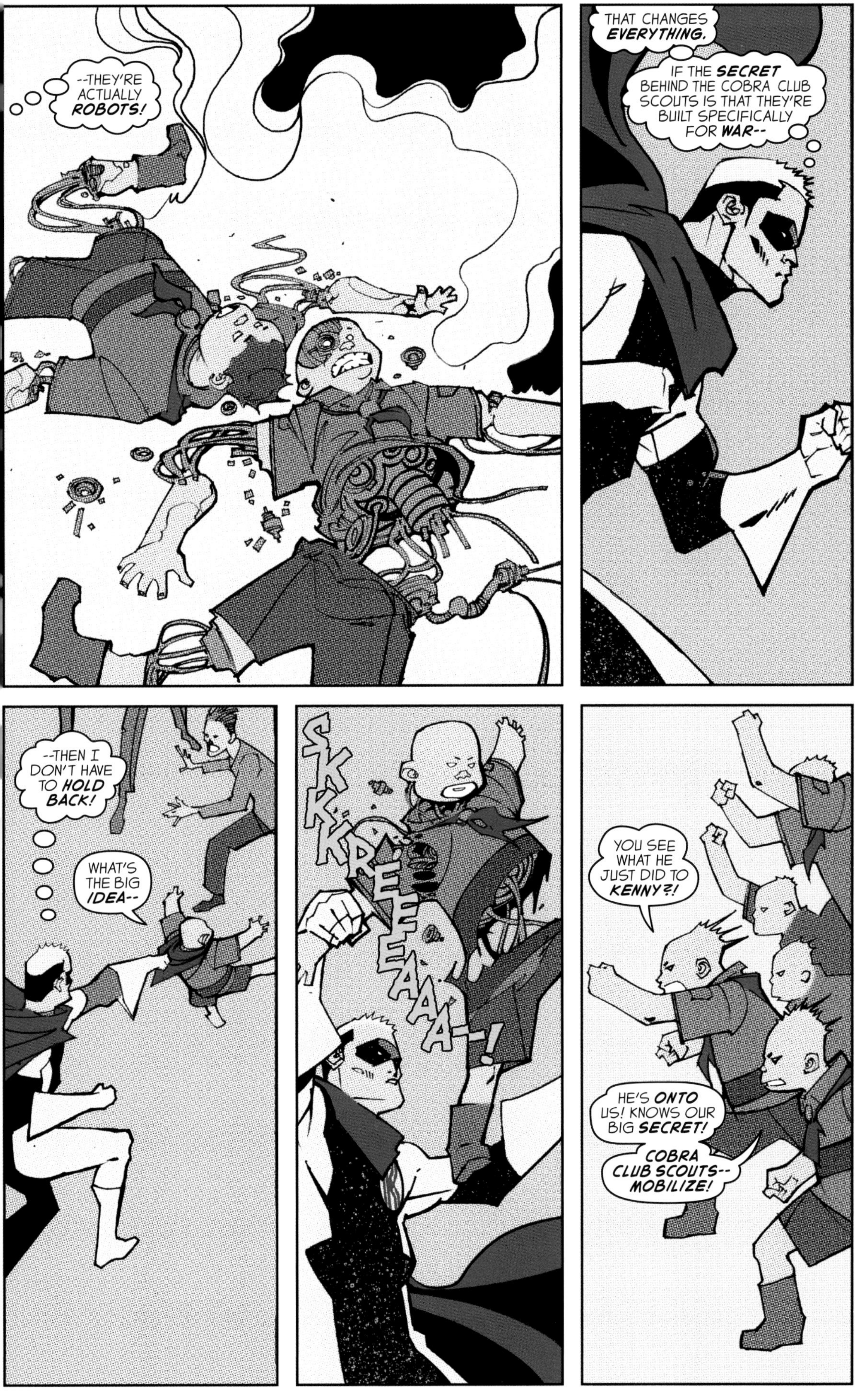
--THEY'RE ACTUALLY ROBOTS!
THAT CHANGES EVERYTHING.
IF THE SECRET BEHIND THE COBRA CLUB SCOUTS IS THAT THEY'RE BUILT SPECIFICALLY FOR WAR--
--THEN I DON'T HAVE TO HOLD BACK!
WHAT'S THE BIG IDEA--
SKKREEEAAAA--!
YOU SEE WHAT HE JUST DID TO KENNY?!
HE'S ONTO US! KNOWS OUR BIG SECRET!
COBRA CLUB SCOUTS--MOBILIZE!

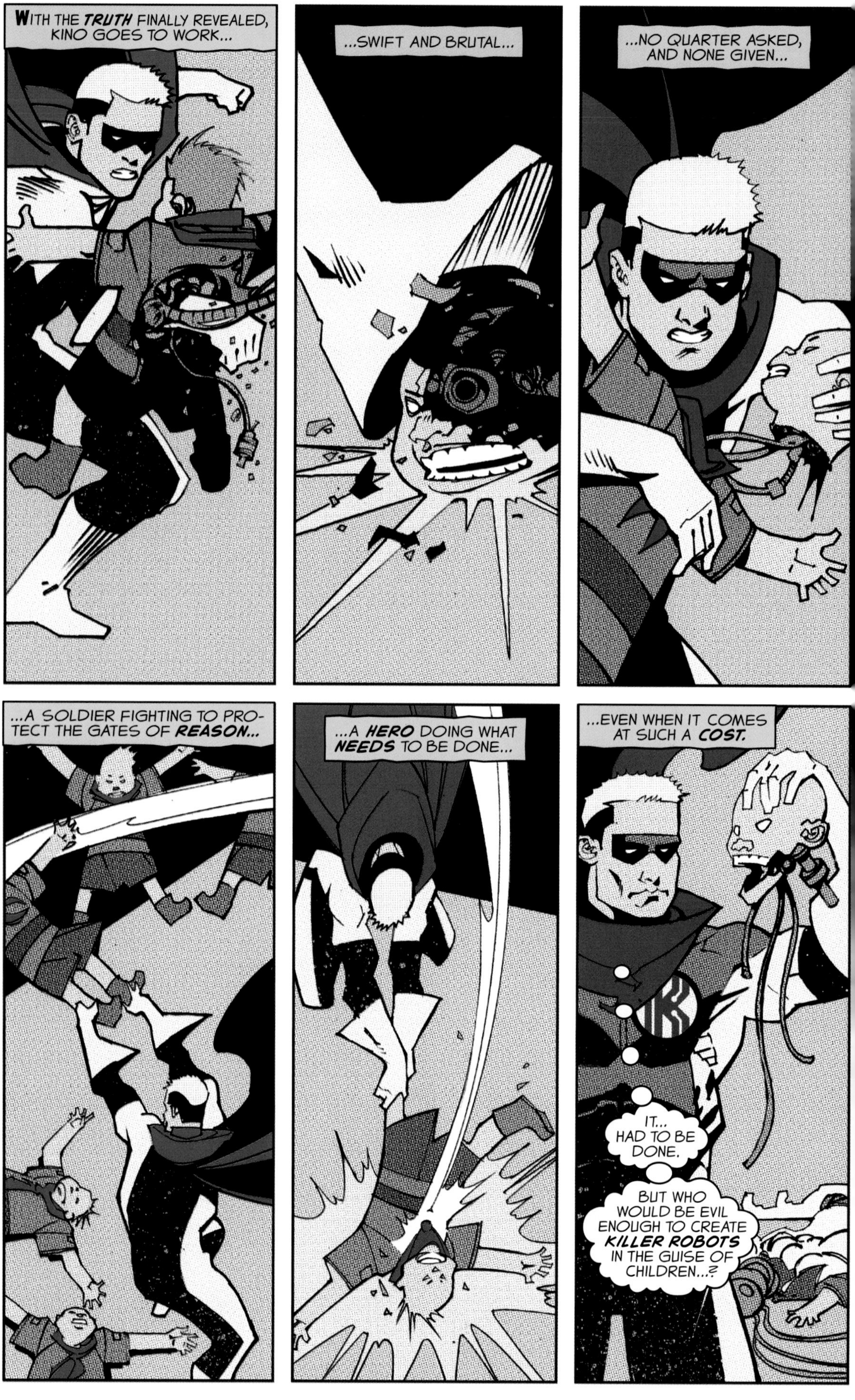
WITH THE TRUTH FINALLY REVEALED, KINO GOES TO WORK...
...SWIFT AND BRUTAL...
...NO QUARTER ASKED, AND NONE GIVEN...
...A SOLDIER FIGHTING TO PROTECT THE GATES OF REASON...
...A HERO DOING WHAT NEEDS TO BE DONE...
...EVEN WHEN IT COMES AT SUCH A COST.
IT... HAD TO BE DONE.
BUT WHO WOULD BE EVIL ENOUGH TO CREATE KILLER ROBOTS IN THE GUISE OF CHILDREN...?

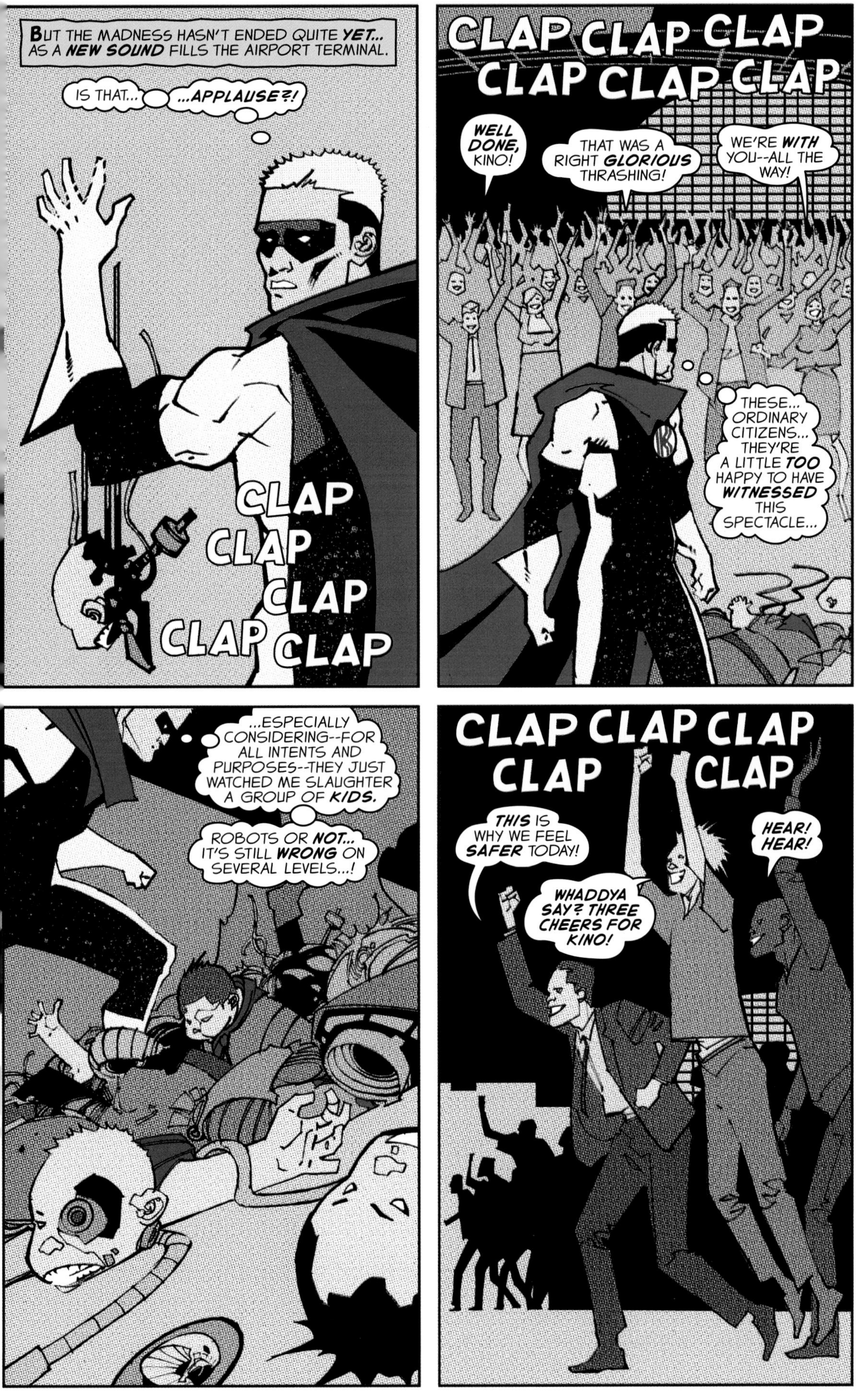

BUT THE MADNESS HASN'T ENDED QUITE YET... AS A NEW SOUND FILLS THE AIRPORT TERMINAL.
IS THAT...
...APPLAUSE?!
CLAP CLAP CLAP CLAP CLAP
CLAP CLAP CLAP CLAP CLAP CLAP
WELL DONE, KINO!
THAT WAS A RIGHT GLORIOUS THRASHING!
WE'RE WITH YOU--ALL THE WAY!
THESE... ORDINARY CITIZENS... THEY'RE A LITTLE TOO HAPPY TO HAVE WITNESSED THIS SPECTACLE...
...ESPECIALLY CONSIDERING--FOR ALL INTENTS AND PURPOSES--THEY JUST WATCHED ME SLAUGHTER A GROUP OF KIDS.
ROBOTS OR NOT... IT'S STILL WRONG ON SEVERAL LEVELS...!
CLAP CLAP CLAP CLAP CLAP
THIS IS WHY WE FEEL SAFER TODAY!
HEAR! HEAR!
WHADDYA SAY? THREE CHEERS FOR KINO!

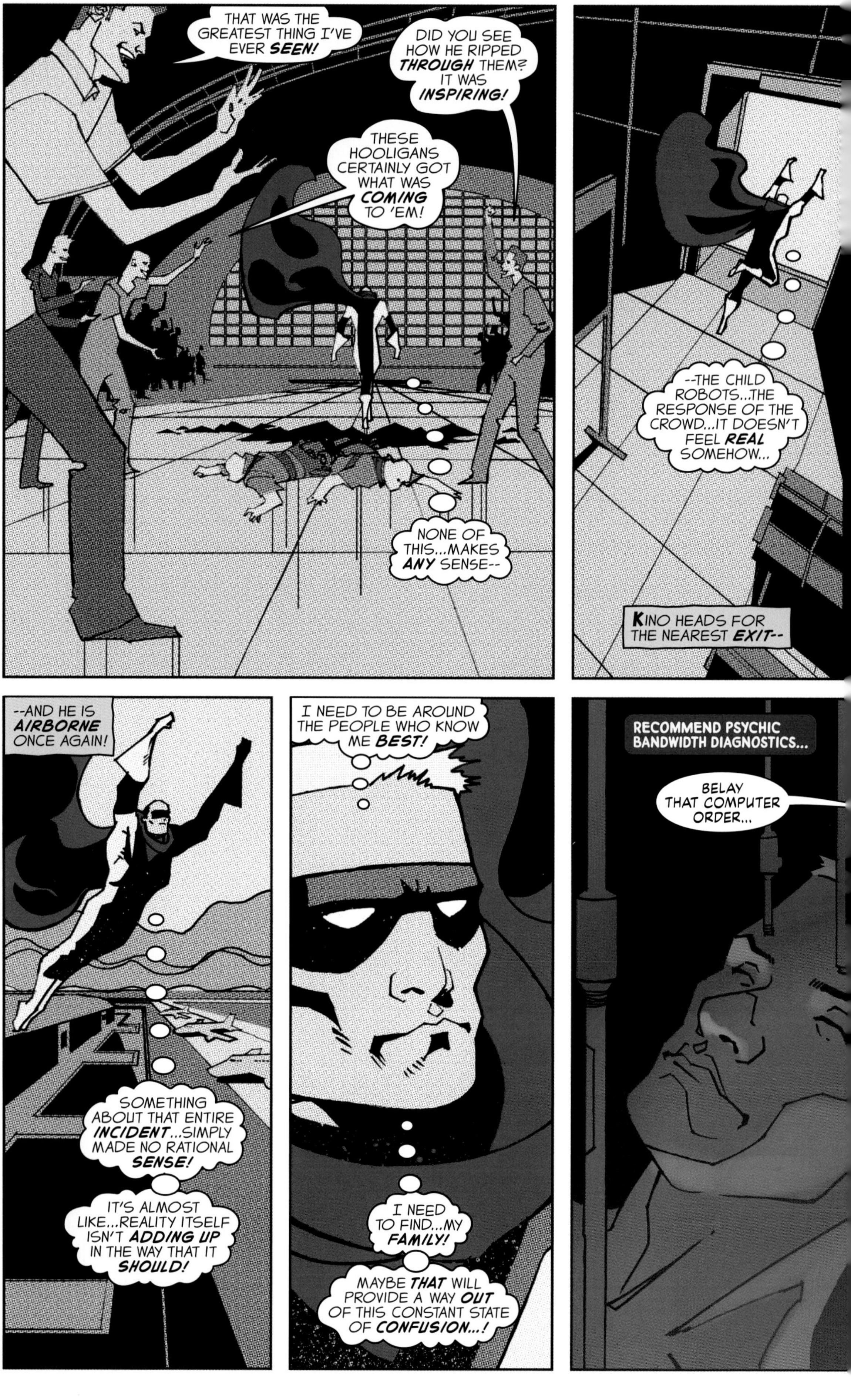
THAT WAS THE GREATEST THING I'VE EVER SEEN!
DID YOU SEE HOW HE RIPPED THROUGH THEM? IT WAS INSPIRING!
THESE HOOLIGANS CERTAINLY GOT WHAT WAS COMING TO 'EM!
NONE OF THIS...MAKES ANY SENSE--
--THE CHILD ROBOTS...THE RESPONSE OF THE CROWD...IT DOESN'T FEEL REAL SOMEHOW...
KINO HEADS FOR THE NEAREST EXIT--
--AND HE IS AIRBORNE ONCE AGAIN!
SOMETHING ABOUT THAT ENTIRE INCIDENT...SIMPLY MADE NO RATIONAL SENSE!
IT'S ALMOST LIKE...REALITY ITSELF ISN'T ADDING UP IN THE WAY THAT IT SHOULD!
I NEED TO BE AROUND THE PEOPLE WHO KNOW ME BEST!
I NEED TO FIND...MY FAMILY!
MAYBE THAT WILL PROVIDE A WAY OUT OF THIS CONSTANT STATE OF CONFUSION...!
RECOMMEND PSYCHIC BANDWIDTH DIAGNOSTICS...
BELAY THAT COMPUTER ORDER...

...THIS IS NOT THE TIME TO **BACK OFF.**

BUT **SIR**...WE CAN'T TRACK THE RATE OF CORTEXTUAL ASSIMILATION WITHOUT PERIODIC AUTO-SAVES...

NONSENSE. RUN THE COMPENSATION SOFTWARE TO CLOSE ANY RELEVANT GAPS IN THE NEURO-NETSCAPE.

BUT, IN THEORY, THE REINTEGRATION PROCESS--

YOU DON'T SEEM TO **UNDER-STAND...**

...WE'RE **BEYOND** THE THEORETICAL PHASE. **FAR** BEYOND IT, IN FACT.

HE'S CREATING SELF-PERPETUATING SCENARIOS...AND YET HE CANNOT **CONTROL** THEM.

FASCINATING.

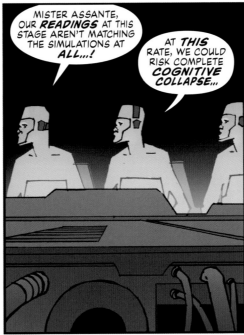

MISTER ASSANTE, OUR **READINGS** AT THIS STAGE AREN'T MATCHING THE SIMULATIONS AT **ALL...!**

AT **THIS** RATE, WE COULD RISK COMPLETE **COGNITIVE COLLAPSE...**

...UNLESS WE **SHUT DOWN** AND RECONFIGURE THE RATE SYSTEMS.

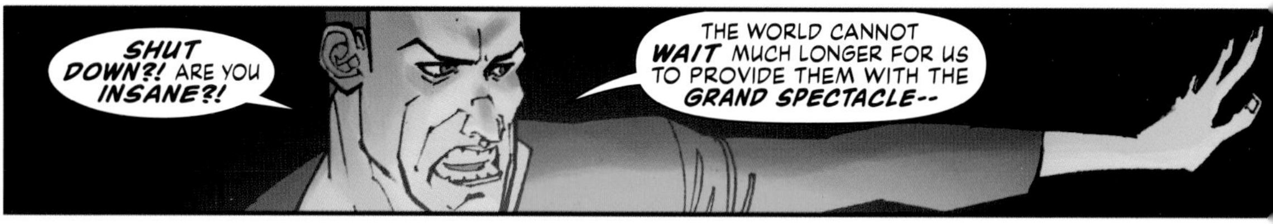
SHUT DOWN?! ARE YOU INSANE?!
THE WORLD CANNOT WAIT MUCH LONGER FOR US TO PROVIDE THEM WITH THE GRAND SPECTACLE--

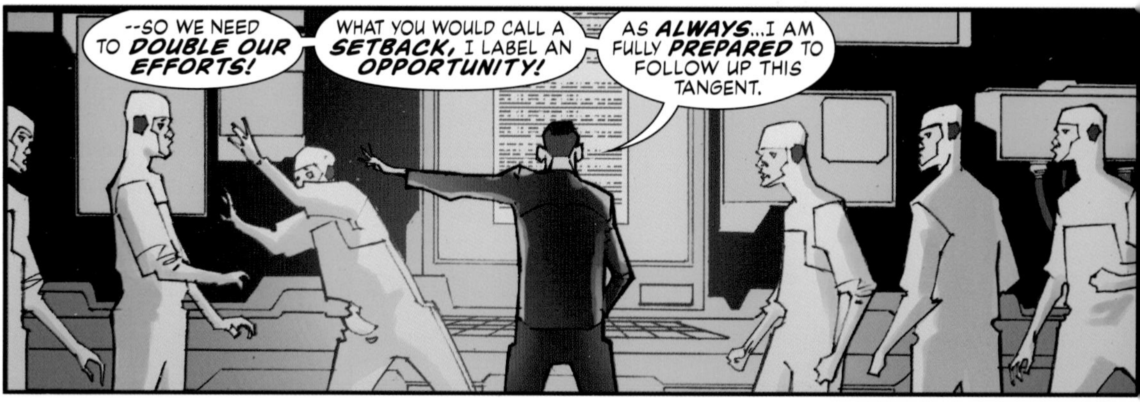
--SO WE NEED TO DOUBLE OUR EFFORTS!
WHAT YOU WOULD CALL A SETBACK, I LABEL AN OPPORTUNITY!
AS ALWAYS...I AM FULLY PREPARED TO FOLLOW UP THIS TANGENT.

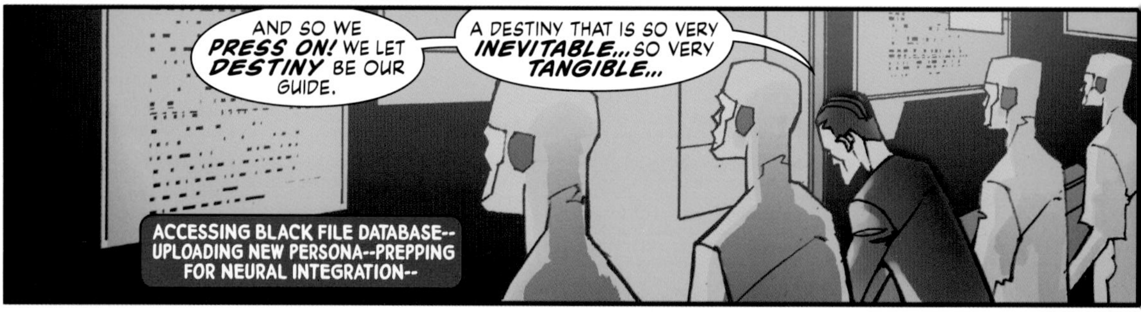
AND SO WE PRESS ON! WE LET DESTINY BE OUR GUIDE.
A DESTINY THAT IS SO VERY INEVITABLE...SO VERY TANGIBLE...
ACCESSING BLACK FILE DATABASE-- UPLOADING NEW PERSONA--PREPPING FOR NEURAL INTEGRATION--

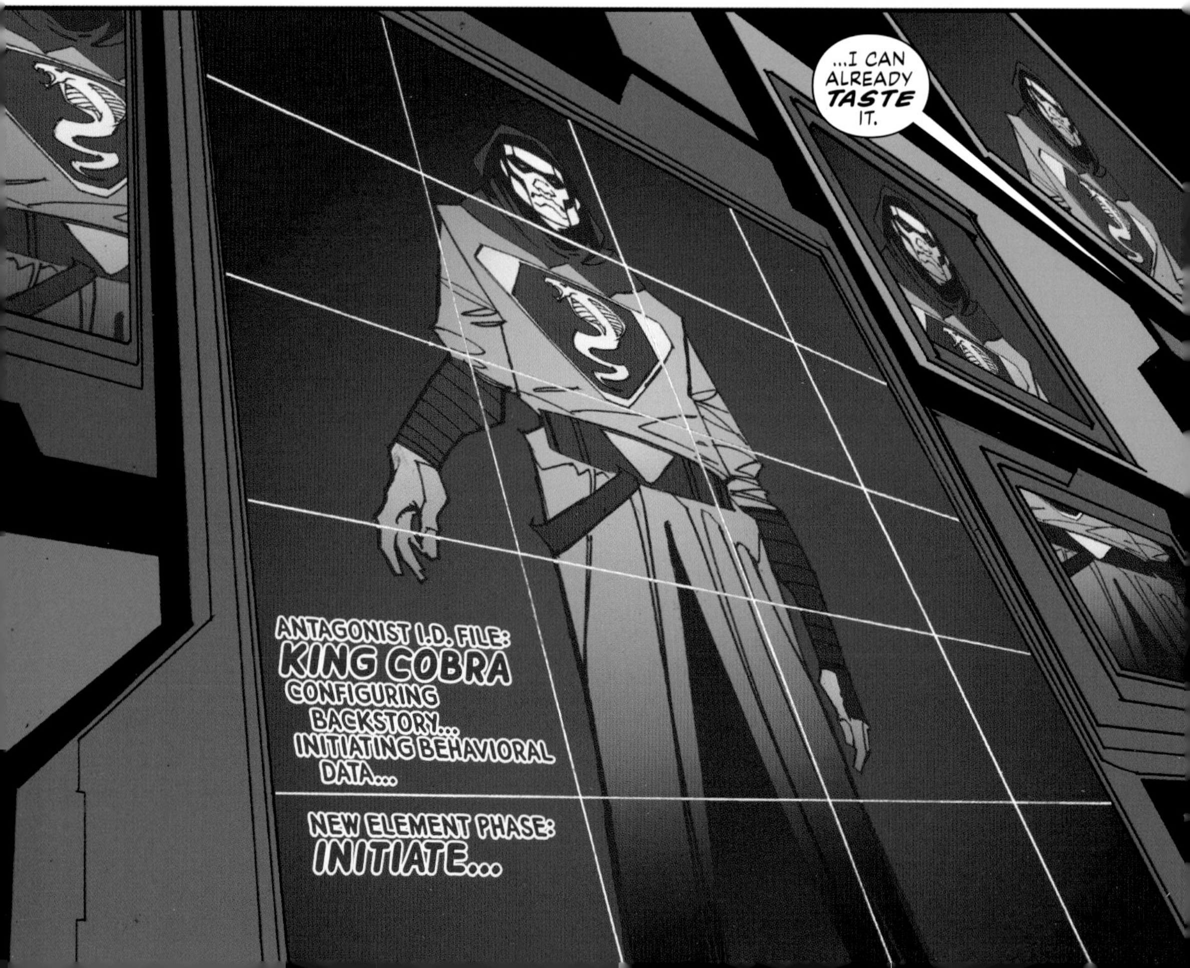
...I CAN ALREADY TASTE IT.
ANTAGONIST I.D. FILE: KING COBRA
CONFIGURING BACKSTORY... INITIATING BEHAVIORAL DATA...
NEW ELEMENT PHASE: INITIATE...

CHAPTER FOUR

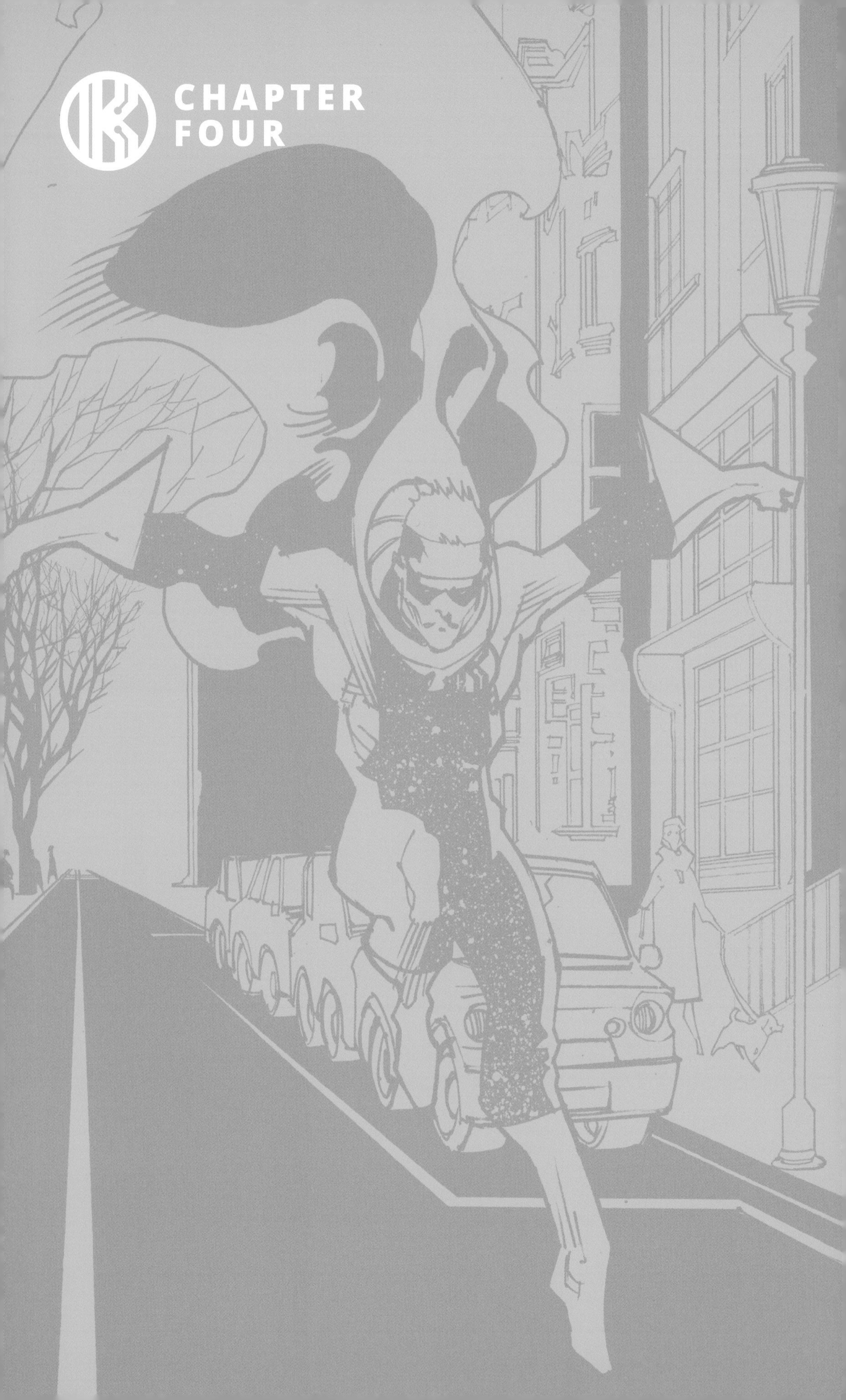

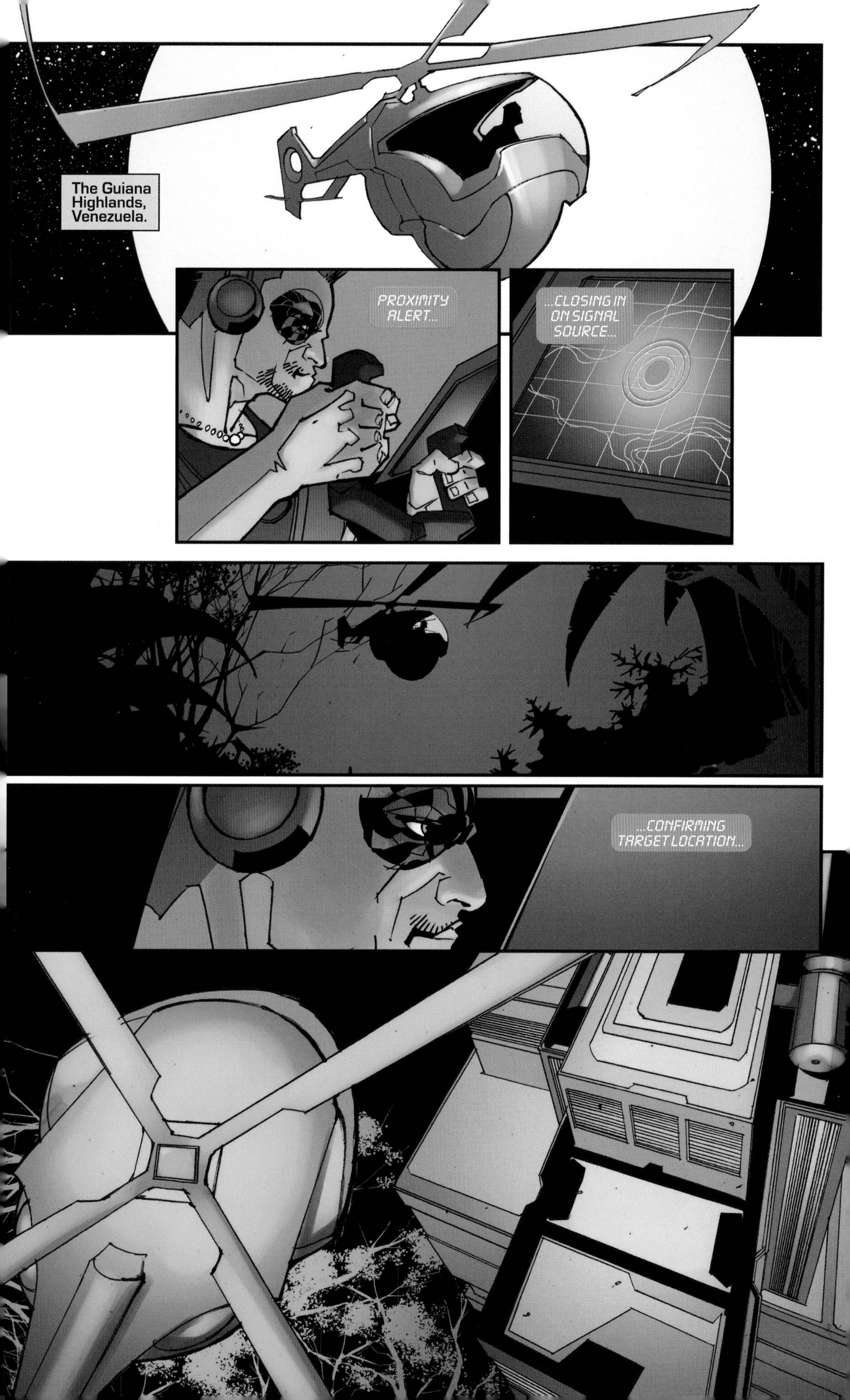

The Guiana Highlands, Venezuela.
PROXIMITY ALERT...
...CLOSING IN ON SIGNAL SOURCE...
...CONFIRMING TARGET LOCATION...

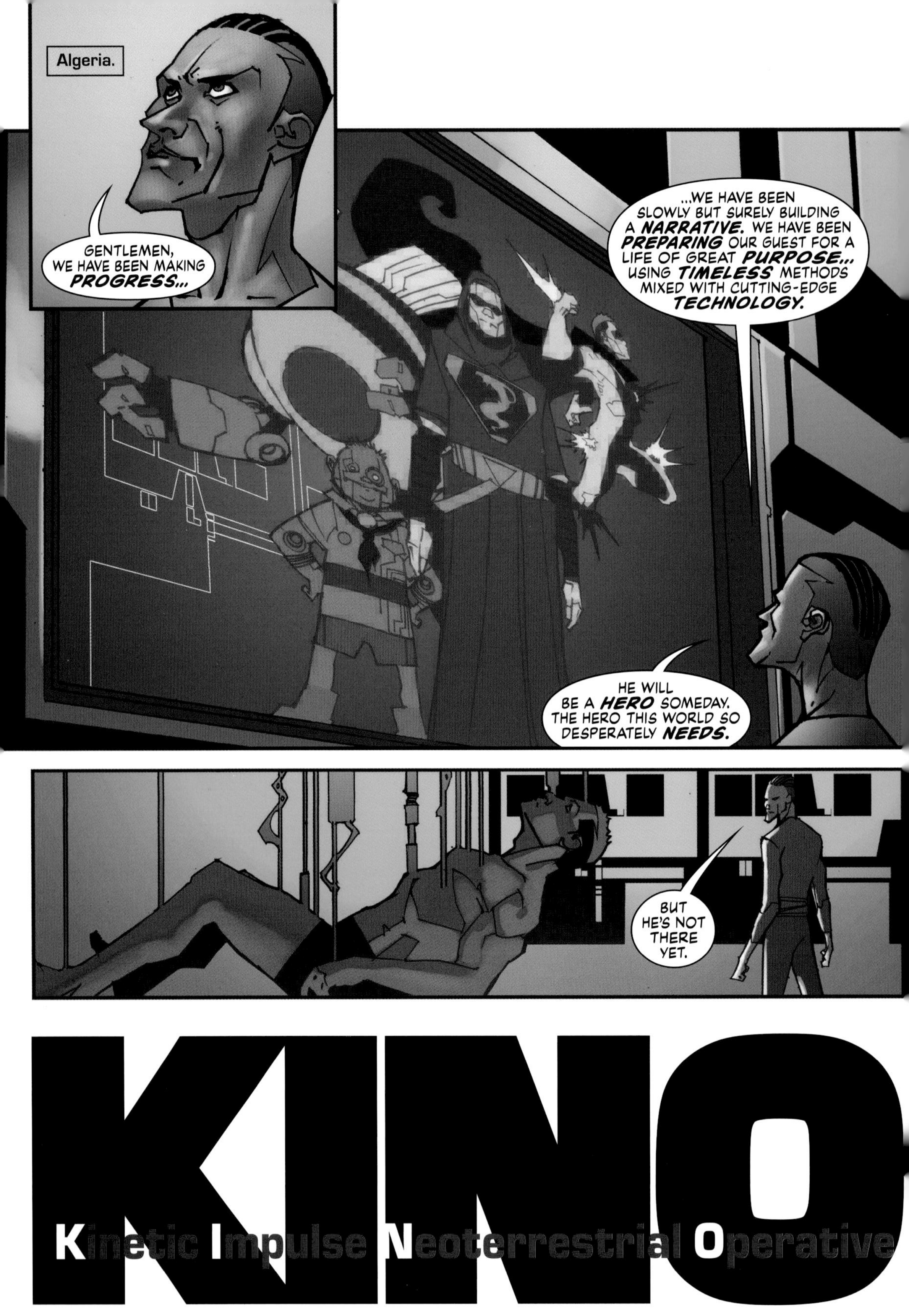
Algeria.
GENTLEMEN, WE HAVE BEEN MAKING PROGRESS...
...WE HAVE BEEN SLOWLY BUT SURELY BUILDING A NARRATIVE. WE HAVE BEEN PREPARING OUR GUEST FOR A LIFE OF GREAT PURPOSE... USING TIMELESS METHODS MIXED WITH CUTTING-EDGE TECHNOLOGY.
HE WILL BE A HERO SOMEDAY. THE HERO THIS WORLD SO DESPERATELY NEEDS.
BUT HE'S NOT THERE YET.

KINO

Kinetic Impulse Neoterrestrial Operative

CHAPTER FOUR:

The Record Skip

YOU'RE CLOSELY MONITORING HIS *VITALS,* YES...?

AT THE MOMENT, THE SELF-PERPETUATING ALGORITHMS SEEM TO BE FLUCTUATING AT RANDOM INTERVALS.

IT'S...DIFFICULT TO KNOW WHAT'S GOING ON INSIDE THE SUBJECT'S *MIND* AT THE MOMENT, WHETHER OR NOT HE'S ACTUALLY *FOLLOWING* THE PROGRAMMING WE'VE ESTABLISHED.

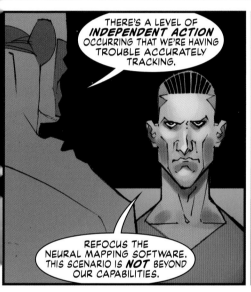

THERE'S A LEVEL OF *INDEPENDENT ACTION* OCCURRING THAT WE'RE HAVING TROUBLE ACCURATELY TRACKING.

REFOCUS THE NEURAL MAPPING SOFTWARE. THIS SCENARIO IS *NOT* BEYOND OUR CAPABILITIES.

THERE ARE CONSTANT *EQUATIONS* FORMING WITHIN THIS PROGRAM. COUNTLESS ZEROS AND ONES THAT FEEL--TO HIM-- AS THOUGH IT WERE *LIFE ITSELF.*

IT'S *OUR* JOB TO STAY WELL *AHEAD* OF THOSE EQUATIONS...

...TO MAKE SURE *THIS* REALITY IS ALL HE *KNOWS.*

ACCESSING: VENTROMEDIAL AND DORSOLATERAL PREFRONTAL CORTEX--

--CINGULATE CORTEX REMAINS ACTIVE.

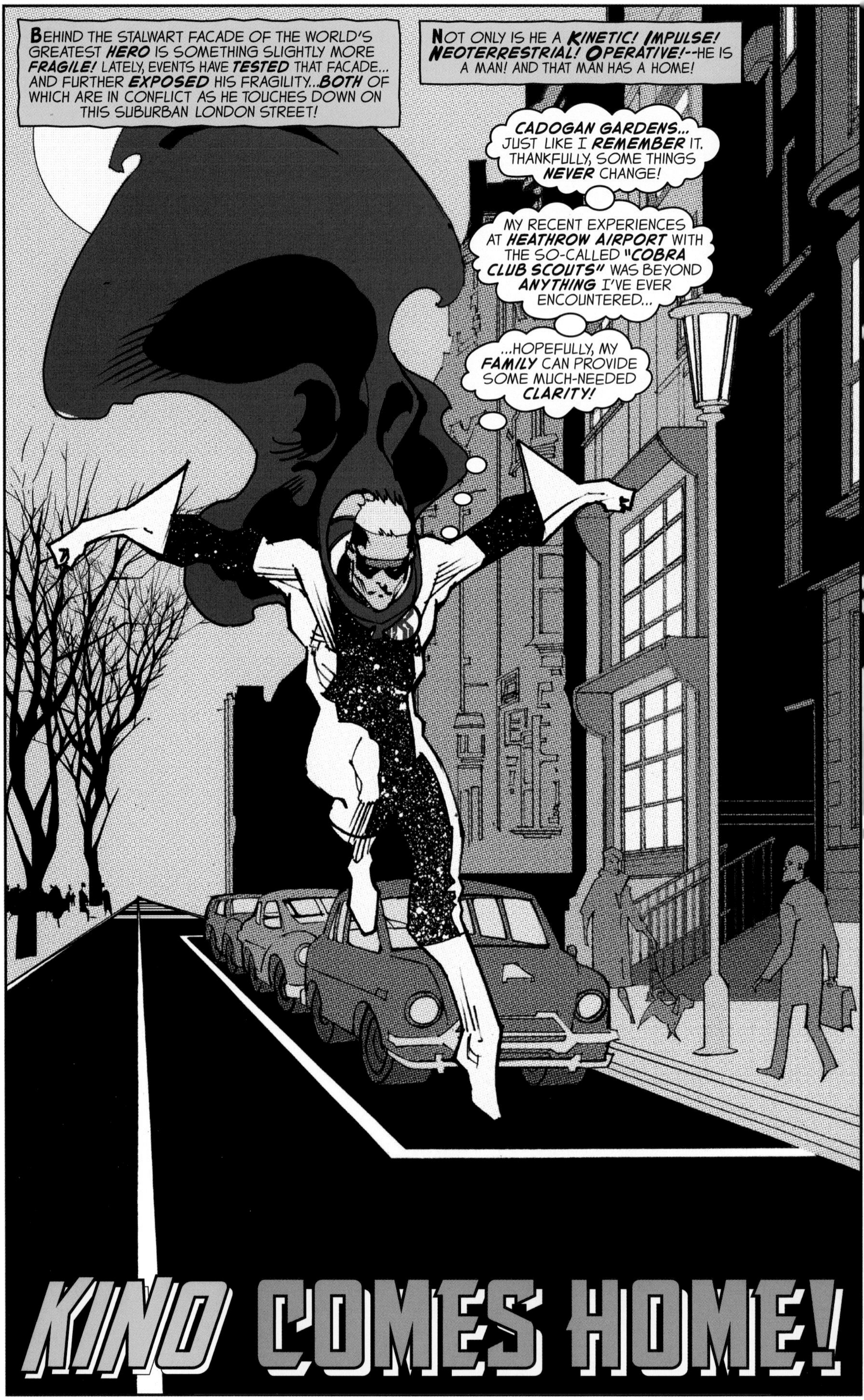
BEHIND THE STALWART FACADE OF THE WORLD'S GREATEST HERO IS SOMETHING SLIGHTLY MORE FRAGILE! LATELY, EVENTS HAVE TESTED THAT FACADE... AND FURTHER EXPOSED HIS FRAGILITY...BOTH OF WHICH ARE IN CONFLICT AS HE TOUCHES DOWN ON THIS SUBURBAN LONDON STREET!
NOT ONLY IS HE A KINETIC! IMPULSE! NEOTERRESTRIAL! OPERATIVE!--HE IS A MAN! AND THAT MAN HAS A HOME!
CADOGAN GARDENS... JUST LIKE I REMEMBER IT. THANKFULLY, SOME THINGS NEVER CHANGE!
MY RECENT EXPERIENCES AT HEATHROW AIRPORT WITH THE SO-CALLED "COBRA CLUB SCOUTS" WAS BEYOND ANYTHING I'VE EVER ENCOUNTERED...
...HOPEFULLY, MY FAMILY CAN PROVIDE SOME MUCH-NEEDED CLARITY!
KINO COMES HOME!

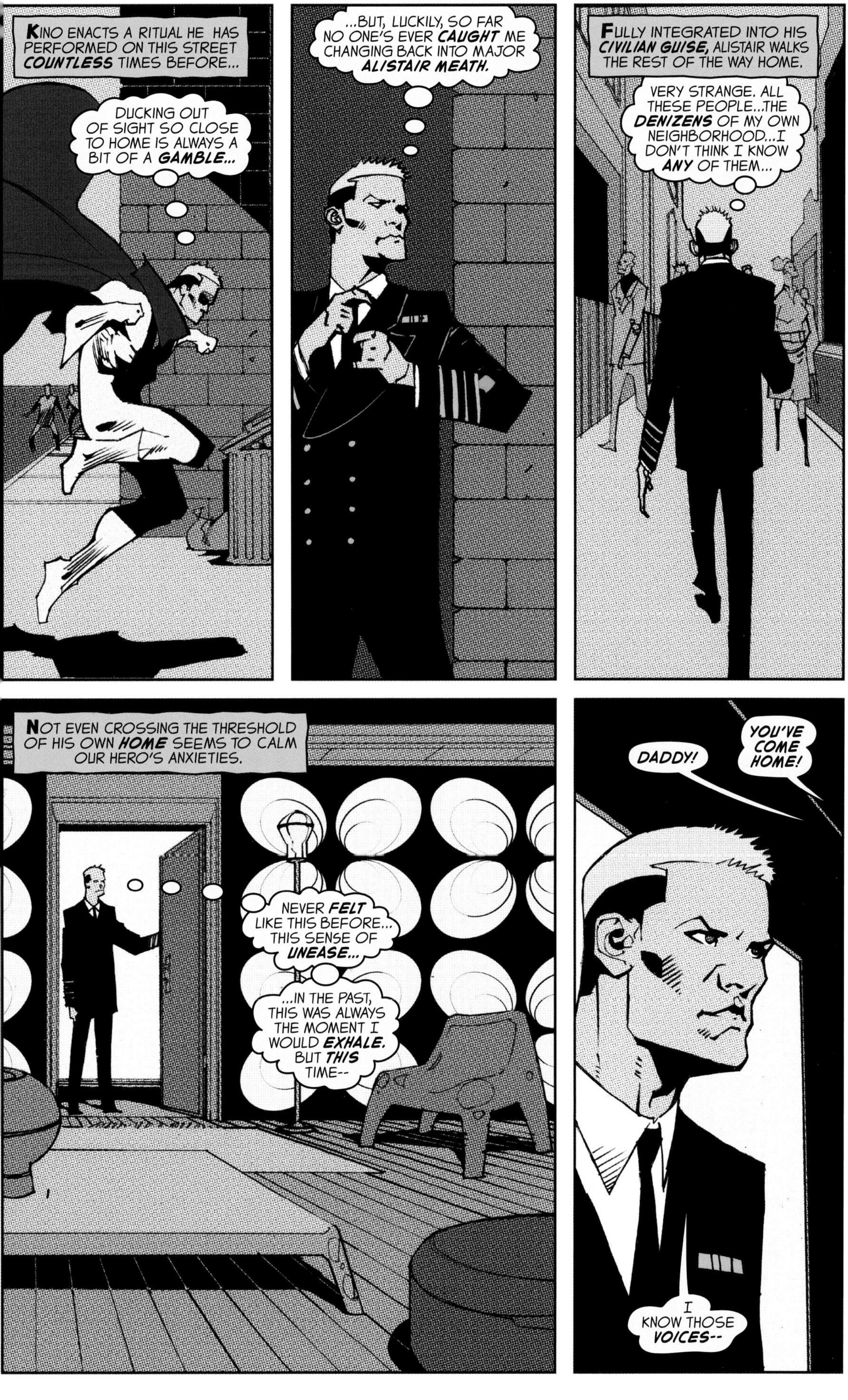
KINO ENACTS A RITUAL HE HAS PERFORMED ON THIS STREET COUNTLESS TIMES BEFORE...
DUCKING OUT OF SIGHT SO CLOSE TO HOME IS ALWAYS A BIT OF A GAMBLE...
...BUT, LUCKILY, SO FAR NO ONE'S EVER CAUGHT ME CHANGING BACK INTO MAJOR ALISTAIR MEATH.
FULLY INTEGRATED INTO HIS CIVILIAN GUISE, ALISTAIR WALKS THE REST OF THE WAY HOME.
VERY STRANGE. ALL THESE PEOPLE...THE DENIZENS OF MY OWN NEIGHBORHOOD...I DON'T THINK I KNOW ANY OF THEM...
NOT EVEN CROSSING THE THRESHOLD OF HIS OWN HOME SEEMS TO CALM OUR HERO'S ANXIETIES.
NEVER FELT LIKE THIS BEFORE... THIS SENSE OF UNEASE...
...IN THE PAST, THIS WAS ALWAYS THE MOMENT I WOULD EXHALE. BUT THIS TIME--
DADDY!
YOU'VE COME HOME!
I KNOW THOSE VOICES--

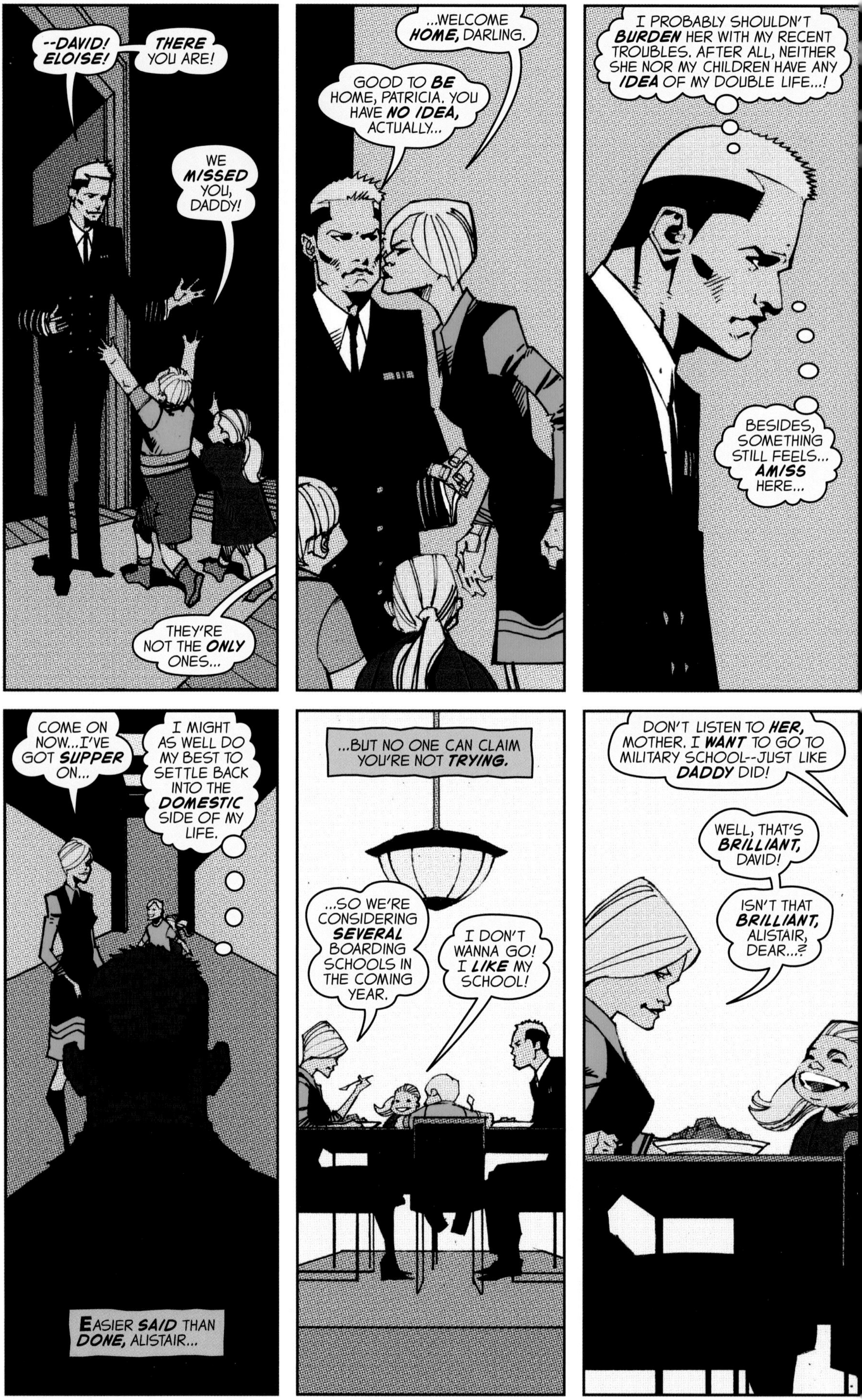
--DAVID! ELOISE!
THERE YOU ARE!
WE MISSED YOU, DADDY!
THEY'RE NOT THE ONLY ONES...
...WELCOME HOME, DARLING.
GOOD TO BE HOME, PATRICIA. YOU HAVE NO IDEA, ACTUALLY...
I PROBABLY SHOULDN'T BURDEN HER WITH MY RECENT TROUBLES. AFTER ALL, NEITHER SHE NOR MY CHILDREN HAVE ANY IDEA OF MY DOUBLE LIFE...!
BESIDES, SOMETHING STILL FEELS... AMISS HERE...
COME ON NOW...I'VE GOT SUPPER ON...
I MIGHT AS WELL DO MY BEST TO SETTLE BACK INTO THE DOMESTIC SIDE OF MY LIFE.
EASIER SAID THAN DONE, ALISTAIR...
...BUT NO ONE CAN CLAIM YOU'RE NOT TRYING.
...SO WE'RE CONSIDERING SEVERAL BOARDING SCHOOLS IN THE COMING YEAR.
I DON'T WANNA GO! I LIKE MY SCHOOL!
DON'T LISTEN TO HER, MOTHER. I WANT TO GO TO MILITARY SCHOOL--JUST LIKE DADDY DID!
WELL, THAT'S BRILLIANT, DAVID!
ISN'T THAT BRILLIANT, ALISTAIR, DEAR...?

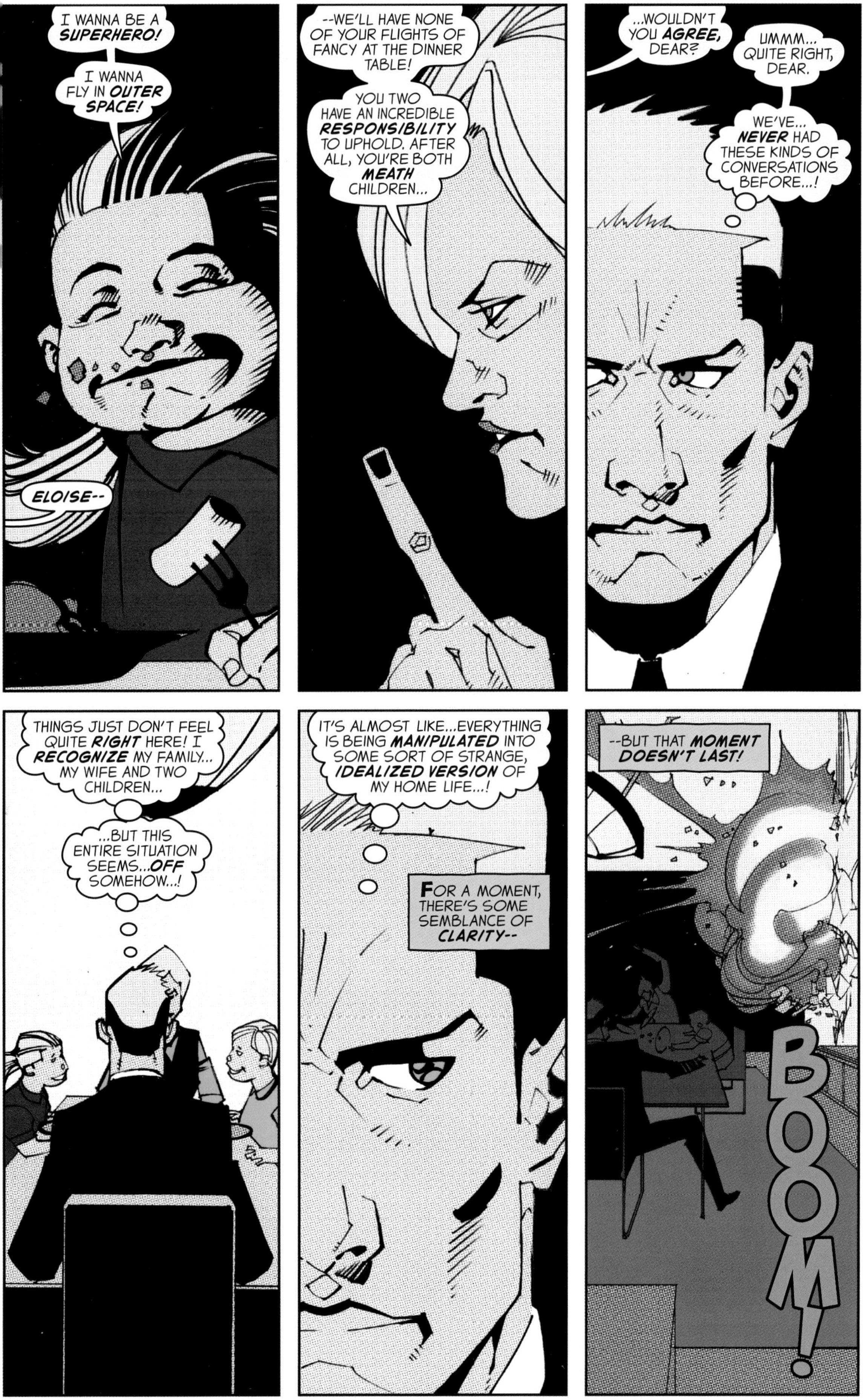
I WANNA BE A SUPERHERO!
I WANNA FLY IN OUTER SPACE!
ELOISE--
--WE'LL HAVE NONE OF YOUR FLIGHTS OF FANCY AT THE DINNER TABLE!
YOU TWO HAVE AN INCREDIBLE RESPONSIBILITY TO UPHOLD. AFTER ALL, YOU'RE BOTH MEATH CHILDREN...
...WOULDN'T YOU AGREE, DEAR?
UMMM... QUITE RIGHT, DEAR.
WE'VE... NEVER HAD THESE KINDS OF CONVERSATIONS BEFORE...!
THINGS JUST DON'T FEEL QUITE RIGHT HERE! I RECOGNIZE MY FAMILY... MY WIFE AND TWO CHILDREN...
...BUT THIS ENTIRE SITUATION SEEMS...OFF SOMEHOW...!
IT'S ALMOST LIKE...EVERYTHING IS BEING MANIPULATED INTO SOME SORT OF STRANGE, IDEALIZED VERSION OF MY HOME LIFE...!
FOR A MOMENT, THERE'S SOME SEMBLANCE OF CLARITY--
--BUT THAT MOMENT DOESN'T LAST!
BOOM!

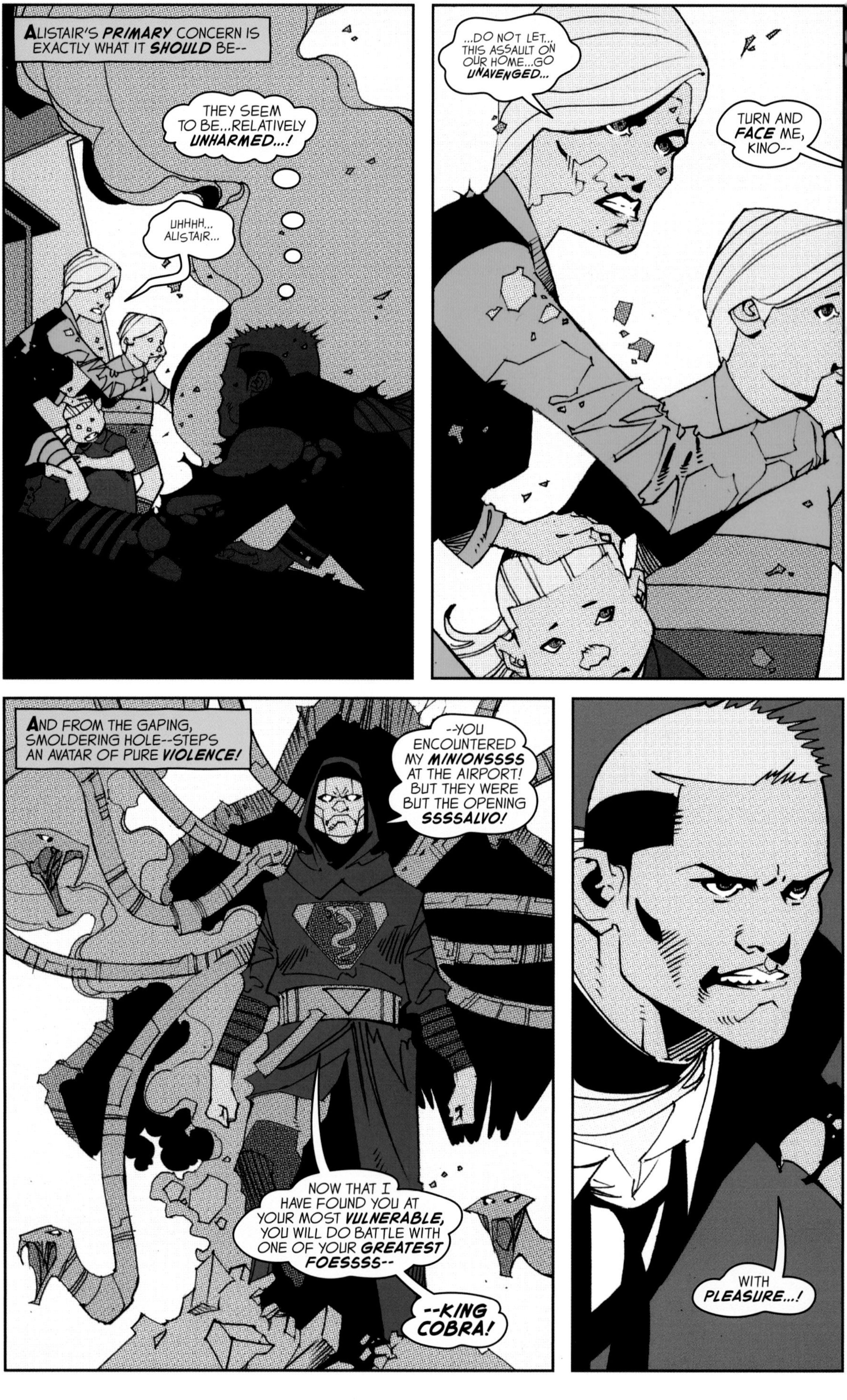
ALISTAIR'S PRIMARY CONCERN IS EXACTLY WHAT IT SHOULD BE--
THEY SEEM TO BE...RELATIVELY UNHARMED...!
UHHHH... ALISTAIR...
...DO NOT LET... THIS ASSAULT ON OUR HOME...GO UNAVENGED...
TURN AND FACE ME, KINO--
AND FROM THE GAPING, SMOLDERING HOLE--STEPS AN AVATAR OF PURE VIOLENCE!
--YOU ENCOUNTERED MY MINIONSSSS AT THE AIRPORT! BUT THEY WERE BUT THE OPENING SSSSALVO!
NOW THAT I HAVE FOUND YOU AT YOUR MOST VULNERABLE, YOU WILL DO BATTLE WITH ONE OF YOUR GREATEST FOESSSS--
--KING COBRA!
WITH PLEASURE...!

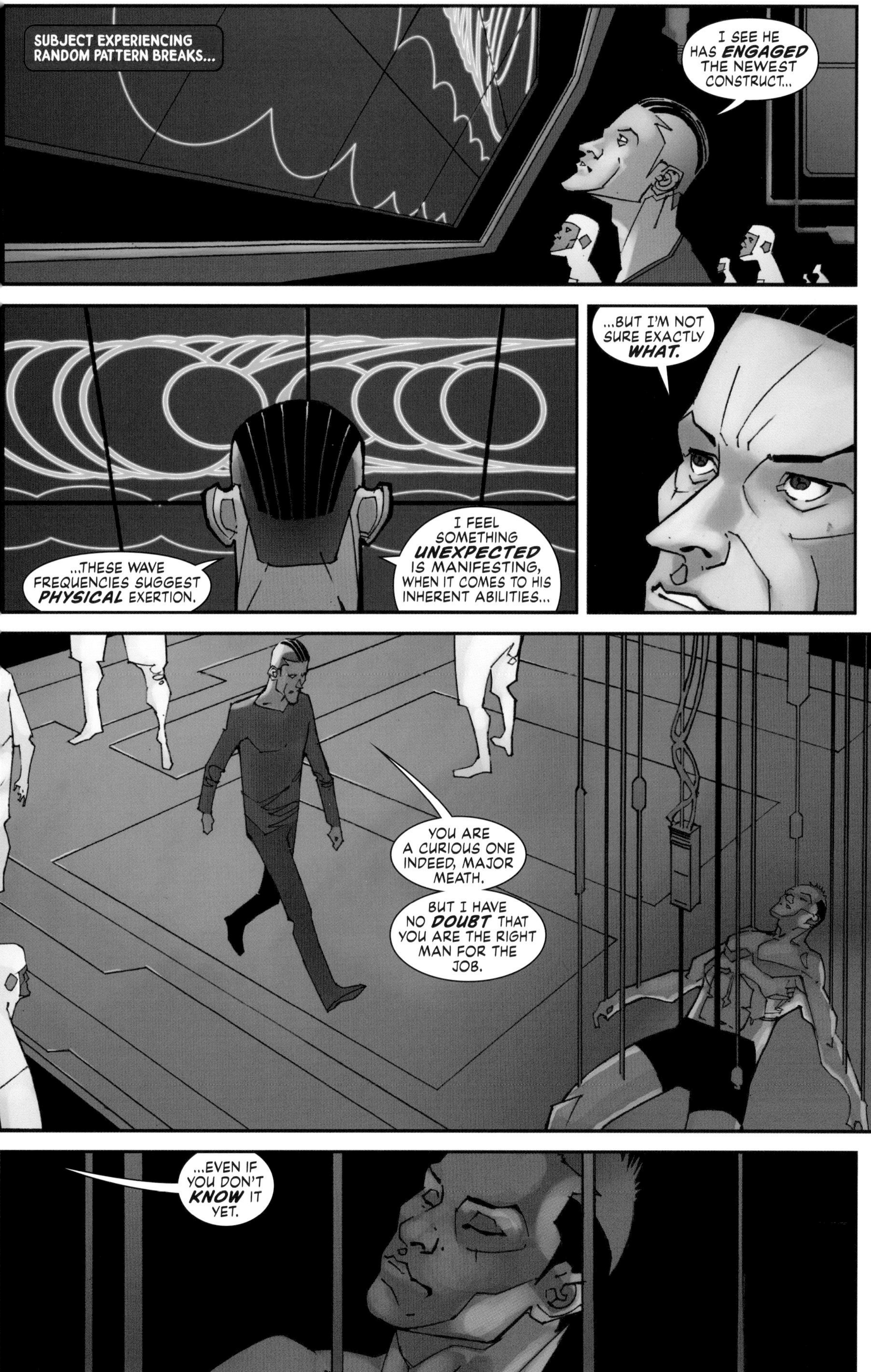
SUBJECT EXPERIENCING RANDOM PATTERN BREAKS...
I SEE HE HAS ENGAGED THE NEWEST CONSTRUCT...
...THESE WAVE FREQUENCIES SUGGEST PHYSICAL EXERTION.
I FEEL SOMETHING UNEXPECTED IS MANIFESTING, WHEN IT COMES TO HIS INHERENT ABILITIES...
...BUT I'M NOT SURE EXACTLY WHAT.
YOU ARE A CURIOUS ONE INDEED, MAJOR MEATH.
BUT I HAVE NO DOUBT THAT YOU ARE THE RIGHT MAN FOR THE JOB.
...EVEN IF YOU DON'T KNOW IT YET.

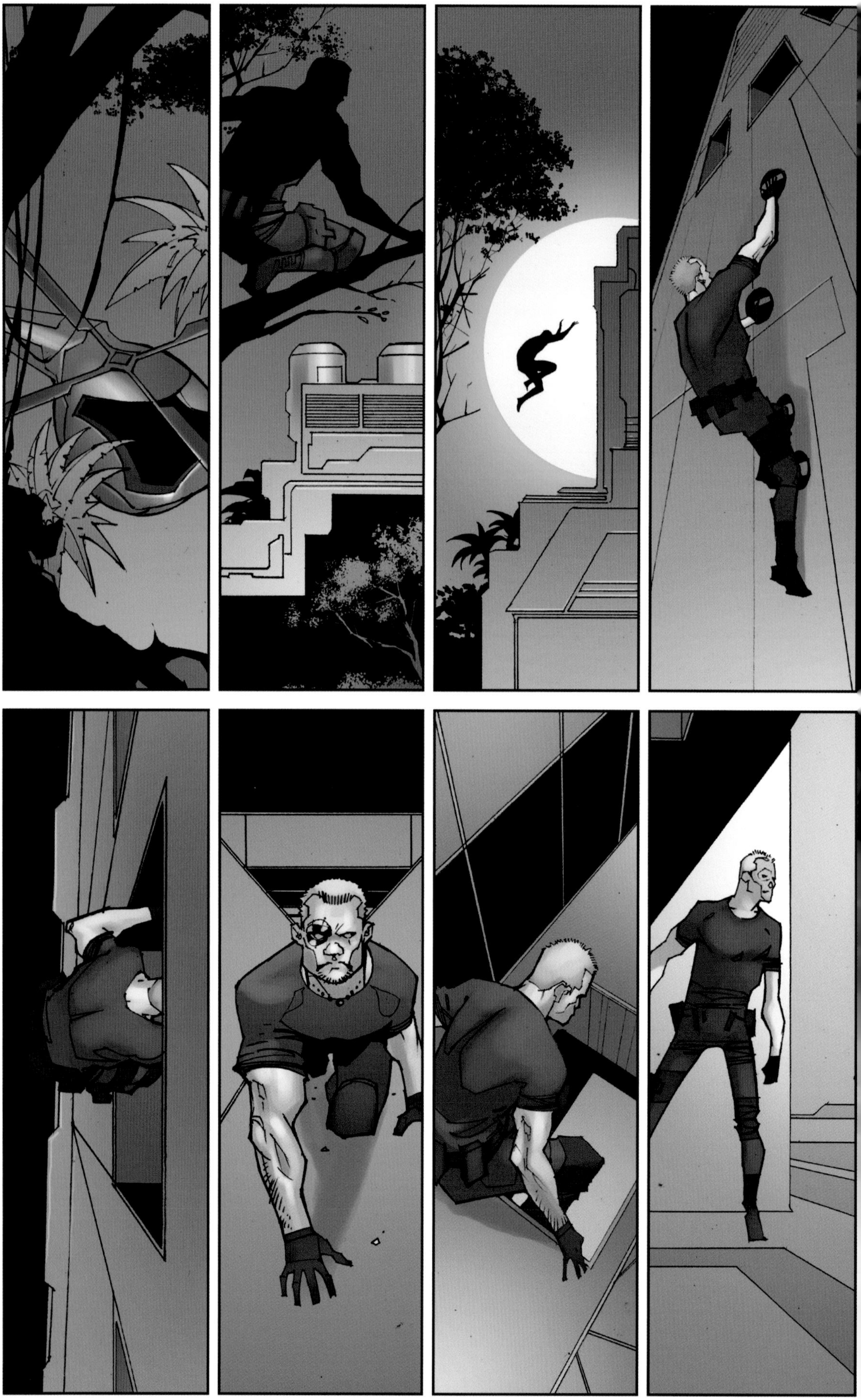

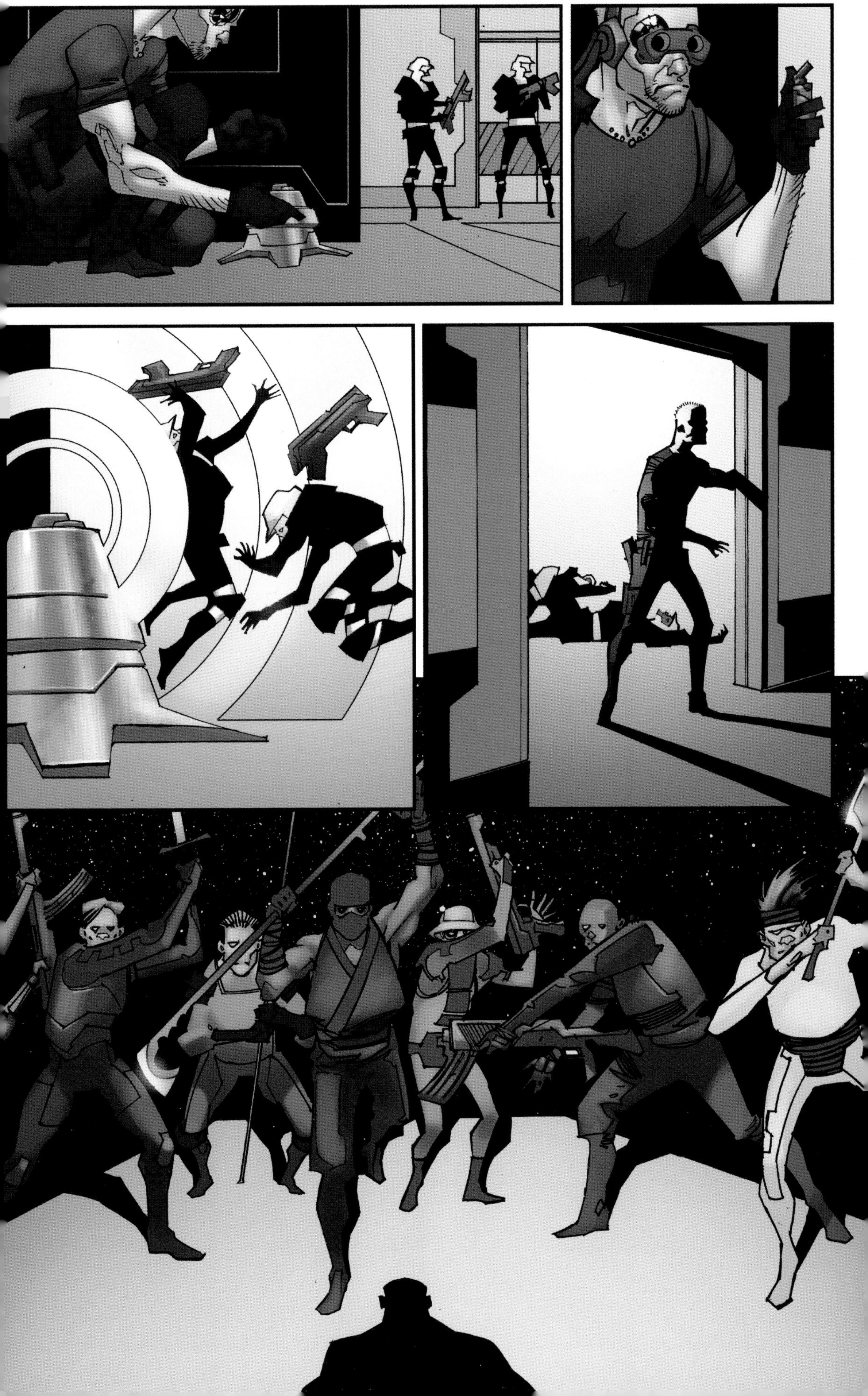

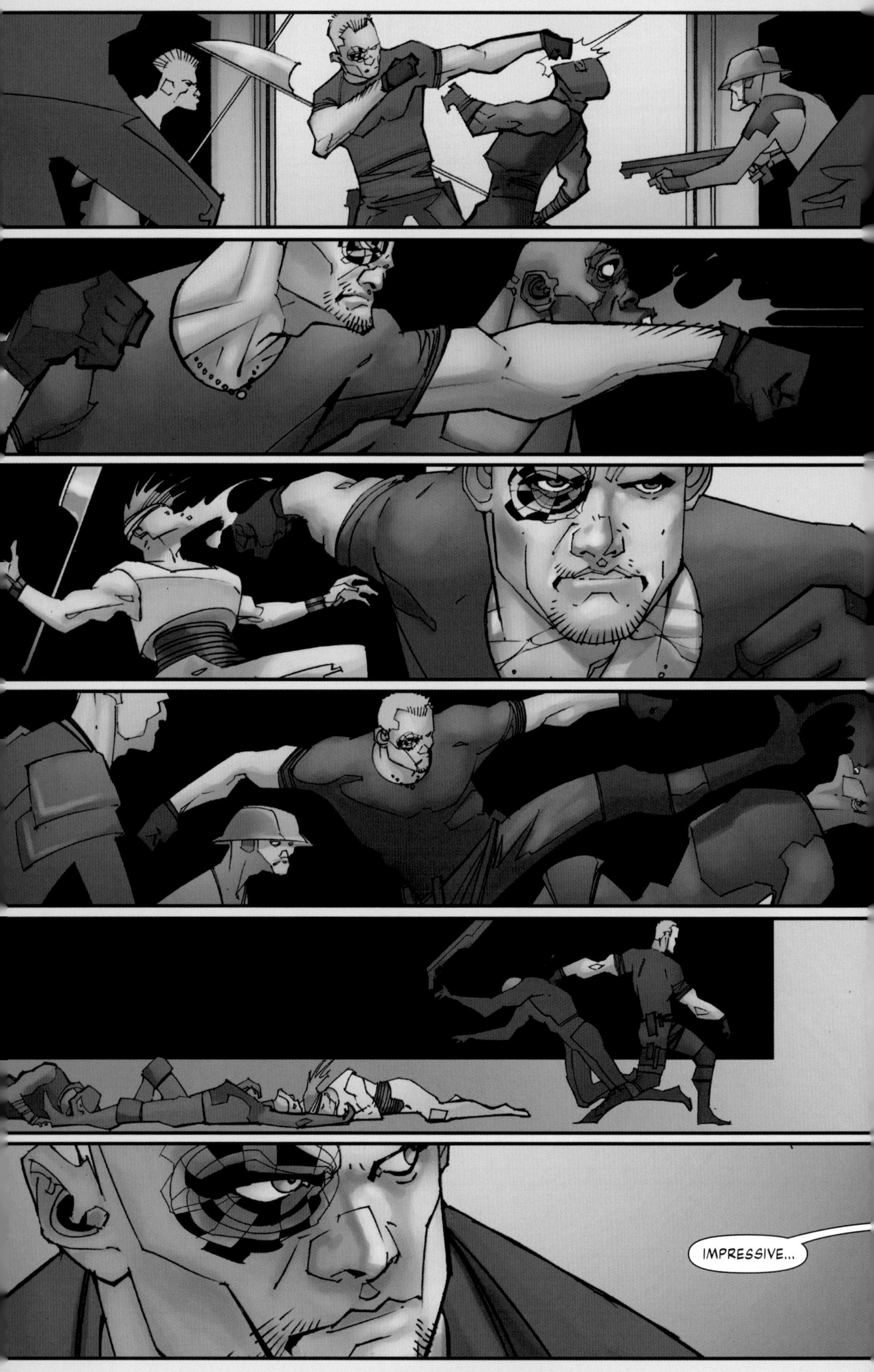
IMPRESSIVE...

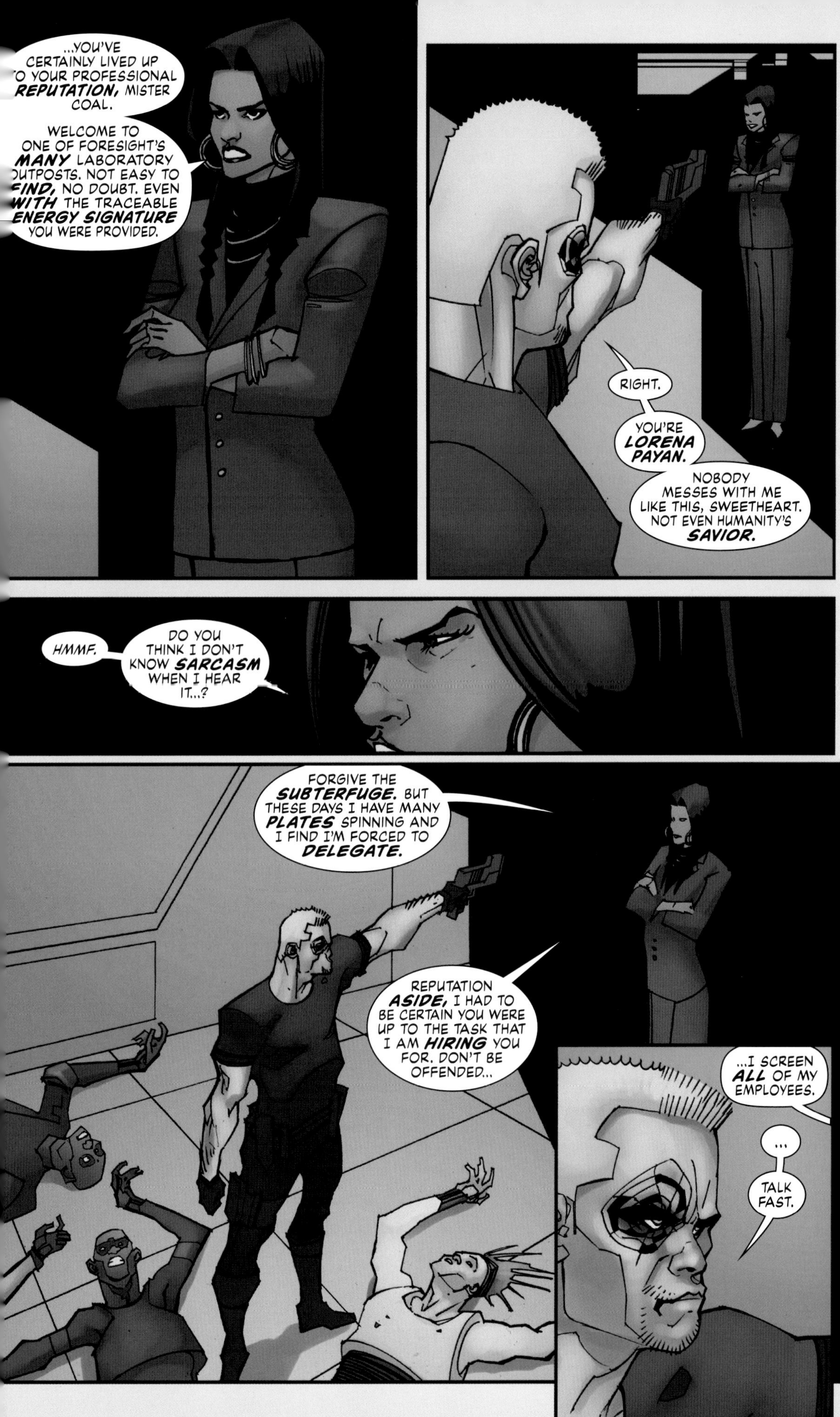
...YOU'VE CERTAINLY LIVED UP TO YOUR PROFESSIONAL REPUTATION, MISTER COAL.
WELCOME TO ONE OF FORESIGHT'S MANY LABORATORY OUTPOSTS. NOT EASY TO FIND, NO DOUBT. EVEN WITH THE TRACEABLE ENERGY SIGNATURE YOU WERE PROVIDED.
RIGHT.
YOU'RE LORENA PAYAN.
NOBODY MESSES WITH ME LIKE THIS, SWEETHEART. NOT EVEN HUMANITY'S SAVIOR.
HMMF.
DO YOU THINK I DON'T KNOW SARCASM WHEN I HEAR IT...?
FORGIVE THE SUBTERFUGE. BUT THESE DAYS I HAVE MANY PLATES SPINNING AND I FIND I'M FORCED TO DELEGATE.
REPUTATION ASIDE, I HAD TO BE CERTAIN YOU WERE UP TO THE TASK THAT I AM HIRING YOU FOR. DON'T BE OFFENDED...
...I SCREEN ALL OF MY EMPLOYEES.
...
TALK FAST.

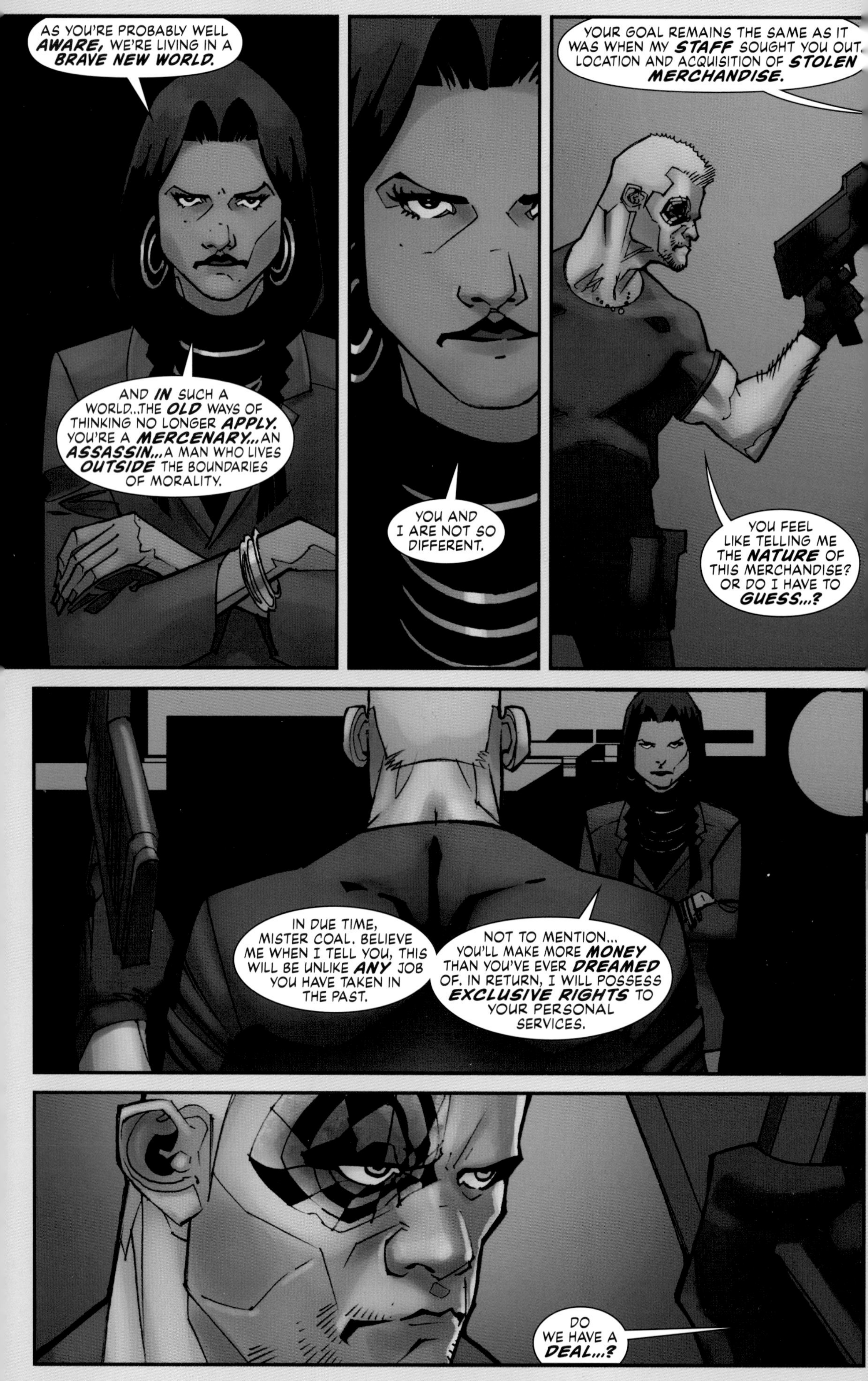
AS YOU'RE PROBABLY WELL AWARE, WE'RE LIVING IN A BRAVE NEW WORLD.
AND IN SUCH A WORLD...THE OLD WAYS OF THINKING NO LONGER APPLY. YOU'RE A MERCENARY...AN ASSASSIN...A MAN WHO LIVES OUTSIDE THE BOUNDARIES OF MORALITY.
YOU AND I ARE NOT SO DIFFERENT.
YOUR GOAL REMAINS THE SAME AS IT WAS WHEN MY STAFF SOUGHT YOU OUT. LOCATION AND ACQUISITION OF STOLEN MERCHANDISE.
YOU FEEL LIKE TELLING ME THE NATURE OF THIS MERCHANDISE? OR DO I HAVE TO GUESS...?
IN DUE TIME, MISTER COAL. BELIEVE ME WHEN I TELL YOU, THIS WILL BE UNLIKE ANY JOB YOU HAVE TAKEN IN THE PAST.
NOT TO MENTION... YOU'LL MAKE MORE MONEY THAN YOU'VE EVER DREAMED OF. IN RETURN, I WILL POSSESS EXCLUSIVE RIGHTS TO YOUR PERSONAL SERVICES.
DO WE HAVE A DEAL...?

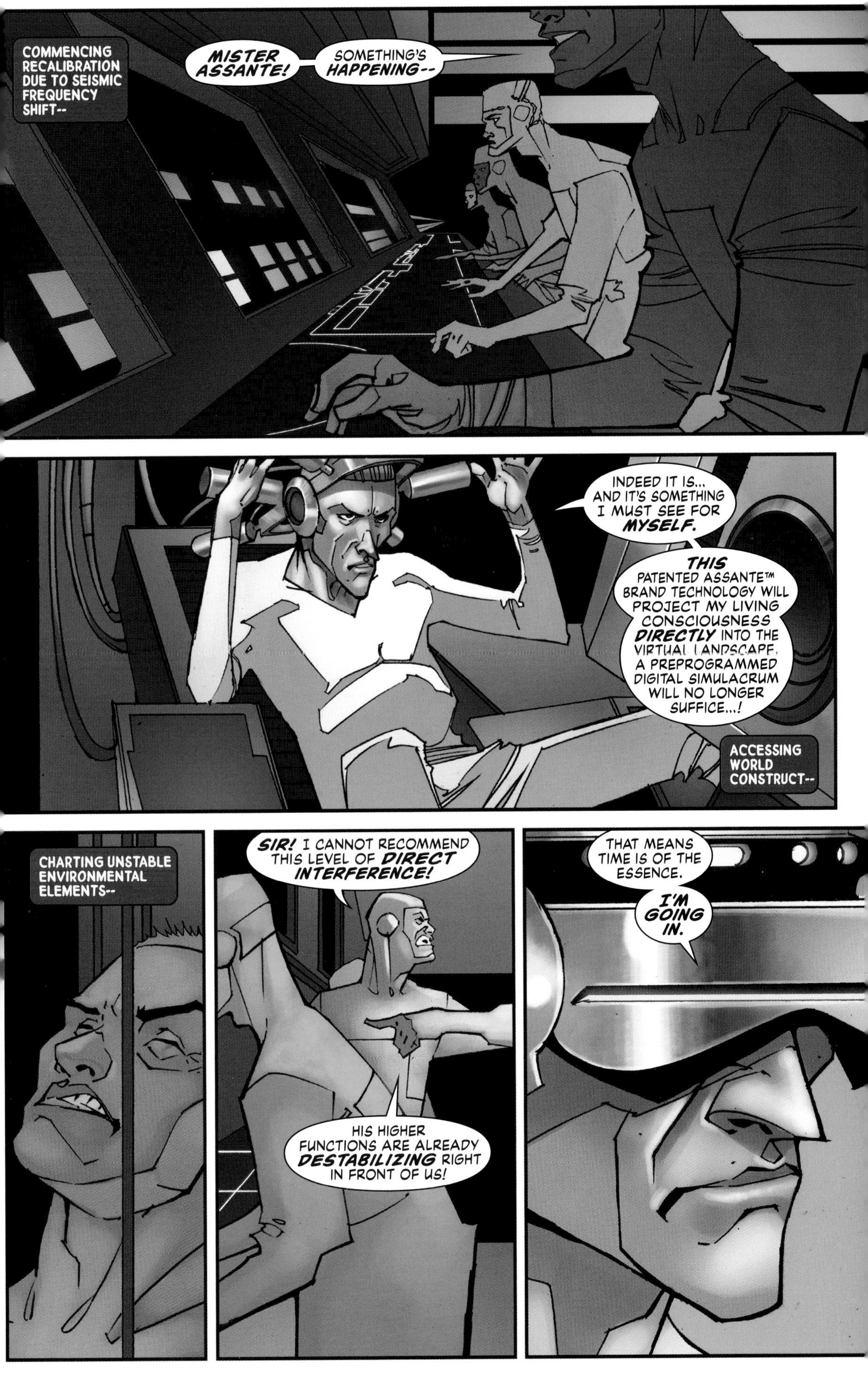
COMMENCING RECALIBRATION DUE TO SEISMIC FREQUENCY SHIFT--
MISTER ASSANTE!
SOMETHING'S HAPPENING--
INDEED IT IS... AND IT'S SOMETHING I MUST SEE FOR MYSELF.
THIS PATENTED ASSANTE™ BRAND TECHNOLOGY WILL PROJECT MY LIVING CONSCIOUSNESS DIRECTLY INTO THE VIRTUAL LANDSCAPE. A PREPROGRAMMED DIGITAL SIMULACRUM WILL NO LONGER SUFFICE...!
ACCESSING WORLD CONSTRUCT--
CHARTING UNSTABLE ENVIRONMENTAL ELEMENTS--
SIR! I CANNOT RECOMMEND THIS LEVEL OF DIRECT INTERFERENCE!
HIS HIGHER FUNCTIONS ARE ALREADY DESTABILIZING RIGHT IN FRONT OF US!
THAT MEANS TIME IS OF THE ESSENCE.
I'M GOING IN.

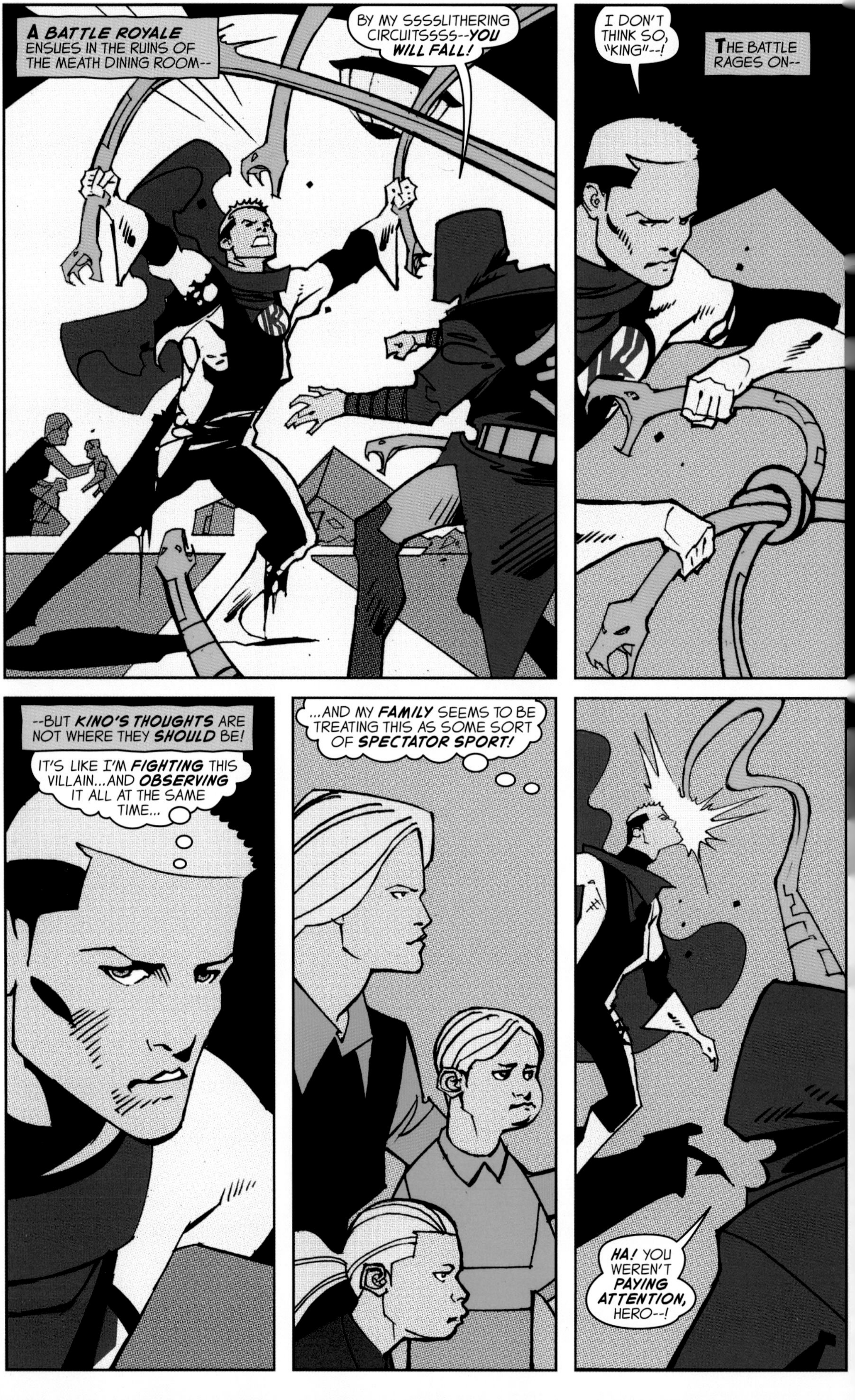
A BATTLE ROYALE ENSUES IN THE RUINS OF THE MEATH DINING ROOM--
BY MY SSSSLITHERING CIRCUITSSSS--YOU WILL FALL!
I DON'T THINK SO, "KING"--!
THE BATTLE RAGES ON--
--BUT KINO'S THOUGHTS ARE NOT WHERE THEY SHOULD BE!
IT'S LIKE I'M FIGHTING THIS VILLAIN...AND OBSERVING IT ALL AT THE SAME TIME...
...AND MY FAMILY SEEMS TO BE TREATING THIS AS SOME SORT OF SPECTATOR SPORT!
HA! YOU WEREN'T PAYING ATTENTION, HERO--!

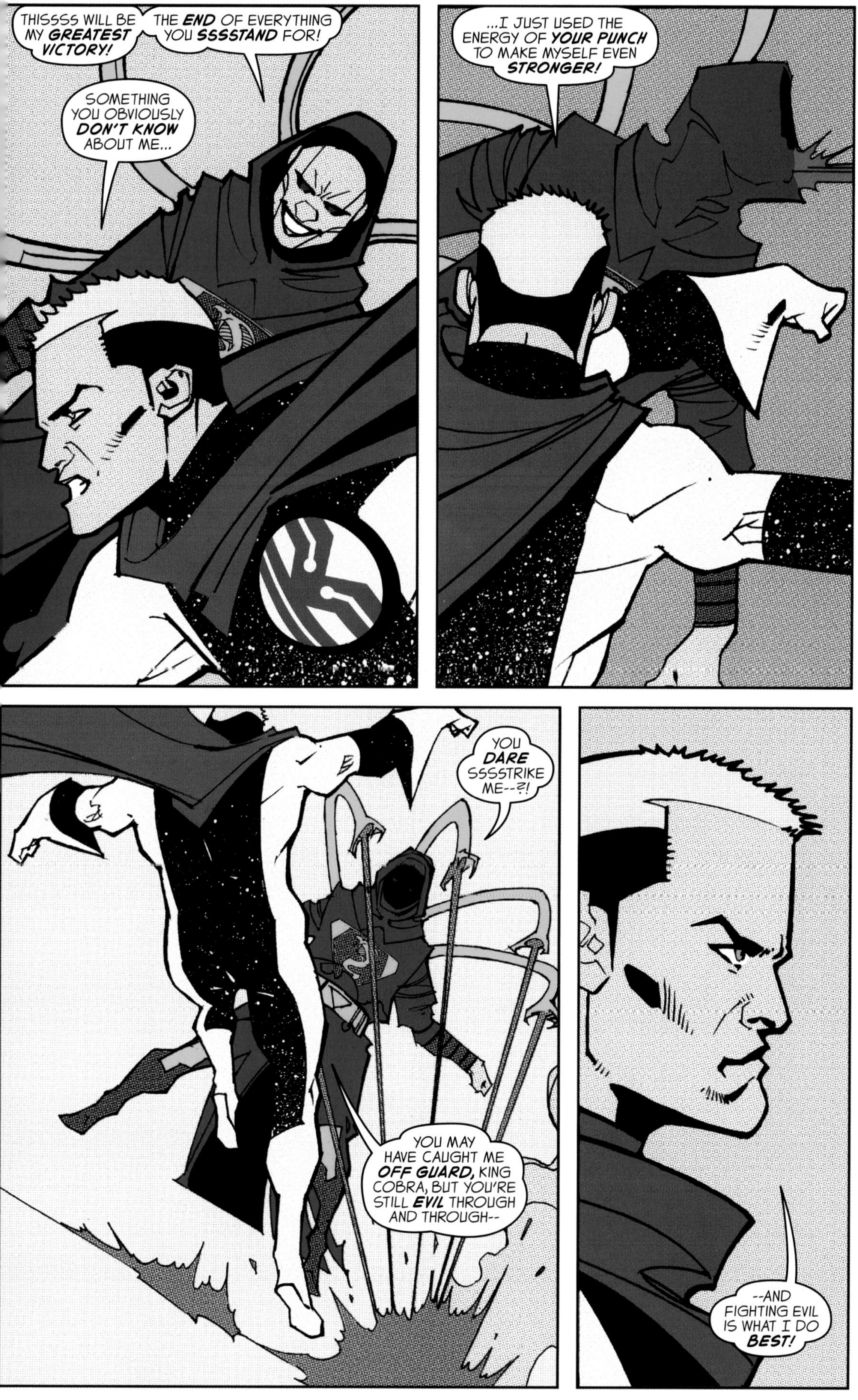
THISSSS WILL BE MY **GREATEST VICTORY!**
THE **END** OF EVERYTHING YOU **SSSSTAND** FOR!
SOMETHING YOU OBVIOUSLY **DON'T KNOW** ABOUT ME...
...I JUST USED THE ENERGY OF **YOUR PUNCH** TO MAKE MYSELF EVEN **STRONGER!**
YOU **DARE** SSSSTRIKE ME--?!
YOU MAY HAVE CAUGHT ME **OFF GUARD,** KING COBRA, BUT YOU'RE STILL **EVIL** THROUGH AND THROUGH--
--AND FIGHTING EVIL IS WHAT I DO **BEST!**

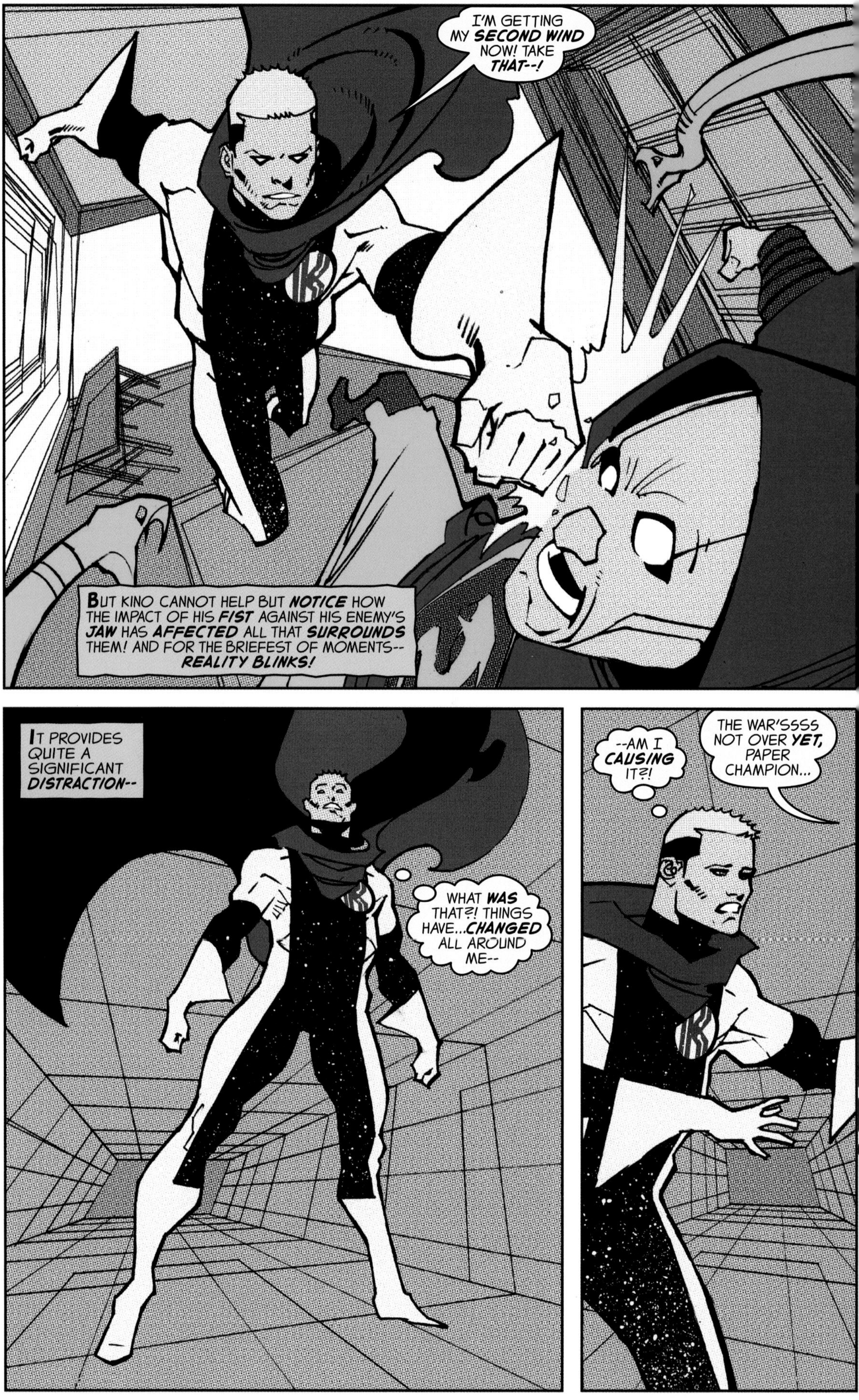
I'M GETTING MY SECOND WIND NOW! TAKE THAT--!
BUT KINO CANNOT HELP BUT NOTICE HOW THE IMPACT OF HIS FIST AGAINST HIS ENEMY'S JAW HAS AFFECTED ALL THAT SURROUNDS THEM! AND FOR THE BRIEFEST OF MOMENTS-- REALITY BLINKS!
IT PROVIDES QUITE A SIGNIFICANT DISTRACTION--
WHAT WAS THAT?! THINGS HAVE...CHANGED ALL AROUND ME--
--AM I CAUSING IT?!
THE WAR'SSSS NOT OVER YET, PAPER CHAMPION...

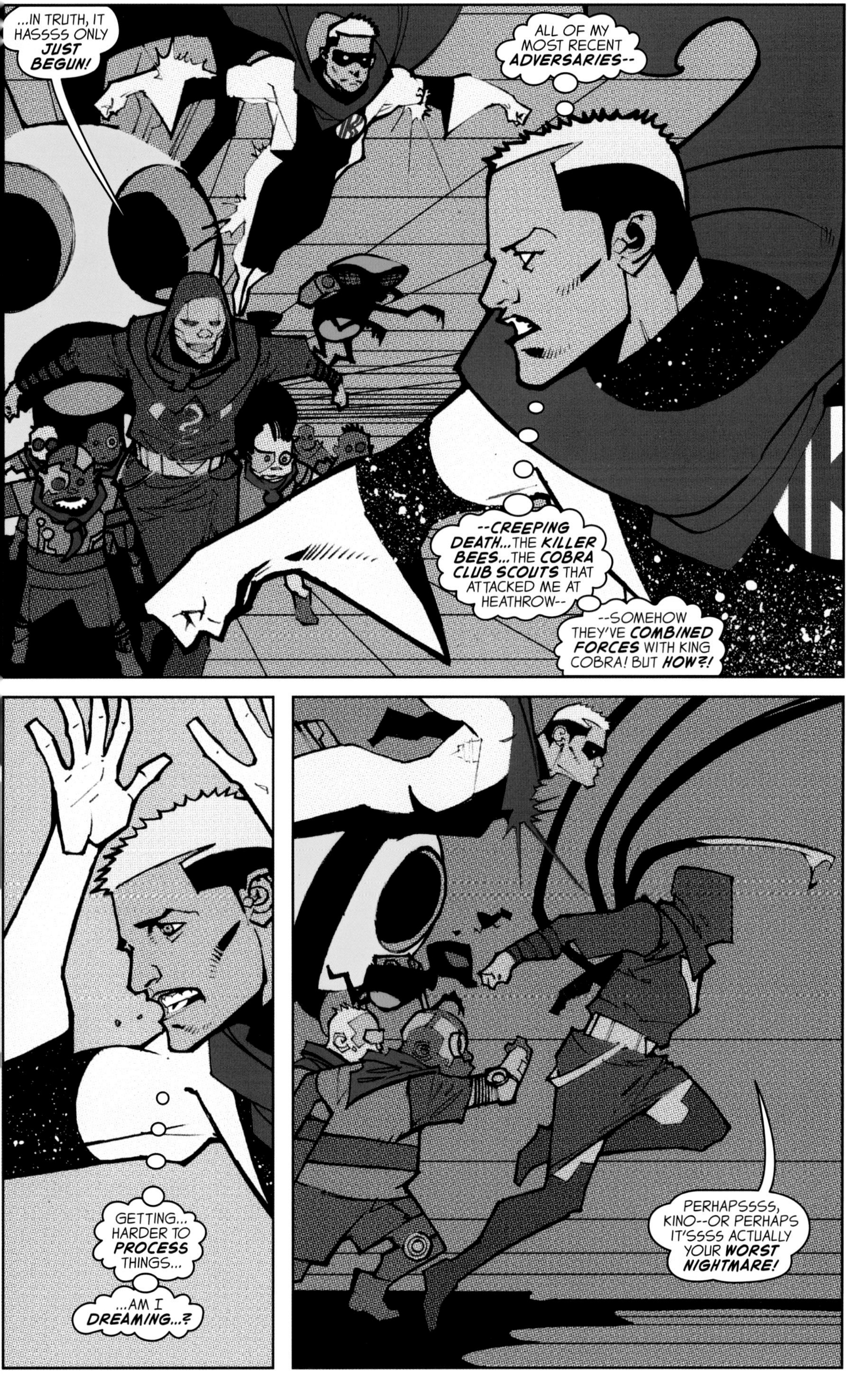
...IN TRUTH, IT HASSSS ONLY JUST BEGUN!
ALL OF MY MOST RECENT ADVERSARIES--
--CREEPING DEATH...THE KILLER BEES...THE COBRA CLUB SCOUTS THAT ATTACKED ME AT HEATHROW--
--SOMEHOW THEY'VE COMBINED FORCES WITH KING COBRA! BUT HOW?!
GETTING... HARDER TO PROCESS THINGS...
...AM I DREAMING...?
PERHAPSSSS, KINO--OR PERHAPS IT'SSSS ACTUALLY YOUR WORST NIGHTMARE!

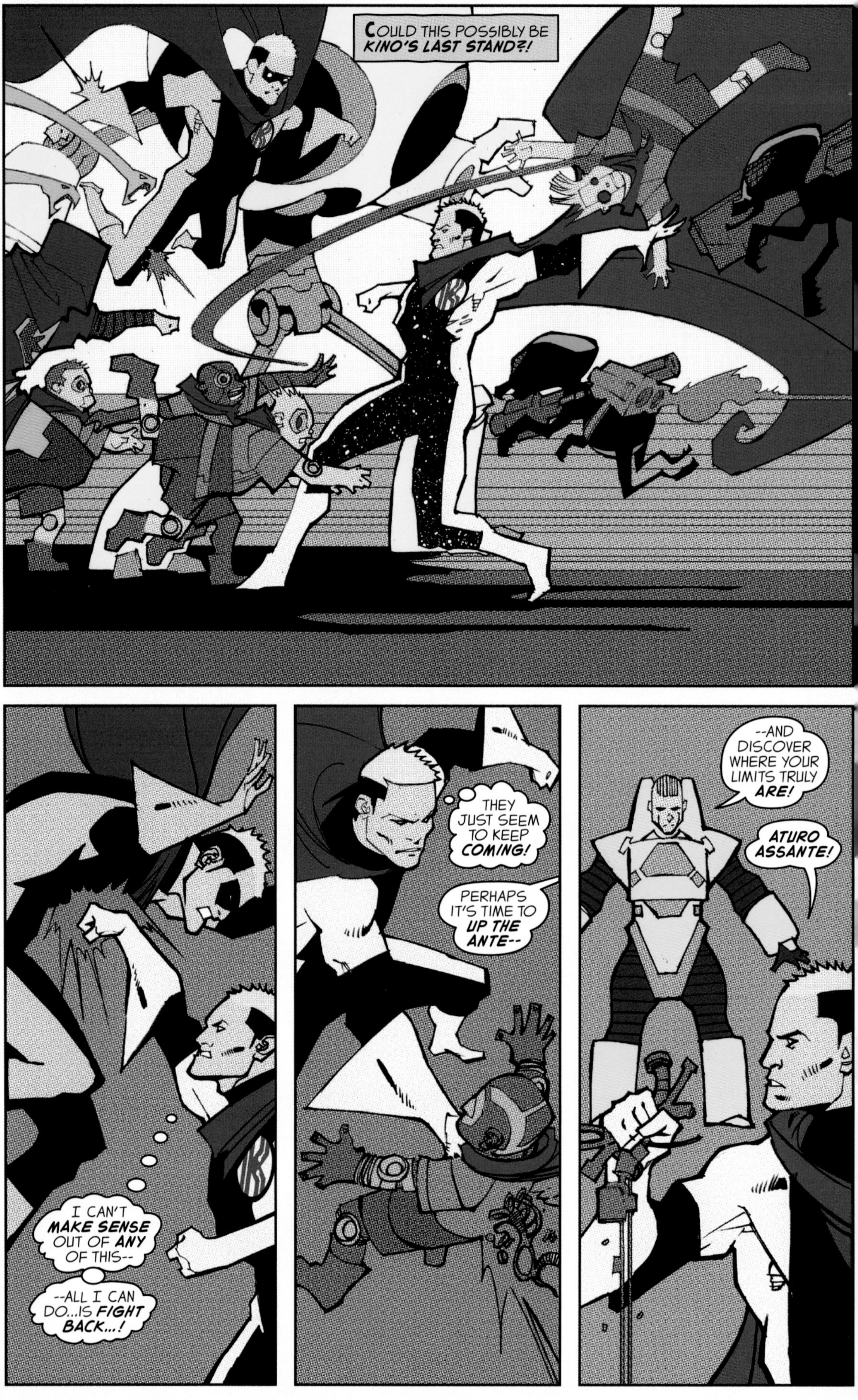
COULD THIS POSSIBLY BE KINO'S LAST STAND?!
I CAN'T MAKE SENSE OUT OF ANY OF THIS--
--ALL I CAN DO...IS FIGHT BACK...!
THEY JUST SEEM TO KEEP COMING!
PERHAPS IT'S TIME TO UP THE ANTE--
--AND DISCOVER WHERE YOUR LIMITS TRULY ARE!
ATURO ASSANTE!

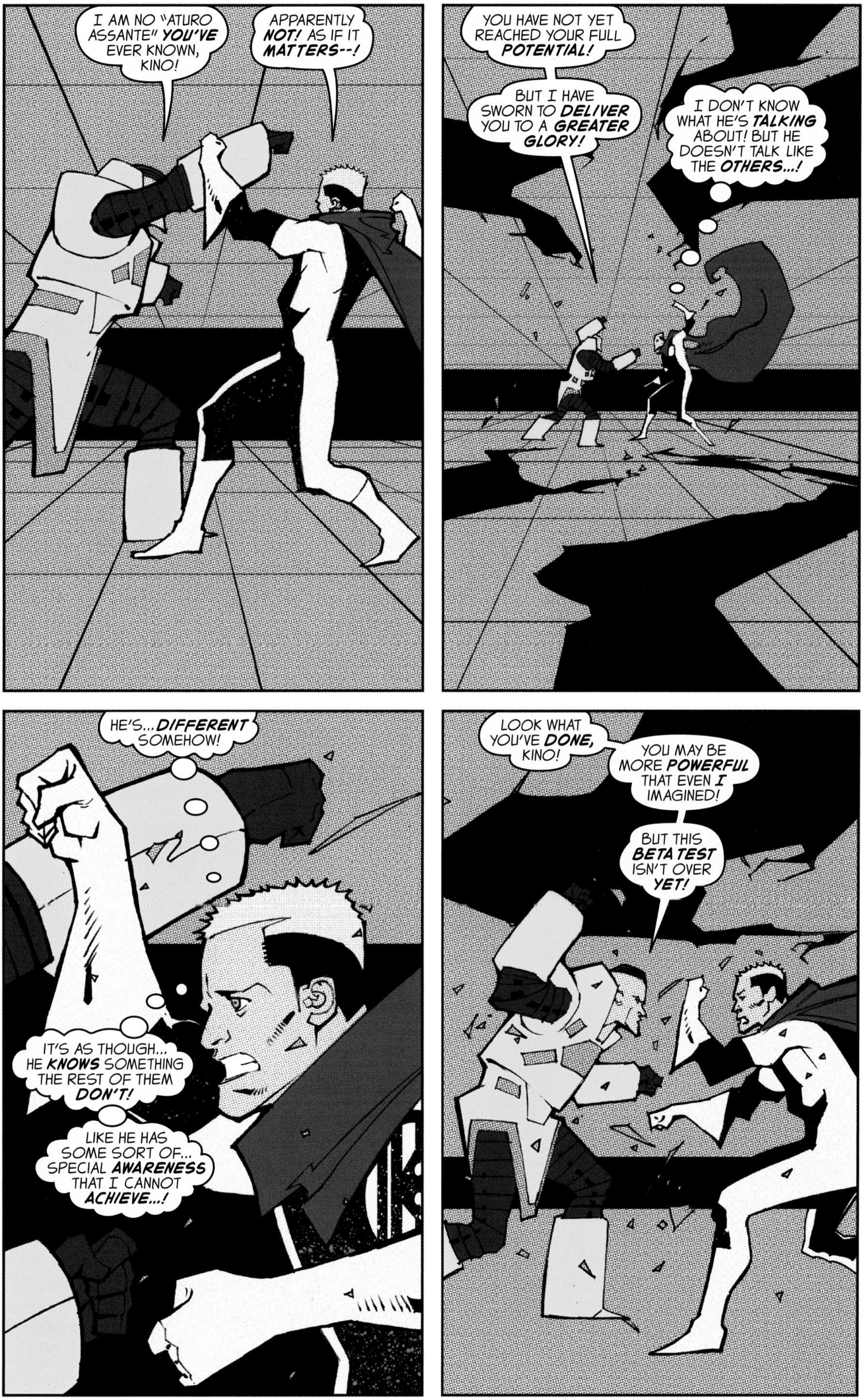
I AM NO "ATURO ASSANTE" ***YOU'VE*** EVER KNOWN, KINO!
APPARENTLY ***NOT!*** AS IF IT ***MATTERS--!***
YOU HAVE NOT YET REACHED YOUR FULL ***POTENTIAL!***
BUT I HAVE SWORN TO ***DELIVER*** YOU TO A ***GREATER GLORY!***
I DON'T KNOW WHAT HE'S ***TALKING*** ABOUT! BUT HE DOESN'T TALK LIKE THE ***OTHERS...!***
HE'S... ***DIFFERENT*** SOMEHOW!
IT'S AS THOUGH... HE ***KNOWS*** SOMETHING THE REST OF THEM ***DON'T!***
LIKE HE HAS SOME SORT OF... SPECIAL ***AWARENESS*** THAT I CANNOT ***ACHIEVE...!***
LOOK WHAT YOU'VE ***DONE,*** KINO!
YOU MAY BE MORE ***POWERFUL*** THAT EVEN ***I*** IMAGINED!
BUT THIS ***BETATEST*** ISN'T OVER ***YET!***

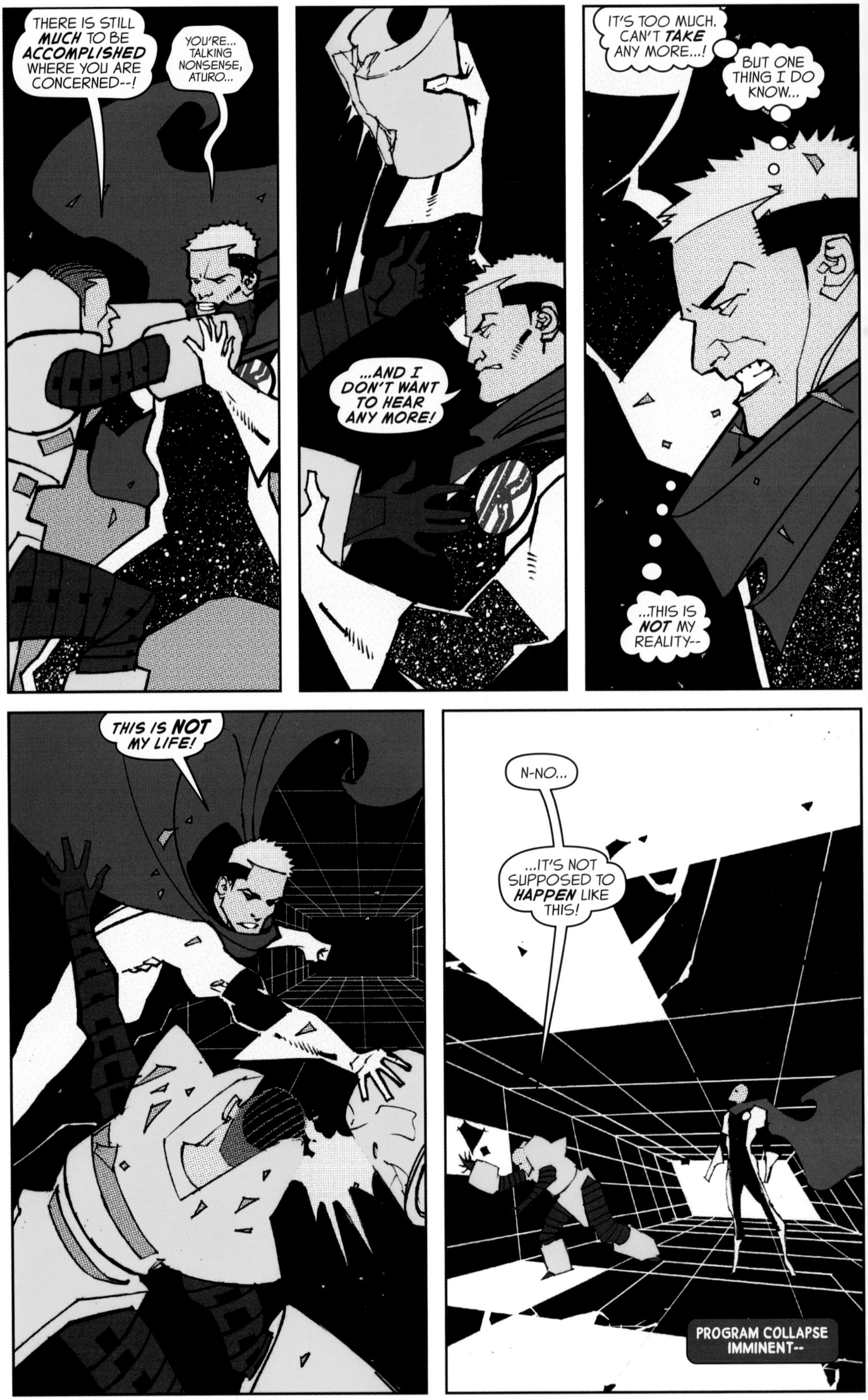
THERE IS STILL **MUCH** TO BE **ACCOMPLISHED** WHERE YOU ARE CONCERNED--!
YOU'RE... TALKING NONSENSE, ATURO...
...AND I DON'T WANT TO HEAR ANY MORE!
IT'S TOO MUCH. CAN'T **TAKE** ANY MORE...!
BUT ONE THING I DO KNOW...
...THIS IS **NOT** MY REALITY--
THIS IS **NOT** MY LIFE!
N-NO...
...IT'S NOT SUPPOSED TO **HAPPEN** LIKE THIS!
PROGRAM COLLAPSE IMMINENT--

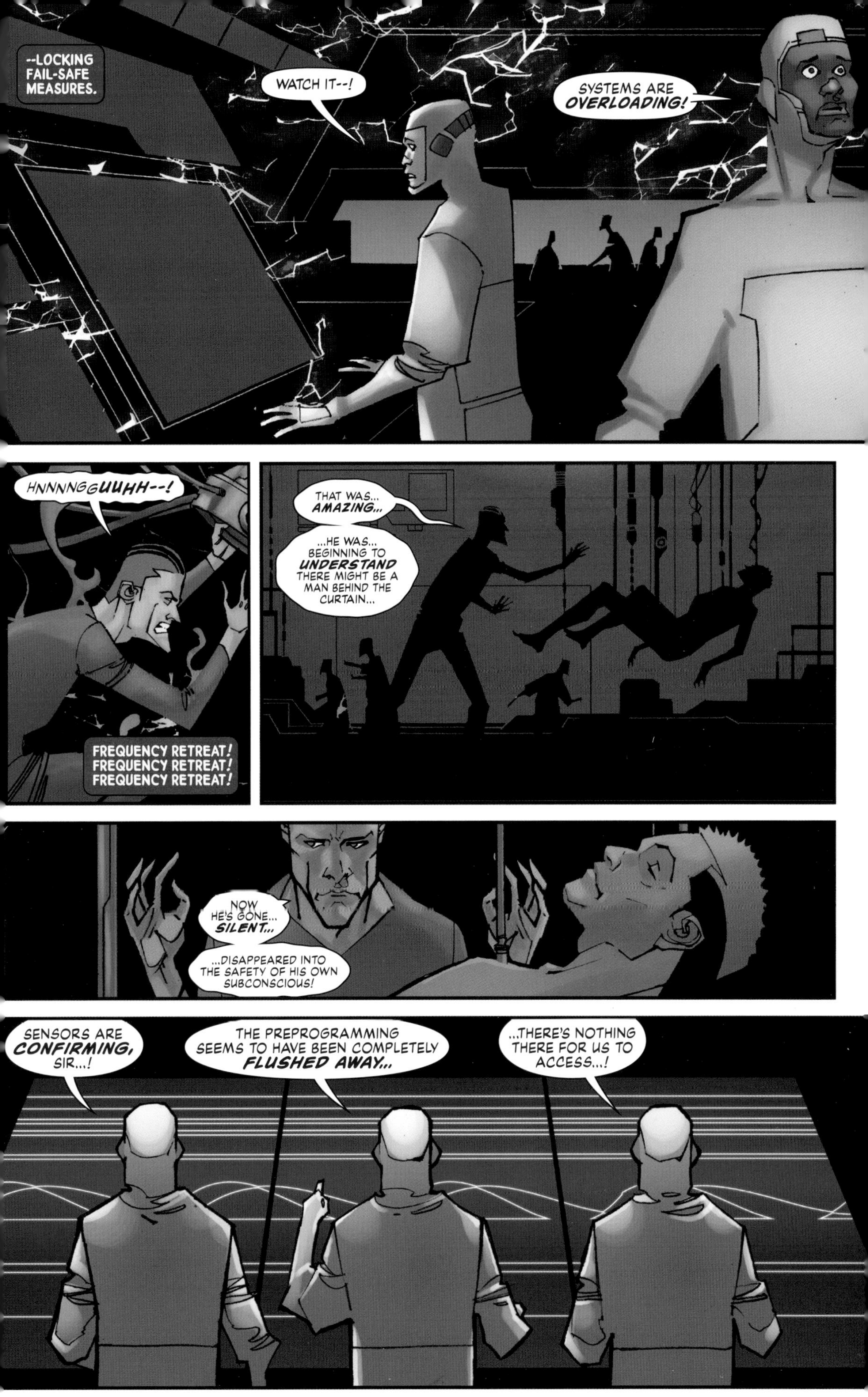
--LOCKING FAIL-SAFE MEASURES.
WATCH IT--!
SYSTEMS ARE OVERLOADING!
HNNNNGGUUHH--!
FREQUENCY RETREAT! FREQUENCY RETREAT! FREQUENCY RETREAT!
THAT WAS... AMAZING...
...HE WAS... BEGINNING TO UNDERSTAND THERE MIGHT BE A MAN BEHIND THE CURTAIN...
NOW HE'S GONE... SILENT...
...DISAPPEARED INTO THE SAFETY OF HIS OWN SUBCONSCIOUS!
SENSORS ARE CONFIRMING, SIR...!
THE PREPROGRAMMING SEEMS TO HAVE BEEN COMPLETELY FLUSHED AWAY...
...THERE'S NOTHING THERE FOR US TO ACCESS...!

ARE YOU **ALL RIGHT,** SIR...?

I'D...NEVER **EXPERIENCED** HIM SO **CLOSELY.** NOT LIKE **THAT...!**

HE WAS... ALMOST EXACTLY WHAT I **NEED** HIM TO BE...!

SIR, WE **CAN'T** CONTINUE THIS PROCESS WITHOUT A FULL DIAGNOSTIC SWEEP. IT COULD TAKE **MONTHS...!**

WE CAN'T BE SURE HOW MUCH OF THE EXPERIENCE HE ACTUALLY **RETAINED...**MUCH LESS **ASSIMILATED...**

YOU'RE MISSING THE **POINT,** I'M AFRAID. FROM EVERYTHING I WITNESSED, THIS IS SOMETHING **BEYOND** SIMPLE BEHAVIORAL PROGRAMMING.

WE CAME SO **CLOSE...**

...PERHAPS WE SIMPLY PUSHED HIM **TOO FAR.**

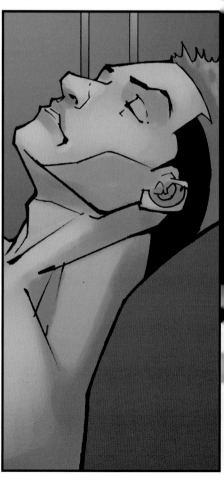

"THE EVENT"

One year before the story of KINO, humanity was on the verge of extinction. An asteroid detected in space was on a collision course with Earth.

Foresight Corporation, the world's most advanced high-tech humanitarian company led by CEO Lorena Payan, developed the science and ships needed to destroy the asteroid.

A team of astronauts flew into space on a suicide mission to save the world.

This is the story of that heroic mission, and "The Event" from which a new generation of heroes emerged in the world.

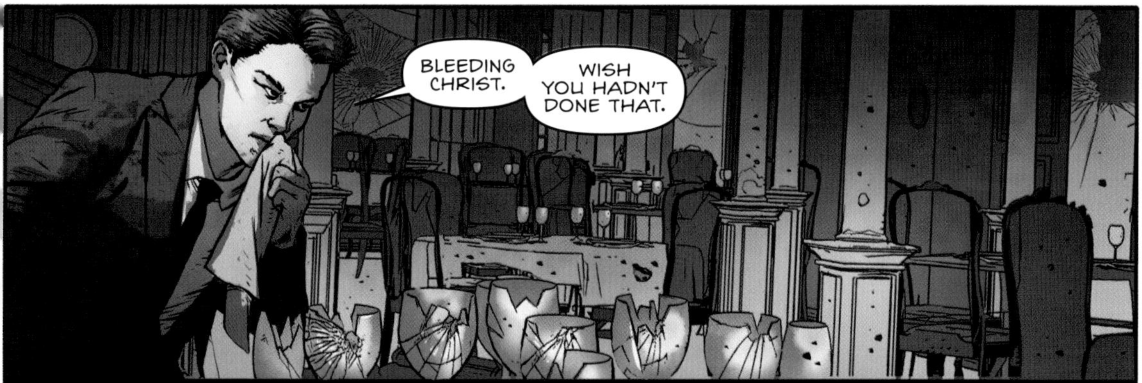
BLEEDING CHRIST.
WISH YOU HADN'T DONE THAT.

"Overture"

ONE YEAR AFTER THE EVENT

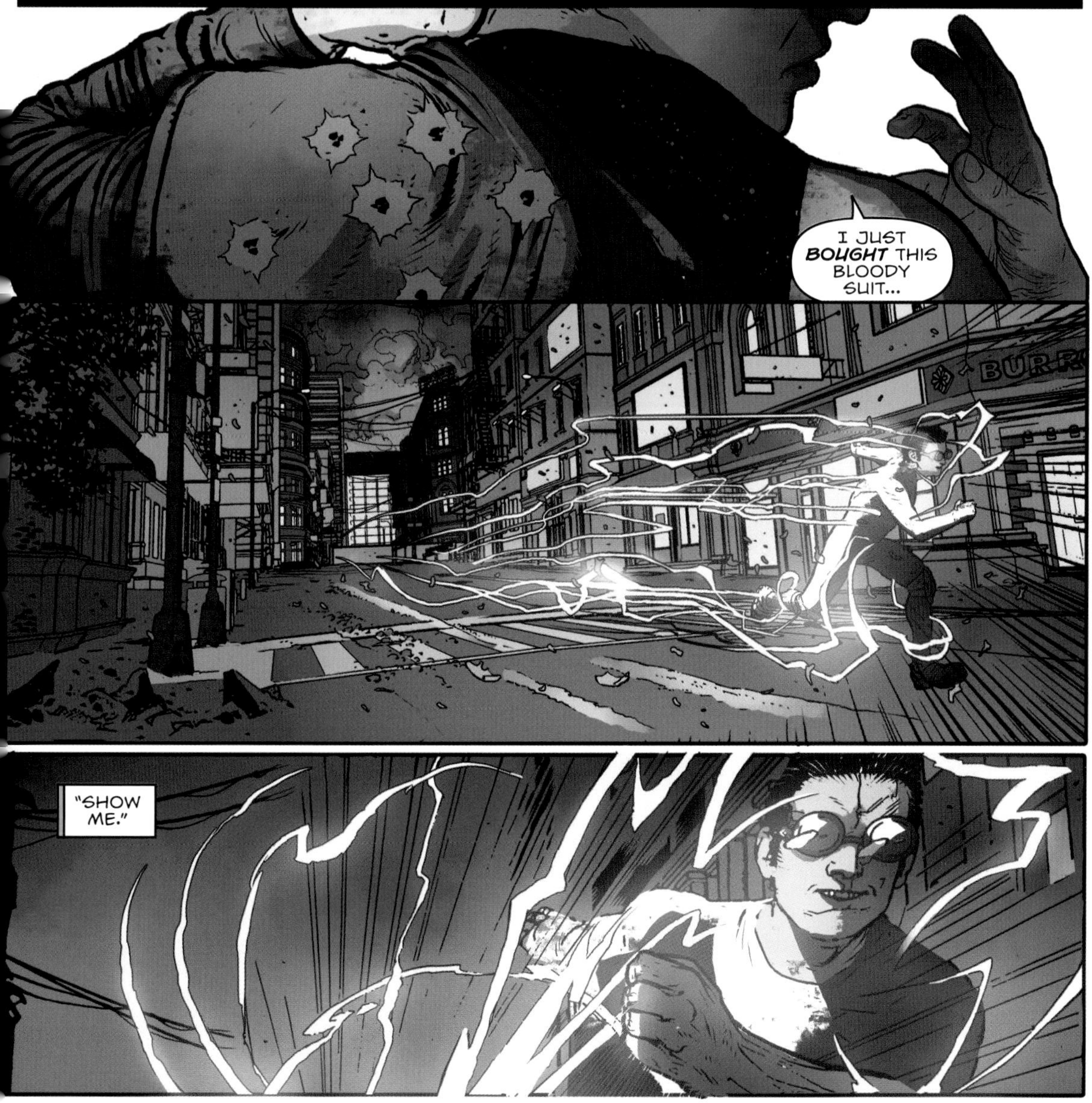
I JUST BOUGHT THIS BLOODY SUIT...
BURR
"SHOW ME."

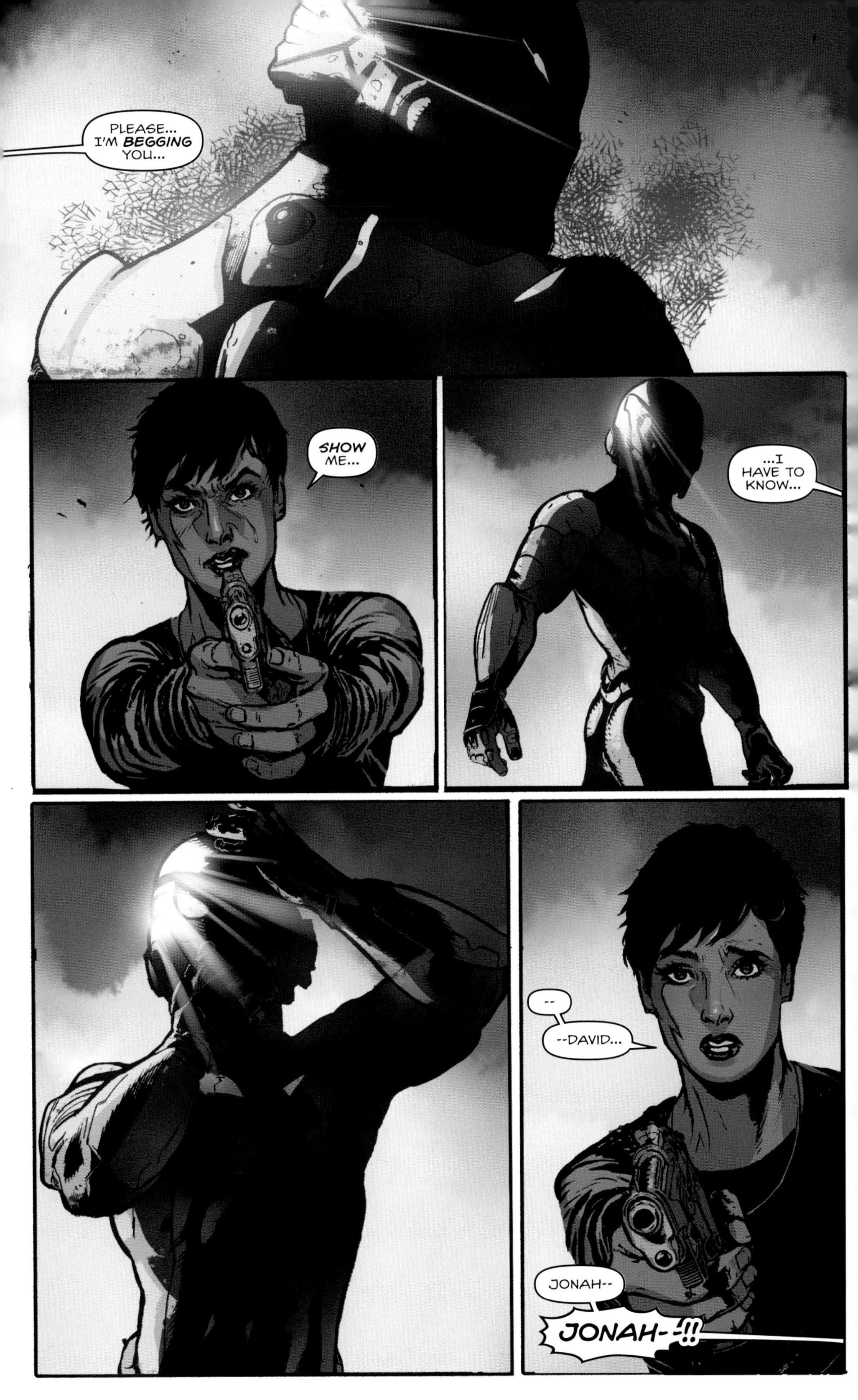
PLEASE... I'M **BEGGING** YOU...
SHOW ME...
...I HAVE TO KNOW...
--
--DAVID...
JONAH--
JONAH--!!

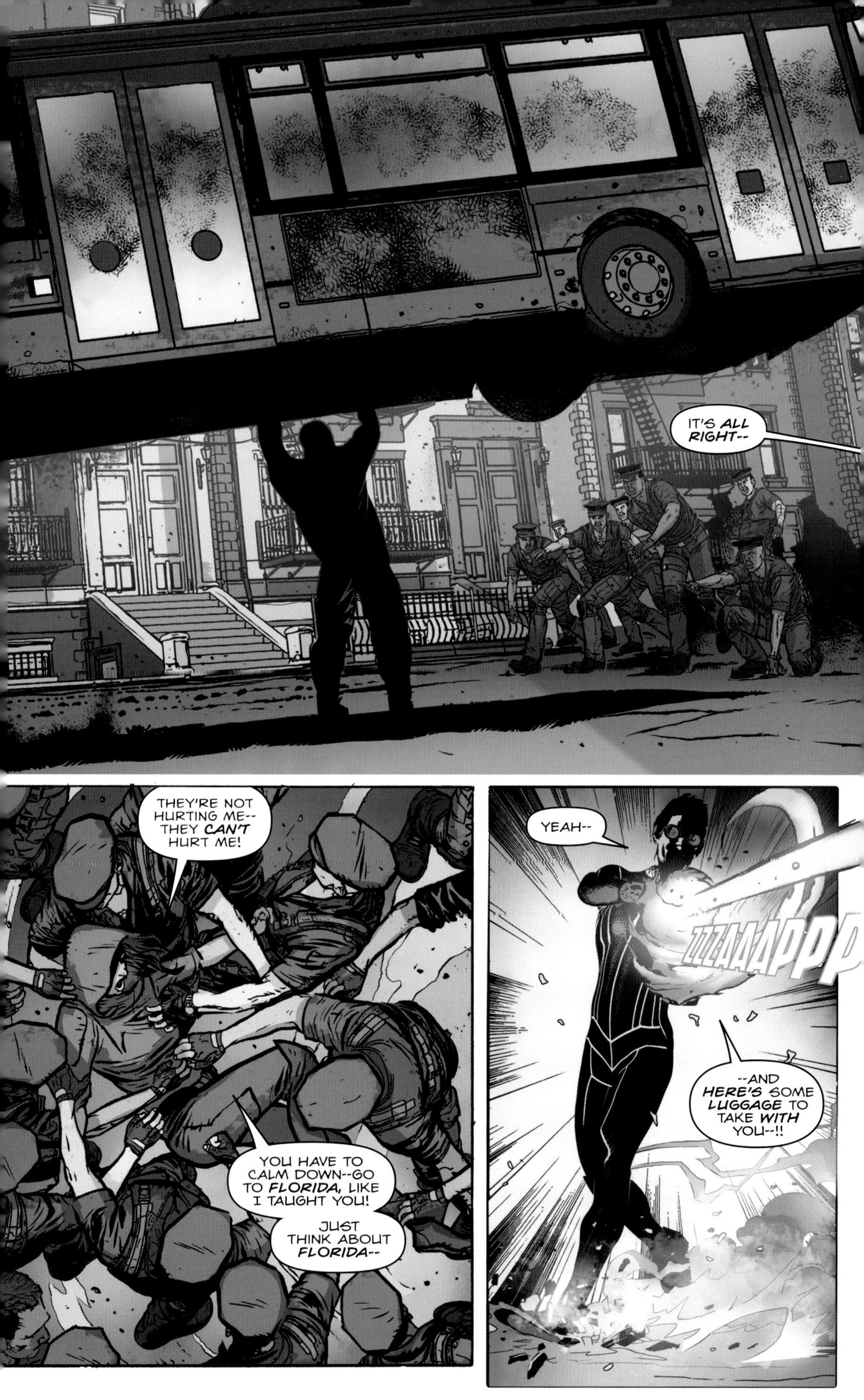
IT'S ALL RIGHT--
THEY'RE NOT HURTING ME-- THEY CAN'T HURT ME!
YOU HAVE TO CALM DOWN--GO TO FLORIDA, LIKE I TAUGHT YOU!
JUST THINK ABOUT FLORIDA--
YEAH--
ZZZAAAPPP
--AND HERE'S SOME LUGGAGE TO TAKE WITH YOU--!!

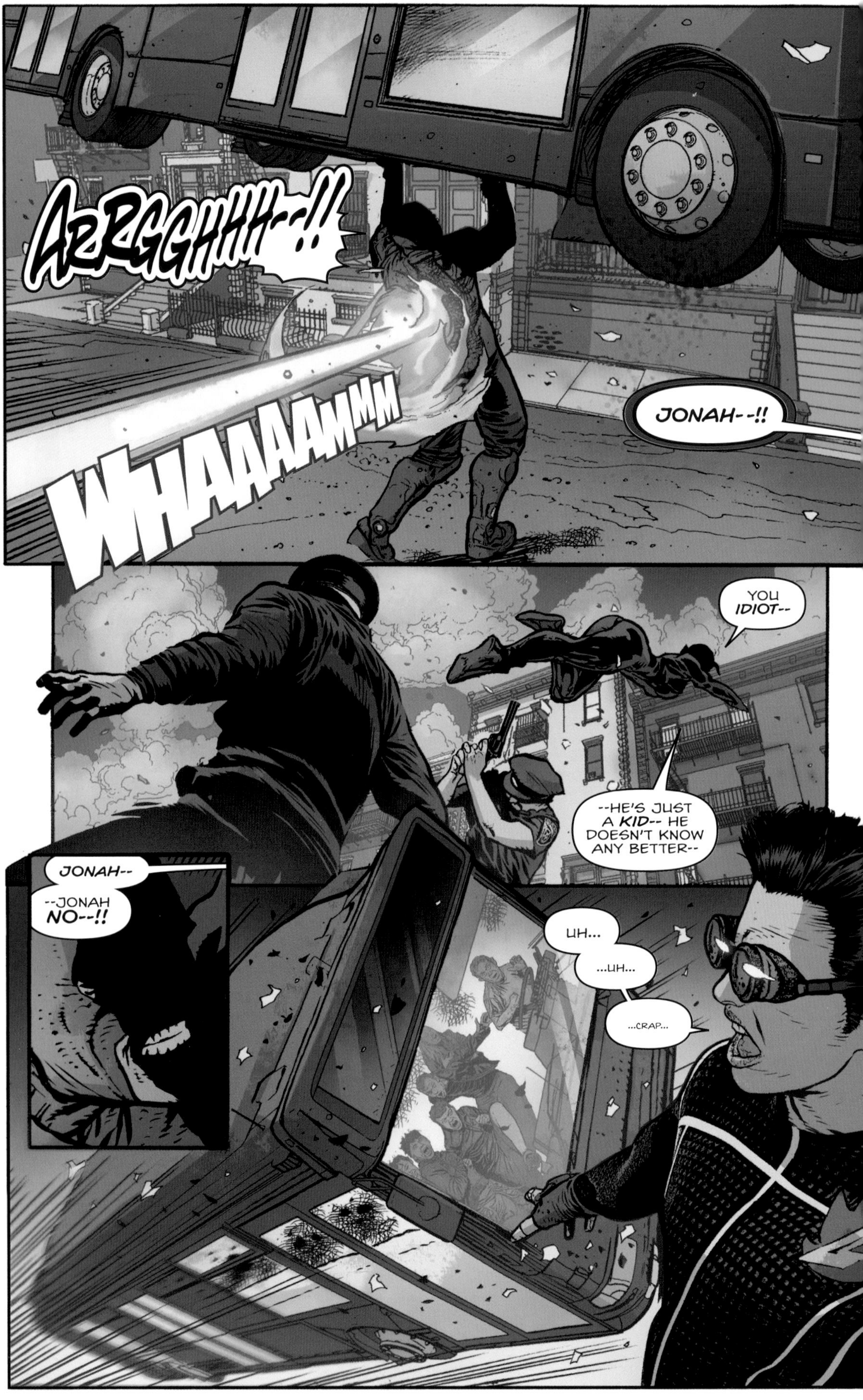
ARRGGHHH--!!
WHAAAAAMMM
JONAH--!!
YOU IDIOT--
--HE'S JUST A KID-- HE DOESN'T KNOW ANY BETTER--
JONAH--
--JONAH NO--!!
UH...
...UH...
...CRAP...

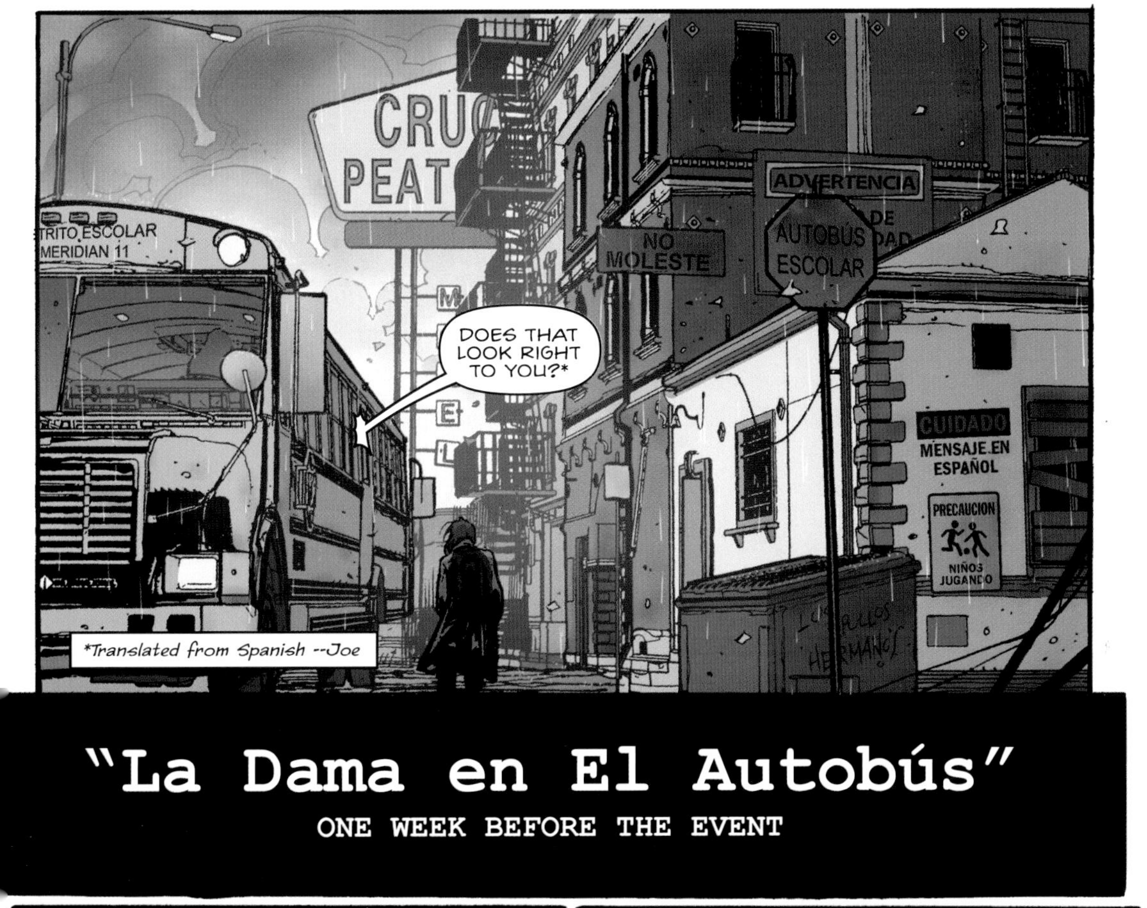
ADVERTENCIA
NO MOLESTE
AUTOBUS ESCOLAR
MERIDIAN 11
DOES THAT LOOK RIGHT TO YOU?*
CUIDADO
MENSAJE EN ESPAÑOL
PRECAUCION
NIÑOS JUGANDO
*Translated from Spanish --Joe

"La Dama en El Autobús"

ONE WEEK BEFORE THE EVENT

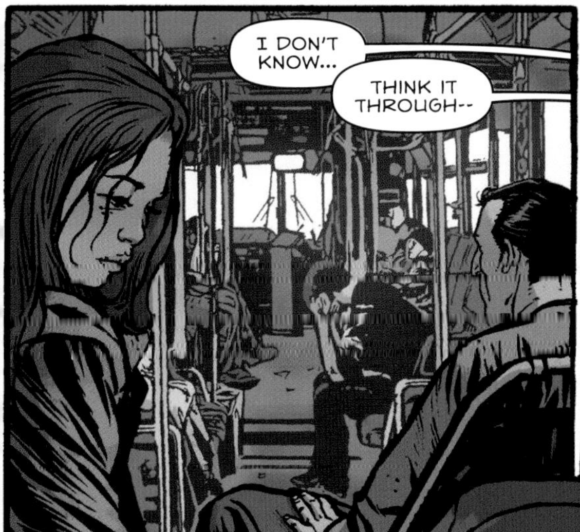
I DON'T KNOW...
THINK IT THROUGH--

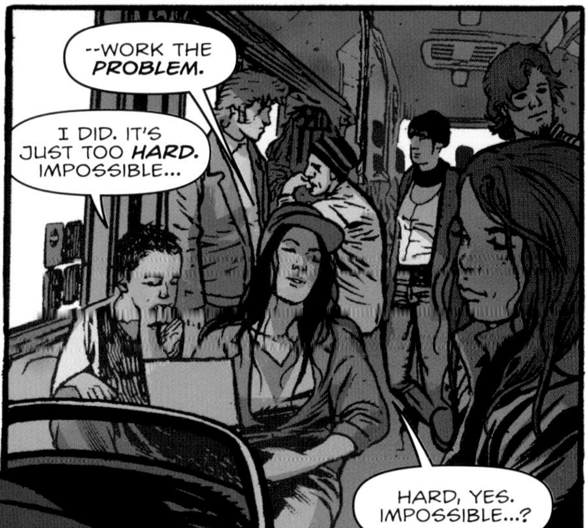
--WORK THE **PROBLEM.**
I DID. IT'S JUST TOO **HARD.** IMPOSSIBLE...
HARD, YES. IMPOSSIBLE...?

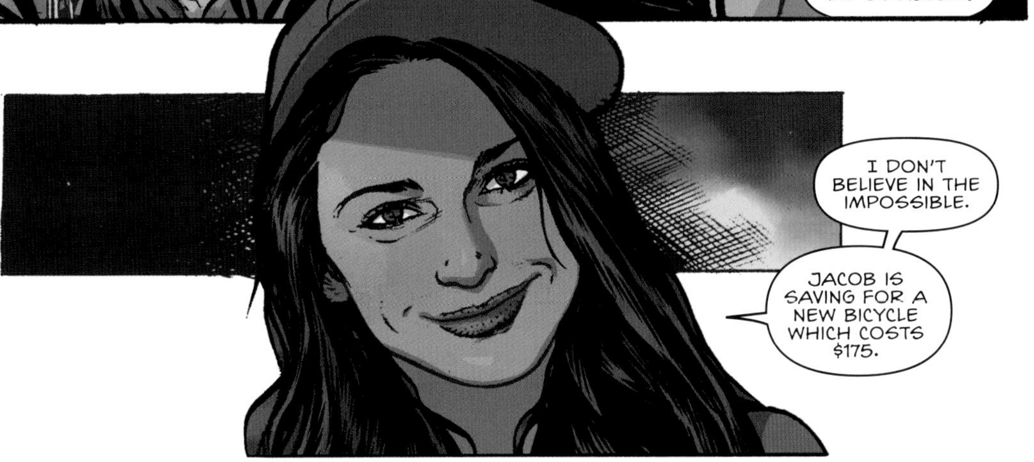
I DON'T BELIEVE IN THE IMPOSSIBLE.
JACOB IS SAVING FOR A NEW BICYCLE WHICH COSTS $175.

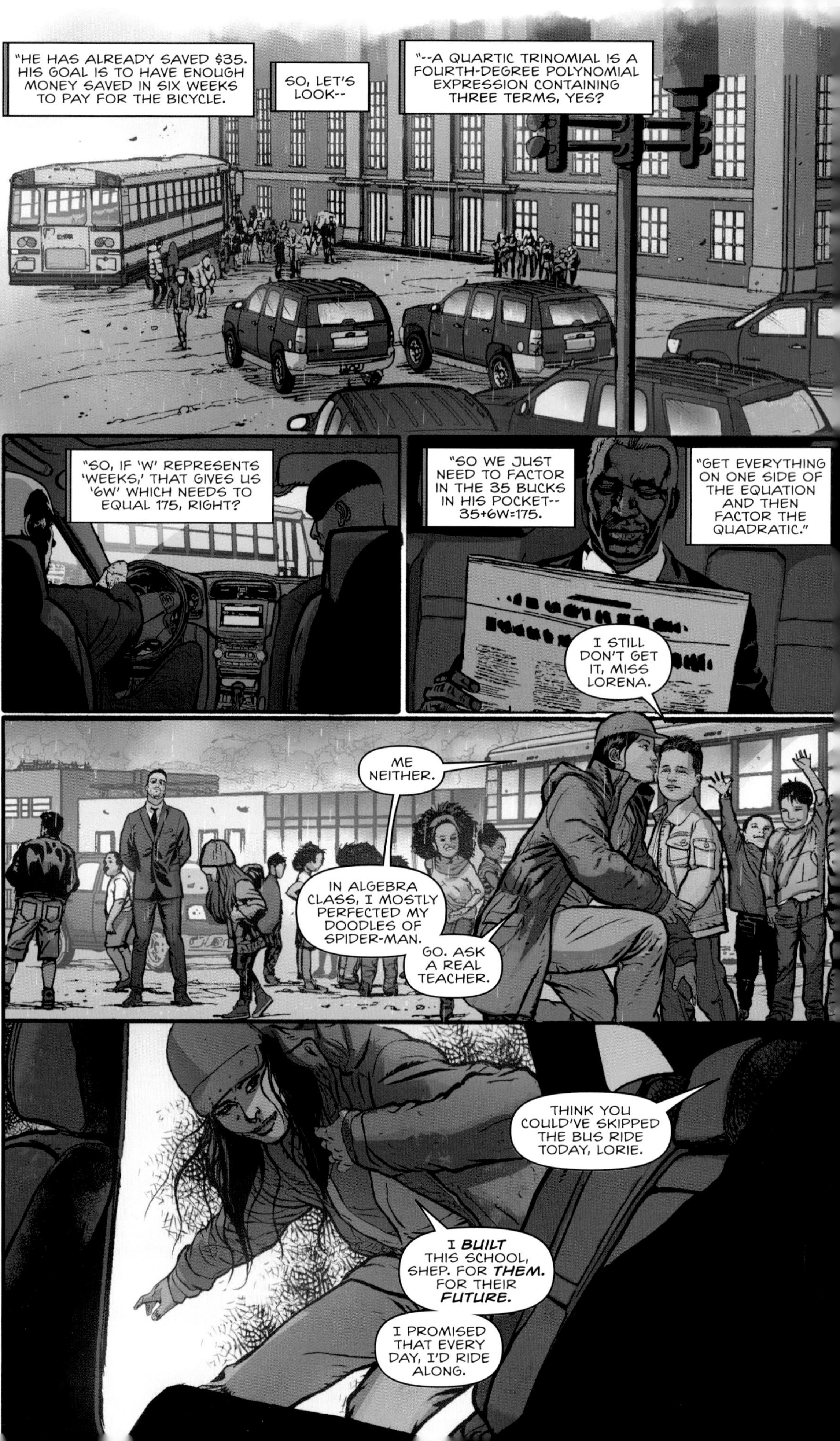

"HE HAS ALREADY SAVED $35. HIS GOAL IS TO HAVE ENOUGH MONEY SAVED IN SIX WEEKS TO PAY FOR THE BICYCLE.
SO, LET'S LOOK--
"--A QUARTIC TRINOMIAL IS A FOURTH-DEGREE POLYNOMIAL EXPRESSION CONTAINING THREE TERMS, YES?
"SO, IF 'W' REPRESENTS 'WEEKS,' THAT GIVES US '6W' WHICH NEEDS TO EQUAL 175, RIGHT?
"SO WE JUST NEED TO FACTOR IN THE 35 BUCKS IN HIS POCKET-- 35+6W=175.
"GET EVERYTHING ON ONE SIDE OF THE EQUATION AND THEN FACTOR THE QUADRATIC."
I STILL DON'T GET IT, MISS LORENA.
ME NEITHER.
IN ALGEBRA CLASS, I MOSTLY PERFECTED MY DOODLES OF SPIDER-MAN.
GO. ASK A REAL TEACHER.
THINK YOU COULD'VE SKIPPED THE BUS RIDE TODAY, LORIE.
I BUILT THIS SCHOOL, SHEP. FOR THEM. FOR THEIR FUTURE.
I PROMISED THAT EVERY DAY, I'D RIDE ALONG.

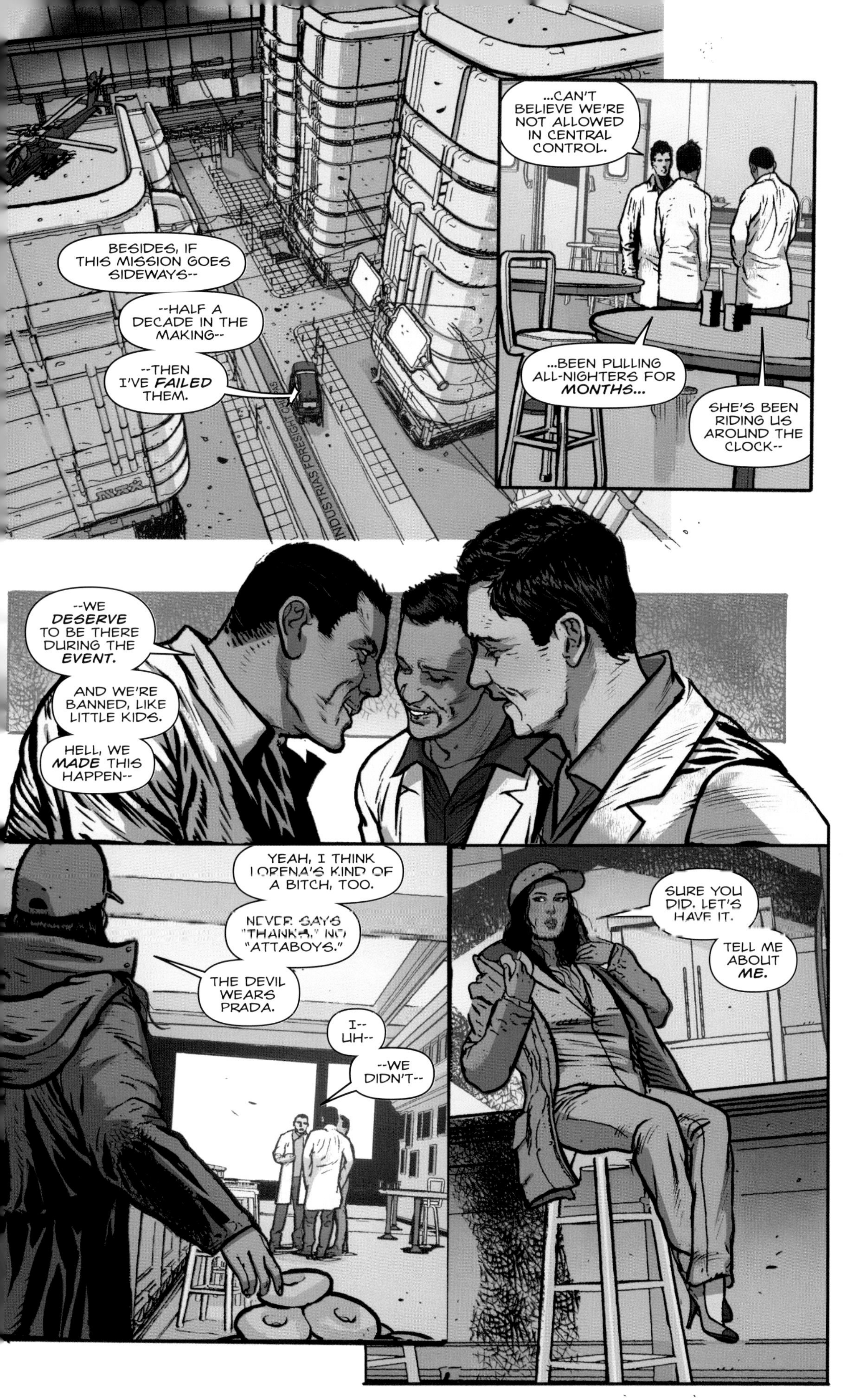
BESIDES, IF THIS MISSION GOES SIDEWAYS--
--HALF A DECADE IN THE MAKING--
--THEN I'VE *FAILED* THEM.
INDUSTRIAS FORESIGHT
...CAN'T BELIEVE WE'RE NOT ALLOWED IN CENTRAL CONTROL.
...BEEN PULLING ALL-NIGHTERS FOR *MONTHS...*
SHE'S BEEN RIDING US AROUND THE CLOCK--
--WE *DESERVE* TO BE THERE DURING THE *EVENT.*
AND WE'RE BANNED, LIKE LITTLE KIDS.
HELL, WE *MADE* THIS HAPPEN--
YEAH, I THINK LORENA'S KIND OF A BITCH, TOO.
NEVER SAYS "THANKS," NO "ATTABOYS."
THE DEVIL WEARS PRADA.
I-- UH--
--WE DIDN'T--
SURE YOU DID. LET'S HAVE IT.
TELL ME ABOUT *ME.*

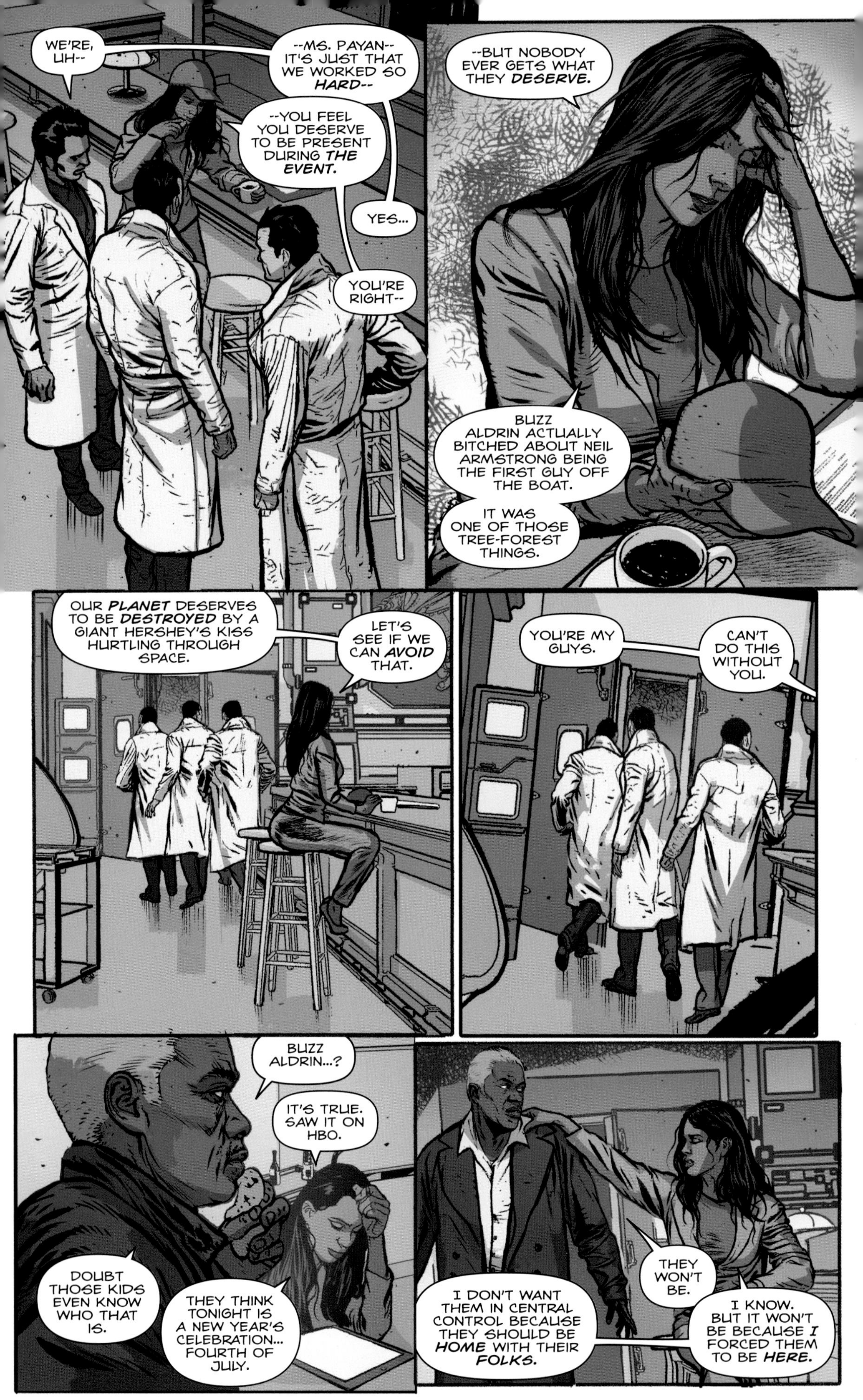
WE'RE, UH--
--MS. PAYAN-- IT'S JUST THAT WE WORKED SO HARD--
--YOU FEEL YOU DESERVE TO BE PRESENT DURING THE EVENT.
YES...
YOU'RE RIGHT--
--BUT NOBODY EVER GETS WHAT THEY DESERVE.
BUZZ ALDRIN ACTUALLY BITCHED ABOUT NEIL ARMSTRONG BEING THE FIRST GUY OFF THE BOAT.
IT WAS ONE OF THOSE TREE-FOREST THINGS.
OUR PLANET DESERVES TO BE DESTROYED BY A GIANT HERSHEY'S KISS HURTLING THROUGH SPACE.
LET'S SEE IF WE CAN AVOID THAT.
YOU'RE MY GUYS.
CAN'T DO THIS WITHOUT YOU.
BUZZ ALDRIN...?
IT'S TRUE. SAW IT ON HBO.
DOUBT THOSE KIDS EVEN KNOW WHO THAT IS.
THEY THINK TONIGHT IS A NEW YEAR'S CELEBRATION... FOURTH OF JULY.
I DON'T WANT THEM IN CENTRAL CONTROL BECAUSE THEY SHOULD BE HOME WITH THEIR FOLKS.
THEY WON'T BE.
I KNOW. BUT IT WON'T BE BECAUSE I FORCED THEM TO BE HERE.

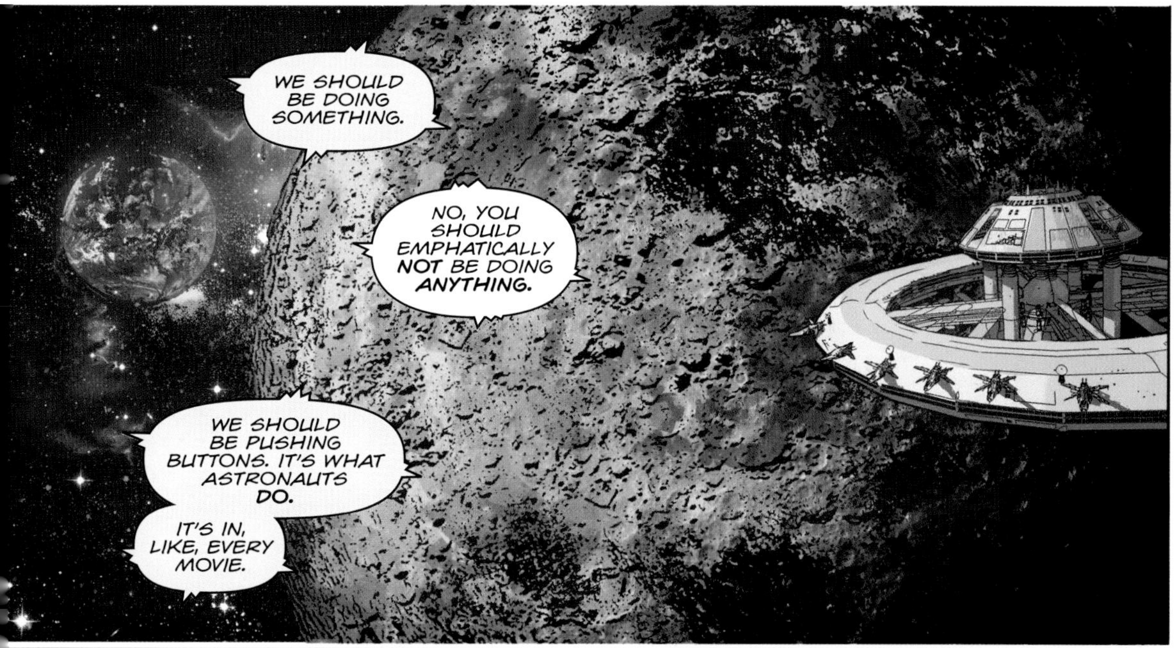
WE SHOULD BE DOING SOMETHING.
NO, YOU SHOULD EMPHATICALLY **NOT** BE DOING **ANYTHING.**
WE SHOULD BE PUSHING BUTTONS. IT'S WHAT ASTRONAUTS **DO.**
IT'S IN, LIKE, EVERY MOVIE.

"Monkeys"

FORESIGHT AMERICO LUNAR PLATFORM
ONE WEEK BEFORE THE EVENT

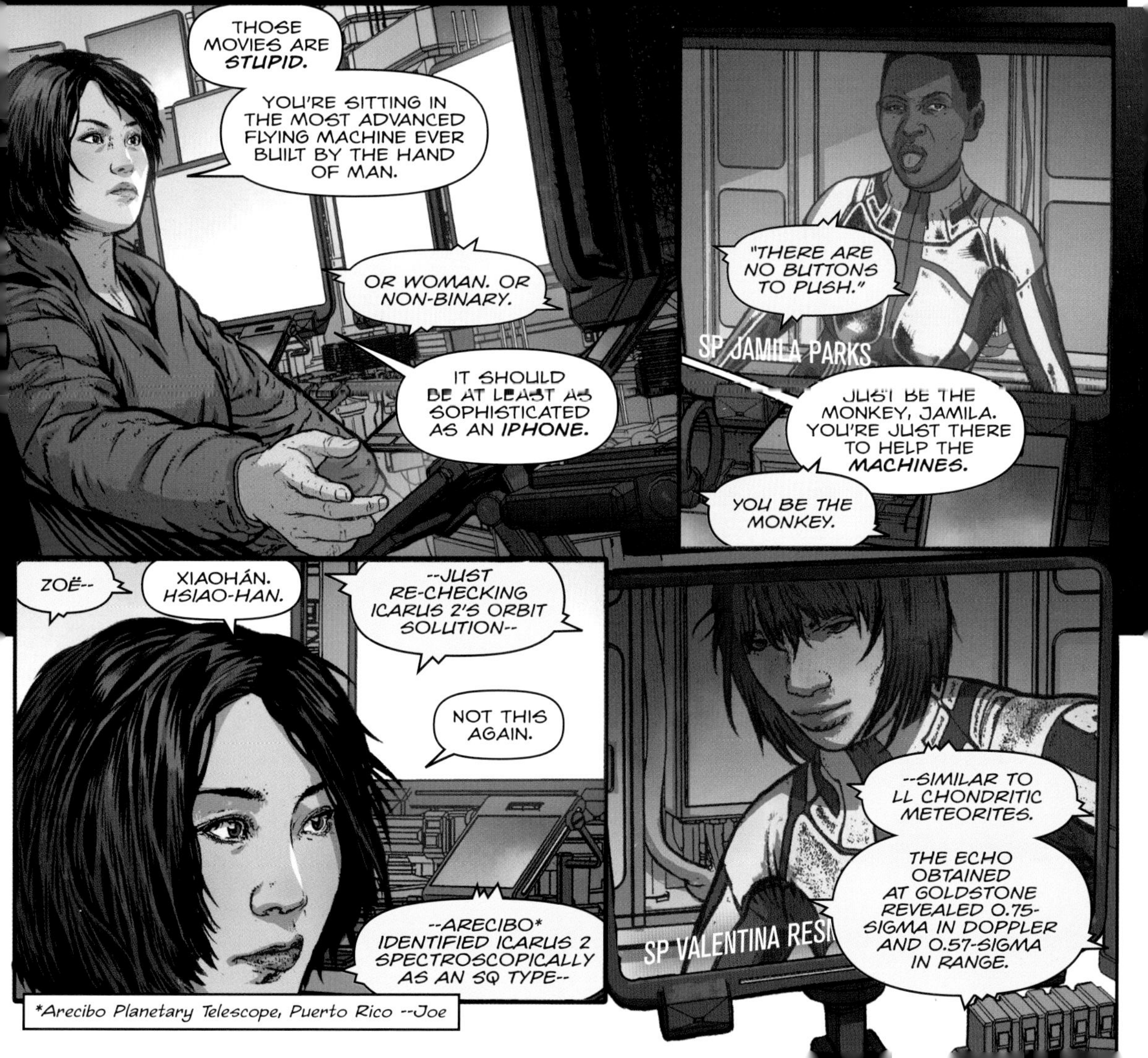
THOSE MOVIES ARE **STUPID.**
YOU'RE SITTING IN THE MOST ADVANCED FLYING MACHINE EVER BUILT BY THE HAND OF MAN.
OR WOMAN. OR NON-BINARY.
IT SHOULD BE AT LEAST AS SOPHISTICATED AS AN ***IPHONE.***
"THERE ARE NO BUTTONS TO PUSH."
SP JAMILA PARKS
JUST BE THE MONKEY, JAMILA. YOU'RE JUST THERE TO HELP THE ***MACHINES.***
YOU BE THE MONKEY.
ZOË--
XIAOHÁN. HSIAO-HAN.
--JUST RE-CHECKING ICARUS 2'S ORBIT SOLUTION--
NOT THIS AGAIN.
--ARECIBO* IDENTIFIED ICARUS 2 SPECTROSCOPICALLY AS AN SQ TYPE--
*Arecibo Planetary Telescope, Puerto Rico --Joe
SP VALENTINA RESI
--SIMILAR TO LL CHONDRITIC METEORITES.
THE ECHO OBTAINED AT GOLDSTONE REVEALED 0.75-SIGMA IN DOPPLER AND 0.57-SIGMA IN RANGE.

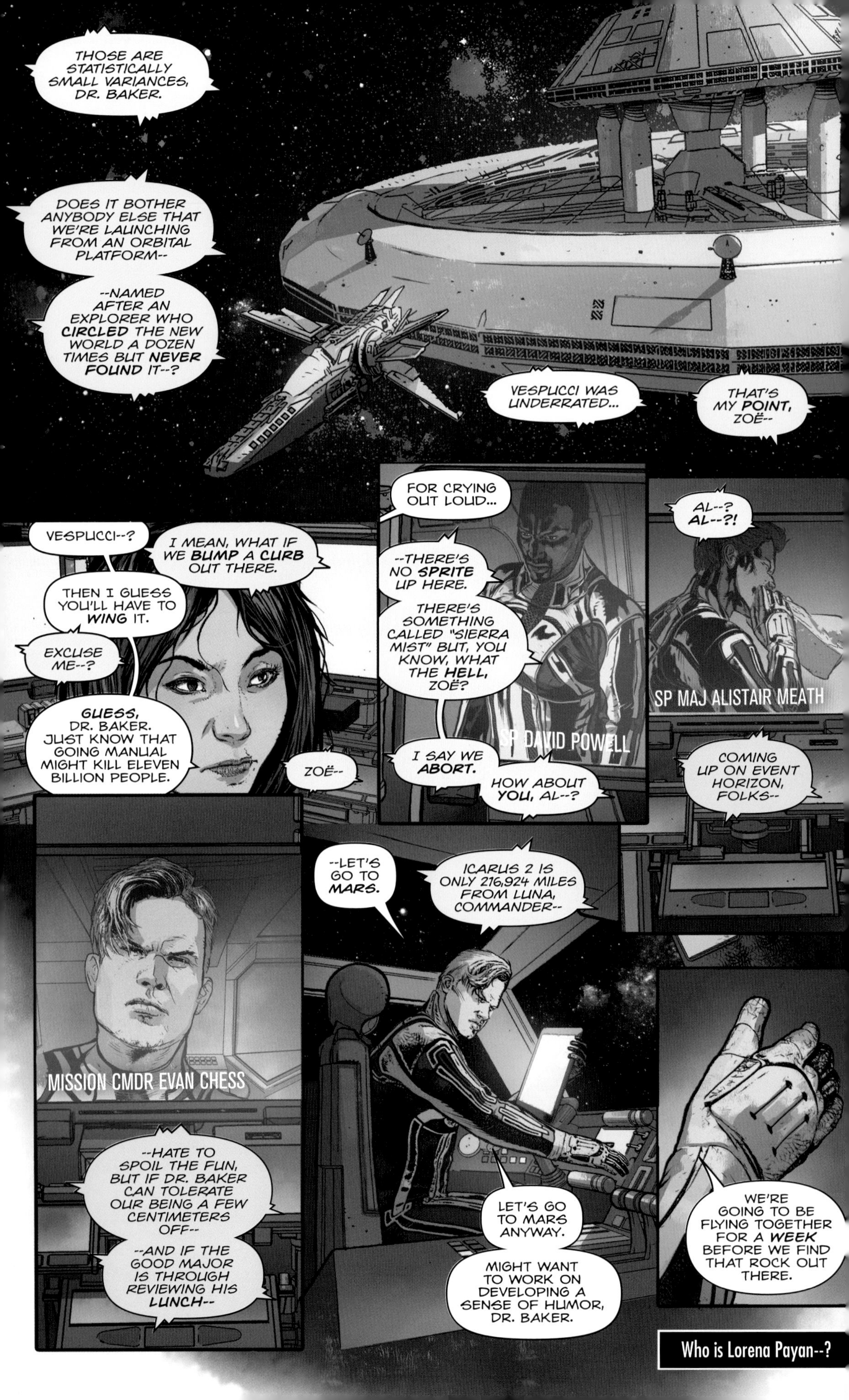
THOSE ARE STATISTICALLY SMALL VARIANCES, DR. BAKER.
DOES IT BOTHER ANYBODY ELSE THAT WE'RE LAUNCHING FROM AN ORBITAL PLATFORM--
--NAMED AFTER AN EXPLORER WHO **CIRCLED** THE NEW WORLD A DOZEN TIMES BUT **NEVER FOUND** IT--?
VESPUCCI WAS UNDERRATED...
THAT'S MY **POINT,** ZOË--
VESPUCCI--?
I MEAN, WHAT IF WE **BUMP A CURB** OUT THERE.
THEN I GUESS YOU'LL HAVE TO **WING** IT.
EXCUSE ME--?
GUESS, DR. BAKER. JUST KNOW THAT GOING MANUAL MIGHT KILL ELEVEN BILLION PEOPLE.
ZOË--
FOR CRYING OUT LOUD...
--THERE'S NO **SPRITE** UP HERE.
THERE'S SOMETHING CALLED "SIERRA MIST" BUT, YOU KNOW, WHAT THE **HELL,** ZOË?
SP DAVID POWELL
I SAY WE **ABORT.**
HOW ABOUT **YOU,** AL--?
AL--? **AL--?!**
SP MAJ ALISTAIR MEATH
COMING UP ON EVENT HORIZON, FOLKS--
MISSION CMDR EVAN CHESS
--HATE TO SPOIL THE FUN, BUT IF DR. BAKER CAN TOLERATE OUR BEING A FEW CENTIMETERS OFF--
--AND IF THE GOOD MAJOR IS THROUGH REVIEWING HIS **LUNCH--**
--LET'S GO TO **MARS.**
ICARUS 2 IS ONLY 216,924 MILES FROM LUNA, COMMANDER--
LET'S GO TO MARS ANYWAY.
MIGHT WANT TO WORK ON DEVELOPING A SENSE OF HUMOR, DR. BAKER.
WE'RE GOING TO BE FLYING TOGETHER FOR A **WEEK** BEFORE WE FIND THAT ROCK OUT THERE.
Who is Lorena Payan--?

GLOBAL NOW

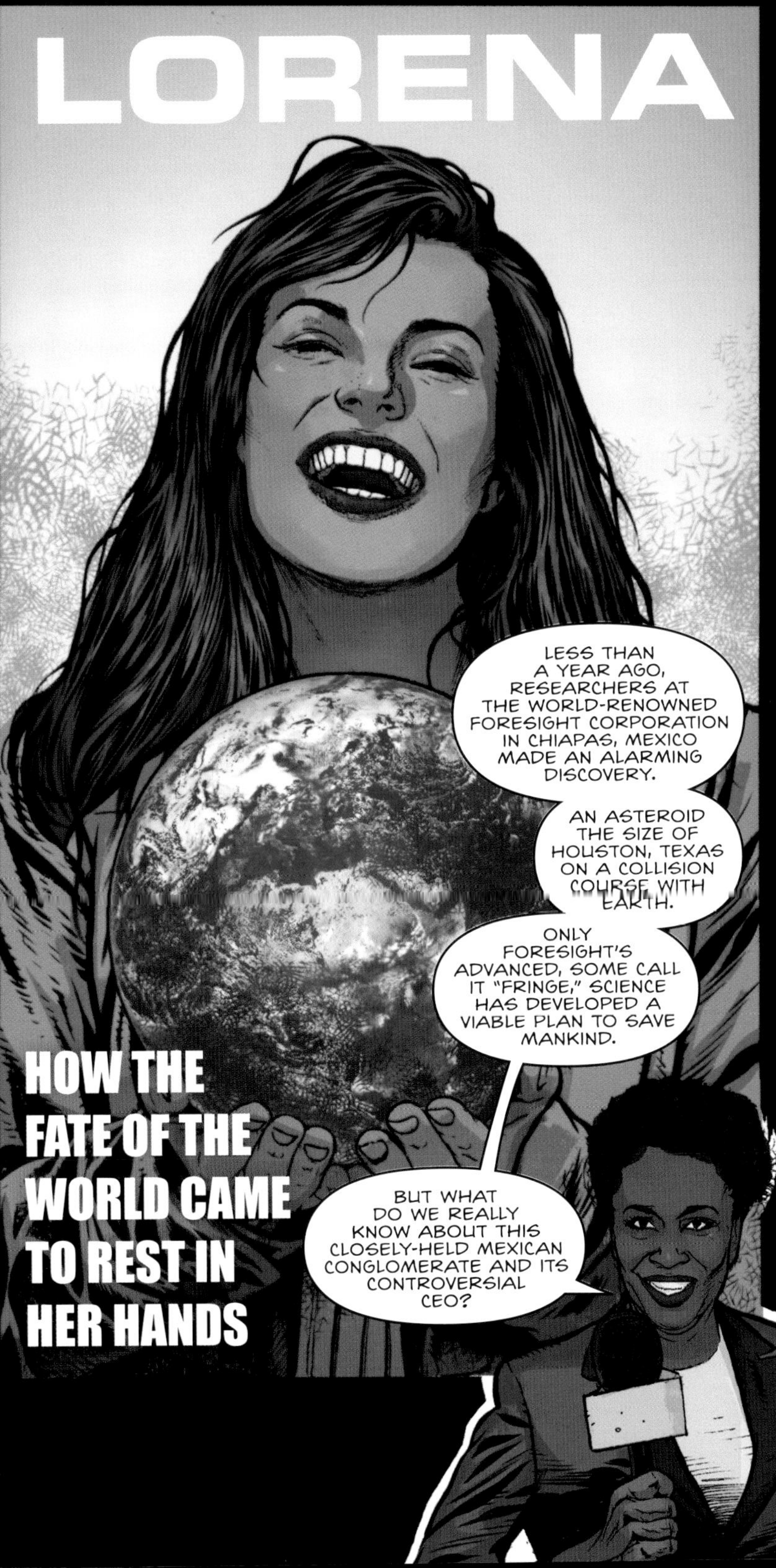
LORENA
LESS THAN A YEAR AGO, RESEARCHERS AT THE WORLD-RENOWNED FORESIGHT CORPORATION IN CHIAPAS, MEXICO MADE AN ALARMING DISCOVERY.
AN ASTEROID THE SIZE OF HOUSTON, TEXAS ON A COLLISION COURSE WITH EARTH.
ONLY FORESIGHT'S ADVANCED, SOME CALL IT "FRINGE," SCIENCE HAS DEVELOPED A VIABLE PLAN TO SAVE MANKIND.
HOW THE FATE OF THE WORLD CAME TO REST IN HER HANDS
BUT WHAT DO WE REALLY KNOW ABOUT THIS CLOSELY-HELD MEXICAN CONGLOMERATE AND ITS CONTROVERSIAL CEO?

In less than ten years, Lorena Payan built the Foresight Corporation into a global titan through innovations in aerospace development, space exploration, and so-called "fringe" science.

A native of the impoverished Mexican state of Chiapas, Payan lost her mother at age twelve. She and her brother Ramon were raised by their paternal grandmother Isabel, while their father Enrique Payan attended M.I.T. in the United States.

Payan's father founded the Foresight Corporation in Silicon Valley when she was a teenager, using wealth accumulated from his various business ventures in Mexico.

After immigrating to America, Payan studied under the tutelage of the eminent physicist, Dr. Parker "Shep" Bingham, who has served as her mentor and most trusted advisor.

While Payan lived in America with her father, her brother returned to Mexico, where Ramon Payan rose within the political structure. While Enrique Payan planted himself and his daughter in the ground of the American Dream, Lorena's brother chose to fight for his people back home, to work within the system to pull Mexico out of corruption and save it from the drug cartels.

Ramon Payan inherited the leadership of Foresight upon their father's death and relocated the corporation's central office to Chiapas. The Payan siblings hired a near 100% Mexican labor force in every section of the company and revolutionized the local economy while bringing global attention to the plight of Chiapas's indigenous tribes and social conflicts. Lorena Payan assumed control of Foresight after her brother was killed in a car bombing.

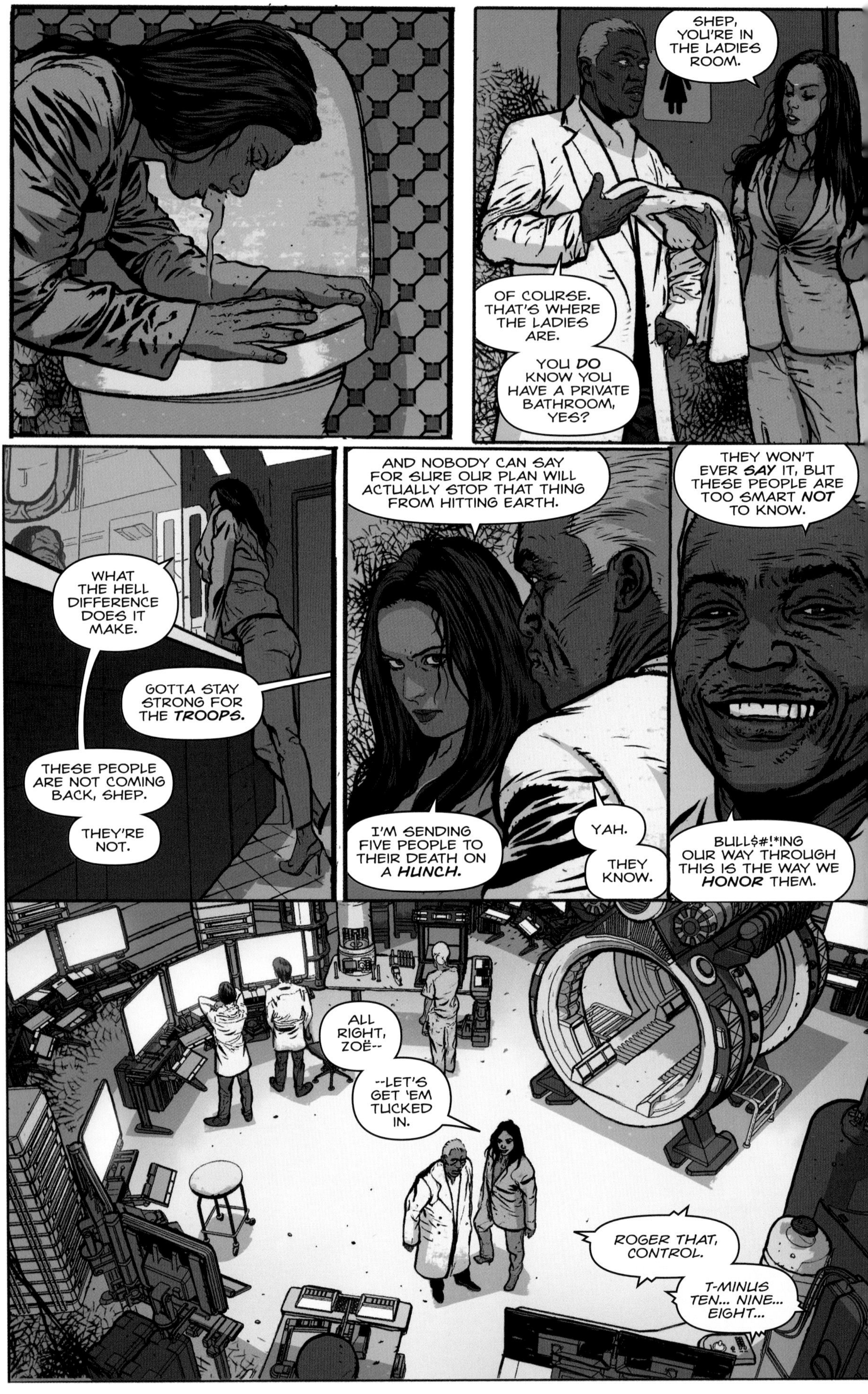
SHEP, YOU'RE IN THE LADIES ROOM.
OF COURSE. THAT'S WHERE THE LADIES ARE.
YOU DO KNOW YOU HAVE A PRIVATE BATHROOM, YES?
WHAT THE HELL DIFFERENCE DOES IT MAKE.
GOTTA STAY STRONG FOR THE TROOPS.
THESE PEOPLE ARE NOT COMING BACK, SHEP.
THEY'RE NOT.
AND NOBODY CAN SAY FOR SURE OUR PLAN WILL ACTUALLY STOP THAT THING FROM HITTING EARTH.
I'M SENDING FIVE PEOPLE TO THEIR DEATH ON A HUNCH.
YAH.
THEY KNOW.
THEY WON'T EVER SAY IT, BUT THESE PEOPLE ARE TOO SMART NOT TO KNOW.
BULL$#!*ING OUR WAY THROUGH THIS IS THE WAY WE HONOR THEM.
ALL RIGHT, ZOË--
--LET'S GET 'EM TUCKED IN.
ROGER THAT, CONTROL.
T-MINUS TEN... NINE... EIGHT...

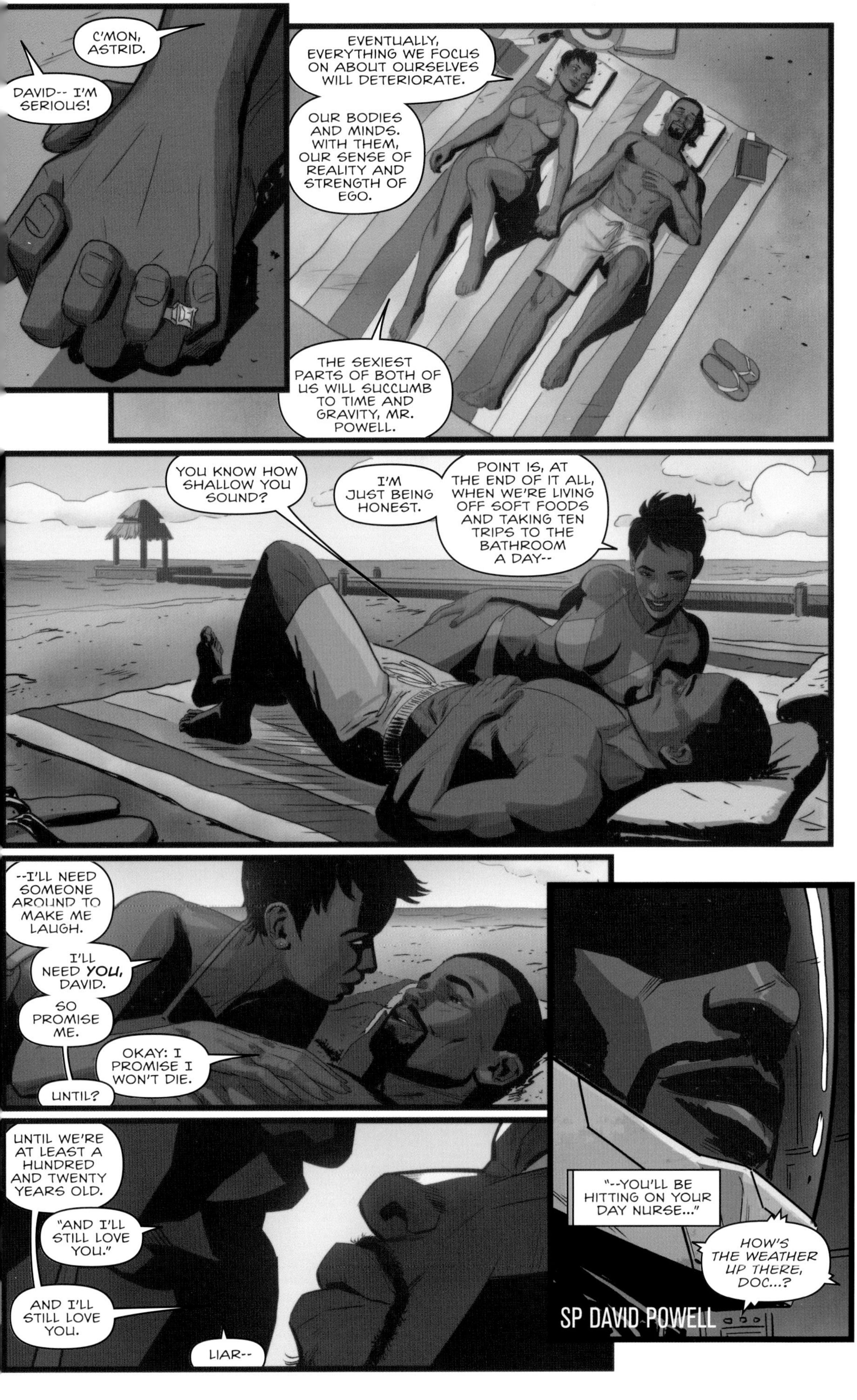
C'MON, ASTRID.
DAVID-- I'M SERIOUS!
EVENTUALLY, EVERYTHING WE FOCUS ON ABOUT OURSELVES WILL DETERIORATE.
OUR BODIES AND MINDS. WITH THEM, OUR SENSE OF REALITY AND STRENGTH OF EGO.
THE SEXIEST PARTS OF BOTH OF US WILL SUCCUMB TO TIME AND GRAVITY, MR. POWELL.
YOU KNOW HOW SHALLOW YOU SOUND?
I'M JUST BEING HONEST.
POINT IS, AT THE END OF IT ALL, WHEN WE'RE LIVING OFF SOFT FOODS AND TAKING TEN TRIPS TO THE BATHROOM A DAY--
--I'LL NEED SOMEONE AROUND TO MAKE ME LAUGH.
I'LL NEED YOU, DAVID.
SO PROMISE ME.
OKAY: I PROMISE I WON'T DIE.
UNTIL?
UNTIL WE'RE AT LEAST A HUNDRED AND TWENTY YEARS OLD.
"AND I'LL STILL LOVE YOU."
AND I'LL STILL LOVE YOU.
LIAR--
"--YOU'LL BE HITTING ON YOUR DAY NURSE..."
HOW'S THE WEATHER UP THERE, DOC...?
SP DAVID POWELL

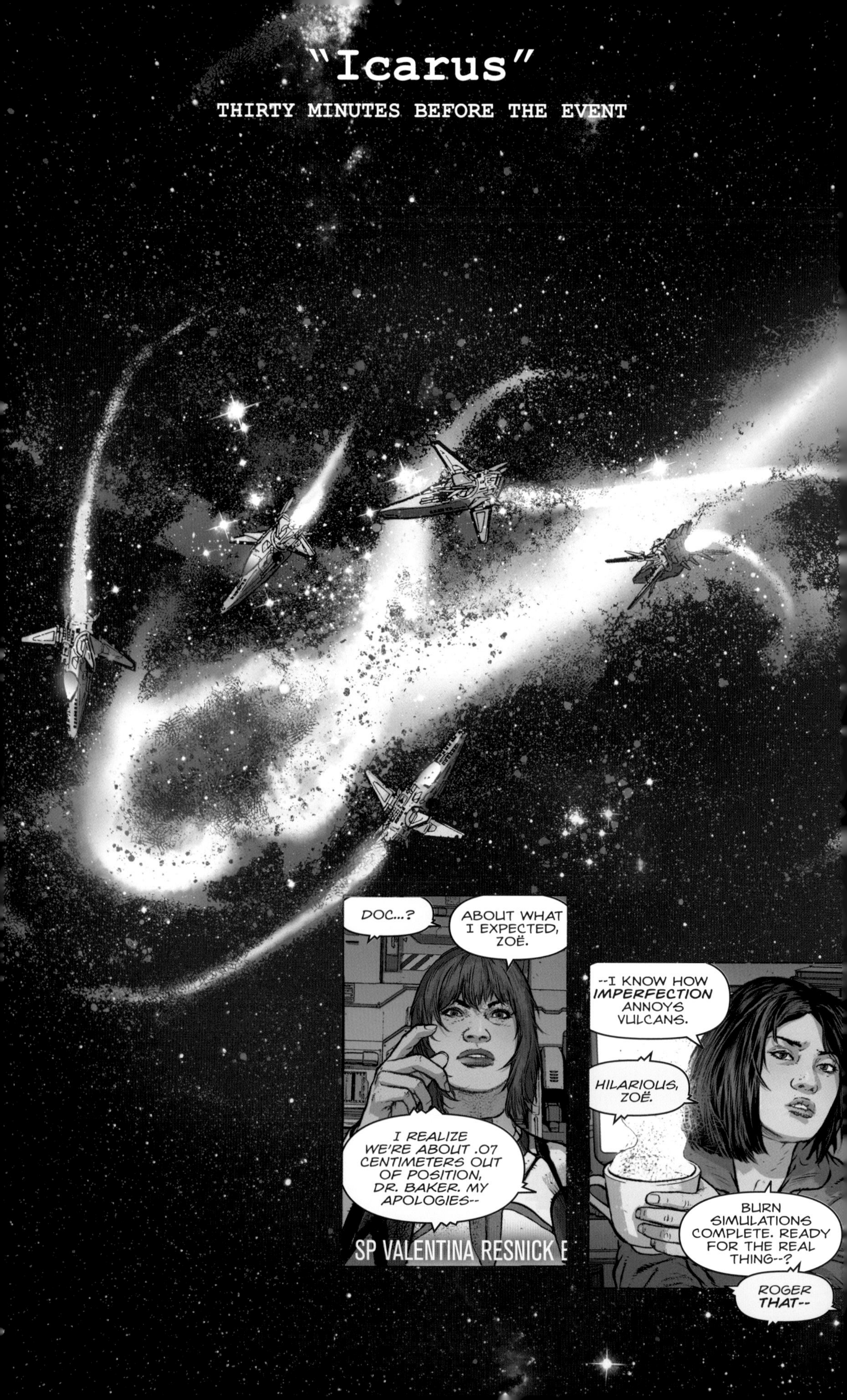
"Icarus"
THIRTY MINUTES BEFORE THE EVENT
DOC...?
ABOUT WHAT I EXPECTED, ZOË.
I REALIZE WE'RE ABOUT .07 CENTIMETERS OUT OF POSITION, DR. BAKER. MY APOLOGIES--
SP VALENTINA RESNICK
--I KNOW HOW IMPERFECTION ANNOYS VULCANS.
HILARIOUS, ZOË.
BURN SIMULATIONS COMPLETE. READY FOR THE REAL THING--?
ROGER THAT--

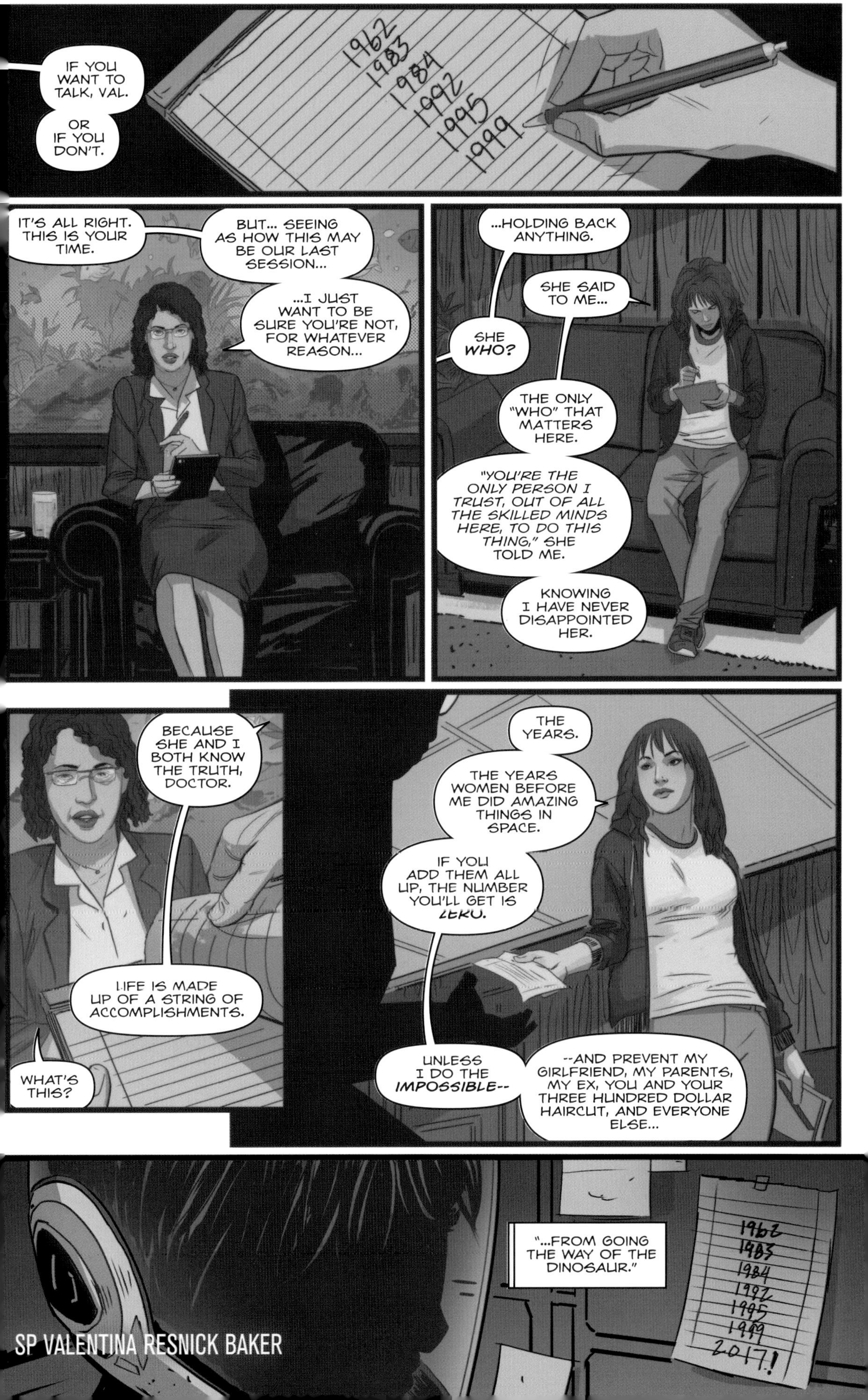
IF YOU WANT TO TALK, VAL.
OR IF YOU DON'T.
1962
1983
1984
1992
1995
1999
IT'S ALL RIGHT. THIS IS YOUR TIME.
BUT... SEEING AS HOW THIS MAY BE OUR LAST SESSION...
...I JUST WANT TO BE SURE YOU'RE NOT, FOR WHATEVER REASON...
...HOLDING BACK ANYTHING.
SHE SAID TO ME...
SHE *WHO?*
THE ONLY "WHO" THAT MATTERS HERE.
"YOU'RE THE ONLY PERSON I TRUST, OUT OF ALL THE SKILLED MINDS HERE, TO DO THIS THING," SHE TOLD ME.
KNOWING I HAVE NEVER DISAPPOINTED HER.
BECAUSE SHE AND I BOTH KNOW THE TRUTH, DOCTOR.
LIFE IS MADE UP OF A STRING OF ACCOMPLISHMENTS.
WHAT'S THIS?
THE YEARS.
THE YEARS WOMEN BEFORE ME DID AMAZING THINGS IN SPACE.
IF YOU ADD THEM ALL UP, THE NUMBER YOU'LL GET IS *ZERO.*
UNLESS I DO THE *IMPOSSIBLE--*
--AND PREVENT MY GIRLFRIEND, MY PARENTS, MY EX, YOU AND YOUR THREE HUNDRED DOLLAR HAIRCUT, AND EVERYONE ELSE...
"...FROM GOING THE WAY OF THE DINOSAUR."
1962
1983
1984
1992
1995
1999
2017!
SP VALENTINA RESNICK BAKER

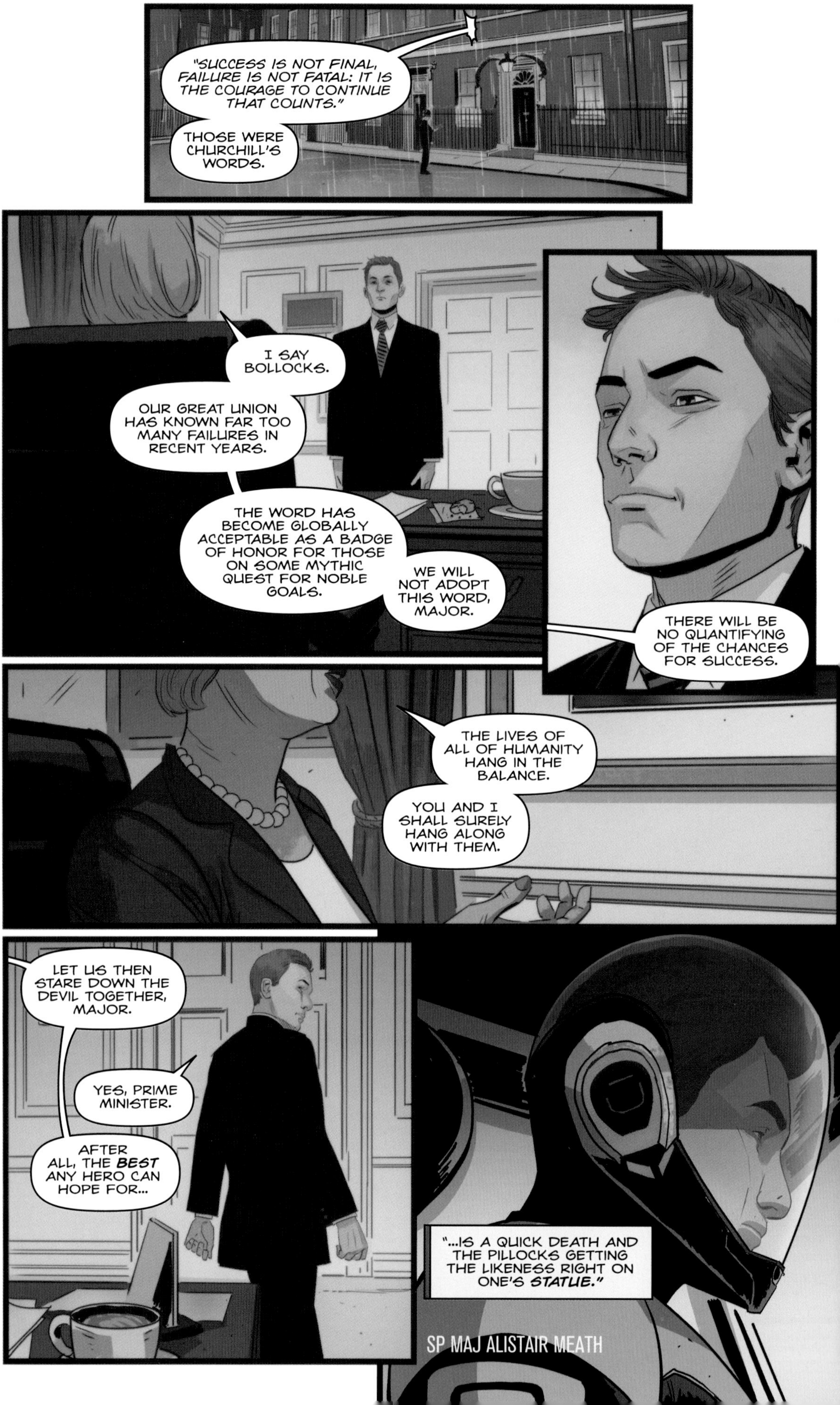
"*SUCCESS IS NOT FINAL, FAILURE IS NOT FATAL: IT IS THE COURAGE TO CONTINUE THAT COUNTS.*"
THOSE WERE CHURCHILL'S WORDS.
I SAY BOLLOCKS.
OUR GREAT UNION HAS KNOWN FAR TOO MANY FAILURES IN RECENT YEARS.
THE WORD HAS BECOME GLOBALLY ACCEPTABLE AS A BADGE OF HONOR FOR THOSE ON SOME MYTHIC QUEST FOR NOBLE GOALS.
WE WILL NOT ADOPT THIS WORD, MAJOR.
THERE WILL BE NO QUANTIFYING OF THE CHANCES FOR SUCCESS.
THE LIVES OF ALL OF HUMANITY HANG IN THE BALANCE.
YOU AND I SHALL SURELY HANG ALONG WITH THEM.
LET US THEN STARE DOWN THE DEVIL TOGETHER, MAJOR.
YES, PRIME MINISTER.
AFTER ALL, THE **BEST** ANY HERO CAN HOPE FOR...
"...IS A QUICK DEATH AND THE PILLOCKS GETTING THE LIKENESS RIGHT ON ONE'S ***STATUE.***"
SP MAJ ALISTAIR MEATH

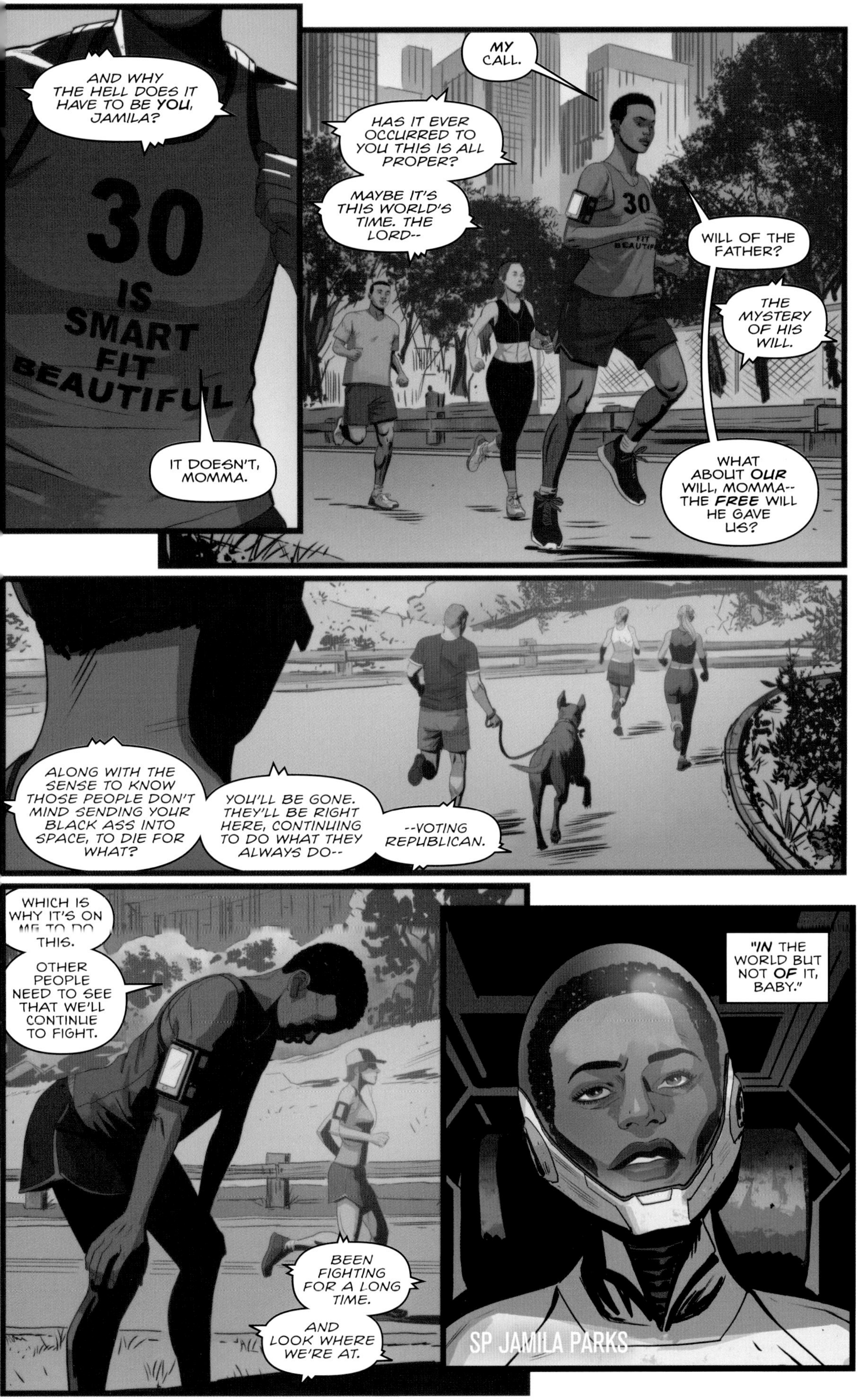
AND WHY THE HELL DOES IT HAVE TO BE YOU, JAMILA?
30 IS SMART FIT BEAUTIFUL
IT DOESN'T, MOMMA.
MY CALL.
HAS IT EVER OCCURRED TO YOU THIS IS ALL PROPER?
MAYBE IT'S THIS WORLD'S TIME. THE LORD--
WILL OF THE FATHER?
THE MYSTERY OF HIS WILL.
WHAT ABOUT OUR WILL, MOMMA-- THE FREE WILL HE GAVE US?
ALONG WITH THE SENSE TO KNOW THOSE PEOPLE DON'T MIND SENDING YOUR BLACK ASS INTO SPACE, TO DIE FOR WHAT?
YOU'LL BE GONE. THEY'LL BE RIGHT HERE, CONTINUING TO DO WHAT THEY ALWAYS DO--
--VOTING REPUBLICAN.
WHICH IS WHY IT'S ON ME TO DO THIS.
OTHER PEOPLE NEED TO SEE THAT WE'LL CONTINUE TO FIGHT.
BEEN FIGHTING FOR A LONG TIME.
AND LOOK WHERE WE'RE AT.
"IN THE WORLD BUT NOT OF IT, BABY."
SP JAMILA PARKS

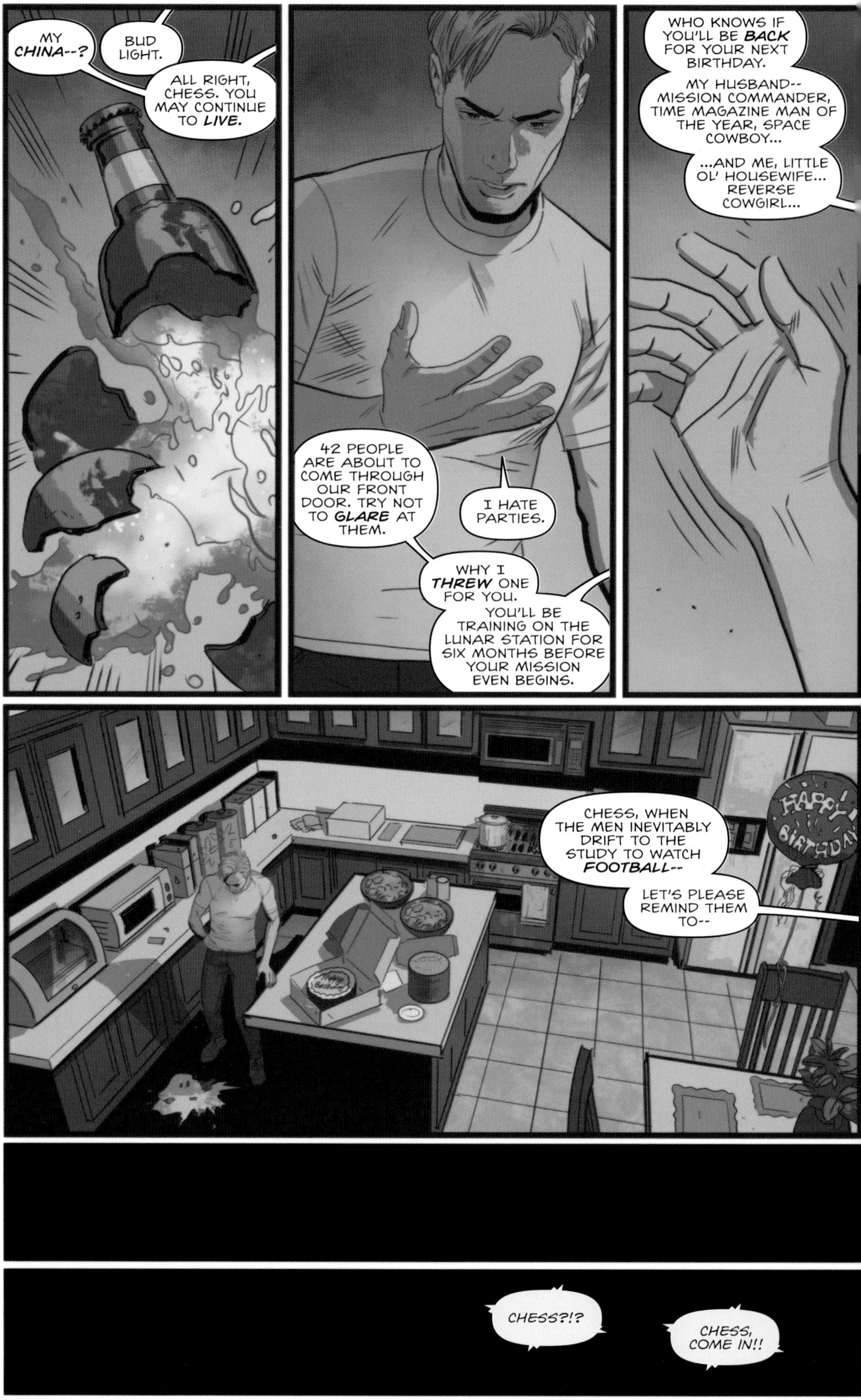
MY CHINA--?
BUD LIGHT.
ALL RIGHT, CHESS. YOU MAY CONTINUE TO LIVE.
42 PEOPLE ARE ABOUT TO COME THROUGH OUR FRONT DOOR. TRY NOT TO GLARE AT THEM.
I HATE PARTIES.
WHY I THREW ONE FOR YOU.
YOU'LL BE TRAINING ON THE LUNAR STATION FOR SIX MONTHS BEFORE YOUR MISSION EVEN BEGINS.
WHO KNOWS IF YOU'LL BE BACK FOR YOUR NEXT BIRTHDAY.
MY HUSBAND-- MISSION COMMANDER, TIME MAGAZINE MAN OF THE YEAR, SPACE COWBOY...
...AND ME, LITTLE OL' HOUSEWIFE... REVERSE COWGIRL...
HAPPY BIRTHDAY
CHESS, WHEN THE MEN INEVITABLY DRIFT TO THE STUDY TO WATCH FOOTBALL--
LET'S PLEASE REMIND THEM TO--
CHESS?!?
CHESS, COME IN!!

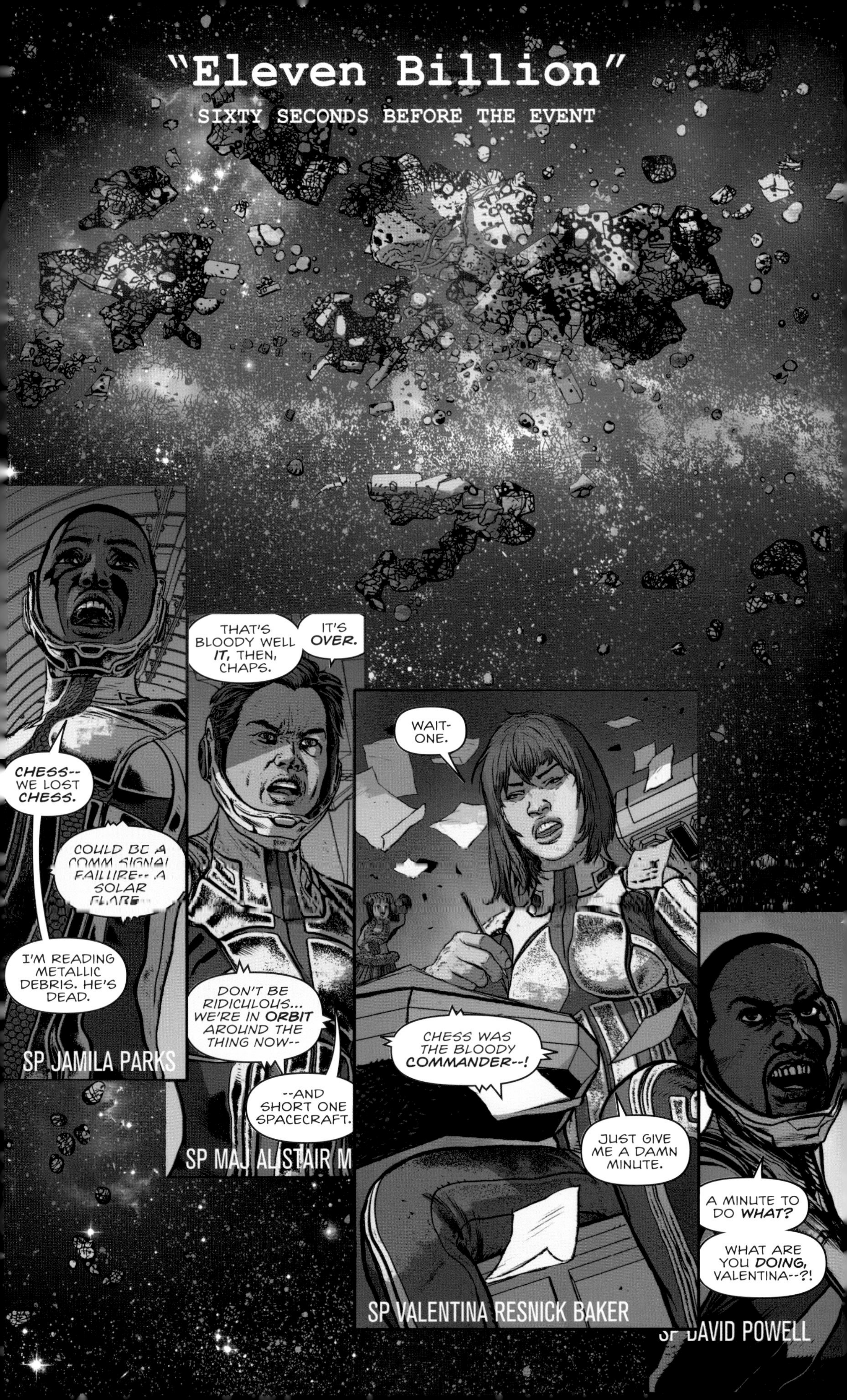
"Eleven Billion"
SIXTY SECONDS BEFORE THE EVENT
CHESS-- WE LOST CHESS.
COULD BE A COMM SIGNAL FAILURE-- A SOLAR FLARE--
I'M READING METALLIC DEBRIS. HE'S DEAD.
SP JAMILA PARKS
THAT'S BLOODY WELL IT, THEN, CHAPS.
IT'S OVER.
DON'T BE RIDICULOUS... WE'RE IN ORBIT AROUND THE THING NOW--
--AND SHORT ONE SPACECRAFT.
SP MAJ ALISTAIR M
WAIT-ONE.
CHESS WAS THE BLOODY COMMANDER--!
JUST GIVE ME A DAMN MINUTE.
SP VALENTINA RESNICK BAKER
A MINUTE TO DO WHAT?
WHAT ARE YOU DOING, VALENTINA--?!
DAVID POWELL

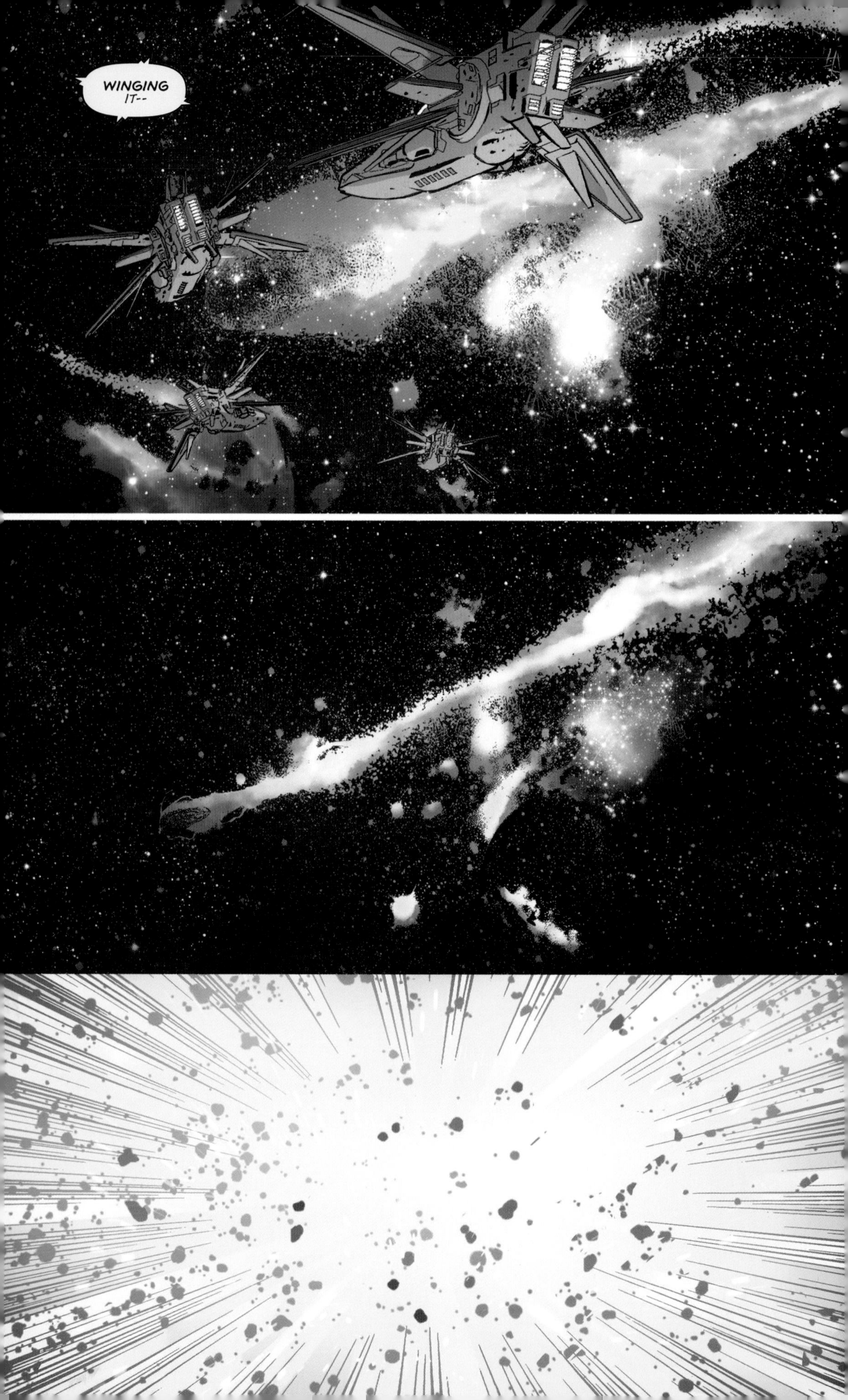
WINGING IT--

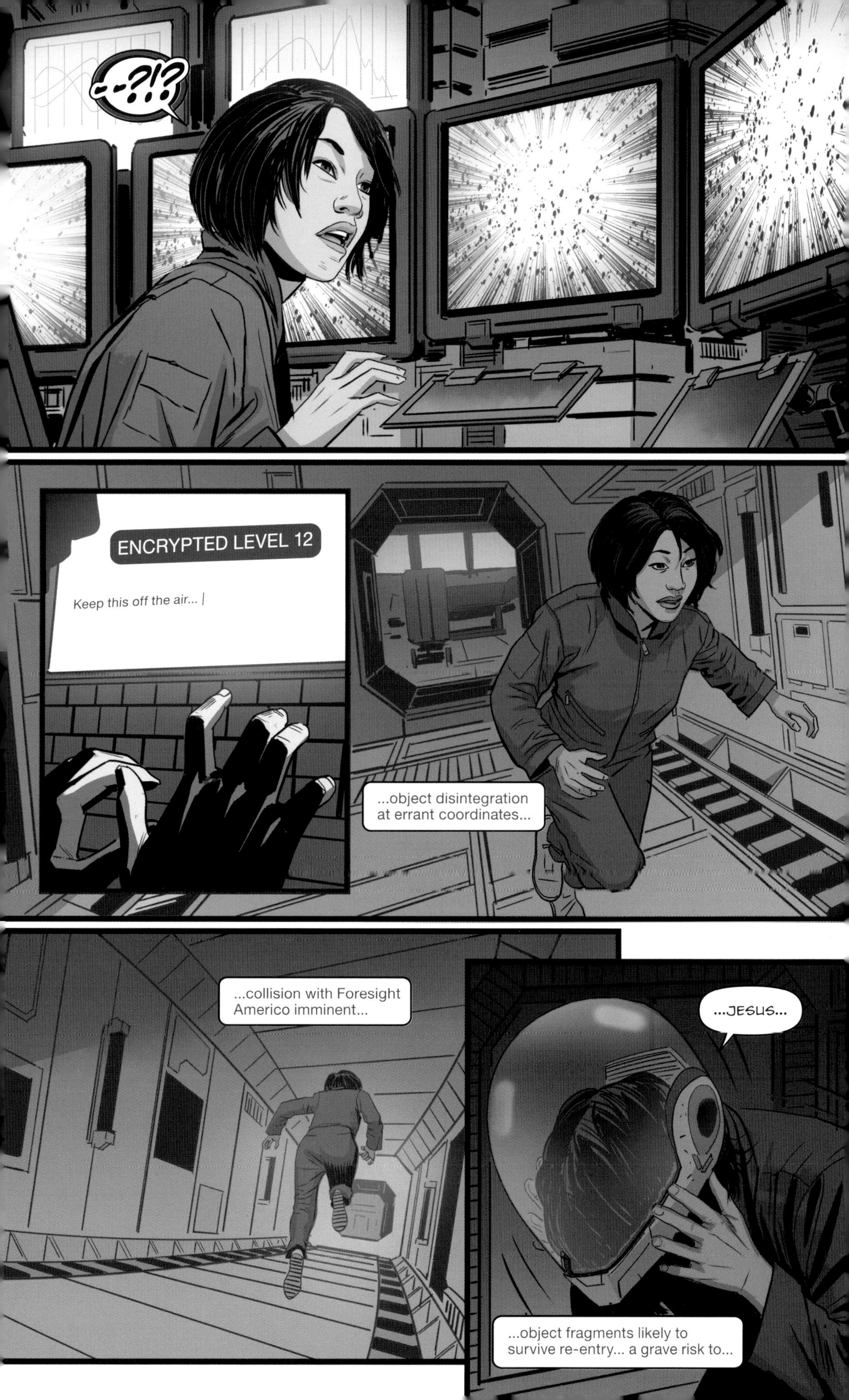
--?!?
ENCRYPTED LEVEL 12
Keep this off the air... |
...object disintegration at errant coordinates...
...collision with Foresight Americo imminent...
...JESUS...
...object fragments likely to survive re-entry... a grave risk to...

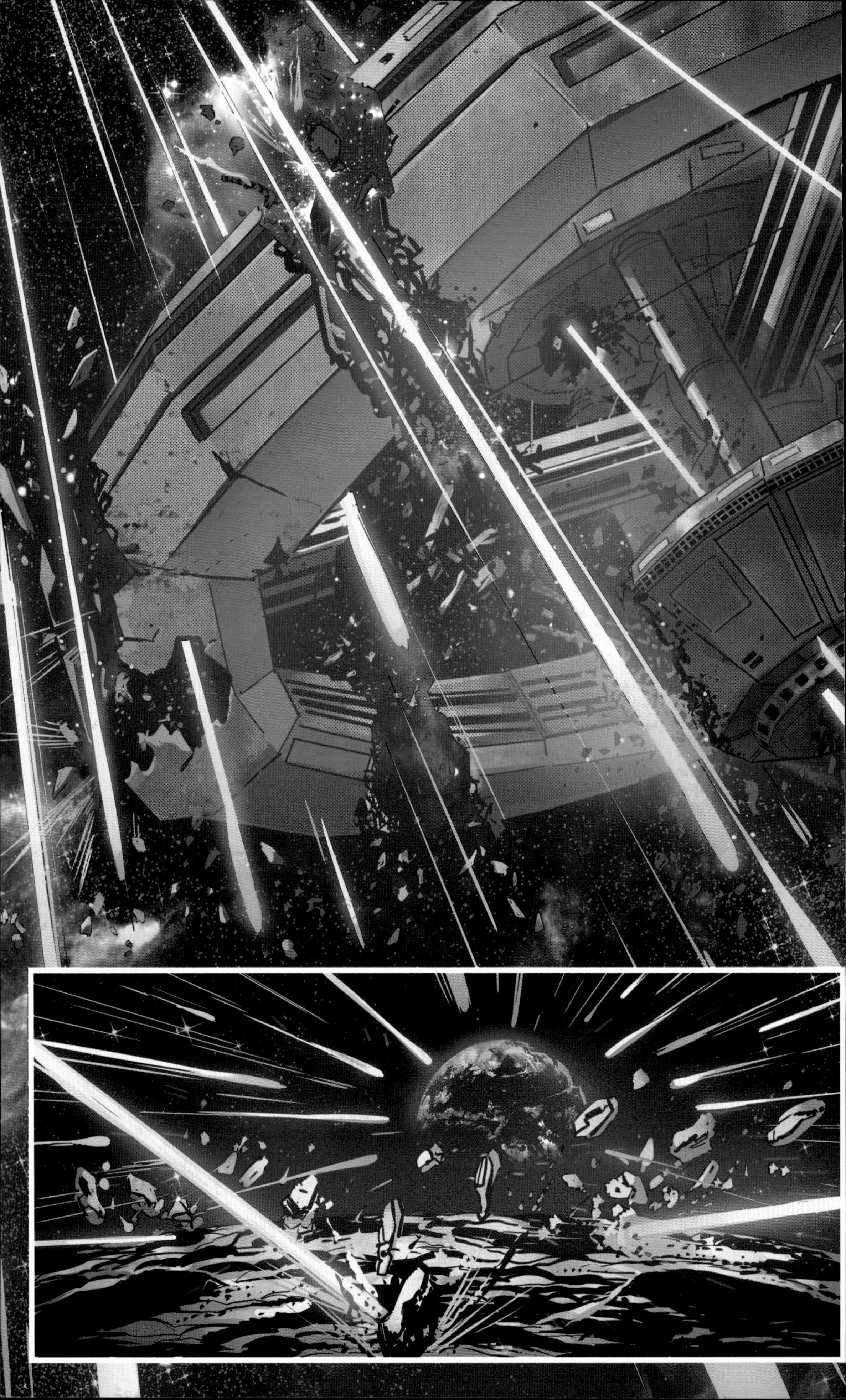

“The Beginning”

THE EVENT

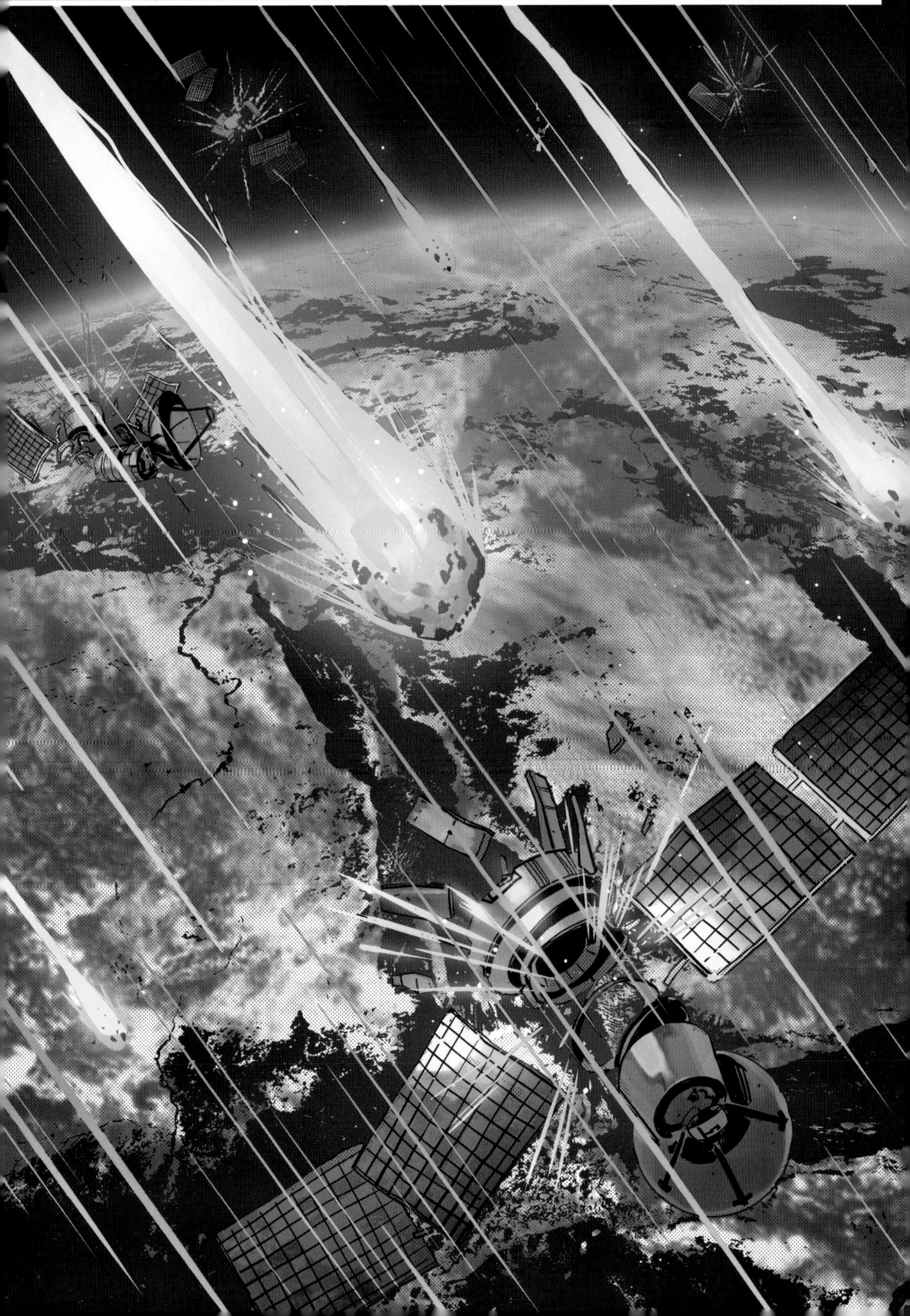

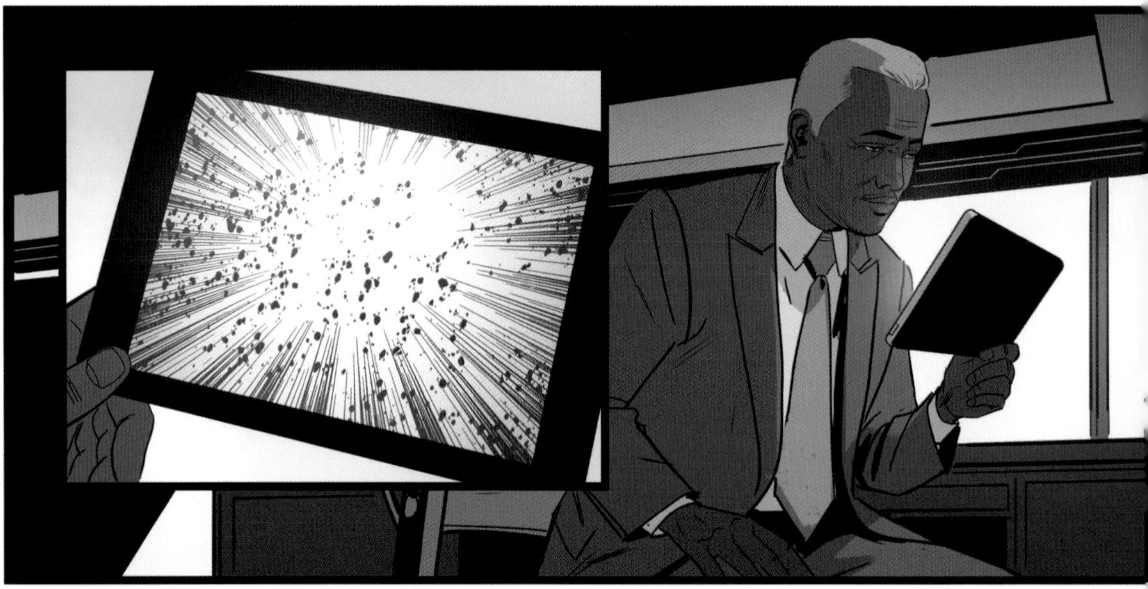

"Clouds"

TWO WEEKS AFTER THE EVENT

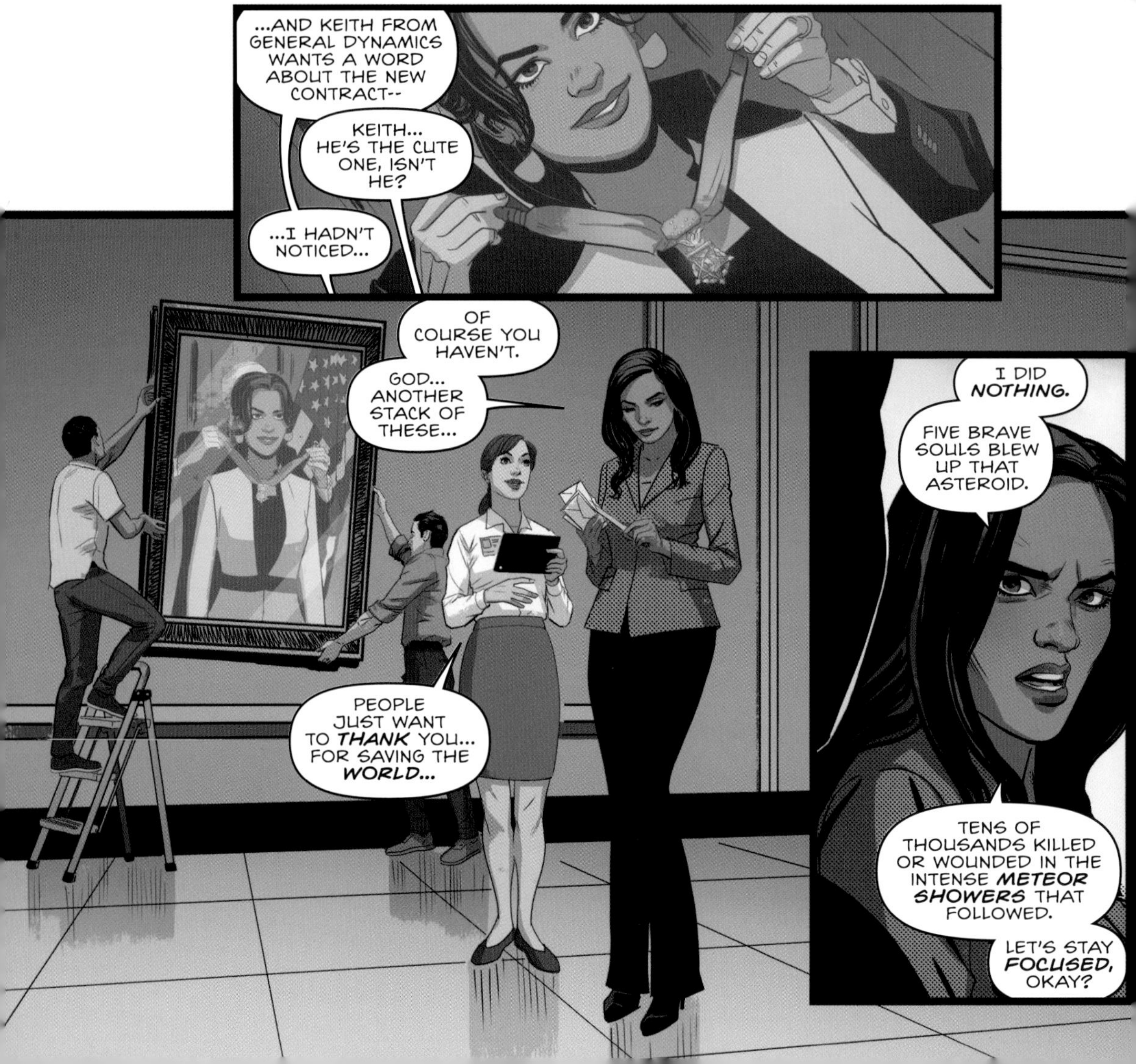

...AND KEITH FROM GENERAL DYNAMICS WANTS A WORD ABOUT THE NEW CONTRACT--
KEITH... HE'S THE CUTE ONE, ISN'T HE?
...I HADN'T NOTICED...
OF COURSE YOU HAVEN'T.
GOD... ANOTHER STACK OF THESE...
PEOPLE JUST WANT TO ***THANK*** YOU... FOR SAVING THE ***WORLD...***
I DID ***NOTHING.***
FIVE BRAVE SOULS BLEW UP THAT ASTEROID.
TENS OF THOUSANDS KILLED OR WOUNDED IN THE INTENSE ***METEOR SHOWERS*** THAT FOLLOWED.
LET'S STAY ***FOCUSED,*** OKAY?

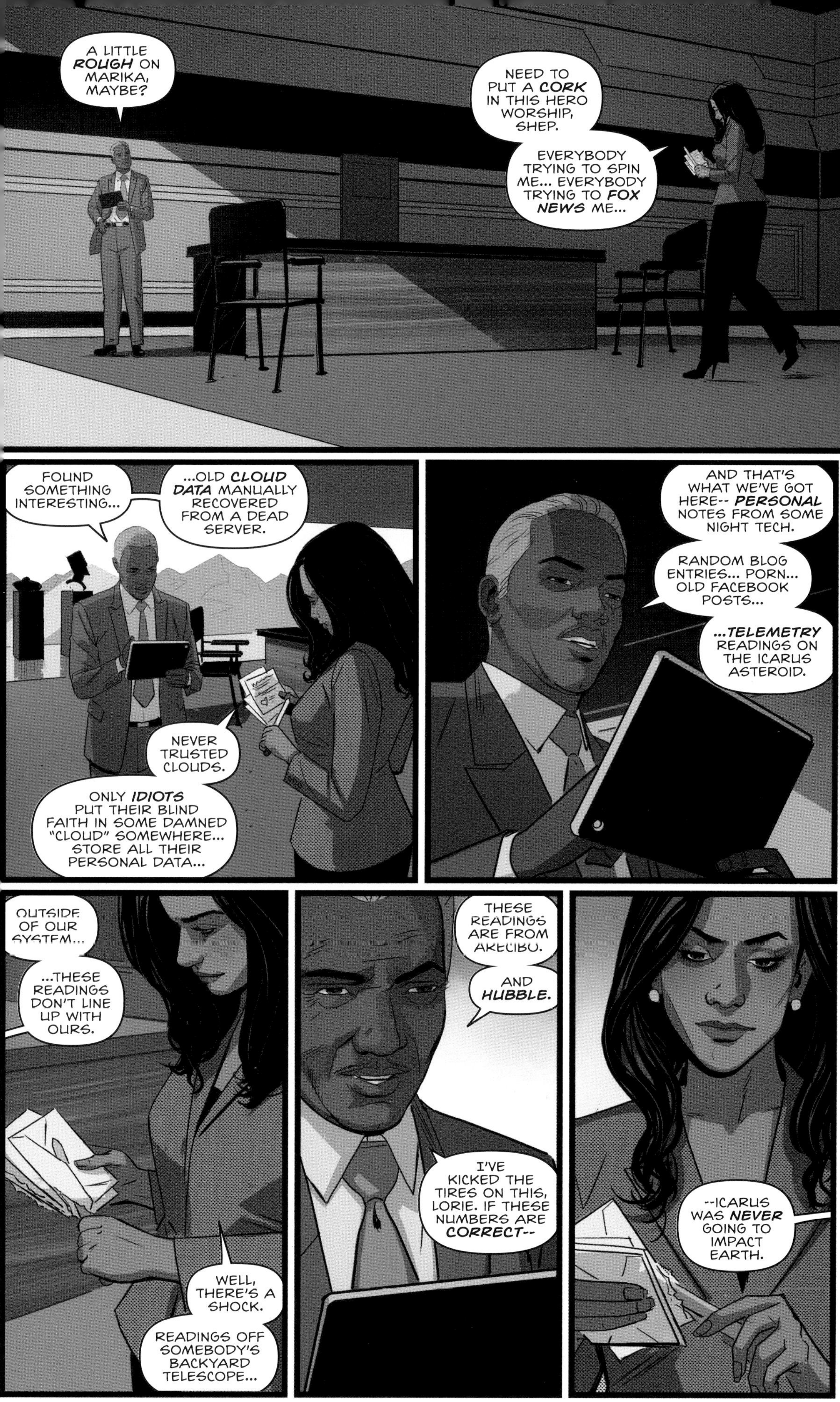
A LITTLE ROUGH ON MARIKA, MAYBE?
NEED TO PUT A CORK IN THIS HERO WORSHIP, SHEP.
EVERYBODY TRYING TO SPIN ME... EVERYBODY TRYING TO FOX NEWS ME...
FOUND SOMETHING INTERESTING...
...OLD CLOUD DATA MANUALLY RECOVERED FROM A DEAD SERVER.
NEVER TRUSTED CLOUDS.
ONLY IDIOTS PUT THEIR BLIND FAITH IN SOME DAMNED "CLOUD" SOMEWHERE... STORE ALL THEIR PERSONAL DATA...
AND THAT'S WHAT WE'VE GOT HERE-- PERSONAL NOTES FROM SOME NIGHT TECH.
RANDOM BLOG ENTRIES... PORN... OLD FACEBOOK POSTS...
...TELEMETRY READINGS ON THE ICARUS ASTEROID.
OUTSIDE OF OUR SYSTEM...
...THESE READINGS DON'T LINE UP WITH OURS.
WELL, THERE'S A SHOCK.
READINGS OFF SOMEBODY'S BACKYARD TELESCOPE...
THESE READINGS ARE FROM ARECIBO.
AND HUBBLE.
I'VE KICKED THE TIRES ON THIS, LORIE. IF THESE NUMBERS ARE CORRECT--
--ICARUS WAS NEVER GOING TO IMPACT EARTH.

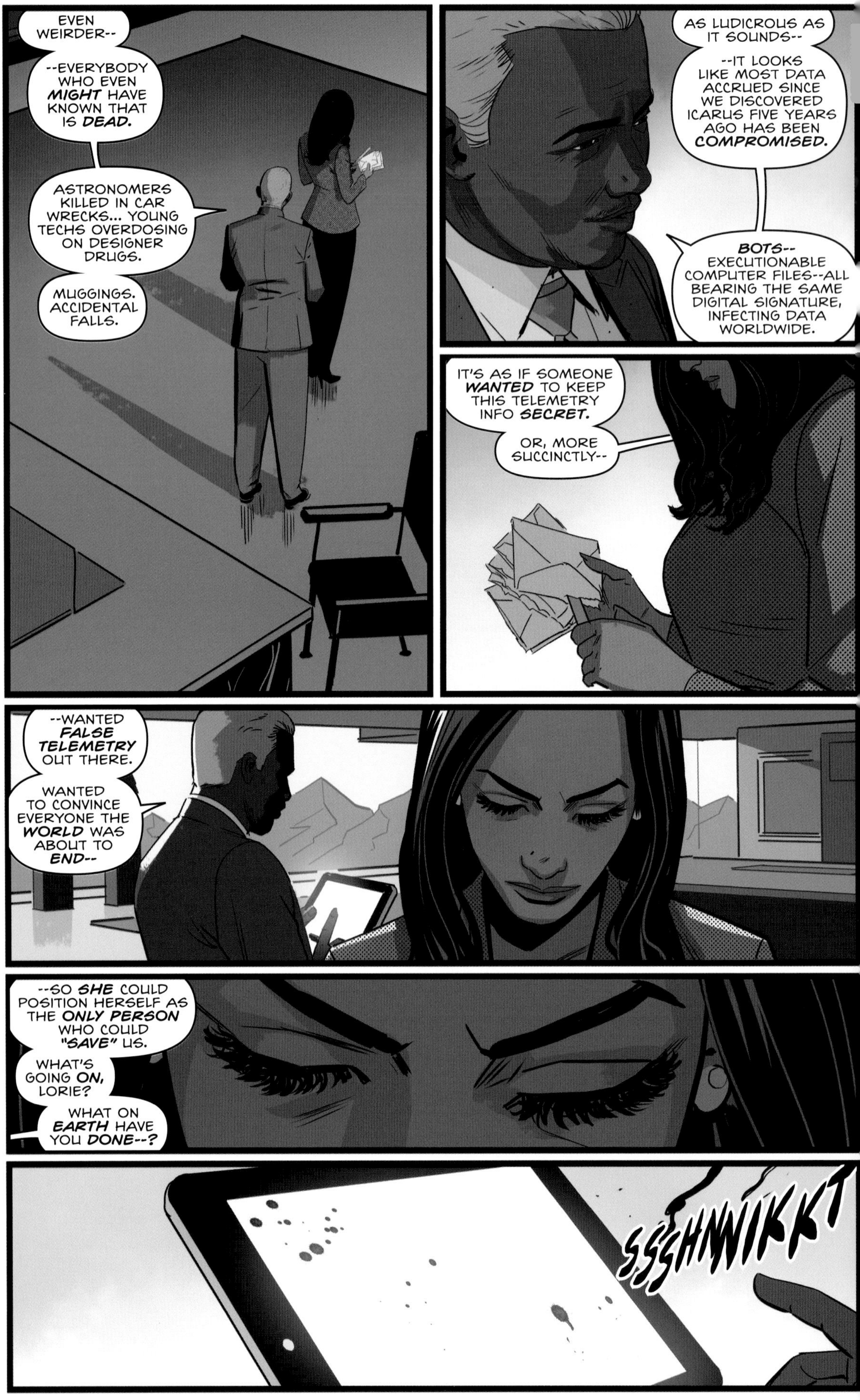
EVEN WEIRDER--
--EVERYBODY WHO EVEN MIGHT HAVE KNOWN THAT IS DEAD.
ASTRONOMERS KILLED IN CAR WRECKS... YOUNG TECHS OVERDOSING ON DESIGNER DRUGS.
MUGGINGS. ACCIDENTAL FALLS.
AS LUDICROUS AS IT SOUNDS--
--IT LOOKS LIKE MOST DATA ACCRUED SINCE WE DISCOVERED ICARUS FIVE YEARS AGO HAS BEEN COMPROMISED.
BOTS--EXECUTIONABLE COMPUTER FILES--ALL BEARING THE SAME DIGITAL SIGNATURE, INFECTING DATA WORLDWIDE.
IT'S AS IF SOMEONE WANTED TO KEEP THIS TELEMETRY INFO SECRET.
OR, MORE SUCCINCTLY--
--WANTED FALSE TELEMETRY OUT THERE.
WANTED TO CONVINCE EVERYONE THE WORLD WAS ABOUT TO END--
--SO SHE COULD POSITION HERSELF AS THE ONLY PERSON WHO COULD "SAVE" US.
WHAT'S GOING ON, LORIE?
WHAT ON EARTH HAVE YOU DONE--?
SSSHNIKKT

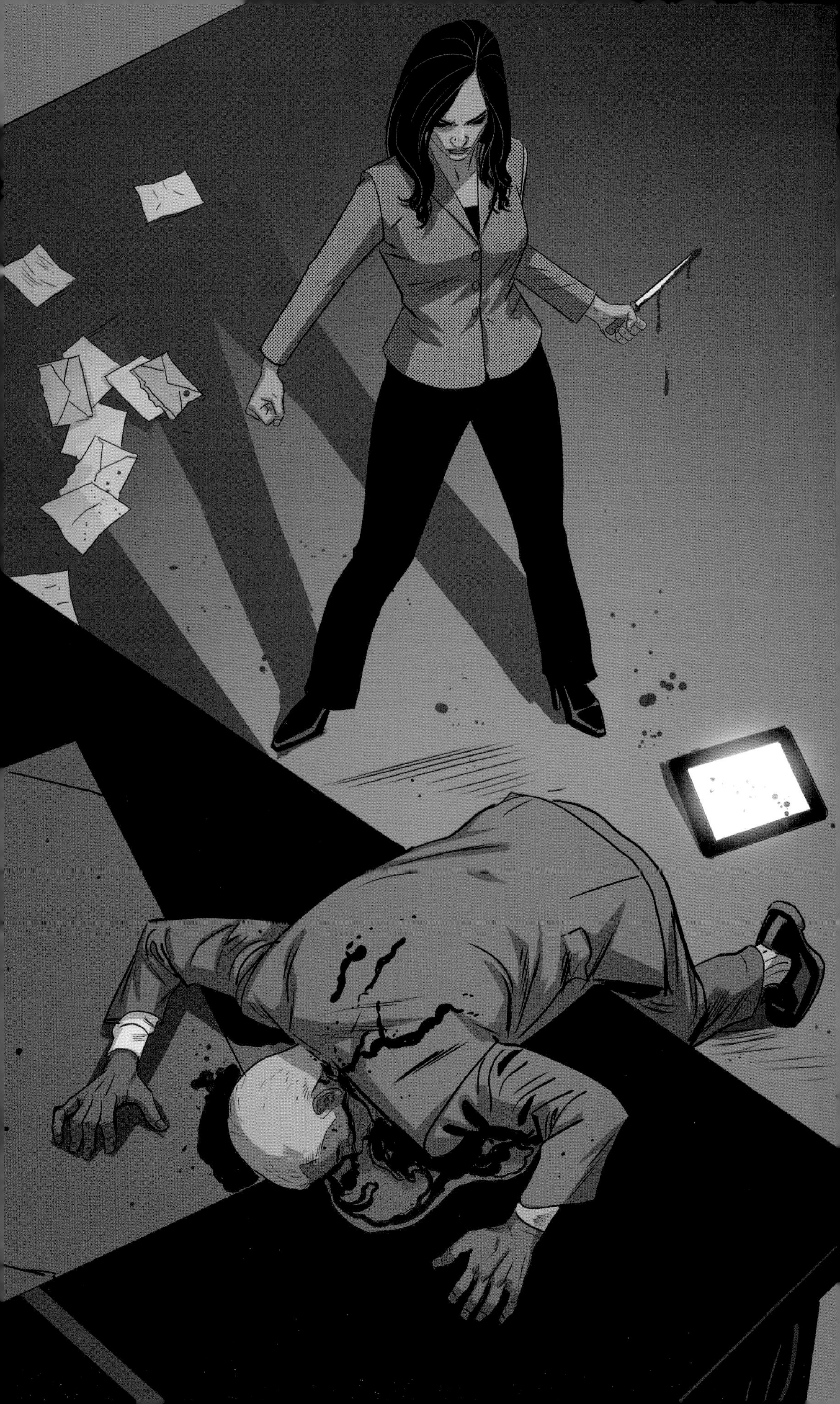

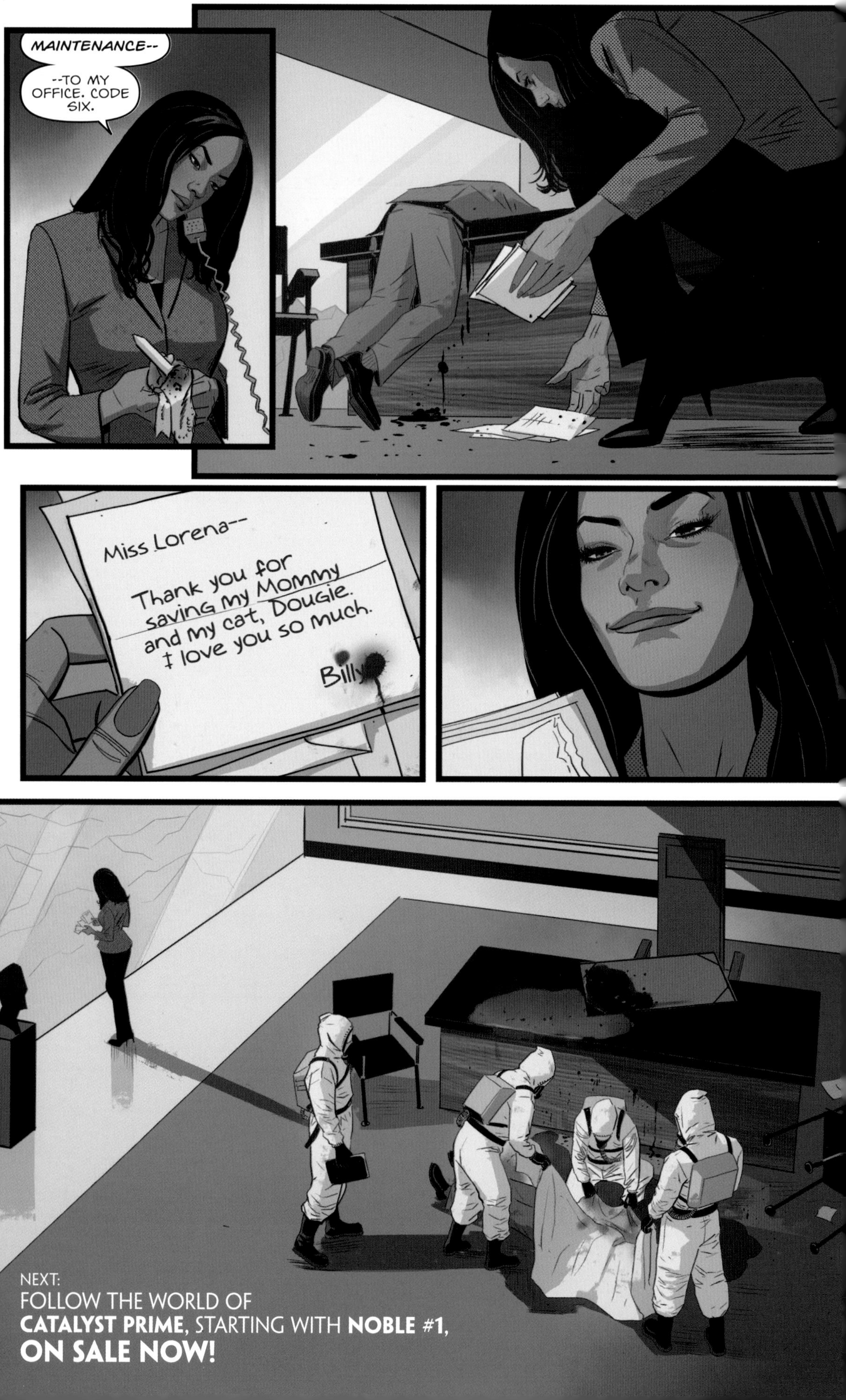
MAINTENANCE--
--TO MY OFFICE. CODE SIX.
Miss Lorena--
Thank you for saving my Mommy and my cat, Dougie. I love you so much.
Billy
NEXT:
FOLLOW THE WORLD OF CATALYST PRIME, STARTING WITH NOBLE #1, ON SALE NOW!

COVER GALLERY

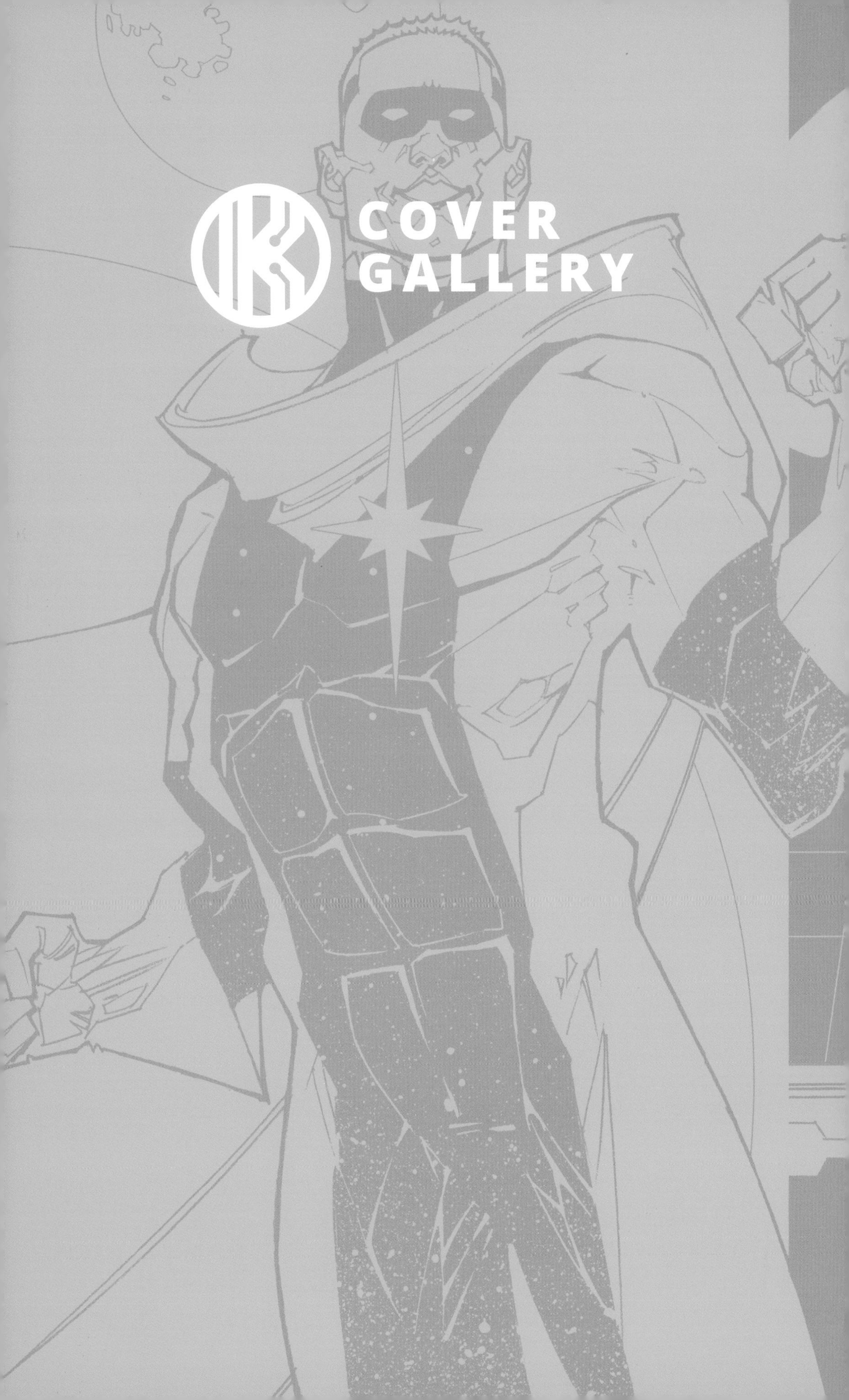

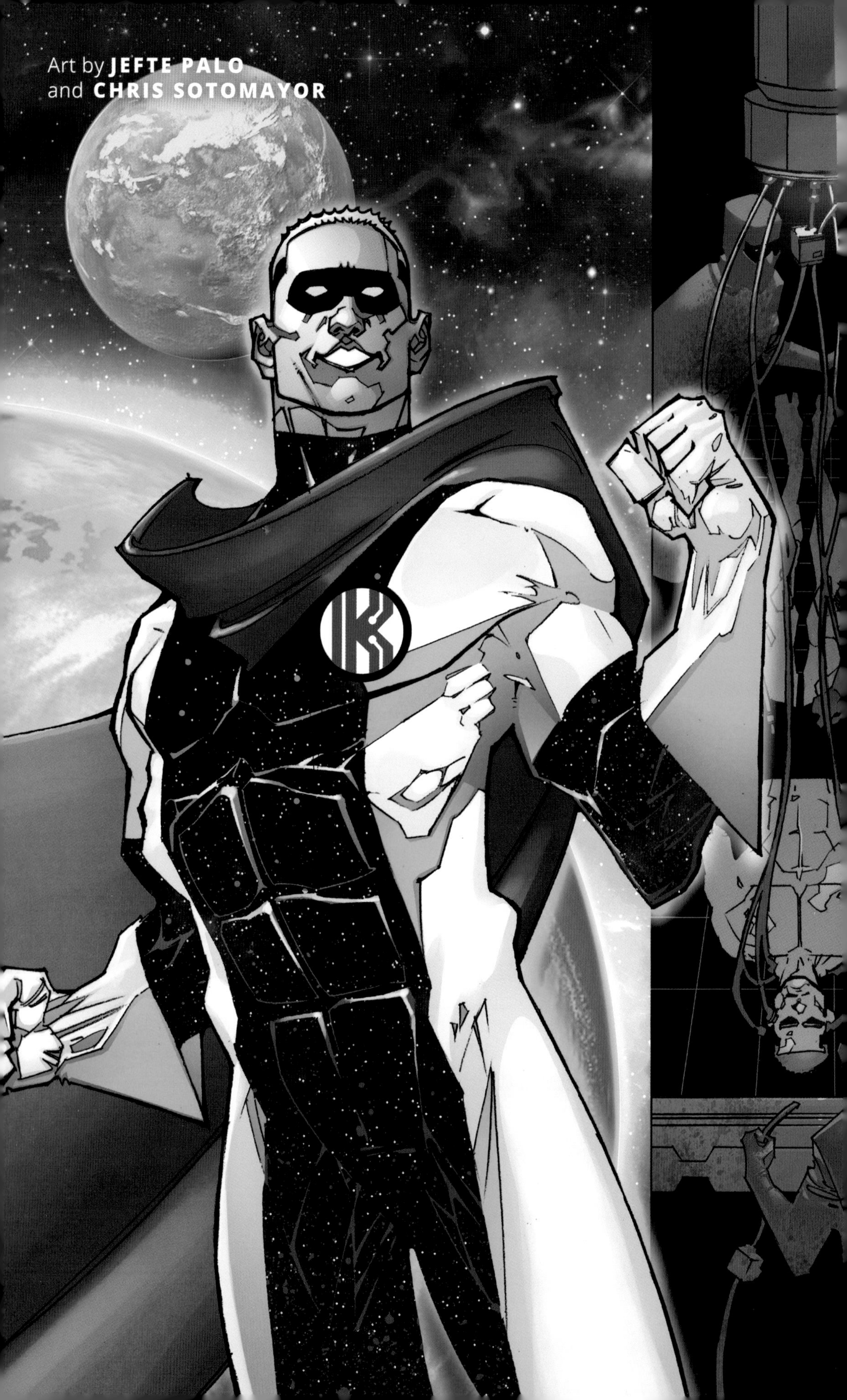
Art by JEFTE PALO
and CHRIS SOTOMAYOR

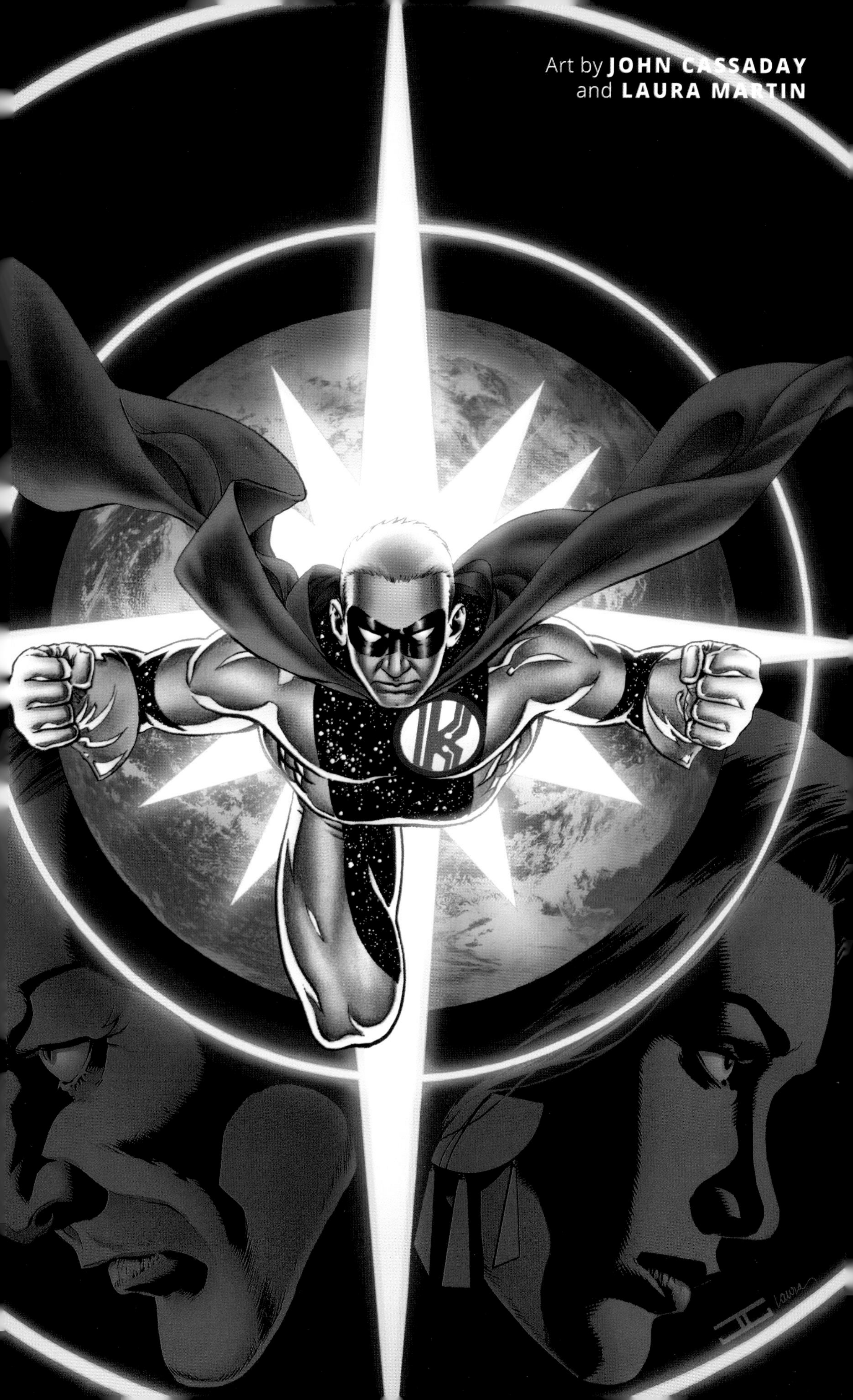

Art by **JOHN CASSADAY**
and **LAURA MARTIN**

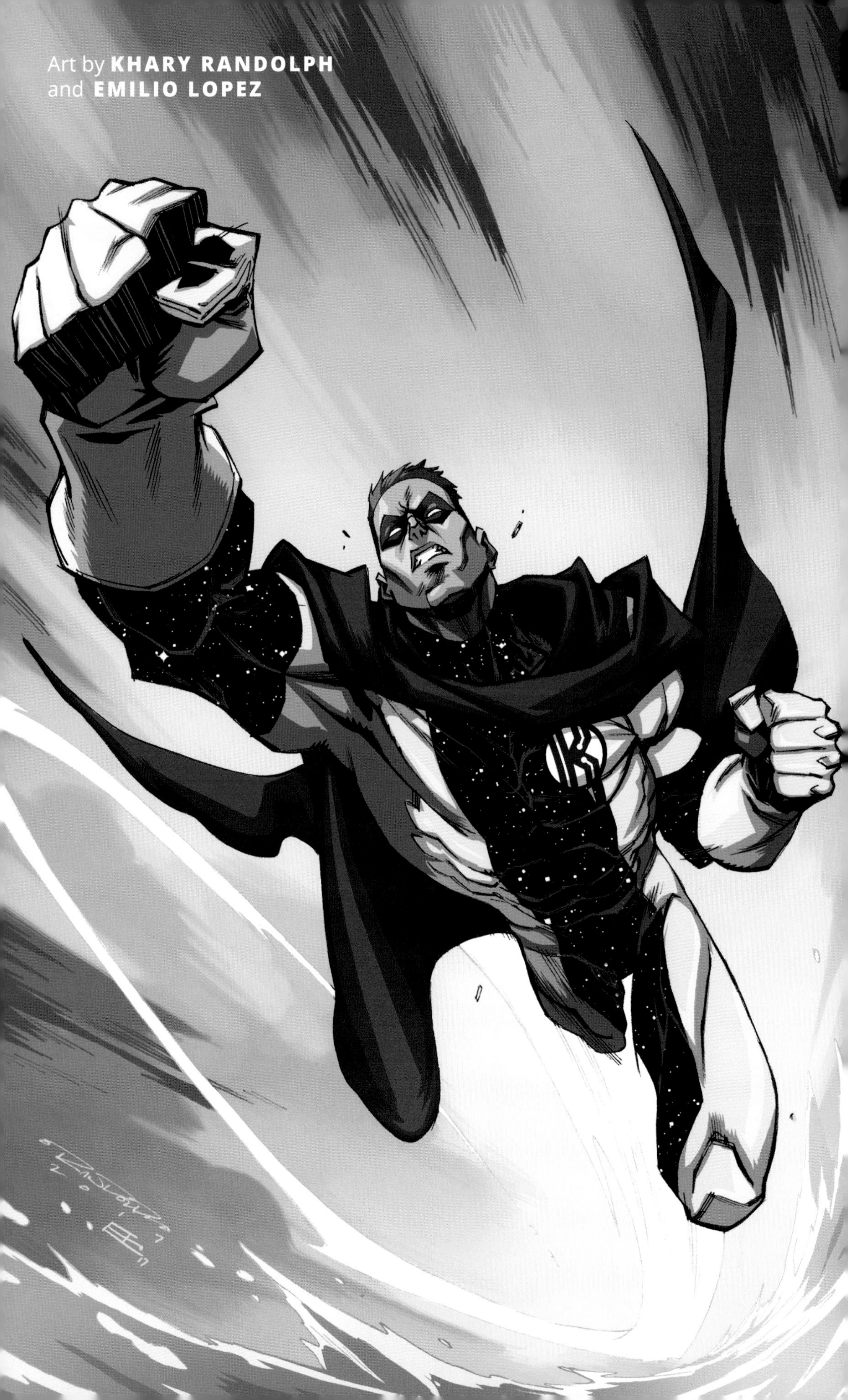

Art by **KHARY RANDOLPH**
and **EMILIO LOPEZ**

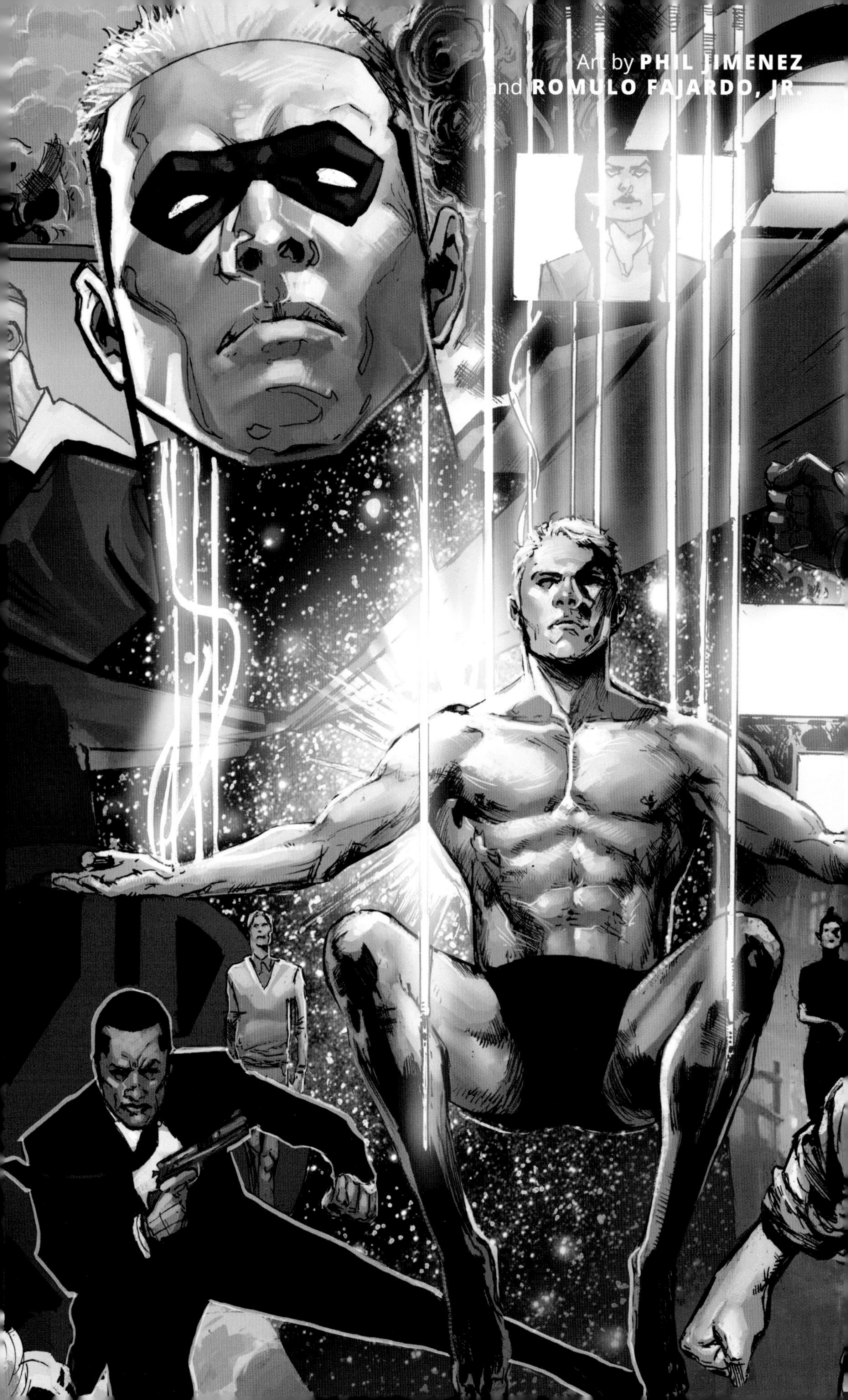
Art by **PHIL JIMENEZ**
and **ROMULO FAJARDO, JR.**

Art by **JEFTE PALO**
and **CHRIS SOTOMAYOR**

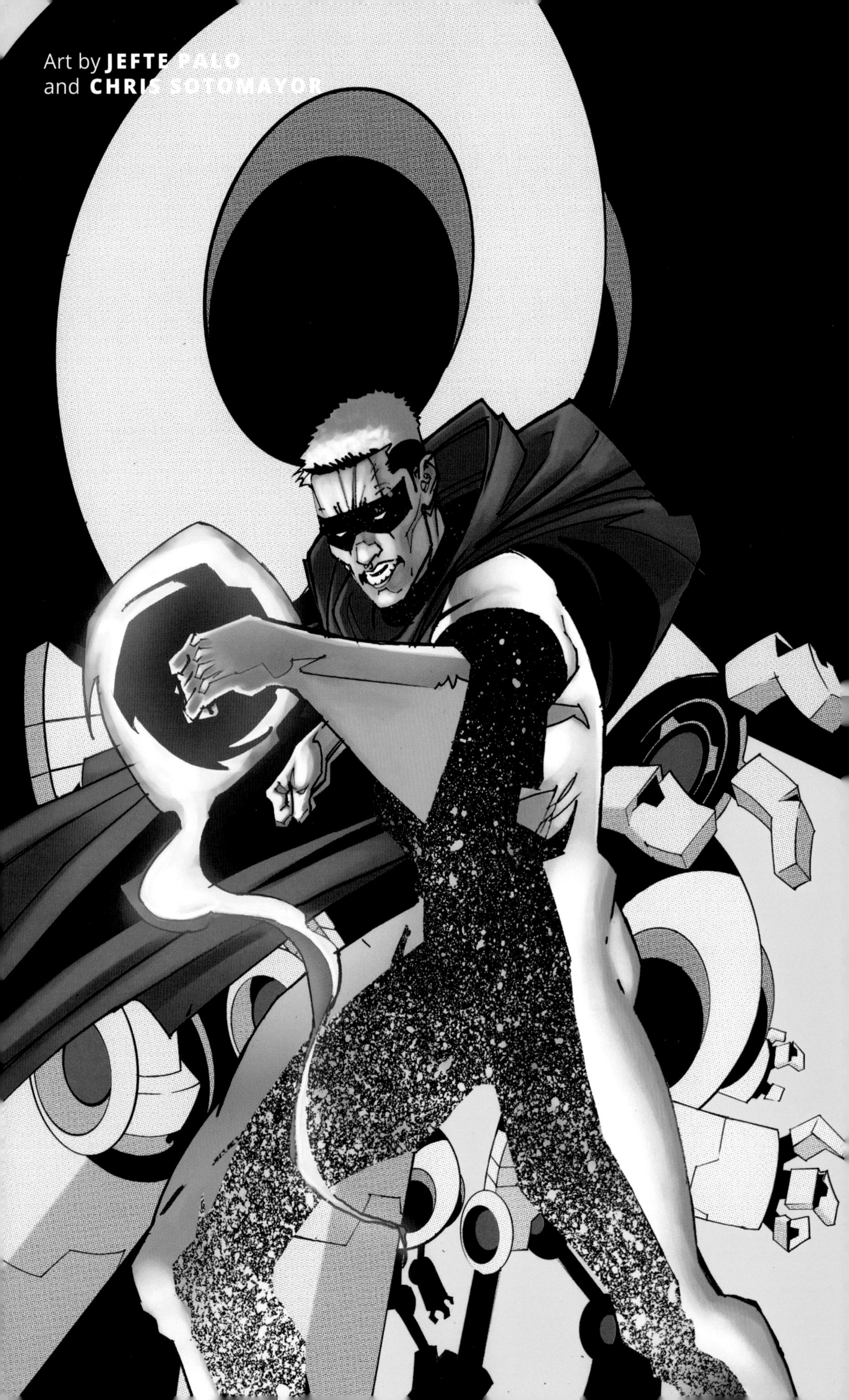

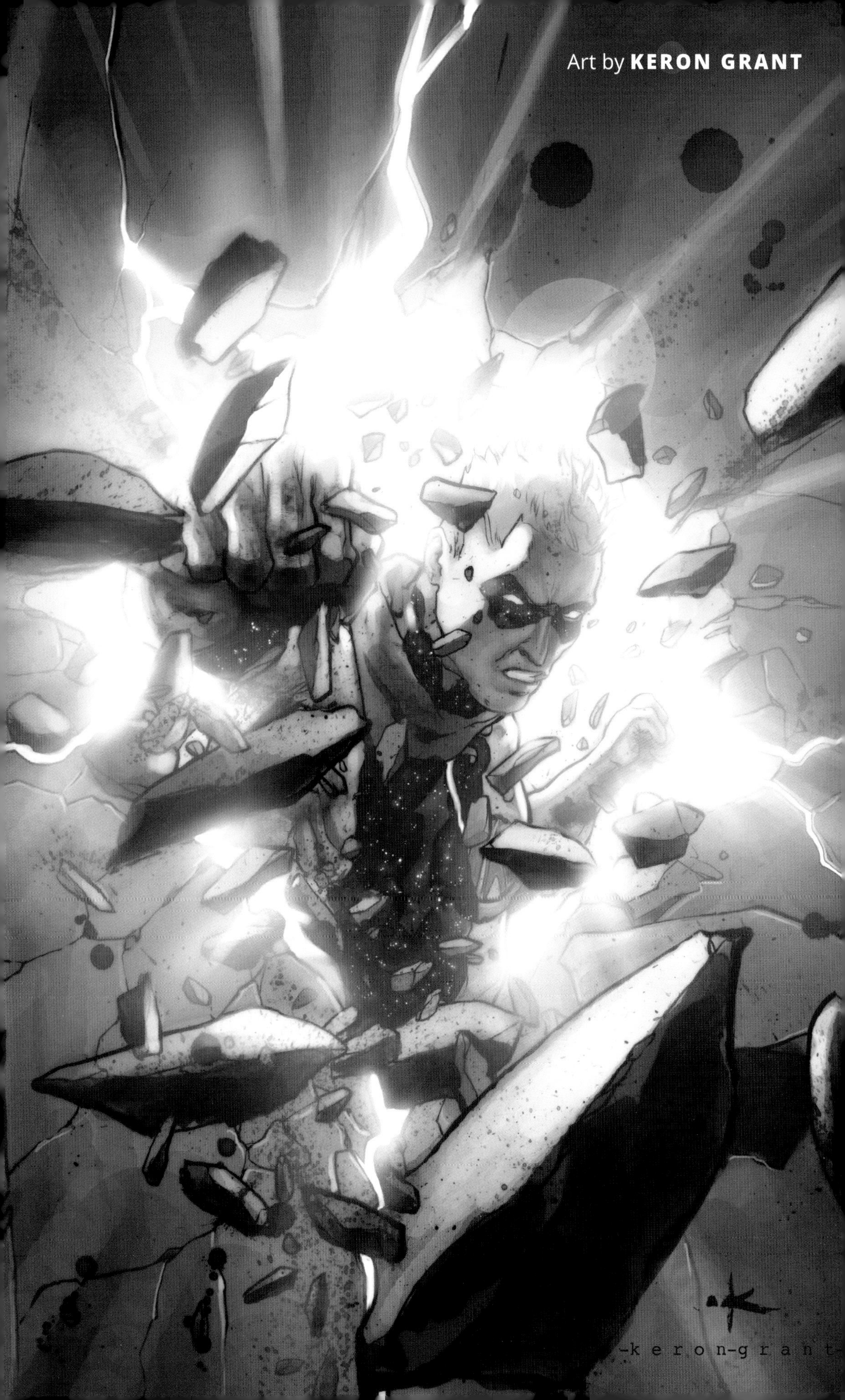
-keron-grant-
Art by **KERON GRANT**

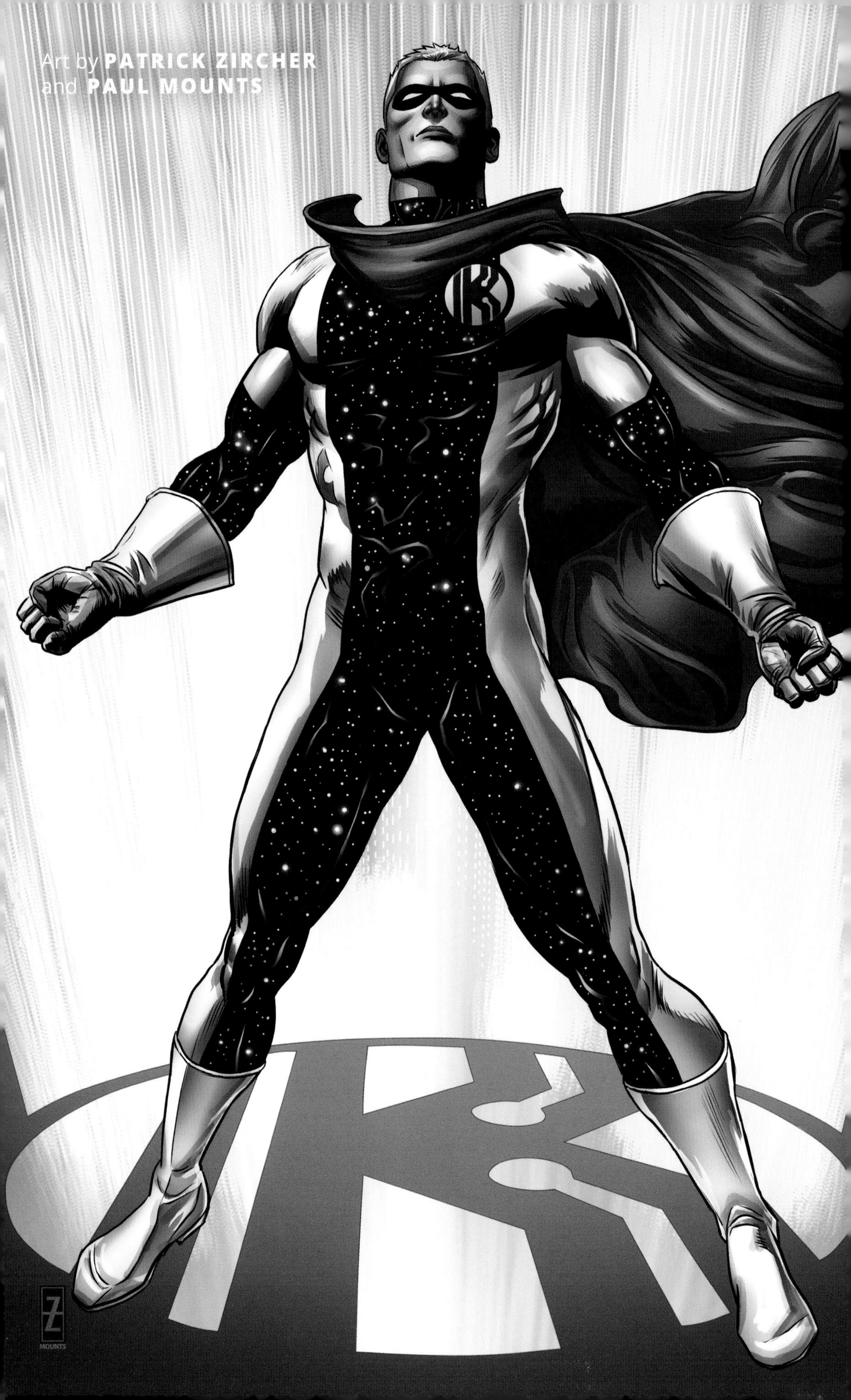
MOUNTS
Art by **PATRICK ZIRCHER**
and **PAUL MOUNTS**

Art by **JEFTE PALO**
and **CHRIS SOTOMAYOR**

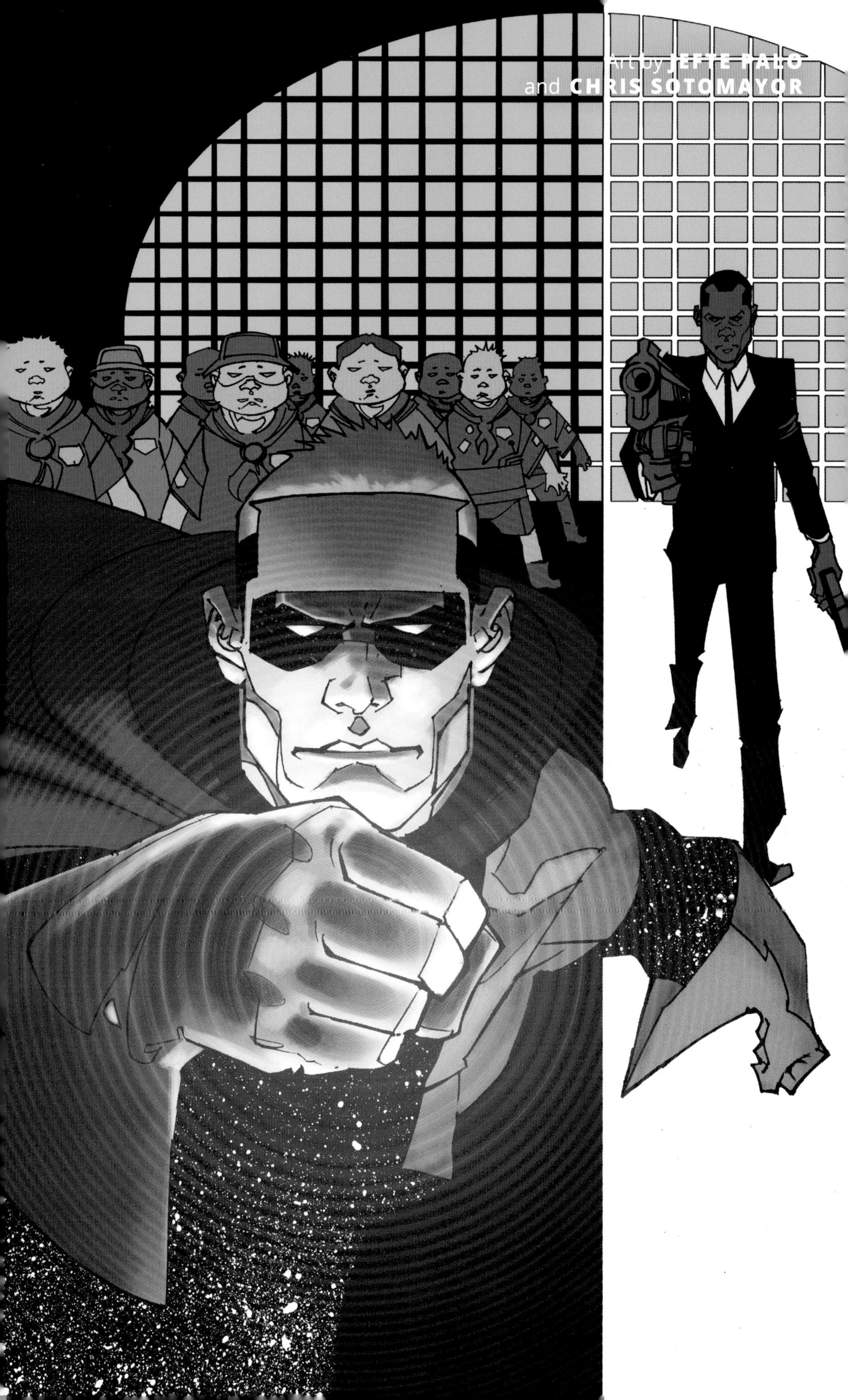

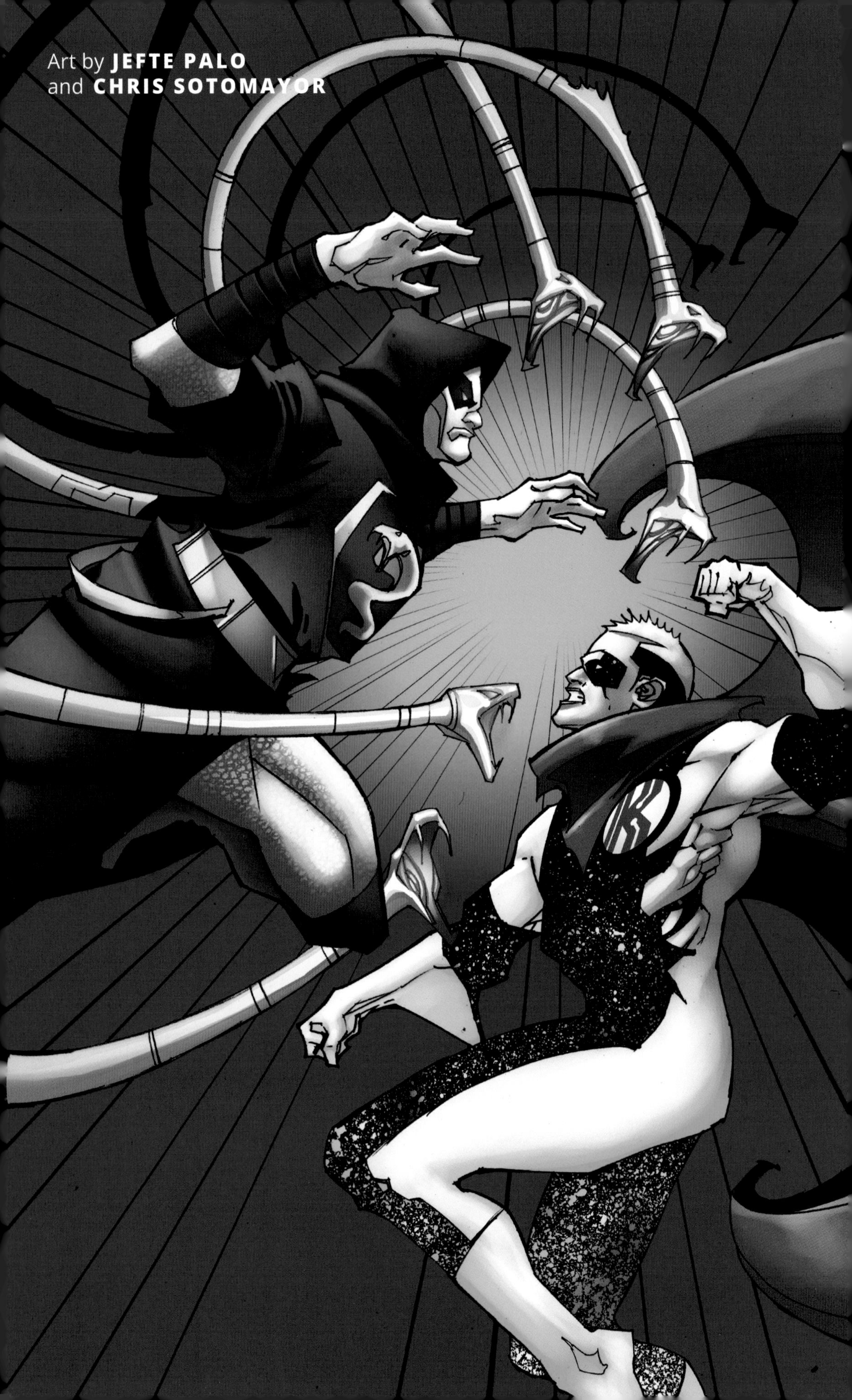

Art by **JEFTE PALO**
and **CHRIS SOTOMAYOR**

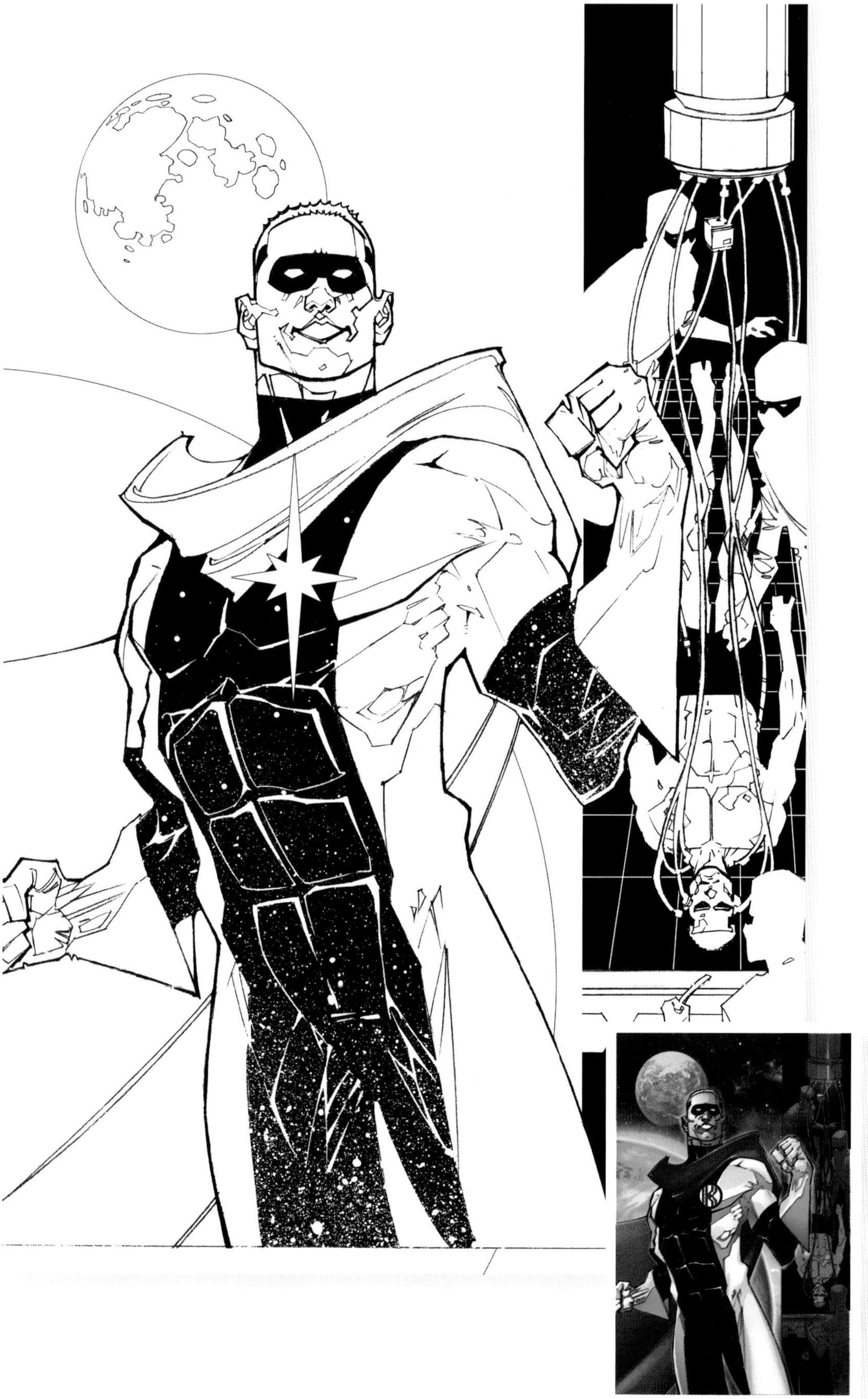

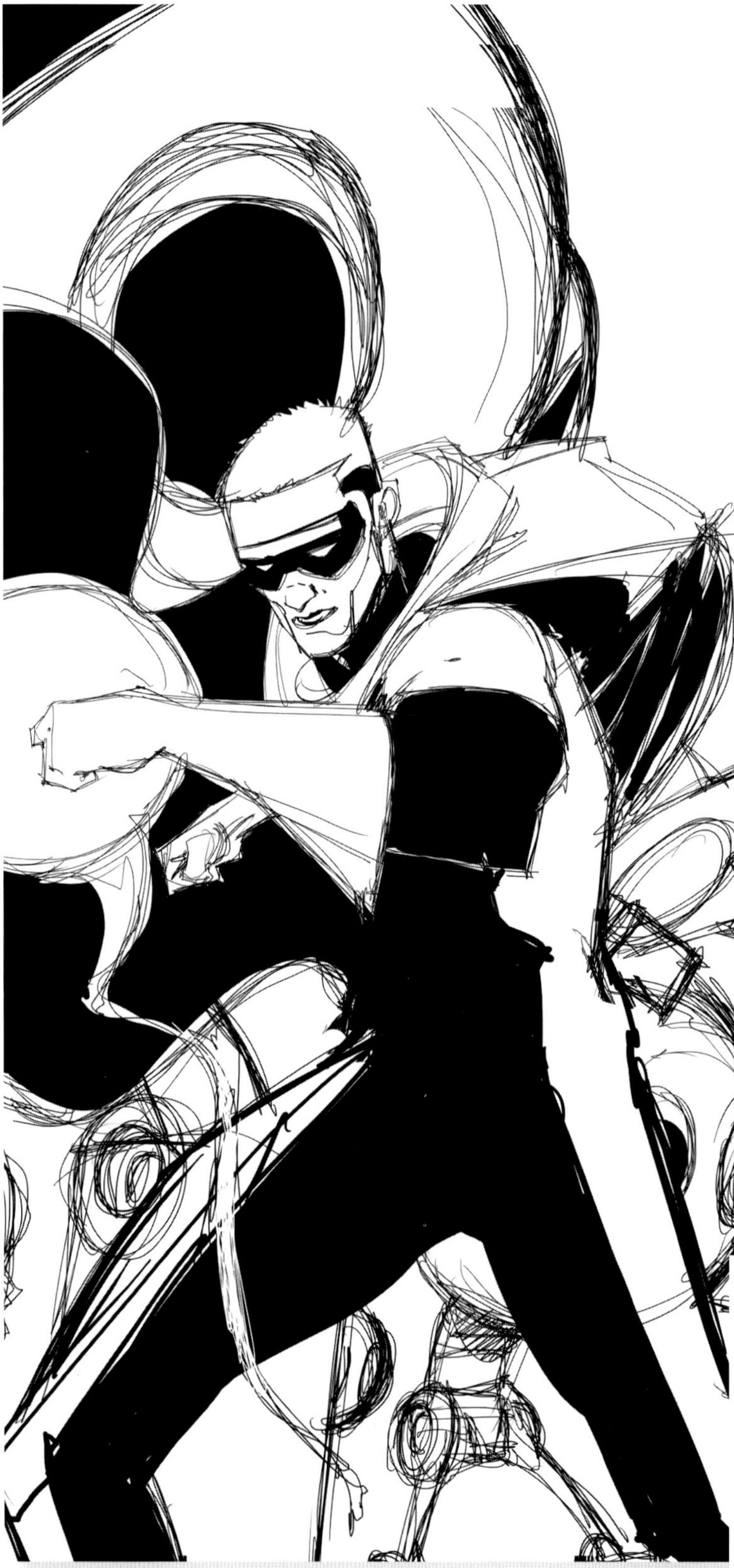
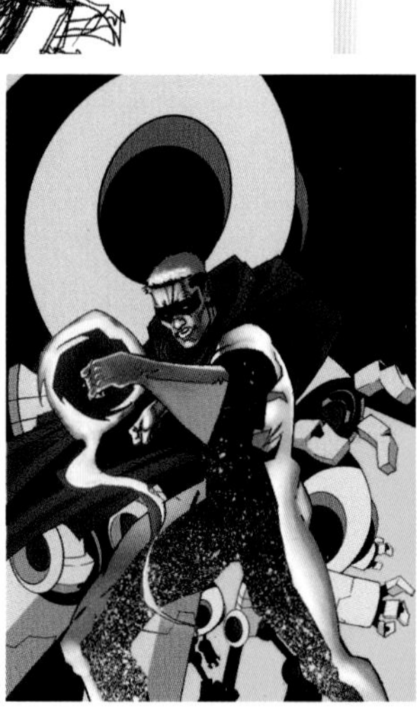

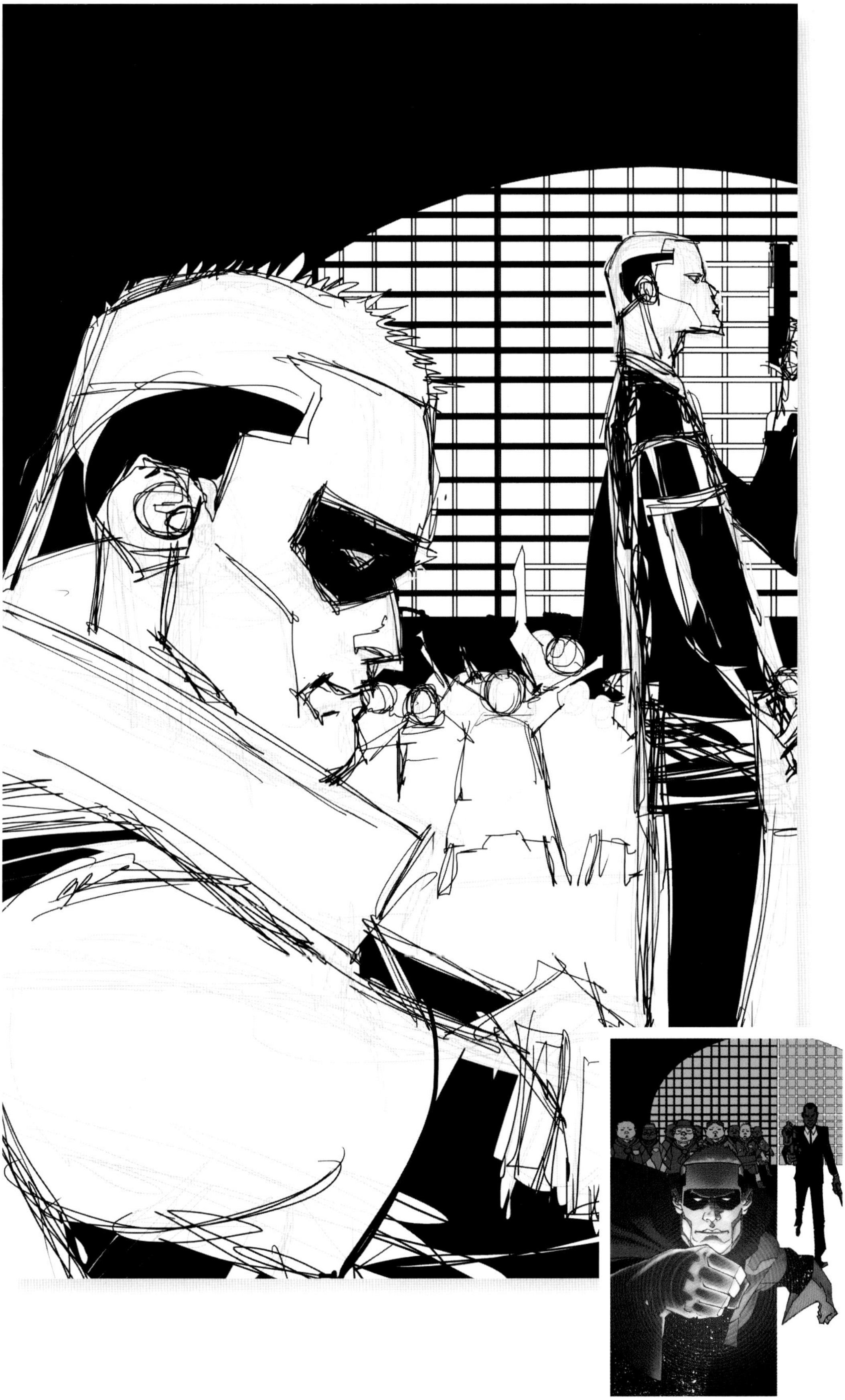

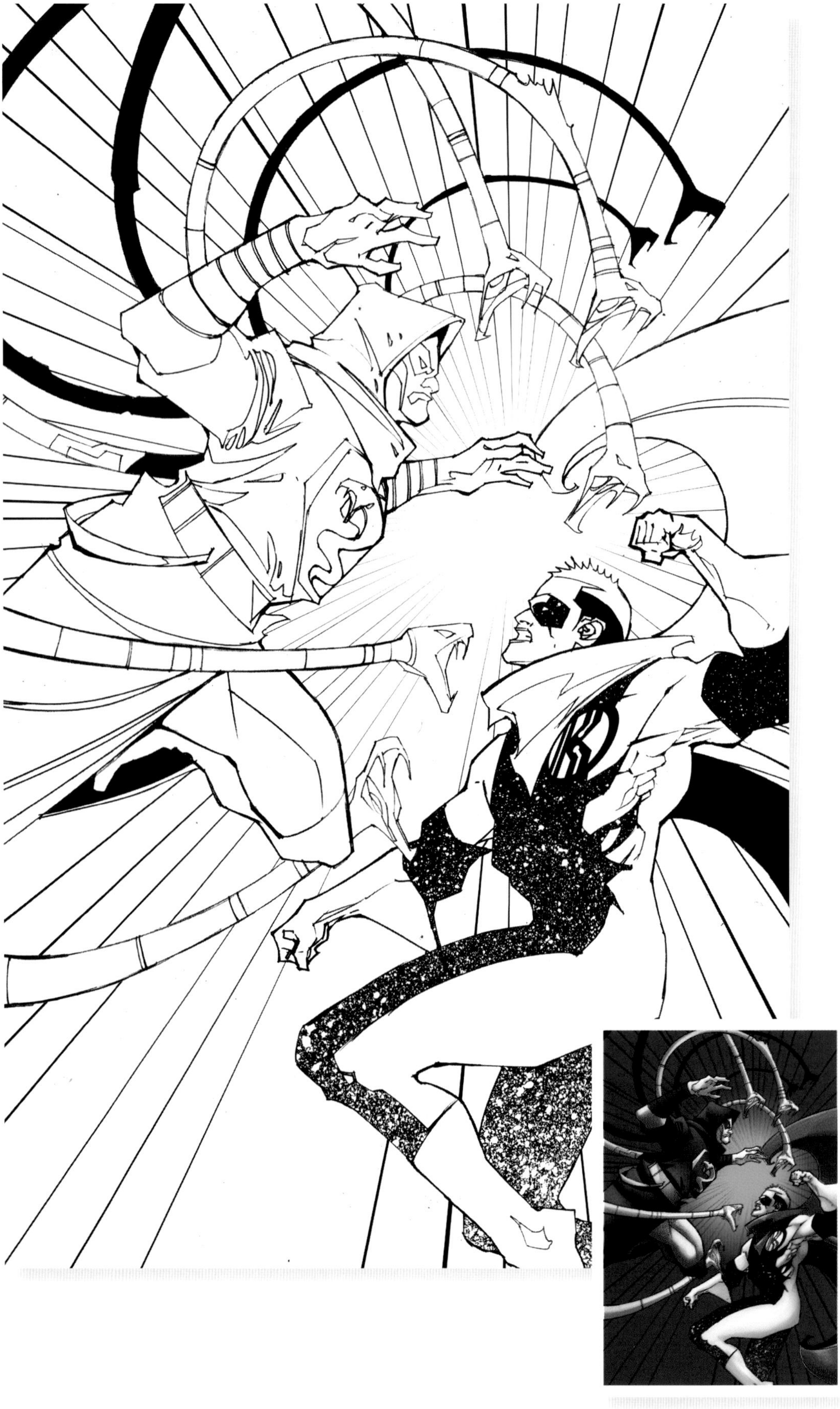

ASSANTE

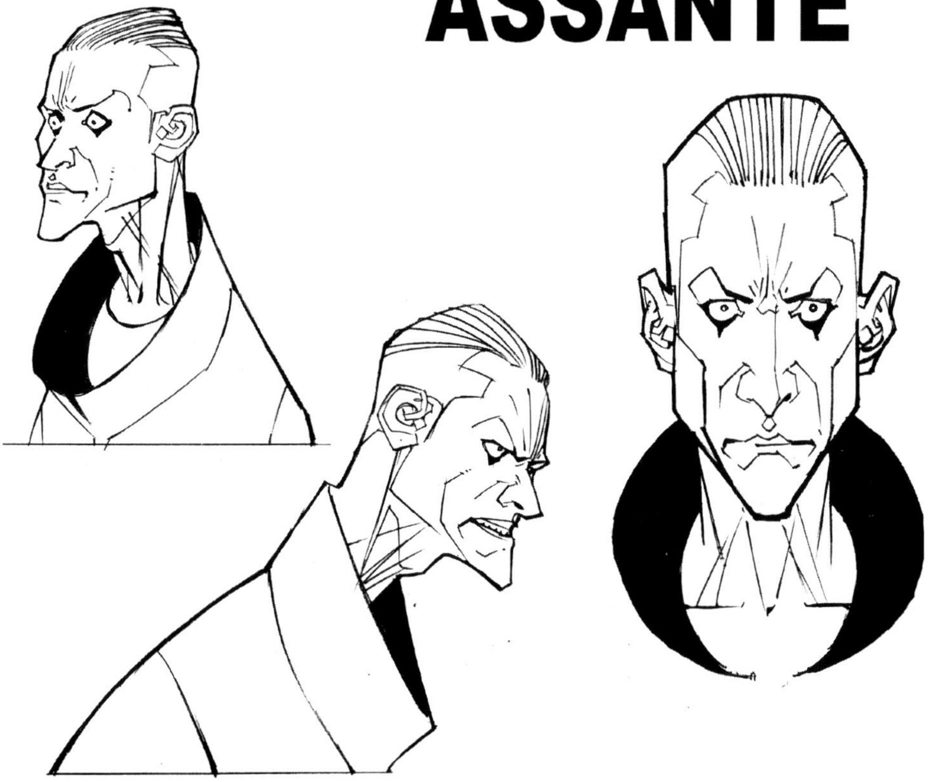

GILMOUR

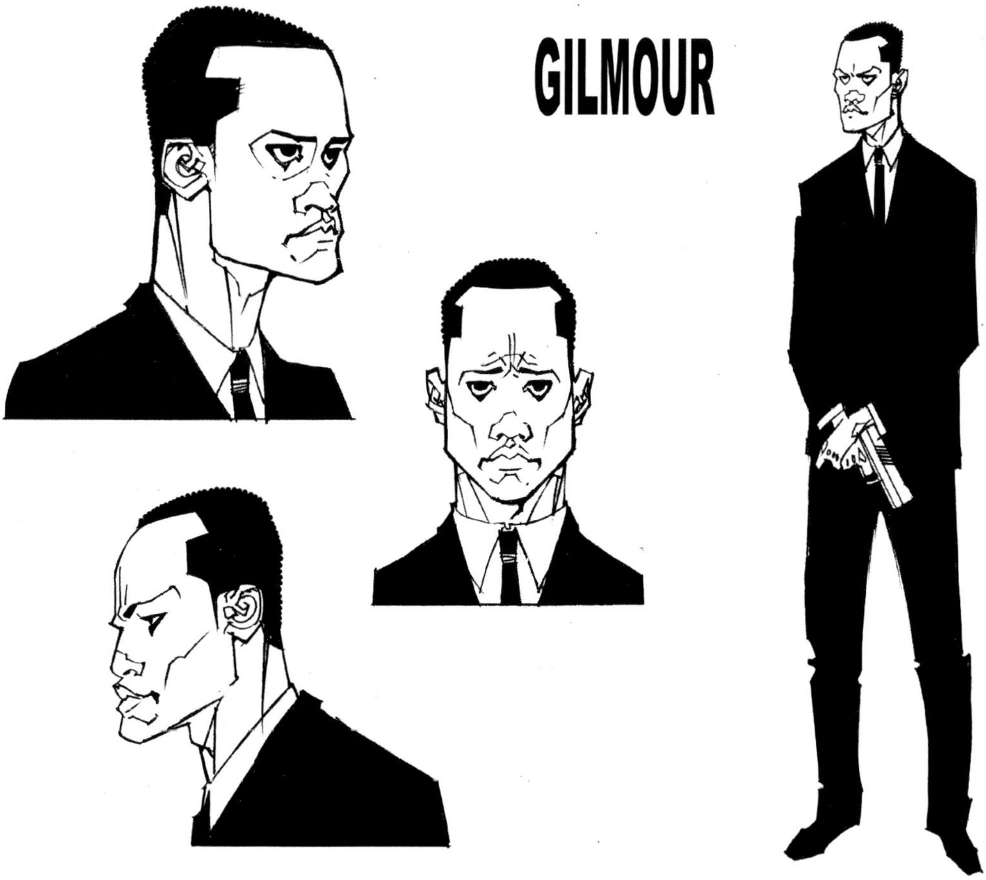

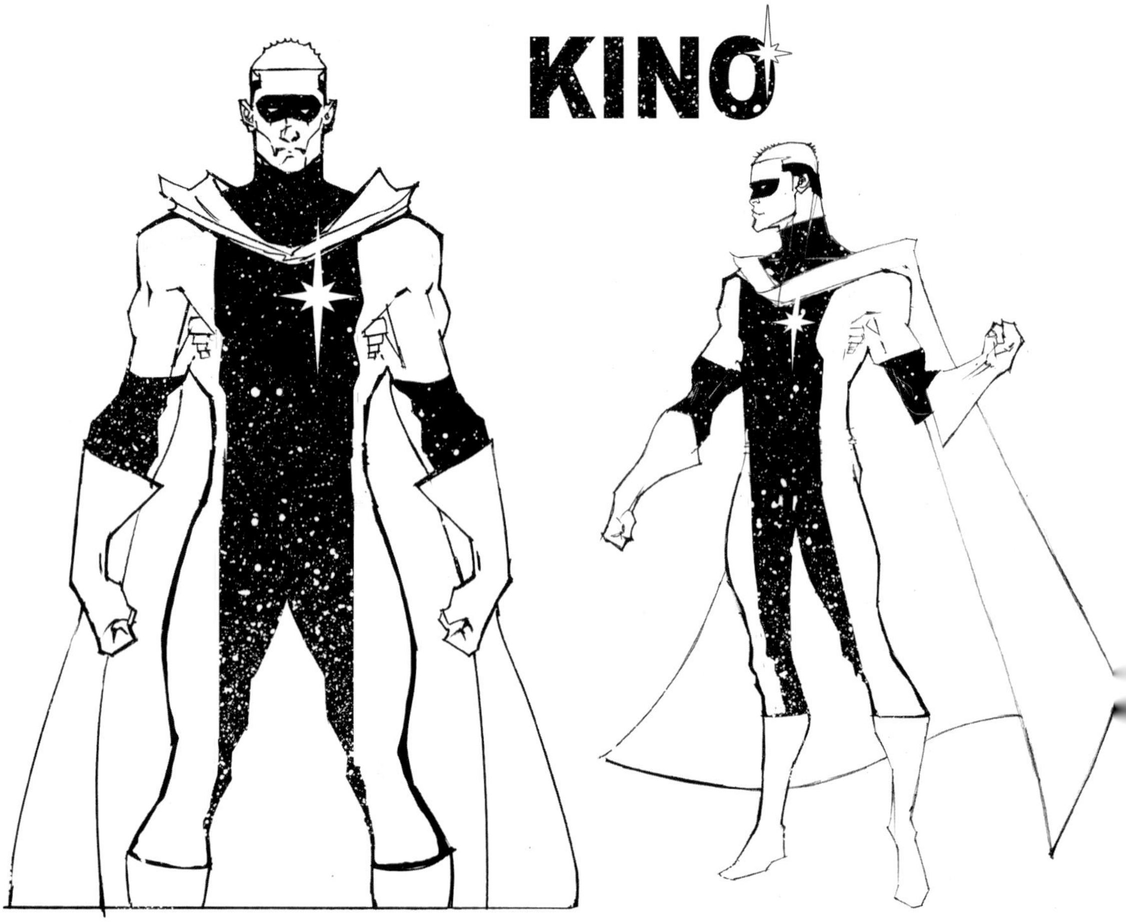
KINO

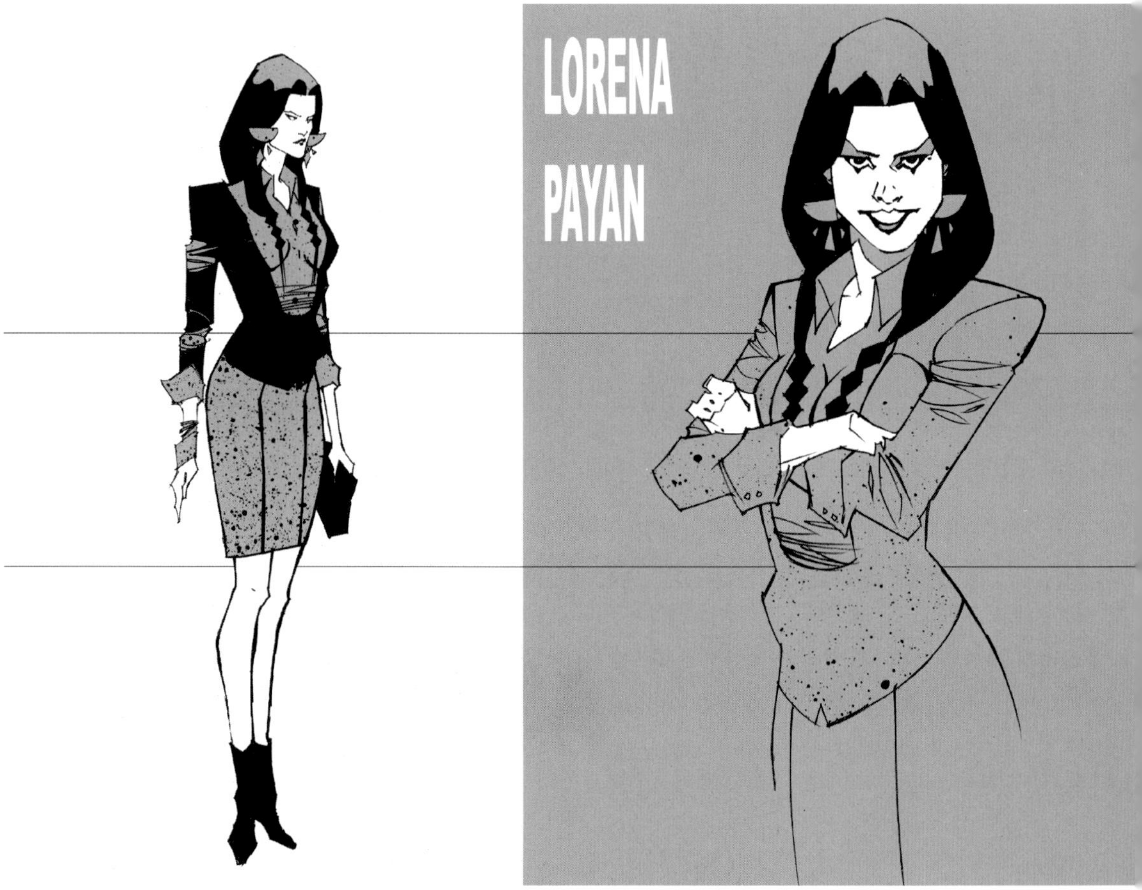
LORENA
PAYAN